Y0-BTW-451

Reflecting on Practice in Elementary School Mathematics

Readings from NCTM's School-Based Journals and Other Publications

Edited by
Anne R. Teppo
Montana State University—Bozeman
Bozeman, Montana

National Council of Teachers of Mathematics
Reston, Virginia

The special contents of this book are
Copyright © 1999 by
The National Council of Teachers of Mathematics, Inc.
1906 Association Drive, Reston, VA 20191-9988
All rights reserved

Library of Congress Cataloging-in-Publication Data

Reflecting on practice in elementary school mathematics : readings from
    NCTM's school-based journals and other publications / edited by Anne
    R. Teppo.
        p.   cm.
    Includes bibliographical references.
    ISBN 0-87353-477-8
    1. Mathematics—Study and teaching (Elementary)—United States.
I. Teppo, Anne R.
QA135.5.R426   1999
372.7'0973—dc21   99-44869
                                                                    CIP

The publications of the National Council of Teachers of Mathematics present a variety of viewpoints. The views expressed or implied in this publication, unless otherwise noted, should not be interpreted as official positions of the Council

Printed in the United States of America

Contents

Part 2: Mathematical Content

Introduction

This collection of articles about elementary school mathematics education is selected from the following publications of the National Council of Teachers of Mathematics (NCTM): *Arithmetic Teacher; Teaching Children Mathematics* (which supersedes the *Arithmetic Teacher*); *Mathematics Teaching in the Middle School; Curriculum and Evaluation Standards for School Mathematics* (1989); *Professional Standards for Teaching Mathematics* (1991); *New Directions for Elementary School Mathematics,* 1989 Yearbook; and *NCTM Xchange.* The articles were chosen for their ability to promote reflection about the processes of teaching and learning mathematics consistent with the vision put forth in the NCTM *Standards.* They are designed to help bridge the gap between readers' past experiences as learners of (often traditional) school mathematics and their roles as teachers within the reform movement. Activities related to certain articles are included to extend the readers' engagement with specific issues.

The articles provide powerful vignettes of children engaged in reform-based elementary school mathematics. They serve as effective tools to help readers think about and make explicit their own beliefs about the nature of mathematics and how it should be taught and learned. The intent of this publication is not to furnish a collection of classroom activities or specific teaching techniques but rather to raise issues about, and deepen insights into, what it means to implement the NCTM Standards.

The articles are divided into eight sections, organized in two parts. Part 1 (Sections 1 through 6) deals with general issues of teaching and learning mathematics. Part 2 (Sections 7 and 8) describes specific mathematics content within the framework of reformed-based elementary and middle school classrooms. The discussions of content focus on concepts rather than on mastering procedures, and they illustrate the connected nature of the mathematics under study. Readers are encouraged to relate the experiences of the children described throughout the eight sections to their own experiences as learners and teachers of mathematics.

Section 1, "Reform in School Mathematics," sets the stage by focusing on issues raised by the NCTM *Standards* documents. A brief summary of the three documents is presented, and a selection of editorial essays provides perspectives from which to consider the reform movement. Section 2, "Children's Invented Strategies," presents examples of classrooms in which children are encouraged to develop their own strategies for arithmetic operations on whole numbers. These articles describe a picture of school mathematics, very different from the traditional classroom, in which children are encouraged to think about mathematics in ways that are meaningful to them.

The articles included in Section 3, "The Reflective Learner," are designed to help readers become aware of, and focus on, their own understandings about the processes of teaching and learning mathematics. Section 4, "Creating a Different Kind of Classroom," discusses the roles of worthwhile mathematical tasks and of different modes of communication and the issue of equity in the reformed classroom. Examples of children engaged in active mathematical discussions and reflective-writing assignments illustrate the importance of these activities for promoting effective learning. The articles in Section 5, "Developing Mathematical Thinking," give examples of students engaged in specific tasks that illustrate the power of mathematical thinking and the importance of developing such thinking. Section 6, "Tools and Technology," presents examples of how calculators and computers can be used as powerful thinking tools in the teaching and learning of mathematics.

Section 7, "The Real-Number System," presents innovative mathematical tasks and descriptions of classroom episodes related to the real-number system. Articles in this section address arithmetic operations on whole numbers and integers, estimation, number theory, rational numbers, and other number bases. The reported examples of children's work in Section 8, "Data, Measurement, and Geometry," indicate the depth of understanding that these students are capable of developing in these topics.

The sequence of the articles allows readers to progress from a general discussion about each topic to more-detailed considerations of specific issues. Reading the sections in order makes it possible to extract richer information from later articles on the basis of insights developed from previous sections. The collection can also be used as a resource to be mined as needed within any given area of interest.

Activities

The readings presented in this collection can be enriched by follow-up activities. Practicing teachers will find the classroom examples described in many articles useful for experimenting with the ideas discussed by the authors. A set of questions and activities coordinated with specific articles is also provided at the end of each section to encourage readers to reflect on and extend the readings. These activities can be used as part of a preservice or in-service course to help participants focus on their experiences as learners and teachers of Standards-based mathematics.

Not every article is accompanied by an activity. Some of the readings are included more to provide information than to stimulate further action. The questions, problems, and suggested activities that are given at the end of each section are designed to encourage deeper engagement with the ideas discussed in particular articles. Rather than form a comprehensive set, these activities offer examples of the variety of ways to extend the classroom use of the readings.

The majority of the activities include prompts for reflective writing. Readers are asked to react to articles, either by relating the information to their own experiences or by commenting on the authors' points of view. Scheibelhut's article in Section 4 discusses the value of such writing for clarifying ideas and actively constructing knowledge. When assigned as part of a preservice or in-service course, reflective writing also serves as an important tool for assessment and communication between participants and instructors.

Activities have been included that require group or whole-class participation. Any of the mathematical problems posed can also be done in groups. In fact, group discussions afford opportunities for richer understandings of the mathematics embedded in each of the problems. Other types of activities include using manipulatives, a review of literature, a Logo computer activity, and calculator problems.

Readers are encouraged to try out any or all of the activities. Some of them are straightforward, and others will present more of a challenge. In addition to the activities included at the end of each section, others can be found within many of the articles to extend and enrich the reading experience.

Part 1
Issues in Teaching and Learning Mathematics

Section 1
Reform in School Mathematics

The vision of school mathematics articulated by the NCTM's Curriculum, Teaching, and Assessment Standards has provided a direction for educational reform. Instead of traditional classrooms with an emphasis on mastering basic procedures and memorizing rules and terminology, school districts are being challenged to create classrooms in which children are actively engaged in doing mathematics—exploring, conjecturing, and reasoning about mathematical ideas.

Implementing such change is a complicated process. How do teachers create classrooms different from those they experienced themselves as learners of mathematics? What is now meant by "doing" mathematics? What kind of mathematics should be emphasized? What is the place of "basics" in the reformed classroom? What tasks promote active involvement with mathematical ideas? What does it really mean to "implement the NCTM Standards," and what roles do students, teachers, parents, and school administrators play in such an implementation?

The readings in this section set the stage for thinking about such questions. A brief summary of the NCTM *Standards* documents is given, including an outline for the K–4 and 5–8 Curriculum Standards. The article by Szemcsak and West presents examples of how the calls for reform have been addressed at the local level. The three essays expressing "One Point of View" and "In My Opinion" provide perspectives for evaluating the recommendations put forth in the NCTM *Standards*. The article by Battista and Larson fleshes out the *Standards* vision of a different kind of school mathematics. The authors describe a constructivist view of learning that focuses on how children think. Tasks that facilitate mathematical thinking and research related to such tasks are described.

Change is a process, and the first step in this process is to become aware of the nature of the proposed changes. Thus, the articles in this section were selected not to provide answers but to initiate thinking about more-effective ways to promote learning. Succeeding sections will furnish specific information about different components of the new directions for school mathematics and help the reader to become a reflective participant in the reform movement.

NCTM *Standards* Documents

Curriculum and Evaluation Standards for School Mathematics

In 1989 the National Council of Teachers of Mathematics (NCTM) published the *Curriculum and Evaluation Standards for School Mathematics*. This document presents a vision of the mathematics students should know and be able to do in order to achieve mathematical literacy in today's rapidly changing world. The five general goals that underlie the Curriculum Standards are that all students—

♦ learn to value mathematics;

♦ become confident in their ability to do mathematics;

♦ become mathematical problem solvers;

♦ learn to communicate mathematically;

♦ learn to reason mathematically.

The *Curriculum and Evaluation Standards* envisions classrooms in which students are actively engaged in exploring interesting problems by using important mathematical ideas; where they read, write, and discuss mathematics and conjecture and test ideas by using mathematical reasoning. These experiences are aimed at helping students develop mathematical power (NCTM 1989, p. 5):

[Mathematical power] denotes an individual's abilities to explore, conjecture, and reason logically, as well as the ability to use a variety of mathematical methods effectively to solve nonroutine problems. This notion is based on the recognition of mathematics as more than a collection of concepts and skills to be mastered; it includes methods of investigating and reasoning, means of communication, and notions of context. In addition, for each individual, mathematical power involves the development of personal self-confidence.

The document presents sets of thirteen to fourteen standards each within the categories of grades K–4, 5–8, and 9–12 that describe the "basic skills and understandings students should have in numbers and number theory, geometry, measurement, probability and statistics, patterns and functions, discrete mathematics, algebra, and beyond" (NCTM n.d., p. 7). Examples of specific problems are provided to illustrate the nature of the mathematics described in each standard. Running through all the grade levels are a set of standards that present mathematics as problem solving, communication, reasoning, and connections. A brief outline of the thirteen standards for grades K–4 and 5–8 is presented in Section 1.

Professional Standards for Teaching Mathematics

In 1991 the NCTM followed the *Curriculum and Evaluation Standards* with the *Professional Standards for Teaching Mathematics*. This document describes standards for teaching mathematics, for the evaluation of such teaching, for the professional development of teachers of mathematics, and for the support and development of teachers and teaching. Suggestions for implementing each standard are illustrated by short classroom vignettes. The standards for teaching mathematics include—

♦ selecting worthwhile mathematical tasks;

♦ orchestrating classroom discourse;

♦ creating learning environments that foster the development of each student's mathematical power;

♦ engaging in ongoing analysis of one's own teaching and the assessment of the students' learning.

Assessment Standards for School Mathematics

The *Assessment Standards for School Mathematics,* published by NCTM in 1995, provides a set of principles for developing new assessment strategies and practices "that will enable teachers and others to assess students' performance in a manner that reflects the NCTM's reform vision for school mathematics" (NCTM 1995, p. 1). These standards recommend that assessment should—

♦ reflect the mathematics that all students need to know and be able to do;

♦ enhance mathematics learning;

♦ promote equity;

♦ be an open process;

♦ promote valid inferences about mathematics learning;

♦ be a coherent process.

The document also provides classroom vignettes to illustrate the four purposes for which assessment can be used:

♦ To monitor students' progress

♦ To make instructional decisions

♦ To evaluate students' achievement

♦ To evaluate programs

Together, the Curriculum, Teaching, and Assessment Standards present a coordinated vision of how all aspects of school mathematics—content, teaching, and assessment—need to change on a systemic basis. Included in this vision are the following:

♦ A shift in the mathematical content that students are expected to learn …

♦ A shift in the vision of learning mathematics toward investigating, formulating, representing, reasoning, and applying a variety of strategies to the solution of problems—then reflecting on these uses of mathematics—and away from being shown or told, memorizing, and repeating …

♦ A shift in the role of teachers toward "questioning and listening" as their classrooms become stimulating intellectual learning communities and away from "telling" students what to do …

♦ A shift in the vision of evaluation toward a system based on evidence from multiple sources and away from relying on evidence from a single test (NCTM 1995, p. 2)

References

National Council of Teachers of Mathematics. *Assessment Standards for School Mathematics.* Reston, Va.: National Council of Teachers of Mathematics, 1995.

———. *Curriculum and Evaluation Standards for School Mathematics.* Reston, Va.: National Council of Teachers of Mathematics, 1989.

———. *Mathematics: Making a Living, Making a Life.* Reston, Va.: National Council of Teachers of Mathematics, n.d.

———. *Professional Standards for Teaching Mathematics.* Reston, Va.: National Council of Teachers of Mathematics, 1991.

Summary of the Curriculum Standards for Grades K–4

Standard 1: Mathematics as Problem Solving

The study of mathematics should emphasize problem solving so that students can—

♦ use problem-solving approaches to investigate and understand mathematical content;

♦ formulate problems from everyday and mathematical situations;

♦ develop and apply strategies to solve a wide variety of problems;

♦ verify and interpret results with respect to the original problem;

♦ acquire confidence in using mathematics meaningfully.

Standard 2: Mathematics as Communication

The study of mathematics should include numerous opportunities for communication so that students can—

♦ relate physical materials, pictures, and diagrams to mathematical ideas;

♦ reflect on and clarify their thinking about mathematical ideas and situations;

♦ relate their everyday language to mathematical language and symbols;

♦ realize that representing, discussing, reading, writing, and listening to mathematics are a vital part of learning and using mathematics.

Standard 3: Mathematics as Reasoning

The study of mathematics should emphasize reasoning so that students can—

♦ draw logical conclusions about mathematics;

♦ use models, known facts, properties, and relationships to explain their thinking;

♦ justify their answers and solution processes;

♦ use patterns and relationships to analyze mathematical situations;

♦ believe that mathematics makes sense.

Standard 4: Mathematical Connections

The study of mathematics should include opportunities to make connections so that students can—

♦ link conceptual and procedural knowledge;

♦ relate various representations of concepts or procedures to one another;

♦ recognize relationships among different topics in mathematics;

♦ use mathematics in other curriculum areas;

♦ use mathematics in their daily lives.

Standard 5: Estimation

The curriculum should include estimation so students can—

♦ explore estimation strategies;

♦ recognize when an estimation is appropriate;

♦ determine the reasonableness of results;

♦ apply estimation in working with quantities, measurement, computation, and problem solving.

Standard 6: Number Sense and Numeration

The mathematics curriculum should include whole number concepts and skills so that students can—

- construct number meanings through real-world experiences and the use of physical materials;
- understand our numeration system by relating counting, grouping, and place-value concepts;
- develop number sense;
- interpret the multiple uses of numbers encountered in the real world.

Standard 7: Concepts of Whole Number Operations

The mathematics curriculum should include concepts of addition, subtraction, multiplication, and division of whole numbers so that students can—

- develop meaning for the operations by modeling and discussing a rich variety of problem situations;
- relate the mathematical language and symbolism of operations to problem situations and informal language;
- recognize that a wide variety of problem structures can be represented by a single operation;
- develop operation sense.

Standard 8: Whole Number Computation

The mathematics curriculum should develop whole number computation so that students can—

- model, explain, and develop reasonable proficiency with basic facts and algorithms;
- use a variety of mental computation and estimation techniques;
- use calculators in appropriate computational situations;
- select and use computation techniques appropriate to specific problems and determine whether the results are reasonable.

Standard 9: Geometry and Spatial Sense

The mathematics curriculum should include two- and three-dimensional geometry so that students can—

- describe, model, draw, and classify shapes;
- investigate and predict the results of combining, subdividing, and changing shapes;
- develop spatial sense;
- relate geometric ideas to number and measurement ideas;
- recognize and appreciate geometry in their world.

Standard 10: Measurement

The mathematics curriculum should include measurement so that students can—

- understand the attributes of length, capacity, weight, mass, area, volume, time, temperature, and angle;
- develop the process of measuring and concepts related to units of measurement;
- make and use estimates of measurement;
- make and use measurements in problem and everyday situations.

Standard 11: Statistics and Probability

The mathematics curriculum should include experiences with data analysis and probability so that students can—

- collect, organize, and describe data;
- construct, read, and interpret displays of data;
- formulate and solve problems that involve collecting and analyzing data;
- explore concepts of chance.

Standard 12: Fractions and Decimals

The mathematics curriculum should include fractions and decimals so that students can—

- develop concepts of fractions, mixed numbers, and decimals;
- develop number sense for fractions and decimals;
- use models to relate fractions to decimals and to find equivalent fractions;
- use models to explore operations on fractions and decimals;
- apply fractions and decimals to problem situations.

Standard 13: Patterns and Relationships

The mathematics curriculum should include the study of patterns and relationships so that students can—

- recognize, describe, extend, and create a wide variety of patterns;
- represent and describe mathematical relationships;
- explore the use of variables and open sentences to express relationships.

Summary of the Curriculum Standards for Grades 5–8

Standard 1: Mathematics as Problem Solving

The mathematics curriculum should include numerous and varied experiences with problem solving as a method of inquiry and application so that students can—

- ♦ use problem-solving approaches to investigate and understand mathematical content;
- ♦ formulate problems from situations within and outside mathematics;
- ♦ develop and apply a variety of strategies to solve problems, with emphasis on multistep and nonroutine problems;
- ♦ verify and interpret results with respect to the original problem situation;
- ♦ generalize solutions and strategies to new problem situations;
- ♦ acquire confidence in using mathematics meaningfully.

Standard 2: Mathematics as Communication

The study of mathematics should include opportunities to communicate so that students can—

- ♦ model situations using oral, written, concrete, pictorial, graphical, and algebraic methods;
- ♦ reflect on and clarify their own thinking about mathematical ideas and situations;
- ♦ develop common understandings of mathematical ideas, including the role of definitions;
- ♦ use the skills of reading, listening, and viewing to interpret and evaluate mathematical ideas;

- ♦ discuss mathematical ideas and make conjectures and convincing arguments;
- ♦ Appreciate the value of mathematical notation and its role in the development of mathematical ideas.

Standard 3: Mathematics as Reasoning

Reasoning shall permeate the mathematics curriculum so that students can—

- ♦ recognize and apply deductive and inductive reasoning;
- ♦ understand and apply reasoning processes, with special attention to spatial reasoning and reasoning with proportions and graphs;
- ♦ make and evaluate mathematical conjectures and arguments;
- ♦ validate their own thinking;
- ♦ appreciate the pervasive use and power of reasoning as a part of mathematics.

Standard 4: Mathematical Connections

The mathematics curriculum should include the investigation of mathematical connections so that students can—

- ♦ see mathematics as an integrated whole;
- ♦ explore problems and describe results using graphical, numerical, physical, algebraic, and verbal mathematical models or representations;
- ♦ use a mathematical idea to further their understanding of other mathematical ideas;

- apply mathematical thinking and modeling to solve problems that arise in other disciplines, such as art, music, psychology, science, and business;
- value the role of mathematics in our culture and society.

Standard 5: Number and Number Relationships

The mathematics curriculum should include the continued development of number and number relationships so that students can—

- understand, represent, and use numbers in a variety of equivalent forms (integer, fraction, decimal, percent, exponential, and scientific notation) in real-world and mathematical problem situations;
- develop number sense for whole numbers, fractions, decimals, integers, and rational numbers;
- understand and apply ratios, proportions, and percents in a wide variety of situations;
- investigate relationships among fractions, decimals, and percents;
- represent numerical relationships in one- and two-dimensional graphs.

Standard 6: Number Systems and Number Theory

The mathematics curriculum should include the study of number systems and number theory so that students can—

- understand and appreciate the need for numbers beyond the whole numbers;
- develop and use order relations for whole numbers, fractions, decimals, integers, and rational numbers;
- extend their understanding of whole number operations to fractions, decimals, integers, and rational numbers;
- understand how the basic arithmetic operations are related to one another;
- develop and apply number theory concepts (e.g., primes, factors, and multiples) in real-world and mathematical problem situations.

Standard 7: Computation and Estimation

The mathematics curriculum should develop the concepts underlying computation and estimation in various contexts so that students can—

- compute with whole numbers, fractions, decimals, integers, and rational numbers;

- develop, analyze, and explain procedures for computation and techniques for estimation;
- develop, analyze, and explain methods for solving proportions;
- select and use an appropriate method for computing from among mental arithmetic, paper-and-pencil, calculator, and computer methods;
- use computation, estimation, and proportions to solve problems;
- use estimation to check the reasonableness of results.

Standard 8: Patterns and Functions

The mathematics curriculum should include explorations of patterns and functions so that students can—

- describe, extend, analyze, and create a wide variety of patterns;
- describe and represent relationships with tables, graphs, and rules;
- analyze functional relationships to explain how a change in one quantity results in a change in another;
- use patterns and functions to represent and solve problems.

Standard 9: Algebra

The mathematics curriculum should include explorations of algebraic concepts and processes so that students can—

- understand the concepts of variable, expression, and equation;
- represent situations and number patterns with tables, graphs, verbal rules, and equations and explore the interrelationships of these representations;
- analyze tables and graphs to identify properties and relationships;
- develop confidence in solving linear equations using concrete, informal, and formal methods;
- investigate inequalities and nonlinear equations informally;
- apply algebraic methods to solve a variety of real-world and mathematical problems.

Standard 10: Statistics

The mathematics curriculum should include exploration of statistics in real-world situations so that students can—

- systematically collect, organize, and describe data;
- construct, read, and interpret tables, charts, and graphs;
- make inferences and convincing arguments that are based on data analysis;

- evaluate arguments that are based on data analysis;
- develop an appreciation for statistical methods as powerful means for decision making.

Standard 11: Probability

The mathematics curriculum should include explorations of probability in real-world situations so that students can—

- model situations by devising and carrying out experiments or simulations to determine probabilities;
- model situations by constructing a sample space to determine probabilities;
- appreciate the power of using a probability model by comparing experimental results with mathematical expectations;
- make predictions that are based on experimental or theoretical probabilities;
- develop an appreciation for the pervasive use of probability in the real world.

Standard 12: Geometry

The mathematics curriculum should include the study of the geometry of one, two, and three dimensions in a variety of situations so that students can—

- identify, describe, compare, and classify geometric figures;
- visualize and represent geometric figures with special attention to developing spatial sense;
- explore transformations of geometric figures;
- represent and solve problems using geometric models;
- understand and apply geometric properties and relationships;
- develop an appreciation of geometry as a means of describing the physical world.

Standard 13: Measurement

The mathematics curriculum should include extensive concrete experiences using measurement so that students can—

- extend their understanding of the process of measurement;
- estimate, make, and use measurements to describe and compare phenomena;
- select appropriate units and tools to measure to the degree of accuracy required in a particular situation;
- understand the structure and use of systems of measurement;
- extend their understanding of the concepts of perimeter, area, volume, angle measure, capacity, and weight and mass;
- develop the concepts of rates and other derived and indirect measurements;
- develop formulas and procedures for determining measures to solve problems.

The Whole Town Is Talking about It ... "Math Month," That Is

by

Donna DeCasas Szemcsak and Oliver J. West

As most parents are aware, a nationwide concern exists about elementary mathematics instruction. We constantly hear that the United States lags behind other countries in standardized test scores. In response, the president and governors adopted ambitious educational goals in 1990. First, by the year 2000, American students will exit grades 4, 8, and 12 having demonstrated competence in challenging subjects including English, mathematics, science, history, and geography. In addition, this plan will be accomplished with schools' further ensuring that all children will have learned to use their minds capably to become good citizens, active adult learners, and productive employees in the future. Second, United States students will be first in the world in mathematics and science achievement.

This straightforward second goal was set forth after a decade's worth of data and information clearly highlighted that our nation's children are generally lacking in mathematics skills. Greater skills are needed to cope with employment demands and college requirements for mathematical proficiency in prerequisite mathematics skills. This finding is not surprising or unexpected considering recent studies by the National Center for Education Statistics (NCES), whose 1991 document *The State of Mathematics Achievement* acknowledged that textbooks and worksheets still flourish in place of more innovative activities. Most students are never asked to work cooperatively in small groups, do mathematics projects, or use a computer in mathematics classes.

Donna Szemcsak is a mathematics teacher at the Richard M. Teitelman Junior High School, Cape May, NJ 08204. Oliver West is a principal of the Maud Abrams School in Cape May.

Calculators, even in eighth grade, where arithmetic should be entrenched, are not employed. The use of such mathematics tools as geometric shapes and attribute blocks is not widespread. The recommendation made by the NCES is to help all students learn to think mathematically through group and individual projects that stress applying mathematics and incorporating calculators and computers.

The Parent-Student-Teacher Mathematics Coalition

With a clear mandate to update and energize mathematics instruction at the earliest time, the Lower Township Elementary Schools in Cape May County, New Jersey, took a first significant step to address these recommendations. As a result of communications with parents, teachers, students, and the New Jersey Mathematics Coalition, the

Parents share one-half of the cooperative group work.

first Parent-Student-Teacher Math Coalition was formed in the Lower Township school system.

Initially, a group of interested parents, teachers, and administrators organized a Family Math Night so that children and parents could learn together. The high level of excitement, energy, and team spirit demonstrated by parents and teachers during the first meeting was evidence that more time was needed to accomplish group plans. The catalyst for the expansion of the project came from the group's concern that multiple goals needed to be addressed.

As the activities for the proposed family-mathematics night were explored, additional activities began to surface as the mathematics coalition focused on a framework. The need existed to—

- make all parents aware of new mathematics recommendations for instruction coming from the National Council of Teachers of Mathematics.
- make both students and parents aware that mathematics instruction is an immediate priority; the subject matter is important, and the application of mathematics is an evolving concern.
- refocus attention on the wealth of information accessible to teachers concerning mathematics innovations, including that from past district in-service training centered on elementary mathematics instruction.
- acquaint parents, students, and teachers with mathematics initiatives, such as those of the New Jersey Mathematics Coalition and National Council of Teachers of Mathematics, which work to strengthen community understanding of, and support for, reform in mathematics.
- accomplish the goals as a joint venture between parents and teachers. The focus was intended to be specific enough to guide the activities but broad enough to encompass both in-school and at-home mathematics.

Other subgoals surfaced as a result of group meetings under the umbrella of the major goals of the Lower Township Parent-Student-Teacher Math Coalition. A genuine concern evolved that activities reflect new curricular demands but also be motivational, enjoyable, and non-competitive. Second, both informal and formal evaluation of activities should be carried out in the anticipation of continued coalition activities.

The Community Speaks Out

After proposing, discussing, debating, and planning events during several meetings, the coalition issued a calendar of events and selected a list of committees to implement Math Month. The first priority was to establish an all-important link with the home. *Math Madness,* a biweekly newsletter, was prepared by parent volunteers

and sent home with each child every Tuesday and Thursday (see fig. 1). It contained news of school mathematics activities, mind-bending puzzles, and suggestions to parents on how to help their children enjoy and understand mathematics. Concerns were raised about whether the newsletter would reach its destination, so once a week a family-activity page was attached to the newsletter to be completed and returned to a "math box" located in the cafeteria. At the end of the week, a random drawing was held to determine the student who would win an ice-cream party for her or his class.

Family activity pages presented nontraditional mathematical challenges.

The purpose of the activity sheet was not to ask for right or wrong answers but rather to present a nontraditional mathematical challenge that would foster questioning, exploring, conjecturing, and thinking. The activity was also structured to encourage family involvement.

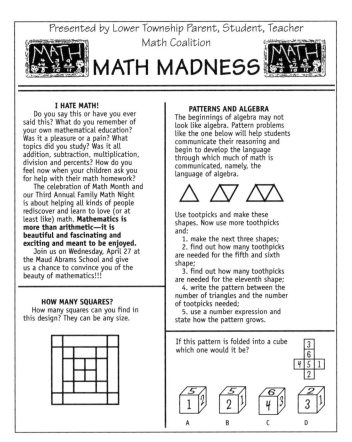

Fig. 1. A *Math Madness* newsletter

One of the first series of activities centered on mathematics speakers. In keeping with its goals, the coalition wanted to ensure that the community was significantly involved. Community members were invited to meet with students to (1) speak about the importance of mathematics in their jobs and (2) relate to children their own experiences as schoolchildren in learning mathematics. The intended message was that not all adults who are proficient users of mathematics were necessarily gifted mathematics students. Mathematics may not be easy at times and so may take extra work and effort to master, but the hard work in school will pay big dividends in the future. From a nominating list of community members compiled by the committee with input from classroom teachers, over forty people were asked to speak. Every profession from computer analyst to salon owner volunteered to help. Over the course of the month, many speakers described using mathematics in their jobs. A person who worked in a restaurant was most impressive and demonstrated amazing addition skills by scribbling two-, three-, or four-digit amounts on the front chalkboard and totaling them almost simultaneously.

Math Bubbles Up!

"Bubble Day," entirely coordinated and planned by parents, offered each child the chance to explore bubble blowing as a mathematics lesson. Why are bubbles spherical? If the width of a bubble changes by a certain amount, does the height change proportionally? What happens when four bubble walls come together? What happens when a bubble is made next to another one of a different size? These mysteries were investigated by each student. In the playground area, over twenty parents set up bubble workstations for each question. Clearly, students found out not only that mathematics can be fun but also that it involves more than paper, pencil, and workbook.

The climate of the school became charged with excitement.

Implications across the Curriculum

As other special mathematics events occurred, the climate of the school became charged with excitement about Math Month. Various activities were carried out in all quarters. A "math good-idea box" became a permanent fixture in the teachers' room. Everyone was invited to share mathematics activities that were effective, motivational, and entertaining. Other teachers, representing art, music, the library, computers, and physical education, added fantastic lessons on graphics, measurement, symmetry, and statistics. The halls were festooned with posters, artwork, and banners.

Family Math Night

Eventually, the end of Math Month was in sight and was scheduled to culminate with Family Math Night. Once again, parental involvement was the key factor in planning all the events for that evening. One key parent, who not only served on the New Jersey Mathematics Coalition but was also a pillar of our Parent-Student-Teacher Math Coalition, served as the program coordinator. All parents and students received information and an invitation to Family Math Night.

On Family Math Night, after an introduction and welcome by the principal and a mathematics update by the parent project coordinator, all participants moved to classrooms for workshop selections. Families attended sessions on using calculators in the classroom (see fig. 2), manipulatives to solve problems, and computer-assisted instruction

---

Wipeout

Teaches: Place value

Objective: To remove one digit from the display without changing any of the other digits

How to play: The teacher picks a number that all players enter into their calculators. The teacher then announces which digit is to be removed. This "wipeout" is done by subtracting one number number from the display and hitting = .

Example: In the display, 876543, wipe out the 7 without changing any other digit.

| Before | After |

Fig. 2. A calculator activity to teach place value

---

to solve multistep problems. A session titled "But Who's Counting?" allowed parents, teachers, administrators, and board members to participate in a game show involving estimation and hypothesis building.

One fourth-grade teacher volunteered her class to prepare the refreshments. The class was divided into groups that were challenged to (1) create a snack recipe, (2) figure out the proportions of the ingredients, (3) write a list of how much of each ingredient was needed so that the teacher could purchase the items, (4) name this creation, (5) write out the recipe so that it could be included in the math-night folders, and (6) taste test the snack. Snacks were a combination of candy, cereal, fruit, crackers, and nuts. The PTA helped to facilitate this activity.

At the end of the evening, the PTA provided an incentive for filling out a necessary evaluation sheet by donating calculators as door prizes. The results of the evaluations were all positive. Comments included, "Great! Must do it again!" "Wish it could be longer!" "My family and I had a great time!" and "Math is fun!" Each family also received a mathematics folder, donated through the New Jersey Mathematics Coalition, Apple Computers, and Public Service Electric and Gas, that was filled with mathematics information and follow-up activities that families could do at home.

Our celebration of mathematics had brought together school, home, and community. It not only piqued the interest and curiosity of the children but prompted many teachers to reevaluate their feelings about mathematics. Many had questions about the NCTM's *Curriculum and Evaluation Standards* (1989) and asked for implementation ideas; the majority wanted to change but were not quite sure how to do so. This program was viewed as a beginning for positive change.

One Parent-Student-Teacher Math Coalition leader related, "At the end of Family Math Night, a child's grandmother came up to me, held my hand, and told me how afraid she had been of computers. After having the opportunity to 'play' with one that night, she loved it. Her grandchild stood proudly beaming at her side. I know we affected at least one family. I'm certain many more realized the potential and importance of mathematics in society and felt assured that our community was moving in the right direction."

As a tribute to the hard work of parents, teachers, and students and to emphasize mathematics education in the community, the local NBC television affiliate featured Family Math Night on its *Nightly News* program.

Conclusions

Clearly, Lower Township Elementary Schools' Math Month served to promote and activate creative thinking about the need to focus on and upgrade mathematics instruction. As a community effort, the planning, implementation, and evaluation of all the mathematics activities brought parents, teachers, administrators, and students together to experiment with and enhance mathematics as both an intellectual activity and a creative adventure. The Lower Township Parent-Student-Teacher Math Coalition joins with others who recommend teaching and learning that rely on applying mathematics to tangible everyday problems. The aim, to encourage thinking that uses imagination while exploring mathematics, was clearly met.

Bibliography

Ashlock, Robert B. "Parents Can Help Children Learn Mathematics." *Arithmetic Teacher* 38 (November 1990):42–46.

Barnes, Sue Jackson. "Involve the Community." *Mathematics Teacher* 86 (September 1993):442–48.

Bayliffe, Janie, Raymond Brie, and Beverly Oliver. "Teaching Mathematics with Technology: Family Math Enhanced through Technology." *Arithmetic Teacher* 41 (November 1993):172–75.

Cassidy, John. *The Unbelievable Bubble Book.* Palo Alto, Calif.: Klutz Press, 1987.

Flexer, Roberta J., and Carolyn L. Topping. "Mathematics on the Home Front." *Arithmetic Teacher* 36 (October 1988):12–19.

Ford, Marilyn Sue, and Caroline Gibson Crew. "Table-Top Mathematics—a Home-Study Program for Early Childhood." *Arithmetic Teacher* 38 (April 1991):6–12.

Franklin, Joyce, and Joyce Krebil. "Take-Home Kits." *Arithmetic Teacher* 40 (April 1993):442–48.

Goldstein, Sue, and Frances A. Campbell. "Parents: A Ready Resource." *Arithmetic Teacher* 38 (February 1991):24–27.

Joseph, Helen. "Teaching Mathematics with Technology: Build Parental Support for Mathematics with Family Computers." *Arithmetic Teacher* 40 (March 1993):412–15.

National Center for Education Statistics (NCES). *The State of Mathematics Achievement Executive Summary.* Washington, D.C.: U.S. Department of Education, 1991.

National Council of Teachers of Mathematics. *Curriculum and Evaluation Standards for School Mathematics.* Reston, Va.: The Council, 1989.

O'Connell, Susan R. "Math Pairs—Parents as Partners." *Arithmetic Teacher* 40 (September 1992):10–12.

Orman, Sheryl A. "Math Backpacks: Making the Home-School Connection." *Arithmetic Teacher* 40 (February 1993):306–8.

Peterson, Winnie. "Principles for Principals: Celebrate Math Month with a Family Math Night." *Arithmetic Teacher* 36 (March 1989):24–25.

Tregaskis, Owen. "Parents and Mathematical Games." *Arithmetic Teacher* 38 (March 1991):14–16.

Zubrowski, Bernie. *Bubbles, a Children's Museum Activity Book.* Boston: Little, Brown & Co. 1979.

One Point of View

The Dangers of Implementing the Standards; or, When Bad Things Happen to Good Ideas

by David J. Whitin

Although I embrace the vision that the *Curriculum and Evaluation Standards for School Mathematics* (NCTM 1989) sets for us in the field of mathematics education, I am already worried about the way many people have begun to interpret it. My concerns echo those in the field of language education who fear the same fate for the writing process and whole language movements. Bad things can happen to good ideas, including the *Curriculum and Evaluation Standards,* unless we are clear about what that document *is* and *is not.* Let me clarify two misconceptions that have the potential to undermine the very heart of these standards:

1. The *Curriculum and Evaluation Standards* is not a methodology but a theory of learning. We can never begin to realize the vision of the *Standards* document by running around trying to collect the best activities we can find. If we consume ourselves in a methodology hunt, falsely assuming that if we search long and hard enough we will be able to secure the right set of activities for all learners, then we are closing the very vision that we are trying to make possible. The kind of mathematical literacy advocated by the Standards will never be found in a workbook, skill sheet, or basal mathematics textbook. No publisher will ever be able to package it, contain it, or sell it, despite their many claims to the contrary. True mathematical literacy must originate not from a methodology but from a theory of learning—one that views learning not as a series

David Whitin teaches at the University of South Carolina, Columbia, SC 29208. He works regularly in an elementary school classroom to create a curriculum that supports mathematical learning through inquiry. He has a special interest in using children's literature as a springboard for mathematical investigations.

of enjoyable activities or problem-solving techniques but as a way of knowing and learning about the world (Whitin, Mills, and O'Keefe 1990).

The *Standards* offers only working hypotheses.

The *Standards* document is a theoretical statement about how people learn; it is based on a belief system that says, among other things, that learners construct their own knowledge; that learners grow by sharing and generating ideas with others; and that learners gain new understandings by representing their ideas in different ways, such as through drawings, written narrative, or oral discourse. From this perspective it is not a static document to be implemented but a growing theory of learning to be tested out, challenged, and refined. It is a theoretical stance toward how people learn and, as such, can offer no fixed answers, only working hypotheses. If we see the *Standards* document as a series of commandments to be carried out without continual questioning and refining, then we are in trouble. The real danger lies in thinking we have all the answers. We will continue to grow as a profession only when we are asking new questions. The *Standards* document presents us with a vehicle for inquiry; it gives us a forum for testing out new questions about the learning process; it calls us to reflect and question, not to receive and accept.

2. The *Curriculum and Evaluation Standards* is not just for teachers but for all learners. If we view the document as a directive only to teachers, then we may not listen to

the important contributions that our students can make to the teaching-learning process. However, if we see students as constructors of their own knowledge and if we value their unique background experiences and interests, then curriculum is not something we do *to* them but *with* them. We become avid kid watchers who celebrate the strategies students employ and highlight the connections that they construct. We value all their interpretations, including their unexpected responses, because we know they are windows into the thinking process. Thus, the focus of the standards is not on teachers or students but on learning. The standards do not imply a hierarchical relationship between student and teacher but call for a collaborative stance toward the teaching-learning process. Inquiry learning is everybody's business—teachers, students, and administrators alike. Each has a unique perspective on the learning process, and all their voices need to be heard.

The *Standards* document offers us an exciting vision for the field of mathematics education. However, we must view it as a theory of learning that invites continual questions by the inquiring voices of both students and teachers. Otherwise, bad things will happen to this good idea and the vision that was will never be.

References

National Council of Teachers of Mathematics. *Curriculum and Evaluation Standards for School Mathematics.* Reston, Va.: The Council, 1989.

Whitin, David J., Heidi Mills, and Timothy O'Keefe. *Living and Learning Mathematics.* Portsmouth, N.H.: Heinemann Books, 1990.

One Point of View

It's Time to Use Our "OOB" Detectors!

by

Phares G. O'Daffer

The NCTM's *Curriculum and Evaluation Standards for School Mathematics* was thoughtfully conceived and continues to influence the school mathematics curriculum. A strength of the document seems to be that the standards strike a reasonable balance between what ought to be and what can be. Because of this, the book has stimulated our thinking and facilitated realistic, positive changes in many schools.

However, as with many reforms, it is easy for us to lose perspective, jump on a bandwagon, and throw the original intent of the reform out of balance. We could invent a new word, *oob* (which is short for out of balance to describe this situation). It is easy to come up with oobs from the past. In the modern mathematics era, an oob could be the heavy focus on mathematical structure. In the seventies, the overemphasis on drill and practice was an obvious oob. We need to take a careful look at what we are doing. What are our possible oobs today? What can we do to control oobs and maintain balance in curricular reform?

One possible oob today may be the lack of concern about mathematics content. In our legitimate zeal to remedy past deficiencies in developing higher-level processes, communication skills, and student attitudes, we may not be giving enough attention to selecting, sequencing, and helping students learn important basic mathematical ideas. An attitude almost seems to prevail in some circles that if students feel good, are talking, and can engage in some higher-level thinking and problem solving, the mathe-

Phares O'Daffer is an author and professor emeritus of mathematics at Illinois State University, Normal, IL 61761. He is active in curriculum development and writes books for K–12 students and teachers.

matics content or how it is sequenced makes little difference. Yet the curriculum standards emphasize mathematical content and NCTM's *Professional Standards for Teaching Mathematics* (1991) indicates that the teacher should pose tasks based on "sound and significant mathematics." To avoid the content oob, we need to strive for balance among content, process, and attitude development.

When is our mathematics curriculum out of balance?

Another possible oob may be a negative stigma attached to memorizing mathematics facts and learning and practicing procedural skills. Some educators seem to think that it is inherently wrong to practice, to give a rule, or to memorize something, and others seem to think it is wrong to do anything but those things. Yet the learning of facts and procedures is a legitimate and important part of a student's education, including mathematics. The key is to not overemphasize them. We need to achieve a proper balance among learning concepts, facts, procedural skills, generalizations, and higher level processes.

Other possible oobs today may come in the realm of pedagogy. Even the idea that students should actively construct their own meanings in mathematics might be carried to extremes. It is not yet clear how widespread acceptance of this theory of learning will affect a balanced curriculum. Also, learning in small groups is currently getting a lot of attention. Anything done in small groups qualifies, from mechanically following instructions to solving open-ended problems. For some instructors, it is the only way to teach.

Many benefits are derived from this approach to learning, but direct instruction, teacher-whole-class discussion, and individual work are still valuable. The need is not for "more of this and less of that" but rather for a consideration of "when." We need to seek a balance using the most appropriate instructional approach for a given situation.

We can sometimes detect potential oobs by looking at buzz words. When someone says "connections," "cooperative learning," "multicultural," "communication," "mathematical power," "project unit," or "doing mathematics," we can almost hear others say "amen!" Everything seems fine if these labels are included. Later we may find that almost anything qualifies as an example of what these words mean. We need to take a careful look at our favorite buzz words, be sure we really know what they mean, and study the impact of these popular ideas on a balanced mathematics curriculum.

We need to analyze what our buzz words really mean.

Finally, although some oobs may be necessary and beneficial in effecting positive change, we can maintain control of oobs with an *evolutionary* rather than a *revolutionary* approach to change in our local school mathematics programs. Revolutionary *experimental* programs are necessary catalysts for change. But an experimental program should be tested extensively and revised over time before being pushed for widespread use in regular classrooms. When revolutionary experimental programs have been prematurely foisted on the average teacher, they have often created undesirable oobs in our mathematics curriculum. Evaluations of such programs usually contain such statements as "teachers were resistant to change," "it was ahead of its time," "teachers weren't prepared to teach it," or "it sounded like a good idea, but it just didn't work." Is it possible that curricular changes that affect all students and teachers will be more successful when they result from an evolutionary process that minimizes oobs and builds carefully on current successes?

We want to prepare students to be citizens and work in various jobs that will require mathematics in the twenty-first century. To do so will require a balanced mathematics curriculum. Now is the time to bring out our oob detectors!

References

National Council of Teachers of Mathematics. *Curriculum and Evaluation Standards for School Mathematics.* Reston, Va.: The Council, 1989.

———. *Professional Standards for Teaching Mathematics.* Reston, Va.: The Council, 1991.

Timed Tests

In My Opinion

by

Marilyn Burns

Dee Uyeda, a teacher in Mill Valley, California, told her class of third graders that they were going to take a test. Mrs. Uyeda was interested in the progress the children were making in their mathematics learning.

Tommy's hand shot up. "Is this a timed test?" he asked.

Mrs. Uyeda had not intended to impose a time limit on the children's work and was surprised by the question. Before giving the children her test, she encouraged them to talk about their experiences with timed tests. The responses poured from the children. After hearing some of their reactions, Mrs. Uyeda asked the children to write about their feelings.

Jess wrote this response:

> I don't like timed tests because the teachers never give you enough time and when I have a timed test I start to tremble with fear.

Emily wrote the following:

> I hate time tests when I try to do them I think oh no the time is running out and I look at the paper next to me and it's half way done and I've only done one problem and after that I hate math.

And from Elizabeth came this passionate plea:

> The teacher passes out the paper. Thats when the butterflys began! Your heart is in your throt! You want to get all the math problems rigs. But there is no time to think! There is a blur of proloms to be done. Your head gets dizy, rushing

Marilyn Burns is creator of Math Solutions in-service courses and president of Marilyn Burns Education Associates, Sausalito, CA 94965. She is interested in developing and writing mathematic curriculum units, articles for teachers, and books for children.

you try to finsh. No time to check over. It will have to do. I don't think I ever got all the prolmems in a timed test rigs. You get so nervs that you can't think, your palms swet. That feeling in your stomick is too bad for words. The dreaded time test …

Timed tests have long been used to monitor children's proficiency with basic mathematics facts and skills. Even with a nationwide shift in mathematics education to a curriculum that calls for teaching for understanding and instruction that emphasizes thinking, reasoning, and solving problems, giving timed tests still persists as standard classroom procedure in many school districts.

Teachers who use timed tests believe that the tests help children learn basic facts. This perspective makes no instructional sense. Children who perform well under time pressure display their skills. Children who have difficulty with skills or who work more slowly run the risk of reinforcing wrong practices under pressure. Also, they can become fearful about, and negative toward, their mathematics learning.

Also, timed tests do not measure children's understanding. An analysis of the National Assessment of Educational Progress's (NAEP) tests have demonstrated that children's ability to perform arithmetic skills does not ensure their ability to use those skills in problem-solving situations. As stated in California's *Mathematics Model Curriculum Guide* (CDSE 1987, 10), "[i]f a child does not have an understanding of the concept represented by a symbol, no amount of practice working with that symbol will help to develop that concept."

From a regimen of timed tests, children learn that it is important not only to be able to recall mathematics facts and skills but also to do so quickly. Yet speed with arithmetic skills has little, if anything, to do with mathematical power. The more important measure of children's mathematical prowess is their ability to use numbers to solve problems, confidently analyze situations that call for the use of numerical calculations, and arrive at reasonable numerical decisions that they can explain and justify. Expecting any less is educationally foolish and shortsighted.

Educational Leadership (Brandt 1988) conducted an interview with Lauren Resnick, codirector of the Learning Research and Development Center at the University of Pittsburgh. She expressed the following thoughts in response to a question about drill and practice and tests (pp. 13–14):

> If you believe that mathematics is a collection of specific pieces of knowledge, it is very reasonable to build tests that sample that knowledge…. And those tests encourage teaching that emphasizes bits of knowledge because that's how you improve students' scores. With the kind of teaching those tests promote, children come to believe that mathematics is a collection of questions to which one can find the answer within about a minute, or not at all. And that is contradictory to the goal of having children come to believe

that mathematics is an organized system of thought that they are capable of figuring out.

It *is* important for students to learn the addition and multiplication facts. However, learning facts must follow developing understanding of the concept. Having children memorize addition facts or times tables when they are learning new ideas may communicate to children that immediate recall of facts is the true message of mathematical success. Instead, the message to children about their mathematics learning should be that it is important to be able to apply numerical reasoning in a variety of problem situations. Timed tests do not help children learn.

References

Brandt, Ron. "On Learning Research: A Conversation with Lauren Resnick." *Educational Leadership* 46 (December 1988/January 1989):12–16.

California State Department of Education (CDSE). *Mathematics Model Curriculum Guide, Kindergarten through Grade Eight.* Sacramento, Calif.: CDSE, 1987.

The Role of *JRME* in Advancing Learning and Teaching Elementary School Mathematics

by

Michael T. Battista and Carol Novillis Larson

The *Journal for Research in Mathematics Education* (*JRME*) is the research journal of the National Council of Teachers of Mathematics. It is a "forum for disciplined inquiry into the learning and teaching of mathematics at all levels—from preschool through adult" (*JRME* Editorial Board 1993, 3). *JRME*'s twenty-fifth anniversary year is 1994. As part of the celebration of this event, members of *JRME*'s editorial panel have written articles for the Council's other journals that describe the role that *JRME* and research have played in promoting teaching and learning mathematics. This article will focus on *JRME*'s contribution to the view of learning and teaching elementary school mathematics embodied in current curricular recommendations for school mathematics.

Research on Children's Learning

Research in *JRME* illustrates how prevailing theories about how students learn mathematics have moved away from a behaviorist tradition, which focuses on what students do, to a more constructivist view, which focuses on how students think. According to a constructivist view, students learn mathematics meaningfully as they personally construct mental structures and operations that enable

Michael Battista teaches at Kent State University, Kent, OH 44242. He is currently involved with research and curriculum-development projects in elementary school mathematics. Carol Novillis Larson teaches at the University of Arizona, Tucson, AZ 85721. Both authors are former members of the Editorial Panel of the Journal for Research in Mathematics Education.

them to deal with problematic situations, organize their ideas about the world, and make sense of their interactions with others. The constructive process occurs as students reflect on and abstract the mental and physical actions they perform on their current representations of the world (see, e.g., Clement [1991]; Cobb et al. [1991]; Cobb et al. [1992]).

In a constructivist approach to teaching, the goal is to guide students in building mathematical structures that are more complex, abstract, and powerful than those they already possess. Such guidance can occur only if it is based on a knowledge of what conceptual structures the students might make and how the students might change during the course of instruction (Cobb et al. 1991). Along this line, *JRME* has reported much research that has investigated the cognitive structures and operations that students bring to bear on problems in elementary school mathematics. In this article, several important themes that recur in the research will be described, an example of an essential concept in mathematics whose in-depth research analysis has important implications for curriculum redesign will be given, and some specific classroom applications of the research will be listed.

Recurrent themes

- Students often apply informal, common-sense knowledge rather than formal, school-taught procedures when solving mathematical problems. Sometimes this informal knowledge is powerful enough to solve the problems; sometimes it is not. For instance, students in grades 1–3 often solve addition and subtraction word problems by employing informally learned counting strategies to model the actions described in the problems (Carpenter and Moser 1984; De Corte and Verschaffel 1987). Similarly, for a pictorially presented problem, Lamon (1993) asked sixth graders if 19 food pellets would be enough for 9 aliens, given that 3 aliens need 5 pellets. She found that rather than comparing ratios, most students modeled the problem by matching 3 aliens with 5 pellets three times, correctly determining that 4 pellets were left over. However, both Lamon (1993) and Mack (1990) found that many of the students' informal procedures were inadequate for solving more-complex fraction and ratio problems. Moreover, Clements and Battista (1990) found that fourth graders have many informal, everyday conceptualizations of geometric ideas that actually compete with formal concepts. For instance, students often think of angles as tilted lines, straight as meaning perpendicular, and a rectangle as having two long sides and two short sides, which means that for them a square is not a rectangle.

- Students' informal, intuitive ideas are, for the most part, unconnected to the formal concepts, procedures, and symbols they learn in school. For example, when asked which is bigger, 1/6 or 1/8, four of five students who had just correctly solved an analogous verbal problem involving pizzas chose 1/8 (Mack 1990). Explaining why similar types of errors, such as using the wrong operation, occurred in primary-age children's solution of verbal addition and subtraction problems, Carpenter, Hiebert, and Moser (1981) blamed traditional instruction in operations and word problems: "Because the operations are initially learned outside the context of verbal problems and children are simply told that addition and subtraction can be used to solve these problems, they have no basis for using their natural intuition to relate the problem structure to the operations they have learned" (p. 37).

- Learning the procedures taught in school often interferes with students' efforts to make sense of mathematics (Mack 1990; Wearne and Hiebert 1988). For instance, for problems involving fractions, Mack found that students' use of procedures either preempted their attempts to apply informal knowledge or yielded incorrect answers that they trusted more than informally reasoned, correct answers. "The evidence suggests that learners who possess well-practiced, automatic rules for manipulating symbols are reluctant to connect the rules with other representations that might give them meaning" (Hiebert and Carpenter 1992, 78). In fact, the traditional focus on teaching algorithmic procedures causes students to develop the belief that learning mathematics means following rules that someone else presents (Cobb et al. 1992).

- In a traditional curriculum, many techniques taught for solving problems are based on surface characteristics of problems, like looking for key words that correspond to operations (Carpenter and Moser 1984).

Such techniques encourage superficial analysis of problems, and their continued use leads to insufficient development of problem-solving skills.

- Classrooms that have adopted a constructivist approach to instruction have proved quite successful. For instance, when compared with students in traditionally taught classes, students in second-grade classes taking a constructivist approach were similar in computational skills but had higher levels of conceptual understanding, were more motivated by a desire to understand or to make sense of their mathematical experiences, and showed signs of developing intellectual autonomy (Cobb et al.1991; Yackel, Cobb, and Wood 1991).

The role of units in elementary mathematics

Investigating the role and nature of *units* has been a recurrent theme in research on place value, multidigit addition and subtraction, and fractions. The notion is also essential in students' understanding of whole-number multiplication and division and of decimals, making it a natural idea with which to make *connections* across the mathematics curriculum, as suggested by the NCTM's *Curriculum and Evaluation Standards for School Mathematics* (1989).

Searching for key words is insufficient for developing problem-solving skills.

Fuson (1990) and Baroody (1990) agree that to understand place value, students need to develop *multiunit conceptual structures*. It is not enough for them to think of 70 as a collection of seventy units; they need to form new units of ten so that they can also think of 70 as seven units, each of which is a collection of ten. That is, students have constructed a multiunit, or *abstract composite unit,* of ten when they can take sets of ten as single entities while simultaneously maintaining their "tenness." Baroody (1990) systematically describes a sequence of activities using different concrete embodiments that can help students develop multiunits of ten, hundred, and thousand: (1) using interlocking blocks to group 10 ones into a ten, (2) using base-ten blocks to trade 10 ones for a pregrouped ten, (3) using colored chips for trading in 10 ones for a different-looking ten marker, and (4) using trading boards to trade in 10 ones for an identical marker that represents ten because of its position on the board. Also see Cobb, Yackel, and Wood's (1992) discussion of "The Candy Factory" instructional sequence.

On the basis of studies, in particular Fuson and Briars (1990), Fuson (1990) recommends changes in the traditional textbook placement of place-value topics and in teaching practices. She thinks that multidigit addition and subtraction should first be introduced in second rather than first grade. From the beginning, students should be given multidigit problems with and without regrouping. Fuson and Briars (1990) report that using base-ten blocks to solve a wide variety of problems helped the second graders in their research study begin to develop the concepts of multiunits that are essential to understanding our numeration system. Once students have constructed these multiunits, they are better able to apply place-value concepts in such other circumstances as multiplication and division.

Studies illustrate the cognitive complexity of seemingly simple concepts.

Another area in which "seeing" units is essential is in understanding fractions. Being able to identify the unit, or one, for any given fraction situation and recognizing how that unit is partitioned are crucial to developing an understanding of fractions as "numbers." For instance, fourth graders have little difficulty successfully partitioning a set into equivalent subsets, that is, sharing 28 cookies fairly among 4 dolls. Yet when trying to find 1/5 of 5 eggs, some of these students cannot employ their partitioning strategy because their concept of *whole* is one continuous object (Hunting 1983). To understand fractional parts of a set, students need to recognize that the collection is the unit, or one. That is, in all elementary school students' work with representing whole numbers, each object in a set is one, or a unit. However, when working with fractional parts of sets, students must think of the whole set as the unit. For example, a six-pack of cola comprises six cans; one-half of the *whole set* contains three cans.

The number-line model for fractions also requires students to refine their concept of unit, especially when the number line is longer than one unit. For example, in figure 1, students have more difficulty locating or identifying what number is represented by position *X* on number line B than on A (Bright et al. 1988). On number line B, some students associate "1/6" with point *X* because they assume that the unit is the total length of the visible portion of the number line rather than the segment from 0 to 1. The confusion seems to arise from students' thinking of the number line as a line-segment model for fractions, as shown in figure 2, causing them to lose track of the unit.

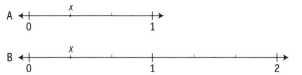

Fig. 1. What number is represented by *x* on these number lines?

In the line segment model, the complete segment, regardless of length, is treated as the unit; in this example, each of the three subsegments is labeled 1/3. On the scaled number line, in contrast, 1/3 is the result of partitioning each *marked* unit into three equivalent lengths, with endpoints of segments of length 1/3 being labeled 1/3, 2/3, 1, and so on. Complicating matters even further, Bright and others note that "on the number line there is no visual discreetness between consecutive units" (1988, 215).

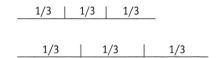

Fig. 2. Two line-segment models for one-third

Many other studies in *JRME* discuss in detail students' learning of specific topics. Readers are encouraged to examine *JRME* articles for details. As in the foregoing discussion of units, most of the studies illustrate the cognitive complexity of seemingly simple mathematical concepts and suggest that students require many diverse experiences before they can transfer learning from one type of situation, problem, or concrete model to another (e.g., Behr et al. [1984]; Kouba [1989]; Mack [1990]).

Classroom Applications

In addition to the instructional hints given in our discussion of units, several practical suggestions for improving mathematics instruction can be derived from research.

- An essential ingredient for encouraging students' constructive activity in mathematics instruction is a set of properly chosen problem-solving tasks. To be effective, these tasks should represent genuine, but doable, problems for students who are functioning within a wide range of conceptual levels and should elicit variety in students' solution strategies and thinking (Cobb et al. 1991; Lamon 1993). For example, students could solve concretely or pictorially the aliens problem described earlier; they could use multiplication, reasoning that because 5 times 3 is 15, only 15 pellets are needed; or they could set up a proportion. All viable student strategies should be accepted as correct; adopting more sophisticated strategies is encouraged as students publicly discuss their strategies and solve additional problems.

- Instruction should promote a climate of sense making, inquiry, and reflection in the classroom. One way to accomplish this goal is to involve students first in small-group collaborative mathematical investigations then in teacher-orchestrated class discussions in which students understand that their role is to make sense of, discuss, explain, critique, and justify mathematical ideas (Cobb et al. 1991).

Students' informal mathematical ideas cannot be ignored.

- Word problems should not be treated as applications of previously learned computational procedures but as opportunities for problem solving and sense making. They should be viewed as a way to introduce new mathematical concepts. For example, students in the Lamon (1993) study were able to discover viable methods for solving the aliens problem before they had been formally introduced to ratio and proportion concepts.

- Mathematical ideas reside in students' minds, not in concrete materials or in mathematical symbols. These materials and symbols become meaningful when students can use them as tools to support their personal mathematical thinking (Cobb, Yackel, and Wood 1992). For example, because of their tendency to understand addition and subtraction word problems in terms of the action described, first graders were very successful in learning to solve such problems using open number sentences (Bebout 1990). Open sentences, such as $5 + n = 12$, permitted students to express meaningfully their intuitive understanding of such problems as "John had 5 marbles. After Mary gave him some more marbles, he had 12. How many marbles did Mary give to John?" Similarly, base-ten blocks become meaningful to a student as he or she learns to let a tens block represent the act of counting ten cubes and mentally grouping them into a unit.

- Students' informal mathematical ideas cannot be ignored. These informal ideas, along with previously learned formal ideas, form the current experiential mathematical reality of students. This reality must serve as the starting point for the construction of more-sophisticated mathematical structures (Cobb, Yackel, and Wood 1992). Only after students have created these structures and developed meaning for symbols should they be practicing symbolic routines (Wearne and Hiebert 1988).

Conclusion

The striking similarity between the conclusions drawn from research and the basic tenets underlying the reform movement and the NCTM's *Curriculum and Evaluation Standards* (1989) is not a coincidence. Research in mathematics education has been essential in exposing shortcomings of past practice and suggesting avenues for improving mathematics instruction. The *Journal for Research in Mathematics Education* has played a leading role in supporting this endeavor.

References

Baroody, Arthur J. "How and When Should Place-Value Concepts and Skills Be Taught?" *Journal for Research in Mathematics Education* 21 (July 1990):281–86.

Bebout, Harriett C. "Children's Symbolic Representation of Addition and Subtraction Word Problems." *Journal for Research in Mathematics Education* 21 (March 1990):123–31.

Behr, Merlyn J., Ipke Wachsmuth, Thomas R. Post, and Richard Lesh. "Order and Equivalence of Rational Numbers: A Clinical Teaching Experiment." *Journal for Research in Mathematics Education* 15 (November 1984):323–41.

Bright, George W., Merlyn Behr, Thomas R. Post, and Ipke Wachsmuth. "Identifying Fractions on Number Lines." *Journal for Research in Mathematics Education* 19 (May 1988):215–32.

Carpenter, Thomas P., James Hiebert, and James M. Moser. "Problem Structure and First-Grade Children's Initial Solution Processes for Simple Addition and Subtraction Problems." *Journal for Research in Mathematics Education* 12 (January 1981):27–39.

Carpenter, Thomas P., and James M. Moser. "The Acquisition of Addition and Subtraction Concepts in Grades One through Three." *Journal for Research in Mathematics Education* 15 (May 1984):179–202.

Clement, John. "Constructivism in the Classroom—a Review of Transforming Children's Mathematics Education: International Perspectives, edited by Leslie P. Steffe and Terry Wood." *Journal for Research in Mathematics Education* 22 (November 1991):422–28.

Clements, Douglas H., and Michael T. Battista. "The Effects of Logo on Children's Conceptualizations of Angle and Polygons." *Journal for Research in Mathematics Education* 21 (November 1990):356–71.

Cobb, Paul, Terry Wood, Erna Yackel, and Betsy McNeal. "Characteristics of Classroom Mathematics Traditions: An Interactional Analysis." *American Educational Research Journal* 29 (1992):573–604.

Cobb, Paul, Terry Wood, Erna Yackel, John Nicholls, Grayson Wheatley, Beatriz Trigatti, and Marcella Perlwitz. "Assessment of a Problem-Centered Second-Grade Mathematics Project." *Journal for Research in Mathematics Education* 22 (January 1991):3–29.

Cobb, Paul, Erna Yackel, and Terry Wood. "A Constructivist Alternative to the Representational View of Mind in Mathematics Education." *Journal for Research in Mathematics Education* 23 (January 1992):2–33.

De Corte, Erik, and Lieven Verschaffel. "The Effect of Semantic Structure on First Graders' Strategies for Solving Addition and Subtraction Word Problems." *Journal for Research in Mathematics Education* 18 (November 1987):363–81.

Fuson, Karen. "Issues in Place-Value and Multidigit Addition and Subtraction Learning and Teaching." *Journal for Research in Mathematics Education* 21 (July 1990):273–80.

Fuson, Karen C., and Diane J. Briars. "Using a Base-Ten Blocks Learning/Teaching Approach for First- and Second-Grade Place-Value and Multidigit Addition and Subtraction." *Journal for Research in Mathematics Education* 21 (March 1990):180–206.

Hiebert, James, and Thomas P. Carpenter. "Learning and Teaching with Understanding." In *Handbook of Research on Mathematics Teaching and Learning,* edited by Douglas A. Grouws, 65–97. Reston, Va.: National Council of Teachers of Mathematics/Macmillan, 1992.

Hunting, Robert P. "Alan: A Case Study of Knowledge of Units and Performance with Fractions." *Journal for Research in Mathematics Education* 14 (May 1983):182–97.

JRME Editorial Board. "Information for Contributors." *Journal for Research in Mathematics Education* 24 (January 1993):3–7.

Kouba, Vicky L. "Children's Solution Strategies for Equivalent Set Multiplication and Division Word Problems." *Journal for Research in Mathematics Education* 20 (March 1989):147–58.

Lamon, Susan J. "Ratio and Proportion: Connecting Content and Children's Thinking." *Journal for Research in Mathematics Education* 24 (January 1993):41–61.

Mack, Nancy K. "Learning Fractions with Understanding: Building on Informal Knowledge." *Journal for Research in Mathematics Education* 21 (January 1990):16–32.

National Council of Teachers of Mathematics. *Curriculum and Evaluation Standards for School Mathematics.* Reston, Va.: The Council, 1989.

Wearne, Diana, and James Hiebert. "A Cognitive Approach to Meaningful Mathematics Instruction: Testing a Local Theory Using Decimal Numbers." *Journal for Research in Mathematics Education* 19 (November 1988):371–84.

Yackel, Erna, Paul Cobb, and Terry Wood. "Small Group Interactions as a Source of Learning Opportunities in Second-Grade Mathematics." *Journal for Research in Mathematics Education* 22 (November 1991):390–408.

Activities

Reform in School Mathematics

Battista and Larson, "The Role of JRME in Advancing Learning and Teaching Elementary School Mathematics"

The authors discuss the constructivist theory of learning and the recommendation that students be encouraged to build on the knowledge they already possess.

(*a*) Describe an incident from your own learning experiences in which you developed a way of doing some aspect of mathematics that was different from that "told" you by your teacher.

(*b*) Reflect on how this incident illustrates the constructivist theory of learning.

Section 2
Children's Invented Strategies

The articles in this section present both research findings and descriptions of innovative classrooms that illustrate the effectiveness of instruction built around children's invented computational strategies. Researchers in mathematics education have long been interested in how children develop their understandings of number and arithmetic operations. Findings from their research and the development of constructivist theories of learning have led to recommendations for new types of classroom instruction. Children's learning is perceived to be individually as well as socially constructed, built on previous knowledge, and evolved from children's in-school as well as out-of-school experiences. Research has found not only that children enter school with intuitive notions of mathematics but that they are able to invent individually meaningful computational strategies from these ideas. Instruction that builds on children's existing knowledge and encourages children's invented processes has been shown to provide effective learning opportunities.

Hankes describes work done by the Cognitively Guided Instruction project that uses knowledge of how children learn as an integral part of instructional strategies. Simple word problems are presented that illustrate the structure of addition, subtraction, multiplication, and division and the strategies that children use when solving such problems. Classroom vignettes show teachers using this information to make instructional decisions and assess children's learning.

Chambers emphasizes the importance of allowing children to use strategies they understand to solve problems. By directly modeling the relationships and actions in a given situation or by inventing strategies to deal with more-complex problems, children gain confidence in their ability to do mathematics. Examples of children's solution strategies illustrate their abilities to solve problems successfully before mastering number facts or computational algorithms.

The article by Kamii, Lewis, and Livingston presents the results of research on the use of computational algorithms with second and fourth graders. The findings show that students who were allowed to invent their own strategies for whole-number calculations developed better number sense and a greater understanding of place value than those children who began multidigit calculations after first being taught algorithms. The authors describe the teaching approach they use to encourage child-invented processes and give examples of the strategies that children have produced.

The final article by Philipp presents a discussion of alternative algorithms for the addition, subtraction, multiplication, and division of whole numbers. These algorithms, collected by preservice elementary school teachers in a mathematics methods course, show the variations in "standard" procedures that exist across cultures. The author describes how collecting and studying these alternatives promoted discussion about the meanings of the operations involved and why each algorithm worked.

Reading the four articles in this section offers insights into our own ways of thinking about computational processes. It is not easy to understand sets of procedures that are different from the familiar pencil-and-paper ones that we learned in school. In fact, we might be hard pressed to explain why our particular sets of rules work. The act of understanding unfamiliar strategies emphasizes the point made by all the authors in this section—that we understand best the ideas we construct ourselves rather than those others tell us.

An Alternative to Basic-Skills Remediation

by

Judith E. Hankes

Three students stand out vividly when recalling twenty years of teaching. The first one is Josh, a second grader who had been labeled as educable mentally retarded by his kindergarten and first-grade teachers. Josh had serious problems with symbols. He could not memorize his addition and subtraction facts, and at times he seemed not to understand that the numeral 7 stood for the quantity seven. However, Josh enthusiastically related that he only had to work two more weeks to pay off a go-cart. He explained that he owed $10 on it and that he was paid $5 each week for his help in the barn. It was impressive that Josh's out-of-school mathematics was clearly superior to his in-school mathematics.

The second student is Phil, a high school sophomore who was assigned to a tutorial program for help with general mathematics. Phil had given up on school. He explained that he just was not smart enough and that it was a waste of time to try to teach him. What seemed unusual about Phil was that he could use a calculator to figure the cost of feed for forty-eight milk cows or the amount of seed corn needed to plant a twenty-acre field and then estimate the profit for a good year. Phil dropped out of school in his junior year. His father had died, and he needed to run the farm.

All children come to school with an impressive amount of knowledge.

The third student is the author's son, Kurt. Like Josh, he reversed numbers and had difficulty recalling computational procedures. He was diagnosed as dyslexic in fourth grade. However, at that grade, although failing in arithmetic, he was able to figure the amount of change that he should receive after making a purchase; work for hours on mathematically based computer programs, such as Lemonade Stand, The Stock Market, or Flight Simulation; and play chess with skill.

How are these three students somehow connected? Josh, Phil, and Kurt, all labeled as learning disabled, had two things in common: they all experienced failure when computation was not related to meaningful context and they all were far more cognitively capable than traditional school assessments indicated. As would be expected, all three boys were placed in remedial programs that focused on deficit skills, and they were never given the opportunity to use their intuitive higher-order-thinking strategies to compensate.

Judith Hankes is a research assistant with the Cognitively Guided Instruction project, University of Wisconsin—Madison, Madison, WI 53706. She is especially interested in investigating the impact of the NCTM's Standards on minority and learning-disabled students.

This material is based on work supported in part by the National Science Foundation under grant no. MDR-8955346; the Wisconsin Center for Education Research; and the School of Education, University of Wisconsin—Madison. The opinions expressed in this publication are those of the author and do not necessarily reflect the views of the institutions.

Questioning Traditional Remediation Techniques

Why does the wide discrepancy between the inability to master basic skills and the ability to reason exist for some students? This question has perplexed teachers and specialists for a long time. How best to facilitate the understanding and learning of educationally disadvantaged students is being actively investigated, and the wisdom of focusing on skill deficits for remediation is being questioned (Griffin and Cole 1987; Behrend 1994).

It is easy to understand how such compensatory methods developed. The majority of this century's educational practices have been based on the fundamental assumption that certain skills are "basic" and must be mastered before students receive instruction on more "advanced" skills. Consequently, adherence to this assumption, particularly with those deemed most at risk of school failure, produced instruction that emphasized teaching discrete lower-level skills to the exclusion of higher-order-mathematical thinking (Arlington and McGill-Franzen 1989; Oakes 1986). Students in traditional remedial programs are not expected to do even simple mathematics-related problems until they have mastered their number facts and routine arithmetic procedures. Typically, students are drilled on the same operations year after year; demonstrated success at basic skills becomes a hurdle to overcome before the student receives instruction based on comprehension and reasoning (Means and Knapp 1991).

A Shift in Learning Theory

Research from mathematics education leads to quite a different view of children's learning and appropriate instruction (Carpenter 1985; Fennema, Carpenter, and Peterson 1989; Ginsburg 1983; Lave 1988). By discarding assumptions about skill hierarchies and attempting to understand children's knowledge as constructed and evolving both inside and outside school, researchers are developing models of both instruction and intervention that start with what children know and then build on that knowledge by allowing access for participation in advanced or higher-order activities. Instead of starting with a list of academic skills, administering formal assessment, and cataloging children's achievements and deficits, cognitively based instruction starts with the conviction that children from all socioeconomic and cultural backgrounds and with all levels of abilities come to school having already gained an impressive amount of knowledge.

A Shift in Instruction

One example of a cognitive-based approach to teaching mathematics is Cognitively Guided Instruction (CGI).

This primary-grade-mathematics program integrates research findings on how children think about mathematics with findings on how teachers use this knowledge when making instructional decisions. Over the last eight years, the CGI staff has accumulated an extensive body of research on the development of basic addition, subtraction, multiplication, and division concepts and skills in primary-school children (Carpenter, Fennema, and Franke 1992). This research shows that even before receiving any formal instruction with such concepts, children are consistently able to solve simple word problems by modeling, counting, or inventing solutions that are not tied to traditional arithmetic computation. Children interpret and make sense of new knowledge in light of their existing knowledge. Therefore, problem-solving experiences that encourage inventive solution strategies, usually in the form of word problems situated within a story context, form the basis for the development of basic arithmetic concepts and skills within this approach.

Instruction shifts from telling to listening.

Teachers who successfully use CGI in their classrooms base their mathematics instruction on two distinct but related bodies of knowledge: knowledge of the structure of addition, subtraction, multiplication, and division (see figs. 1 and 2) and knowledge of the developmental solution strategies that children employ when solving mathematics problems (see fig. 3).

Example of a CGI lesson

The following vignette describes how the integration of this knowledge informs instruction.

During the first few minutes of the day, Mrs. White asked how many children wanted hot lunch that day. Eighteen children raised their hands. Six children were going to eat cold lunch. Mrs. White asked, "How many children are going to eat lunch here today?"

By starting with 18 and counting on, several children got to the answer of 24. One child got out counters and counted out a set of 6. He then counted all of them and said, "Twenty-four."

Mrs. White then asked, "How many more children are eating hot lunch than are eating cold lunch?"

Several children counted back from 18 to 12. The child with the blocks matched some of his 18 blocks with 6 blocks and counted the blocks left over.

Mrs. White asked those children who had volunteered an answer to tell the rest of the class how they

Problem Type	Addition and Subtraction		
I. Join	A. Connie had 5 marbles. Jim gave her 8 more marbles. How many does Connie have all together? (result unknown)	B. Connie has 5 marbles. How many more marbles does she need to have 13 marbles all together? (change unknown)	C. Connie had some marbles. Jim gave her 5 more marbles. Now she has 13 marbles. How many marbles did Connie have to start with? (start unknown)
II. Separate	A. Connie had 13 marbles. She gave 5 marbles to Jim. How many marbles does she have left? (result unknown)	B. Connie had 13 marbles. She gave some to Jim. Now she has 5 marbles. How many did Connie give to Jim? (change unknown)	C. Connie had some marbles. She gave 5 to Jim. Now she has 8 marbles left. How many marbles did Connie have to start with? (start unknown)
III. Part-part-whole	A. Connie has 5 red marbles and 8 blue marbles. How many marbles does she have?	B. Connie has 13 marbles. Five are red and the rest are blue. How many blue marbles does Connie have?	
IV. Compare	A. Connie has 13 marbles. Jim has 5 marbles. How many more marbles does Connie have than Jim?	B. Jim has 5 marbles. Connie has 8 more than Jim. How many marbles does Connie have?	C. Connie has 13 marbles. She has 5 more marbles than Jim. How many marbles does Jim have?

(Source: Carpenter, Fennema, and Franke 1994)

Fig. 1. Classification of word problems

Multiplication	Megan has 5 bags of cookies. There are 3 cookies in each bag. How many cookies does Megan have altogether?
Measurement division	Megan has 15 cookies. She puts 3 cookies in each bag. How many bags can she fill?
Partitive division	Megan has 15 cookies. She put the cookies into 5 bags with the same number of cookies in each bag. How many cookies are in each bag?

(Source: Carpenter, Fennema, and Franke 1994)

Fig. 2. Multiplication, measurement-division, and partitive-division problems

had arrived at it. Mrs. White continued to ask for different solutions until no one could think of a new way to solve the problem (Peterson, Carpenter, and Fennema 1989a).

The teacher's knowledge of problem types and her knowledge of children's solution strategies are evident in this example. First, Mrs. White posed a part-part-whole-with-whole-unknown problem (refer to fig. 1): "How many children are going to eat lunch here today?" Later, she asked a compare-with-difference-unknown question: "How many more children are eating hot lunch than are eating cold lunch?" The teacher also encouraged the children to solve the problems in ways that made sense to them; some directly modeled them by using counters and some used counting strategies. The children were also encouraged to share their solutions with the rest of the class.

Students are encouraged to invent strategies.

To implement Cognitively Guided Instruction successfully takes time. The developers of this approach state that a teacher, like a child, makes sense of new knowledge in light of existing knowledge and beliefs. To change, the teacher must become a risk taker who is willing to move from the role of direct instructor—from telling to listening, from text dependence to content confidence, and from merely grading students' written work to asking probing questions as a way to gain knowledge of each child's understanding.

A Shift in Staff Development

Rather than use research to prescribe a program of instruction, the developers of CGI share research-based findings about children's knowledge and thinking about mathematics with teachers and let them interpret how it might influence their instructional decisions (Peterson, Carpenter, and Fennema 1989b). Since teachers feel free to interpret and implement CGI ideas based on their own understanding and classroom practice, classrooms reflect individual choices and styles of the teachers. However, CGI classrooms have in common at least three key elements. Teachers believe (1) that all children know something about mathematics and that

Direct Modeling Strategies

Strategy	Description
Joining all Ellen had 3 tomatoes. She picked 5 more tomatoes. How many tomatoes does Ellen have now?	Using objects or fingers, a set of 3 objects and a set of 5 objects are constructed. The sets are joined and the union of the two sets is counted.
Separating from There were 8 seals playing. Three seals swam away. How many seals were still playing?	Using objects or fingers, a set of 8 objects is constructed. 3 objects are removed. The answer is the number of remaining objects.
Separating to There were 8 people on the bus. Some people got off. Now there are 3 people on the bus. How many people got off the bus?	A set of 8 objects is counted out. Objects are removed from it until the number of objects remaining is equal to 3. The answer is the number of objects removed.
Joining to Chuck had 3 peanuts. Clara gave him some more peanuts. Now Chuck has 8 peanuts. How many peanuts did Clara give him?	A set of 3 objects is constructed. Objects are added to this set until there is a total of 8 objects. The answer is found by counting the number of objects added.
Matching Megan has 3 stickers. Randy has 8 stickers. How many more stickers does Randy have than Megan?	A set of 3 objects and a set of 8 objects are matched one-to-one until one set is used up. The answer is the number of objects remaining in the unmatched set.
Trial and error Deborah had some books. She went to the library and got 3 more books. Now she has 8 books altogether. How many books did she have to start with?	A set of objects is constructed. A set of 3 objects is added to or removed, and the resulting set is counted. If the final count is 8, then the number of elements in the initial set is the answer. If it is not 8, a different initial set is tried.

Counting Strategies

Strategy	Description
Counting on from first Ellen had 3 tomatoes. She picked 5 more tomatoes. How many tomatoes does she have now?	The counting sequence begins with 3 and continues on 5 counts. The answer is the last term in the counting sequence.
Counting on from larger Ellen had 3 tomatoes. She picked 5 more tomatoes. How many tomatoes does she have now?	The counting sequence begins with 5 and continues on 3 counts. The answer is the last term in the counting sequence.
Counting down There were 8 seals playing. Three seals swam away. How many seals were still playing?	A backward counting sequence is initiated from 8. The sequence continues for 3 counts. The last number in the counting sequence is the answer.
Counting down to There were 8 people on the bus. Some people got off. Now there are 3 people on the bus. How many people got off the bus?	A backward counting sequence starts from 8 and continues until 3 is reached. The answer is the number of words in the counting sequence.
Counting on to Chuck had 3 peanuts. Clara gave him some more peanuts. Now Chuck has 8 peanuts. How many peanuts did Clara give to him?	A forward counting sequence starts from 3 and continues until 8 is reached. The answer is the number of counting words in the sequence.

Deriving and Fact Recall Strategies

Strategy	Description
Deriving Six frogs were sitting on lily pads. Eight more frogs joined them. How many frogs were there then?	The child answers "14" almost immediately and explains, "I know because 6 and 6 is 12 and 2 more is 14."
Fact recall Eight birds were sitting in a tree. Five flew away. How many are in the tree now?	The child answers "3" immediately and explains, "I know that 8 take away 5 is 3."

(Source: Carpenter, Fennema, and Franke 1994)

Fig. 3. Children's solution strategies

part of the teacher's role is to attempt to determine that knowledge base so as to plan instruction, (2) that focusing on problem solving helps reveal children's mathematics knowledge, and (3) that encouraging students to invent strategies that make sense to them when solving word problems and sharing such strategies reveals students' thinking as well as facilitates learning.

CGI and the Learning-Disabled Child

The following example from the classroom of a CGI teacher will help explain how these elements can be applied when working with a learning-disabled student (Peterson, Fennema, and Carpenter 1991, 90–91):

Billy was a disadvantaged (a child with learning problems) child who had arrived in Ms. J.'s classroom in the middle of October, six weeks after school had started. He had not been in school previously that year because of a teachers' strike in the community from which he came. When Billy entered Ms. J.'s first grade class, he could neither count nor recognize numerals. Ms. J. and the other children helped Billy learn to count objects, first to five and then to ten. Billy learned to count to ten verbally, and when he continued to have great difficulty recognizing numerals, Ms. J. gave him a number line with each number clearly identified. Billy carried the number line with him continuously, and if he needed to know what a numeral looked like, he would count the marks on the number line and know that the numeral written beside the appropriate mark was the numeral he needed. As soon as Billy could count, Ms. J. began giving him simple word problems to solve. On a sheet of paper, she would write a word problem such as, "If Billy had two pennies, and Maria gave him three more, how many would he have then?" (a joining problem with the result unknown). Either Ms. J. or another child would then read the problem to Billy, who would get some counters and patiently model the problem. In this problem, Billy made a set of two cubes and a set of three cubes and then counted all of the cubes. Ms. J. would then ask Billy to explain how he got his answer. He would tell her what each set meant, and how he had counted them all and gotten five and then counted up his number line to know what five looked like.

During mathematics class, Billy might solve only two or three of these simple problems, but he knew what he was doing, and he was able to report his thinking so that Ms. J. could understand what he had done. When Ms. J. was sure he understood the simple problems such as joining and separating result-unknown problems, she moved onto somewhat harder problems and to somewhat larger numbers. She encouraged Billy to make up his own problems to solve and to give to other children. Almost all of Billy's time in mathematics class during the year was spent in solving problems by direct modeling or in making up problems for other children to solve. When we interviewed Billy near the end of the year, he was solving problems more difficult than

those typically included in most first grade textbooks. Billy had become less reliant on his number line, and he could solve result-unknown and change-unknown problems with numbers up to twenty. Although at that point Billy was not yet able to recall basic arithmetic facts, he nonetheless understood conceptually what addition and subtraction meant, and he could directly model problems to find the answer. Billy was no less proud of himself or excited about mathematics than any other child in the classroom. As he said to the school principal, "Do you know those kids in Ms. J.'s class who love math? Well, I'm one of them."

The case of Billy is true. By the end of first grade, this child, who would have qualified for any program for the disadvantaged, had made progress in learning mathematics, understood the mathematics he was doing, and felt good about himself and about mathematics. In his eyes, and in his teacher's eyes, Billy apparently was a successful learner, and clinical interview data also confirmed his success.

In March 1993, Ms. J. was asked why she had used story problems rather than drill and practice to develop Billy's understanding. Ms. J. responded, "I just don't teach that way, and kids don't learn that way. I did not treat Billy as a learning-disabled child. He was given activities that challenged him and was expected to do what all of the other kids were expected to do: attempt to solve problems in any way that made sense to him, listen to others, and share strategies. In my classroom, all children respect each other, regardless of ability. But I do think that situating mathematical computation within a story problem was extremely helpful for Billy. When seeing naked numbers, he would say, 'Ms. J., would you put those numbers in a story problem for me so that I can do it?' Putting numbers into problems made math real for Billy."

Shifting Teachers' Views of Learning-Disabled Children

The majority of experienced classroom teachers who have shifted from a traditional skill-and procedure-based focus to CGI's problem-based approach express similar feelings about CGI and learning-disabled students. As part of an ongoing data collection project, eight first- and second-grade CGI teachers were interviewed (Chambers and Hankes 1994) and asked if they believed that CGI influenced learning-disabled students. One first-grade teacher with eighteen years of teaching experience said, "Some of the LD kids have done very well in CGI math. I mean exceptionally well. I guess it's because they've had to work hard all along so they know how to do it and figure out those problems. If they can directly model it, they've got it. And what it does for their self-esteem is wonderful! The better they do, the more successful they are, the better they feel about themselves." Another veteran first-grade teacher observed, "The learning-disabled children are especially able to master word problems, maybe not with the efficiency that some of the others do, but they were never there at all before. You know, that's a big jump. They want to keep up, and this way they can. It makes them feel pretty good about themselves." A second-grade teacher candidly shared her thoughts regarding low achievers, "I found that years ago the lowers always stayed real low and they didn't have a lot of confidence. I find that now they have more confidence, and I almost expect them to be in the middle.... I really expect them to do just as much as anybody else, and I find that they do." These comments illuminate the most positive contribution of Cognitively Guided Instruction—the belief that all learners are much more mathematically knowledgeable than once assumed. The message of CGI is that when teachers begin listening to children, they come to realize how much more the children how than they recognized previously. They come to realize that children have a lot of mathematical knowledge on which to build. Teachers can achieve the goals of compensatory mathematics education by building on this knowledge. The following findings of a recent CGI study (Behrend 1994) support this belief:

> These [learning-disabled] students were capable of sharing their strategies, listening to other students, discussing similarities and differences between strategies, justifying their thinking, and helping each other understand word problems.
>
> Since these students had appropriate strategies to solve problems, these results call into question the need for explicit strategy instruction in mathematics for learning disabled students, and provide support for instructional approaches which utilize students' natural problem-solving processes.

One cannot help but wonder how different the school experiences of Josh, Phil, and Kurt might have been if they had been encouraged to build on their cognitive strengths. Josh, like Phil, dropped out of school. Currently, both he and Phil are successful farmers. Kurt entered an alternative-vocational program at fifteen, became a certified underwater welder by nineteen, and is a successful commercial diver. All three men share two realities: (1) as adults they are able to manage successful careers that demand a great deal of mathematical reasoning and (2) they all possess bitter memories of school failure that persist in undermining their self-esteem. One wishes that all three could have been part of a CGI classroom.

References

Allington, Richard L., and Anne McGill-Franzen. "School Response to Reading Failure: Chapter 1 and Special Education Students in Grades 2, 4, and 8." *Elementary School Journal* (May 1989):529–42.

Behrend, Jeanie L. "Mathematical Problem Solving Processes of Primary Grade Students Identified as Learning Disabled." Ph.D diss., University of Wisconsin, 1994.

Carpenter, Thomas P. "Learning to Add and Subtract: An Exercise in Problem Solving." In *Teaching and Learning Mathematical Problem Solving: Multiple Research Perspectives,* edited by Edward A. Silver, 17–40. Hillsdale, N.J.: Lawrence Erlbaum Associates, 1985.

Carpenter, Thomas P., Elizabeth Fennema, and Megan L. Franke. "Cognitively Guided Instruction: Building the Primary Mathematics Curriculum on Children's Informal Mathematical Knowledge." Paper presented at the American Educational Research Association Conference, San Francisco, 1992.

———. *Cognitively Guided Instruction: Children's Thinking about Whole Numbers.* Madison, Wisc.: Wisconsin Center for Education Research, 1994.

Chambers, Donald L., and Judith Elaine Hankes. "Using Knowledge of Children's Thinking to Change Teaching." In *Professional Development for Teaching Mathematics,* 1994 Yearbook of the National Council of Teachers of Mathematics, edited by Douglas B. Aichele, 286–95. Reston, Va.: The Council, 1994.

Fennema, Elizabeth, Thomas P. Carpenter, and Penelope L. Peterson. "Learning Mathematics with Understanding." In *Advances in Research on Teaching,* vol. 1, edited by Jere E. Brophy, 195–221. Greenwich, Conn.: JAI Press, 1989.

Ginsburg, Herbert P., ed. *The Development of Mathematical Thinking.* New York: Academic Press, 1983.

Griffin, Peg, and Michael Cole. "New Technologies, Basic Skills, and the Underside of Education. What's to Be Done?" In *Language, Literacy, and Culture: Issues of Society and Schooling,* edited by Judith A. Langer. Norwood, N.J.: Ablex Publishing Corp., 1987.

Lave, Jean. *Cognition in Practice: Mind, Mathematics and Culture in Everyday Life.* New York: Cambridge University Press, 1988.

Means, Barbara, and Michael S. Knapp. "Introduction: Rethinking Teaching for Disadvantaged Students." In *Teaching Advanced Skills to At-Risk Students.* edited by Barbara Means, Carol Chelmer, and Michael S. Knapp, 1–26. San Francisco: Josey-Bass Publishers, 1991.

Oakes, Jeannie. "Tracking, Inequality, and the Rhetoric of School Reform: Why Schools Don't Change." *Journal of Education* 168 (1986):61–80.

Peterson, Penelope L., Thomas P. Carpenter, and Elizabeth Fennema. "Using Knowledge of How Students Think about Mathematics." *Educational Leadership* 46 (December 1988/January 1989a):42–46.

———. "Teachers' Knowledge of Students' Knowledge in Mathematics Problem Solving: Correlational and Case Analysis." *Journal of Educational Psychology* 81 (December 1989b):558–69.

Peterson, Penelope L., Elizabeth Fennema, and Thomas P. Carpenter. "Using Children's Mathematical Knowledge." In *Teaching Advanced Skills to At-Risk Students,* edited by Barbara Means, Carol Chelmer, and Michael S. Knapp, 68–100. San Francisco: Jossey-Bass Publishers, 1991.

Research into Practice

Direct Modeling and Invented Procedures
Building on Students' Informal Strategies

by

Donald L. Chambers

Young children commonly solve mathematics problems by directly modeling the action or relationship described in the problem. They do not need to be taught how to use direct-modeling strategies, nor do they need such often-assumed prerequisite knowledge as number facts or computational algorithms.

Direct Modeling

An example of direct modeling arose when a third-grade teacher posed this problem:

> On our hospital field trip we saw 12 emergency rooms. Each room had 9 beds in it. How many beds were there?

Pamela counted out twelve groups of blocks with 9 blocks in each group. She then rearranged the blocks into groups of 10, replacing each group of 10 with a tens block. When

Donald Chambers, dlchambe@facstaff.wisc.edu, is a member of the staff of the Cognitively Guided Instruction Project, Wisconsin Center for Education Research, 1025 West Johnson Street, University of Wisconsin—Madison, Madison, WI 53706. His interests include children's informal problem-solving strategies, teaching that builds on children's informal strategies, and teacher education that fosters teaching that builds on children's informal strategies.

The examples in this article were transcribed from videotaped interactions between teachers and students. Most are available as part of the Cognitively Guided Instruction Project videotape series produced by the Wisconsin Center for Education Research, © 1995. Some episodes were edited for the presentation described here.

she got 10 tens blocks, she replaced them with a hundreds block. She got 108. Pamela directly modeled the problem situation, using blocks to represent hospital beds. Pamela's strategy is typical. She does not appear to know the standard multiplication algorithm, but she has devised an effective way to solve this "multiplication" problem.

The ability to solve "multiplication" problems is also common among kindergarten students, as the subsequent example illustrates. A kindergarten teacher posed the following problem:

> A bee has 6 legs. How many legs do 5 bees have?

Sean put out 5 cubes to represent the bees. Then he put out 6 cubes with each bee to represent its legs. He then counted all the legs, but not the bees, and got 30. Jeffrey used a number line. He pointed to the 6 and said, "Six for one bee. That's one." He pointed to the 12 and said, "Six for another bee. That's two." He then counted 6 more on the number line, landing at 18, and said, "Six for another bee. That's three." He continued counting by ones on the number line and keeping track of the number of bees mentally until he got 30 legs for 5 bees. Brianna said that she knew that 6 + 6 = 12. Then, using her fingers, she counted on 6 more from 12 to get 18 and repeated the process until she got 30.

The problem-solving power of these students comes from their ability to model a problem directly. In a study of kindergarten students' problem-solving processes (see Carpenter et al. [1993]), 71 percent correctly solved this problem:

> Robin has 3 packages of gum. There are 6 pieces of gum in each package. How many pieces of gum does Robin have altogether?

Direct modeling is a natural strategy used by many children to solve both routine and nonroutine problems. Over half the kindergarten children in the study cited were able to solve the problem:

> 19 children are taking a minibus to the zoo. They will have to sit either 2 or 3 to a seat. The bus has 7 seats. How many children will have to sit 3 to a seat, and how many can sit 2 to a seat?

This problem is almost impossible for children to solve by using addition and subtraction facts. However, it is easy to model, and modeling readily yields a solution. Children who solve this problem usually draw seven seats and systematically assign children to seats, first putting one on each seat, and then a second, and then a third, until all students are seated. They can then count the number sitting two to a seat and the number sitting three to a seat. High school students are taught an algorithm that can be used to solve this problem, but by using direct modeling, younger students clearly can solve the problem long before the procedure is taught.

Invented Strategies

Direct-modeling strategies using counters are sufficient for problems involving small numbers. As numbers become larger, requiring representations of tens and hundreds, students begin to develop invented strategies. Invented strategies involve mental pictures of the blocks that represent the numbers, or mental calculation with the numbers themselves, or invention of pencil-and-paper notation. Three different invented strategies were used by Lauren and Laurel, second graders, and by Joel, a first grader, to solve the following problem:

> Max had 46 comic books. For his birthday his father gave him 37 more comic books. How many comic books does Max have now?

All three students solved the problem mentally. Lauren started with 46 and counted by tens, then by ones: 46, 56, 66, 76, 77, 78, 79, 80, 81, 82, 83. Laurel rounded 37 to 40 to simplify the addition. She then adjusted the result by subtracting the 3 that she added earlier: 46 + 40 = 86; 86 − 3 = 83. Joel used a strategy that is very similar to the standard algorithm but, like many children, he worked with the tens first, then the ones: 40 + 30 = 70; 6 + 7 = 13; 70 + 13 = 83.

Standard algorithms typically form the core of the elementary school mathematics program, but instruction of standard algorithms frequently does not build on students' natural ways of thinking. When standard algorithms abruptly displace children's natural direct-modeling strategies and invented procedures, confusion rather than understanding frequently results. In the following example, Gretchen subtracts 23 from 70 by using the standard algorithm. She then uses an invented strategy based on direct modeling. When she gets two different answers, her confusion is apparent.

Teacher: How would you do this problem? [On a piece of paper, she writes:]

$$\begin{array}{r} 70 \\ -\ 23 \\ \hline \end{array}$$

Gretchen: That's easy. [She first writes a 3 below the 0 and the 3, and then writes a 5 below the 7 and the 2.]

Teacher: And your answer is … ?

Gretchen: 53.

Teacher: Could you show me that problem with these [base-ten] blocks?

Gretchen: Okay. [She takes 7 tens blocks. Then she takes away 2 tens blocks and counts 3 units on the next tens block. She then counts the remaining units on that block: 1, 2, 3, 4, 5, 6, 7. She looks at the remaining tens blocks. Then she looks back at her previous answer.] Oh, gee! [She rechecks her previous work with pencil and paper.] I don't get it.

Teacher: What did you get for your answer with the blocks?

Gretchen: [Rechecks her work, exactly the same way, with the same result.] Over here [with the blocks] I get 47, but over here … [with the pencil and paper]. Okay, 0 take away 3, yeah, that's 3. Okay. 7 take away 2 equals 5. So I put 3 there [pointing to the 3 she wrote earlier] and 5 there [pointing to the 5].

Teacher: And over there [pointing to the blocks] you got what?

Gretchen: 47. I don't get it.

Teacher: Which one do you think is right?

Gretchen: [Taps the 53 with a tens block she still holds in her hand.]

Gretchen has been taught the standard subtraction algorithm. She does not understand it, but she believes in its power. When confronted with her own conceptually based explanation with tens blocks, she rejects it in favor of her algorithmic answer.

Gretchen believes in the power of the standard algorithm.

If we had seen Gretchen's solution with the blocks but not her paper-and-pencil solution, we would probably believe that Gretchen understands subtraction with regrouping. If we had not seen Gretchen reject the blocks-based solution in favor of her pencil-and-paper solution, we would probably believe that such a blocks-based demonstration would persuade her that her pencil-and-paper solution was wrong.

According to the National Assessment of Educational Progress (Kouba, Carpenter, and Swafford 1989), 70 percent of third graders in the spring semester could solve this subtraction problem:

$$\begin{array}{r} 54 \\ -37 \\ \hline \end{array}$$

Only 65 percent could solve 44 – 6. A study of beginning second-grade students who had not yet been taught the subtraction algorithm in school found that 76 percent could correctly solve a two-digit-subtraction-with-regrouping problem by using invented strategies. Performance among third-grade students who had one and one-half additional years of instruction was lower. Why?

Young children understand the strategies they invent. They frequently do not understand standard algorithms, even when conceptually based explanations are included as part of the instruction. When students do not understand an algorithm, they may unintentionally modify it. Without understanding, they have no way to know whether their strategy is flawed.

Teaching

Students gain confidence in their ability to do mathematics when they use strategies that they understand. Students understand the strategies they have invented to solve problems in their prior experience. Teachers are naturally eager to see their students use strategies that are efficient, and efficiency is a feature of standard algorithms. But efficiency without understanding leads to errors, and errors lead to lack of confidence.

Teachers can capitalize on children's ability to use direct-modeling strategies and invented algorithms by valuing them as valid strategies, just as they would value strategies using standard algorithms. In a timely manner, teachers may want to try to move individual students away from direct modeling toward invented strategies, as the teacher does in the following example from a third-grade classroom.

Teacher: A room had 327 cavity-filling caramels and 465 invisible chocolate bars. How many pieces of candy were in that room?

Shannon: Here's my 465 [she shows her 4 hundreds blocks, 6 tens blocks, and 5 ones blocks], and here's my 327 [she shows her 3 hundreds blocks, 2 tens blocks, and 7 ones blocks]. I

took out the tens counters and the ones counters. I added the hundreds counters first: 100, 200, 300, 400, 500, 600, 700 [she stacks the hundreds blocks as she counts by hundreds]; 710, 720, 730, 740, 750, 760, 770, 780 [she counts on by tens from 700 as she puts each tens block with the hundreds blocks]; 781, 782, 783, 784, 785, 786, 787, 788, 789, 790, 791, 792 [she counts on by ones from 780 as she puts each ones block with the hundreds blocks and tens blocks].

Teacher: Nice. Now, you started with the hundreds first, then you went to the tens, then you went to the ones. Now, did you do this in your head?

Shannon: No.

Teacher: Do you want to try it in your head? Now remember what you did here [pointing to the blocks]. You did the hundreds first, right? Then you did the tens. Then the ones. Let's see what you could do.

Shannon: Well, I could add the 300 and the 400 together. That would be 700. And then I could add the 60 and 20 together: 60, 70, that would be 80. And then 5, 6, 7, 8, 9, 10, 11, 12. And that would be 780, 792.

Teacher: Nice job. See, you really didn't need these [base-ten blocks], did you?

Where understanding is valued, few students will use a strategy they do not understand, regardless of its efficiency.

Teachers find that students in their classrooms typically use various strategies for a given problem when allowed to do so. This freedom gives the teacher the opportunity to have students share different strategies with the class. Students listen to other students describe their strategies, and any student may decide to begin using another student's strategy. In this way, all strategies are valued, and students tend to prefer the most efficient strategy they understand. Students typically move from direct-modeling strategies to invented strategies using counting or recalled facts, and eventually, to standard algorithms. In an environment where understanding is valued, few students will use a strategy they do not understand, regardless of its efficiency. Trouble arises when students perceive the use of standard algorithms as being the only strategy the teacher will accept.

Action Research Idea

Think of a computational procedure that your students will learn later this year, or in a later grade. Examples include multiplication or division in grades K–1, subtraction with regrouping in grade 2, multidigit multiplication or division in grades 3–4, and adding or subtracting integers in grades 5–6. Create a problem that might be solved using that procedure, situated in a context that is familiar to your students. Pose the problem and encourage the students to find at least two ways to solve it. Make available various manipulative materials and writing materials.

Circulate among the students as they work, noting which are using direct-modeling strategies with manipulatives, which are using mental or written invented strategies, and which are using a standard algorithm. Assess the students' understanding of their strategies by asking them to explain the reasons for each step in their solutions. Then have students present their various solutions to the class. Only students who understand their solution may explain it to the class; this restriction is especially important for students using a standard algorithm. Invite other students to discuss and evaluate each strategy. Try to avoid indicating that you value one strategy more than another.

At spaced intervals over the next several months, pose a similar problem. By attending to the strategies used by individual students, determine whether each student's understanding increases and whether students exhibit a tendency to progress naturally toward more efficient strategies.

References

Carpenter, Thomas P., Ellen Ansell, Megan L. Franke, Elizabeth Fennema, and Linda Weisbeck. "Models of Problem Solving: A Study of Kindergarten Children's Problem-Solving Processes." *Journal for Research in Mathematics Education* 24 (November 1993):427–40.

Kouba, Vicky L., Thomas P. Carpenter, and Jane O. Swafford. "Numbers and Operations." In *Results from the Fourth Mathematics Assessment of the National Assessment of Educational Progress,* edited by Mary Montgomery Lindquist, 64–93. Reston, Va.: National Council of Teachers of Mathematics, 1989.

Primary Arithmetic
Children Inventing Their Own Procedures

by

Constance Kamii, Barbara A. Lewis,
and Sally Jones Livingston

In an article that appeared in the *Arithmetic Teacher*, Madell (1985) described findings from a private school in New York City in which children were not taught any algorithms until the end of the third grade. Without algorithms, the children devised their own ways of solving computation problems. Madell's observation of the children's thinking led him to conclude that "children not only *can* but *should* create their own computational algorithms" (p. 20) and that "children can and should do their own thinking" (p. 22). The purpose of the present article is to reiterate Madell's call for reform, with supporting evidence from a public school near Birmingham, Alabama.

One of Madell's reasons for saying that children should create their own procedures is that in multidigit addition and subtraction, children "*universally* proceed from left to right" Madell (1985, 21). Two of the examples he gave can be seen in figure 1. Readers having trouble understanding these examples should be heartened by Madell's assurance that almost everyone else does, too. The lesson to be learned from our difficulty in understanding children's thinking is that "it is hard to follow the reasoning of others. No wonder so many children ignore the best of explanations of why a particular algorithm works and just follow the rules" (Madell 1985, 21).

Since 1984, at Hall-Kent School in Homewood, Alabama, one of the authors has been developing a primary

Constance Kamii and Barbara A. Lewis teach at the University of Alabama at Birmingham, Birmingham, AL 35294. Sally Jones Livingston is a third-grade teacher at Hall-Kent Elementary School in Homewood, AL 35209. Kamii and Livingston are collaborating at Hall-Kent School to develop a constructivist approach to third-grade arithmetic.

50 – 20 = 30	50 – 20 = 30
30 – 4 = 26	4 – 3 = 1
26 + 3 = 29	30 – 1 = 29

Fig. 1. Two invented procedures for solving 53 – 24 reported by Madell (1985)

school arithmetic program based on the theory of Jean Piaget. Piaget's theory ([1967] 1971, [1970] 1972), constructivism, states that logico-mathematical knowledge is a kind of knowledge that each child must create from within, in interaction with the environment, rather than acquire it directly from the environment by internalization. On the basis of this theory, the authors have been refraining from teaching algorithms and, instead, have been encouraging children to invent their own procedures for all four arithmetical operations.

Our observations have confirmed Madell's findings every year. Working on addition and subtraction, children in the first two grades always proceed from left to right if they have not been taught to work from right to left and are, instead, encouraged to invent their own procedures. In subtraction, the authors have seen solutions such as the following, besides the two reported by Madell:

$$50 - 20 = 30,$$
$$30 + 3 = 33,$$
$$33 - 4 = 29.$$

In two-column addition, the procedures shown in figure 2 have been observed. When multiplication problems such as 125 × 4 are given, children also work from left to right (see fig. 3).

10 + 10 = 20	10 + 10 = 20			10 + 10 = 20
8 + 7 = 15	8 + 2 = another ten			7 + 7 = 14
20 + 10 = 30	20 + 10 = 30			14 + 1 = 15
30 + 5 = 35	30 + 5 = 35			20 + 10 = 30
				30 + 5 = 35

Fig. 2. Three invented procedures for solving 18 + 17

4 × 100 = 400	4 × 100 = 400
4 × 20 = 80	4 × 25 = 100
4 × 5 = 20	400 + 100 = 500
400 + 80 + 20 = 500	

Fig. 3. Two invented procedures for solving 125 × 4

When the problems are in division, the law of the land suddenly changes and the rule decrees that students work from left to right. If they are encouraged to do their own thinking, however, children proceed from right to left, as can be seen in the following examples with the problem 74 ÷ 5:

$$5 + 5 + 5 + 5 + 5 + 5 + \ldots$$

until the total comes close to 74. (Children usually count on their fingers saying, "Five, ten, fifteen, twenty … ")

$$5 + 5 + 5 + 5 + 5 = 25$$

counting on five fingers. If 5 fives is 25, 10 fives is 50. Four more fives is 20, and 50 + 20 = 70. So the answer is 14 fives, with a remainder of 4.

The preceding methods later become shortened to

$$10 \times 5 = 50, 4 \times 5 = 20$$

so the answer is 14 with a remainder of 4.

Getting Children to Invent

The authors' way of teaching is not exactly the same as Madell's, for theoretical reasons. First, we do not let children write anything (until the numbers get too big to remember) because we want them to think and to talk to each other. Second, we do not use base-ten blocks because (a) the source of logico-mathematical knowledge is the child's mental action rather than the objects in the external world and (b) "one ten" is a new, higher-order construction, rather than ten *ones* merely stuck together (Kamii 1989a; Kamii and Joseph 1988).

At the beginning of second grade, the teacher writes one problem after another, such as those in figure 4, on the chalkboard, and asks, "What's a quick and easy way of solving this problem?"

9	4	15	13	18
+ 5	7	+ 6	+ 13	+ 14
	5			
	2			
	5			
	+ 3			

Fig. 4. Problems on the chalkboard

The entire class can work together, or the teacher can work with small groups. The children raise their hands when they have an answer.

When most of the hands are up, the teacher calls on individual children and writes all the answers given by them. Being careful not to say that an answer is right or wrong, the teacher then asks for an explanation of each procedure used by the children. For the first problem (9 + 5 written vertically), for example, if a child says, "I take one from the five to make ten," the teacher crosses out the 5 and the 9 and writes "10" next to the 9. If the child then says, "That makes the five be four," the teacher writes "4" below the 10. If the child concludes by saying, "Ten and four is fourteen," the teacher draws a line below the 4 and writes the answer, "14," below this line as well as below the line in the original problem.

As the teacher thus interacts with the volunteer, he or she encourages the rest of the class to express agreement or disagreement and to speak up immediately if something does not make sense. The exchange of points of view is very important in a constructivist program, and the teacher is careful not to reinforce right answers or to correct wrong ones. If the teacher were to judge correctness of answers, the children would come to depend on him or her to know whether an answer is correct. If the teacher does not say that an answer is correct or incorrect and encourages the children to agree or disagree among themselves, the class will continue to think and to debate until agreement is reached.

Many teachers ask, "What should the teacher do if no one in the class gets the right answer?" The reply is that if this happened, the teacher would know that the problem was too hard for the class and would go on to something else. In the logico-mathematical realm, if children debate long enough, they will eventually get to the correct answer because absolutely nothing is arbitrary in logico-mathematical knowledge. For example, 18 plus 14 equals 32 in every culture because nothing is arbitrary in this relationship. The reader interested in more detail about this point and this method of teaching is referred to Kamii (1989a, 1989b, 1990a, 1990b).

Advantages of Child-Invented Procedures

The authors think it is better for children to invent their own procedures for three reasons. These are summarized first and elaborated on later. When children invent their own ways,

1. they do not have to give up their own thinking;
2. their understanding of place value is strengthened rather than weakened by algorithms; and
3. they develop better number sense.

It must be clear from the previous discussion that when children are encouraged to invent their own ways of solving problems, they do not have to give up their own ways of thinking. Referring to the algorithms that children are made to use, Madell said, "The early focus on memorization in the teaching of arithmetic thoroughly distorts in children's minds the fact that mathematics is primarily reasoning. This damage is often difficult, if not impossible, to undo" (1985, 22). The authors agree with Madell and add that they have learned from experience that the damage is much harder to undo (Kamii and Lewis 1993) than imagined when first reading Madell's article.

The second reason it is better to encourage children to do their own thinking is that when thinking in their own ways, they strengthen their knowledge of place value by using it. When students in the constructivist program solve problems such as

$$\begin{array}{r} 987 \\ +654, \end{array}$$

they think and say, for example, "Nine hundred and six hundred is one thousand five hundred. Eighty and fifty is a hundred thirty; so that's one thousand six hundred thirty. Plus eleven is one thousand six hundred forty-one." By contrast, many of the children who use the algorithm unlearn place value by saying, for example, "Seven and four is eleven. Put one down and one up. One and eight and five is fourteen. Put four down and one up. One and nine is ten, so that's sixteen." Note that this algorithm is convenient for adults, who already know place value. For children, who have a tendency to think about every column as ones, the algorithm reinforces this weakness.

Let us examine the knowledge of place value among the children at Hall-Kent School. As can be seen in the following distribution for 1989–91, the constructivist teachers, who chose not to teach algorithms, tended to be in the lower grades: first grade, four out of four teachers; second grade, two out of three teachers; third grade, one out of three teachers; and fourth grade, none of the four teachers.

Children were assigned to classes as randomly as possible by the principal at the beginning of the school year. In second grade, students were taught algorithms in one of the three classes (class 1) and not in the remaining two. The remaining two classes differed slightly in that the teacher of class 2 did not call parents to discourage their use of home-taught algorithms, whereas the teacher of class 3 did.

In individual interviews in May 1990, the second graders were shown a sheet of paper on which "7 + 52 + 186" was written horizontally. They were asked to solve the problem without paper and pencil, give the answer, and then explain how they got the answer. The interviewer took notes on what each child said.

The children in class 1 used the algorithm and typically said, "Seven and two and six is fifteen. Put down the five, and carry one. One and five and eight is fourteen, put down the four…. This is hard…. I forgot what I put down before." The children in class 3, which will be called the constructivist class, typically said, "One hundred eighty and fifty is two hundred thirty. Two hundred thirty-seven, two hundred thirty-nine, two hundred forty-five."

Insight can be gained about children's understanding of place value by analyzing the wrong answers they gave. In the algorithm class, the wrong answers tended to be very small or very large. Three children got small totals of 29 or 30 by adding all the digits as ones (7 + 5 + 2 + 1 + 8 + 6 = 29). At the other extreme, seven children in the algorithm class gave large totals ranging from 838 to 9308. Totals in the 800s were obtained by adding the 7 and the 1 of 186. If children carried 1 from the tens column, their total came out in the 900s. By contrast, most of the wrong answers found in the constructivist class were more reasonable and ranged from 235 to 255. (The percent getting the correct answer were 12 percent in the algorithms class [class 1] and 45 percent in the constructivist class [class 3].)

Class 2 came out in between, and the wrong answers given by this group fell between the ranges of those of classes 1 and 3. (The percent getting the correct answer was 26.)

Similar results were found by giving a similar problem (6 + 53 + 185) in May 1991 to four fourth-grade classes, all of which had been taught algorithms. The errors of the fourth-grade classes larger than the largest error of 617 produced by the second-grade constructivist class were 713 + 8, 715, 744, 814, and 1300 in one class; 713, 718, 783, 783, 783, 844, 848, and 1215 in the second class; 718, 721, 738, 738, and 791 in the third class; and 745, 835, 838, 838, and 10099 in the fourth class. The fourth graders who were taught algorithms did considerably worse than the second graders who did their own thinking. (The percent of fourth graders who got the correct answer of 244 were only 24, 17, 30, and 19, respectively, in the four classes.)

It is clear from examining the answers given to the preceding problems that children who know place value also have better number sense. Because those who do their own thinking usually start with larger units, such as 180 + 50, they are not likely to get answers in the 700s, 800s, or beyond (for 6 + 53 + 185). When so many fourth graders get answers in the 700s and 800s, it seems apparent that algorithms unteach place value and prevent children from developing number sense.

The better number sense of children who do their own thinking also comes from the fact that they think about entire numbers and not about each column separately. Responses to the following problem illustrate this point:

$$
\begin{array}{r}
504 \\
-306 \\
\hline
\end{array}
$$

Most of the second and third graders (74 percent and 80 percent, respectively) who had never been taught algorithms easily got the correct answer by doing 500 − 300 = 200, 4 − 6 = − 2, 200 − 2 = 198. The fourth graders, who used the algorithm, again did much worse. The percent of correct responses was 29, 38, 39, and 55, respectively, for the four fourth-grade classes.

The children's wrong answers revealed their number sense. The greatest wrong answer found among the constructivist third graders was 202. By contrast, the fourth graders, who used the algorithm, got larger wrong answers, such as 208 (10 percent of all the answers), 298 (6 percent of all the answers), 308, 408, 410, 498, 808, and 898. Whereas the smallest wrong answer found among the constructivist third graders was 190, the fourth graders, who used algorithms, got smaller wrong answers, such as 108 (15 percent of all the answers), 148, and 189 (4 percent of all the answers). Because they thought only of isolated columns, they did not sense anything wrong even when they were unreasonably off the mark.

When third graders were given the multiplication problem 13 × 11, 60 percent of those who had never been taught algorithms got the correct answer by thinking 13 × 10 = 130, 130 + 13 = 143. Although almost all the fourth graders could get the correct answer by using the algorithm, only the following percent of the four classes got the correct answer when they were allowed to use only their heads: 5, 6, 14, and 15. The incorrect answers given by the fourth graders again demonstrated their lack of number sense. The incorrect answers were 11, 13, 23, 26, 33, 42, 44, 45, 64, 66, 113, 123, 131, 133, 140, 141, 155, 1300, and 1313.

The view that children should be encouraged to do their own thinking is now advocated by many other educators and researchers working from a variety of theoretical perspectives. This view is supported not only in the United States (Cobb and Wheatley 1988; Lester 1989) but also in Brazil (Carraher, Carraher, and Schliemann 1985, 1987; Carraher and Schliemann 1985), England (Plunkett 1979), Holland (Gravemeijer 1990; Heege 1978; Streefland 1990; Treffers 1987), Mexico (Ferreiro 1988), and South Africa (Murray and Olivier 1989; Olivier, Murray, and Human 1990, 1991). If we are serious about reform in mathematics education, we must study how young children think and reexamine our fundamental beliefs about teaching.

References

Carraher, Terezinha Nunes, David William Carraher, and Analucia Dias Schliemann. "Mathematics in the Streets and in Schools." *British Journal of Developmental Psychology* 3 (March 1985):21–29.

———. "Written and Oral Mathematics." *Journal for Research in Mathematics Education* 18 (March 1987):83–97.

Carraher, Terezinha Nunes, and Analucia Dias Schliemann. "Computation Routines Prescribed by Schools: Help or Hindrance?" *Journal for Research in Mathematics Education* 16 (January 1985):37–44.

Cobb, Paul, and Grayson Wheatley. "Children's Initial Understanding of Ten." *Focus on Learning Problems in Mathematics* 10 (Summer 1988):1–28.

Ferreiro, Emilia. "O cálculo escolar et o cálculo com o dinheiro em situação inflacionária." In *Alfabetização em Processo*, edited by Emilia Ferreiro, 106–36. São Paulo, Brazil: Cortez Editora, 1988.

Gravemeijer, Koeno. "Context Problems and Realistic Mathematics Instruction." In *Contexts Free Productions Tests and Geometry in Realistic Mathematics Education*, edited by Koeno Gravemeijer, M. van den Heuvel, and Leen Streefland. Utrecht, Netherlands: Research group for Mathematical Education and Educational Computer Centre, State University of Utrecht, 1990.

Heege, Hans ter. "Testing the Maturity for Learning the Algorithm of Multiplication." *Educational Studies in Mathematics* 9 (February 1978):75–83.

Kamii, Constance. *Young Children Continue to Reinvent Arithmetic, Second Grade*. New York: Teachers College Press, 1989a.

———. *Double-Column Addition: A Teacher Uses Piaget's Theory*. New York: Teachers College Press, 1989b. Videotape. (Also NCTM Publication No. 417)

———. *Multiplication of Two-Digit Numbers: Two Teachers Using Piaget's Theory*. New York: Teachers College Press, 1990a. Videotape.

———. *Multidigit Division: Two Teachers Using Piaget's Theory*. New York: Teachers College Press, 1990b. Videotape.

Kamii, Constance, and Linda Joseph. "Teaching Place Value and Double-Column Addition." *Arithmetic Teacher* 35 (February 1988): 48–52.

Kamii, Constance, and Barbara A. Lewis. "The Harmful Effects of Algorithms in Primary Arithmetic." *Teaching K–8* (January 1993): 36–38.

Lester, Frank K., Jr. "Mathematical Problem Solving in and out of School." *Arithmetic Teacher* 37 (November 1989): 33–35.

Madell, Rob. "Children's Natural Processes."*Arithmetic Teacher* 32 (March 1985):20–22.

Murray, Hanlie, and Alwyn Olivier. "A Model of Understanding Two-Digit Numeration and Computation." In *Proceedings of the 13th Annual Meeting of the International Group for the Psychology of Mathematics Education* (IGPME), edited by Gerard Vergnaud, Janine Rogalski, and Michele Artigue, 3–10. Paris: IGPME, 1989.

Olivier, Alwyn, Hanlie Murray, and Piet Human. "Building on Young Children's Informal Arithmetical Knowledge." In *Proceedings of the 14th Annual Meeting of the International Group for the Psychology of Mathematics Education,* vol. 3, edited by G. Booker, P. Cobb, and T. N. Mendicuti, 297–304. Oaxtapec, Mexico: Author, 1990.

———. "Children's Solution Strategies for Division Problems." In *Proceedings of the 13th Annual Meeting of the North American Chapter of the International Group for the Psychology of Mathematics Education* (IGPME), vol. 2, edited by Robert G. Underhill, 15–21. Blacksburg, Va.: IGPME, 1991.

Piaget, Jean. *Biology and Knowledge.* Chicago: University of Chicago Press, 1971.

———. *Genetic Epistemology.* London: Routledge & Kegan Paul, 1972.

Plunkett, Stuart. "Decomposition and All That Rot." *Mathematics in School* 8 (May 1979):2–5.

Streefland, Leen. "Realistic Mathematics Education (RME). What Does It Mean?" In *Contexts Free Productions Tests and Geometry in Realistic Mathematics Education,* edited by Koeno Gravemeijer, M. van den Heuvel, and Leen Streefland. Utrecht, Netherlands: Research group for Mathematical Education and Educational Computer Centre, State University of Utrecht, 1990.

Treffers, A. "Integrated Column Arithmetic According to Progressive Schematisation." *Educational Studies in Mathematics* 18 (May 1987):125–45.

Multicultural Mathematics and Alternative Algorithms

by

Randolph A. Philipp

Up until recently I wasn't even aware that other people in the world did things [arithmetic algorithms] differently. I thought God sent these. That's the way of the world. The first day you [to another teacher] were talking about some way you did things differently in Ireland. It never occurred to me. I thought there was a world standard.

—A sixth-grade teacher reflecting on alternative-mathematical algorithms

A teacher's beliefs about mathematics significantly affect the manner in which he or she teaches (Thompson 1992). Teachers, from school experience, often believe that there is one right way to solve a particular mathematics problem or to apply a computational algorithm for adding, subtracting, multiplying, and dividing. In turn, these beliefs become the beliefs of their students. The NCTM's *Curriculum and Evaluation Standards for School Mathematics* (1989) has called for decreasing the attention paid to isolated treatment of paper-and-pencil computations and the memorization of rules and algorithms and suggests instead that we increase the attention paid to stu-

Randolph Philipp, rphilipp@mail.sdsu.edu, teaches at the Center for Research in Mathematics and Science Education, San Diego State University, San Diego, CA 92120. He researches the relationships among preservice and in-service teachers' mathematics and pedagogical content knowledge, their conceptions of mathematics, and their instructional practices.

The preparation of this article was supported by grants from the National Science Foundation (MDR-8954679 and RED-9358517). Any opinions expressed herein are those of the author and do not necessarily reflect the views of the National Science Foundation.

dents' *creating* algorithms and procedures. Implicit in this suggestion is that the algorithms we have come to learn and to use are not the only way, and may not even be the best way, to compute.

Different cultures use different arithmetic procedures.

Although teachers are usually aware that various cultures have historically used algorithms that are different from those currently taught in United States schools, these teachers may not be aware that various algorithms are being used currently in the United States. Many of these algorithms are culturally based and are used by people with common ethnic and cultural backgrounds. This article describes how preservice elementary school teachers developed an awareness that the algorithms we teach in school are not the only algorithms for operating on numbers and that if they look, they may find alternative algorithms in their community and school.

An Invented Algorithm

Dictionaries define an algorithm as a rule or procedure for solving a problem. Computational algorithms are invented by people to streamline the process by which we compute. The fact that algorithms are a convention is often lost on our students, who come to think of a particular algorithm as *the* way, instead of as *a* way, to compute.

The following example illustrates the role that algorithms play in school mathematics.

A colleague recently told me a story about his third-grade daughter, who came home from school crying because of long division. The girl, whom I shall call Michelle, could not understand why she needed to learn a procedure for 63 ÷ 7 or 88 ÷ 8. After all, she said, "Can't everyone see what the answers to those are?" Michelle was struggling with the procedure for long division taught in class and was getting confused about when to multiply, when to subtract, and when to "bring down the next number." That afternoon her father sat with her and took a fresh approach. He first asked her whether she could explain a way of thinking about 126 divided by 3. Michelle said, "If you share 126 with 3 people, how much would each person get?" Her dad then asked if she could think of another approach, and she said, "How many 3s are in 126?" He told her to think about division that way. He asked her to imagine having a large number of ones, to take out groups of three, and to keep track of how many groups she "moved aside." Michelle thought that the explanation made sense, and without any other prompting, she solved 579 ÷ 3 (see fig. 1).

Although Michelle's dad suggested that she write down only what she needed, Michelle said that it helped her to write "How many 3s are in 579?" so she could remember what she was doing. Notice the unconventional approach that Michelle invented for this problem. This "algorithm," although nonroutine, was based on Michelle's understanding of the meaning of division and her sense for numera-tion. It makes complete sense and involves a deeper mathematical understanding on Michelle's part than would have been necessary in memorizing the conventional algorithm. Whereas Michelle invoked good numeration sense when working her solution, her dad told me that she did not consider place value when working the traditional long-division algorithm. Instead, she treated all the numbers as ones—"How many 3s are in 5?"—instead of in 500, and so on.

Michelle was confused in learning the school's long-division algorithm, which is taught because it is an efficient method for dividing numbers. However, this algorithm, which is often taught as a set of steps by which one will arrive at the correct answer, is often taught instrumentally, that is, without understanding. Michelle, who understood what division meant, was able to invent her own algorithm for solving the division problem. Other examples appear in the literature of students' inventing algorithms for mathematics (Kamii, Lewis, and Livingston 1993), but this article takes a different approach to the role of algorithms. Instead of additional examples from individual students, it presents examples that people from diverse ethnic and cultural backgrounds learned in school.

Culturally Based Alternative Algorithms

Southern California schools in general, and San Diego Unified Schools in particular, comprise a diverse multiethnic, multilingual population. Although teachers are working hard to find ways to incorporate the knowledge of various cultures, it is unclear how this goal might be accomplished in the area of mathematics. To give elementary-mathematics-methods students an opportunity both to acknowledge the mathematical diversity of their students and to challenge the belief that "God sent these [algorithms]," I have devised the "alternative algorithm" assignment. The purposes for this assignment are the following:

1. To develop an appreciation for the fact that various cultures have developed alternative algorithms to those commonly used in the United States

2. To reinforce the view that the algorithms we have come to use are simply a matter of convention and should be seen as *a* way, not *the* way, to compute

3. To support the view that one can make sense of computational algorithms and, in so doing, develop a deeper understanding of place value and the meanings of operations

Student teachers are asked to identify algorithms that are being used in the community but that differ from those taught in the United States. As student teachers locate various algorithms, they are expected to describe

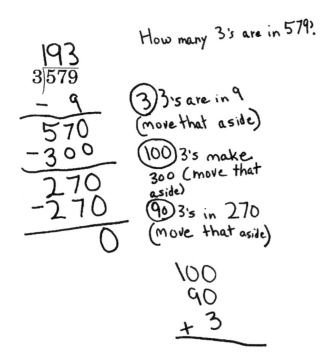

Fig. 1. Michelle's algorithm for 579 ÷ 3

why the algorithms work. In so doing, they must think hard about the underlying mathematical ideas. Some student teachers have found alternative algorithms through students in their own classes, either directly from the students or by asking students to talk with members of the student's family. This system not only legitimizes the mathematics learning of either the child or a member of the child's family but also presents an opportunity to honor this learning in both the child's eyes and, depending on what is done with the information, in the eyes of all the students in the class. This article describes some of the alternative algorithms that have been located by student teachers.

Alternative Algorithms for Addition

The traditional addition algorithm taught in the United States involves writing numbers in columns, then adding the columns, starting with the smallest place value and moving to the left. For example, to add 465 + 190 + 676, the algorithm works as follows:

$$
\begin{array}{r}
{}^{2}\!{}^{1}\!465 \\
190 \\
+676 \\
\hline
1331
\end{array}
$$

In this example, the superscript 1 represents one group of 10 ones, or 10, being "carried," and the superscript 2 represents two groups of 10 tens, or 200, being "carried." Various forms of keeping track of groups of numbers were found among individuals from the Philippines, Japan, Germany, and Ireland. One parent shared the following addition algorithm, demonstrated by adding 98, 24, 99, and 25, that he had learned when he was in second grade in the Philippines:

$$
\begin{array}{r}
-98 \\
24- \\
-99- \\
+25 \\
\hline
246
\end{array}
$$

This algorithm differs from the traditional algorithm used in the United States in two ways. First, a dash is used to notate a group of ten. For example, 8 plus 4 equals 12, but instead of remembering "12," one remembers only "2" and places a dash to indicate that one group of 10 has been reached. The second difference is that the number carried is not written but instead can be determined from the number of dashes. An example of one's thinking while using this algorithm follows:

Eight and 4 is 12 ("-" for 10, leaving 2); 2 and 9 is 11 ("-" for 10, leaving 1); 1 and 5 is 6. So I carry two dashes, or 20. Two (tens) and 9 (tens) is 11 ("-" for 10); 1 and 2 is 3, and 9 is 12 ("-" for 10); 2 and 2 is 4. Carry two dashes, or 200. So the answer is 246.

A woman of Japanese descent was asked to add 87, 65, and 49. She shared the following algorithm, which she had learned in college in Japan. She referred to it as the "scratch technique."

$$
\begin{array}{r}
8\!\!\!/7_{0} \\
6\cancel{5}_{2} \\
+\cancel{4}\cancel{9}_{0}{}_{1} \\
\hline
201
\end{array}
$$

This "scratch method" is similar to the algorithm described in the "Philippine" algorithm. First, as in the "Philippine" algorithm, this algorithm keeps track of groups of tens by overstriking the appropriate digits. However, in addition to keeping track of the groups of tens, this algorithm also keeps track of the leftovers. For example, one might use the following thinking with this algorithm:

Seven plus 5 is 12, which is 10 (strike through the 5) and 2 is left over (subscript 2); 2 and 9 is 11, which is 10 (strike through the 9) and 1 (subscript 1). So we have 1 left, and carry two groups of ten; 2 (tens) and 8 (tens) is 10 (strike through the 8) and 0 (subscript 0); 0 and 6 is 6, and 4 is 10 (strike through the 4) and 0 (subscript 0). So I have 0 tens, and I must carry two groups of 10 tens, or 200. The answer is 201.

Other addition algorithms differed from the traditional United States algorithm only with respect to where the carried digit was written. A young girl of Irish descent shared this algorithm:

$$
\begin{array}{r}
123 \\
+3{}_{1}7{}_{1}8 \\
\hline
501
\end{array}
$$

A twenty-year-old Mexican man explained an addition algorithm in which the numbers to be carried were placed to the side. He called this algorithm "llevamos uno," or "we carry one":

$$
\begin{array}{r}
194 \\
+49 \quad 11 \\
\hline
243
\end{array}
$$

An older man educated in Switzerland and a man schooled in Canada in the early 1970s both demonstrated that they had learned to add by starting from the left-most column. The man from Switzerland worked the following two problems:

$$\begin{array}{r} 59 \\ +16 \\ \hline 60 \\ 15 \\ \hline 75 \end{array} \qquad \begin{array}{r} 481 \\ +926 \\ \hline 1300 \\ 100 \\ 7 \\ \hline 1407 \end{array}$$

This algorithm is the one that many elementary school children in the United States invent when encouraged to do their own thinking. That is, when asked to add multi-digit numbers, most children will naturally begin adding the digits with the largest place value. This procedure is quite natural for adults as well. For example, if two friends emptied their wallets to pool their money, would they first count the $20 bills or the $1 bills?

The American division algorithm is different from others.

Alternative Algorithms for Subtraction

The traditional algorithm for subtraction in the United States involves "borrowing," or regrouping, from the *min-uend*, the quantity from which the subtrahend is subtracted. For example, 347 – 169 can be solved by an individual who subtracts beginning with the ones column and then works toward the *hundreds* column:

$$\begin{array}{r} {}^{2}\!\!\not{3}{}^{13}\!\!\not{4}{}^{1}7 \\ -169 \\ \hline 178 \end{array}$$

People from various countries subtract by using an algorithm different from that used in the United States. Instead of "borrowing," or regrouping, from the minuend, they use what might be referred to as an *equal-addition algorithm*, whereby an equal amount is added to both the minuend and the subtrahend. For example, the previous subtraction problem might be worked as follows:

$$\begin{array}{r} 3{}^{1}4{}^{1}7 \\ -{}^{1}1{}^{1}69 \\ \hline 178 \end{array}$$

The following shows the thinking that might accompany this problem:

> First I want to subtract 9 from 7. I cannot do that, so I will add 10 to the 7, making it 17, and I will add 1 (ten) to the 6 (60) to make it 7 (70). Now I can subtract 9 from 17, and that equals 8. Next I want to subtract 7 (6 + 1) from 4. I cannot do that. So I will add 10 (actually, 10 tens) to the 4 to make it 14, and I will add 1 (100) to the 1 (100) in the subtrahend. Now I can subtract 7 (6 + 1) from 14, leaving 7. Finally I want to subtract 2 (1 + 1) from 3, leaving 1. So the answer is 178.

One way to understand why this technique works is to think of comparing the ages of a fifty-seven-year-old man and his twenty-nine-year-old daughter. In ten years, the father will be sixty-seven years old and his daughter will be thirty-nine years old, but the difference in their ages will not change. This algorithm is based on finding the difference between 57 and 29 by adding the same number to both the minuend and subtrahend.

$$\begin{array}{r} 5{}^{1}7 \\ -{}^{1}29 \\ \hline 28 \end{array}$$

This technique was used by adults from various countries who remembered having been taught this algorithm as children. During this assignment, it became clear that even many adults who had been educated in the United States had learned algorithms that were different from those commonly taught in today's American schools. These adults came from Persia; Panama; Croatia; Germany; Ireland; Riverside, California; and Brooklyn, New York.

Earlier in this century, a discussion involved which method for subtraction ought to be taught in American schools. This controversy was laid to rest after Brownell (1947) and Brownell and Moser (1949) summarized the research evidence, concluding that an interaction existed between the type of subtraction method and the style of teaching. When subtraction was taught procedurally, the second approach, known as "augmenting," or equal addition, was easier to learn. When subtraction was taught conceptually, regrouping, or "borrowing," was easier to learn. This research was instrumental in determining the subtraction algorithm taught in schools.

A man recalled learning the following algorithm while attending primary school in central Italy. When learning addition and subtraction, he was not permitted to write any other numbers on his paper. As a result, he had to perform the computations in his head. To solve 375 – 137, he first mentally subtracted 300 – 100, resulting in 200. Then he mentally subtracted 270 – 30, resulting in 240. Finally he subtracted 245 – 7, which is 238. This process works from left to right and requires one to keep track of place value.

Alternative Algorithms for Multiplication

A ninety-six-year-old German woman, recalling her Russian father's approach to multiplying, demonstrated the following example by multiplying 230 by 17:

2̶3̶0̶	1̶7̶
115	34
57	68
2̶8̶	1̶3̶6̶
1̶4̶	2̶7̶2̶
7	544
3	1088
1	2176
	3910

Starting with the first number in the left-hand column, one keeps dividing each number by 2 while multiplying the corresponding number in the right-hand column by 2. When the left-hand column's number is odd, divide by 2 and drop the remainder. This process continues until a 1 is obtained in the left-hand column. Draw a line through all even numbers in the left-hand column, along with their corresponding numbers in the right-hand column, and then add the right-hand column's numbers that have not been crossed out. The sum of the uncrossed-off numbers in the right-hand column is the product of 230×17. This algorithm works because whenever an even number appears in the left-hand column, dividing it by 2 and multiplying the corresponding right-hand-column number by 2 conserves the product. Conversely, whenever an odd number appears in the left-hand column, dividing it by 2 and dropping the remainder does not conserve the product. To compensate for the dropped remainder, one must add the number in the right-hand column. This algorithm is referred to in the literature as the Russian peasant algorithm and makes it possible to multiply whole numbers by knowing only how to halve and double numbers and add.

People believe that the algorithm they use is the easiest.

An American man of Mexican descent presented the following algorithm for multiplying numbers using the example of 46×37. He does all the calculations in his head:

$$
\begin{array}{r}
46 \\
\times 37 \\
\end{array}
\qquad
\begin{array}{r}
50 - 4 \\
40 - 3 \\
\hline
-150 + 12 \\
+2000 - 160 \\
\hline
2000 - 310 + 12 = 1702
\end{array}
$$

This approach is a direct application of the distributive property and works for exactly the same reasons but in a slightly different way than the traditional multiplication algorithm.

Each of two men, one educated in South Africa and one in Belize, shared an algorithm that started by multiplying the larger digits. Specific examples of how they found partial products are shown for 27×36 and 258×17:

South Africa	Belize
27	258
×36	× 17
810	258
162	1806

Notice in the first example that the first product (27×30) was represented with the 0, whereas in the second example, only the number of tens was written (258×10 was recorded as 258) but their value was remembered in the alignment of the second partial product.

A woman from the Philippines multiplied 48×35 in her head in the following way: 48×35 is 50×35 minus 2×35. Since 50×35 is 50×30, or 1500, plus 50×5, or 250, 50×35 equals 1750. This answer must be reduced by the product of 2×35, or 70, so the answer to 48×35 is 1680.

A woman from Iran and a man from Iraq applied algorithms that are similar to the algorithm generally taught in the United States, with the exception that the numbers to be "carried" are not written in the same location. In the United States, the carried value is written above the column to which the number will subsequently be added, whereas in Iran and Iraq, the numbers to be carried are written off to the side.

Iran		Iraq	
423			2
× 19		755	
3807	2	× 5	
423	2	3775	
8037			

Alternative Algorithms for Division

People all over the world, including many in the United States, use a division algorithm that looks different from the standard algorithm because of the way the numbers are written. In the United States, the typical division algorithm for finding the number of 4s in 260, follows:

$$
\begin{array}{r}
65 \\
4\,\overline{)260} \\
\underline{-24} \\
20 \\
\underline{-20} \\
0
\end{array}
$$

A woman from Laos showed how she learned to divide 65 by 2. Notice that the dividend, 65, is placed on the left, and the divisor, 2, is placed on the right, whereas the quotient, 32.5 (written here as 32,5), is placed under the divisor.

$$
\begin{array}{r|l}
65 & 2 \\
3 & \\ \cline{1-1}
05 & 32{,}5 \\
\underline{-4} & \\ \cline{1-1}
10 & \\
\underline{-10} & \\
0 &
\end{array}
$$

This manner of writing the dividend on the left, the divisor on the right, and the quotient under the divisor was shared by people who learned it in Armenia, Cambodia, Iran, Ireland, Pakistan, Russia, Spain, and Vietnam.

Final Comments

The current mathematics-reform movement in the United States is de-emphasizing the role that procedurally oriented algorithms should play in school. However, in spite of this de-emphasis, students are still taught algorithms by which they are expected to add, subtract, multiply, and divide. This article began with an example of an algorithm invented by a third-grade child who was struggling to make sense of division. Other examples of alternative algorithms have been identified as being used by people from various cultures. Although these people probably did not invent these algorithms, they inherited them as part of their ancestral education. The algorithms we use in school are a matter of convention; they are arbitrary. That is, absolutely nothing is sacred about any of them.

I am neither advocating that teachers teach several different algorithms for a given operation nor suggesting that one algorithm is more "conceptual" than another. I am advocating that teachers allow opportunities for students to present alternative algorithms—whether the students invent them or learn them—and then lead a discussion about the meanings of the operations, with the goal of students' understanding why the algorithm works.

A student in one of my mathematics-methods courses once shared with the class the equal-addition algorithm she had learned for subtraction. After she shared it, many of the students in the class who had been schooled in the traditionally taught algorithm involving "borrowing" expressed their disbelief that their peer would use such a "difficult" algorithm. She replied that her algorithm is not difficult; the one that everyone else is using is difficult. She was quite comfortable with her algorithm and could not figure out how the "borrowing" algorithm worked, which suggests that people have a tendency to believe that the algorithm they use is easiest, regardless of what it is.

It is my hope that teachers not only will become more aware of the diversity of approaches but also might actively seek these approaches among their own students for discussion in their classes. I hope that teachers with students of similar racial and ethnic backgrounds will increase their sensitivity to the many invented algorithms their students might create when learning to operate on numbers and perhaps allow their students a forum for discussing the reasoning that enabled the creation of these different algorithms.

References

Brownell, William A. "The Place of Meaning in the Teaching of Arithmetic." *Elementary School Journal* 47 (January 1947): 256–65.

Brownell, William A., and H. E. Moser. *Meaningful versus Mechanical Learning: A Study in Grade III Subtraction.* Vol. 8 of Duke University Research Studies in Education. Durham, N.C.: Duke University, 1949.

Kamii, Constance, Barbara A. Lewis, and Sally Jones Livingston. "Primary Arithmetic: Children Inventing Their Own Procedures." *Arithmetic Teacher* 41 (December 1993): 200–203.

National Council of Teachers of Mathematics. *Curriculum and Evaluation Standards for School Mathematics.* Reston, Va.: The Council, 1989.

Thompson, Alba G. "Teachers' Beliefs and Conceptions: A Synthesis of the Research." In *Handbook of Research on Mathematics Teaching and Learning*, edited by Douglas A. Grouws, 127–46. New York: Macmillan Publishing Co., and Reston Va.: National Council of Teachers of Mathematics, 1992.

Activities

Children's Invented Strategies

Hankes, "An Alternative to Basic-Skills Remediation"

1. Manipulative activity

   (*a*) For the word problems in figure 1 (and fig. 2), use blocks, beans, or other manipulatives to model the actions children might use to solve each type of problem.

   (*b*) Write a number sentence for each problem.

   (*c*) Explain how the physical actions you performed in Part a relate to the mathematical symbols you wrote in Part b.

2. Write five word problems that use addition or subtraction. Classify them according to the structure given in figure 1.

3. The word problems in figure 1 are differentiated by the subclassifications "result unknown," "change unknown," and "start unknown." Explain the arithmetic structure that these terms represent.

Kamii, Lewis, and Livingston, "Primary Arithmetic: Children Inventing Their Own Procedures"

1. Understanding students' invented procedures

   (*a*) Use each of the strategies described in figure 2 (and fig. 3) to solve two similar problems.

   (*b*) Explain your understanding of the mathematics used in each strategy.

   (*c*) What understanding of mathematics do you think the student that used each strategy is demonstrating?

2. Write about or discuss with a colleague the place for invented strategies in your curriculum.

Philipp, "Multicultural Mathematics and Alternative Algorithms"

1. Explain why the "scratch method" used by Japanese students works when adding 87, 65, and 49. Use this method to find the sum of 36, 68, 83, and 75.

2. Use the Russian method of halving and doubling to multiply 328 by 63. Explain why this algorithm works.

Section 3
The Reflective Learner

In this period of transition from traditional to reformed school mathematics, teachers (both pre-service and in-service) teeter on the shifting edge of change. You will be expected to create dramatically different classroom environments, teaching a kind of mathematics that is different from what you may have experienced in your own background. For many of you, school mathematics is linked to images of a rule-based discipline driven by computational skills and made up of many disconnected topics. You may have perceived your role to be similar to that of teachers from your past in which teaching was telling and learning was memorizing.

In contrast, picture the new type of classroom in which children routinely engage in problem-solving situations, exploring a variety of ways to think about mathematical ideas, explaining their solution strategies, and listening carefully to others. The mathematics these students experience is personal, connected, and based on the long-term development of concepts (Hatfield 1990; Chambers and Hankes 1994).

The readings in this section have been selected to help you make the most of your learning experiences as you wrestle with change. These articles invite an examination of (often implicitly held) beliefs and attitudes toward mathematics and suggest ways to engage in reflective thinking about interactions between the ideas and practices of reformed school mathematics.

Corwin points out the importance for teachers of doing mathematics in a different way—what she calls reflecting "on learning from inside experience." Such experiences help teachers to reorganize their beliefs about the nature of mathematics. Spangler provides specific prompts that can be used to investigate these beliefs and includes discussions of common responses to these prompts.

The other two articles in this section present useful structures for reflection and self-assessment. Greenwood discusses a set of criteria for mathematical thinking and suggests ways to use these items in self-evaluation. Karp and Huinker describe the use of portfolios for documenting mathematical progress. The processes of assembling examples of one's work and reflecting on, and writing about, this activity foster deeper understandings and facilitate further growth.

References

Chambers, Donald L., and Judith Elaine Hankes. "Using Knowledge of Children's Thinking to Change Teaching." In *Professional Development for Teachers of Mathematics,* 1994 Yearbook of the National Council of Teachers of Mathematics, edited by Douglas B. Aichele, pp. 286–95. Reston, Va.: National Council of Teachers of Mathematics, 1994.

Hatfield, Larry L. "Preparing Early Childhood Teachers for Constructive Mathematics Environments." In *Transforming Children's Mathematics Education: International Perspectives,* edited by Leslie Steffe and Terry Wood, pp. 407–14. Hillsdale, N.J.: Lawrence Erlbaum Associates, 1990.

Implementing the *Professional Standards for Teaching Mathematics*

Doing Mathematics Together

Creating a Mathematical Culture

by

Rebecca B. Corwin

Math was when I struggled with remembering which "neighbor" to borrow from, where to place the carried number, and just how many apples Sam had all together. Math was a time for concentrating on the rules of numerical manipulation for addition, subtraction, multiplication, and beginning division. Math was keeping the "show your work" columns straight.

—Rachel, *a fourth-grade teacher*

Rachel's experience of mathematics is typical of that of many elementary school teachers. She experienced it as a collection of rules, rituals, and routines; an arbitrary, unconnected array of procedures; an authority telling her what to do and how to do it. To break the chain that perpetuates this view of mathematics in our society, many changes are needed. Rachel would be the first to agree— she knows that she does not want her students to feel as she did about mathematics. But how can Rachel explore a different, "better" view of mathematics learning and teaching?

Prepared by Rebecca B. Corwin
Technical Education Research Center and Lesley College
Cambridge, MA 02140
Edited by Susan N. Friel
University of North Carolina
Chapel Hill, NC 27599-3345

Rebecca Corwin is professor of education at Lesley College in Cambridge, Massachusetts, where she teaches courses in mathematics education, curriculum development, and computer integration. She is also codirector of the National Science Foundation–funded Talking Mathematics project at the Technology Education Resource Center (TERC) in Cambridge.

To keep our students from having these reactions to mathematics, the National Council of Teachers of Mathematics has developed a vision of more appropriate mathematics teaching toward which the profession must work. The *Professional Standards for Teaching Mathematics* (1991) recommends a shift in classroom environments—

- toward classrooms as mathematical communities— away from classrooms as simply a collection of individuals;

- toward logic and mathematical evidence as verification—away from the teacher as the sole authority for right answers;

- toward mathematical reasoning—away from merely memorizing procedures;

- toward conjecturing, inventing, and problem solving—away from an emphasis on mechanistic answer finding;

- toward connecting mathematics, its ideas, and its applications—away from treating mathematics as a body of isolated concepts and procedures.

This vision of a better classroom environment is very appealing, but how is Rachel, who has not experienced this approach to mathematics, supposed to know what to do? She knows that it's advantageous to de-emphasize right answers. She knows that it is important to treat mathematics as a form of human communication. But she doesn't know *how* to achieve that outcome. More difficult, she has to fly in the face of her own experience to let go of her deepest ideas about what constitutes mathematics. What kinds of professional development experiences might help her as she reconstructs her practice?

The Teaching Standards: A Challenge to Professional Development Programs

Elementary school mathematics educators face a real challenge in these times of mathematics and science reform. We are charged with nothing less than improving the mathematics education of America's children within the next few years—and many approaches have been recommended: Use manipulative materials, support students as they construct their theories, and use activity-based programs. Teach geometry, data analysis, and number concepts in a balanced program. Use problems, projects, and long-term sustained homework assignments. Involve families. Make mathematics relevant to students' lives. Many teachers are working hard toward these goals, but they need support.

On the whole, however, we have seen little change in professional development programs as yet. Although some school systems are telling their teaching faculties about the NCTM's teaching standards, most are doing relatively little. Most school systems are not even furnishing a copy of the *Professional Teaching Standards* in each teacher's room so that the extremely useful dialogues, problems, materials, and approaches can be studied.

Typically, in in-service mathematics programs, elementary school teachers focus on collecting new activities or curricula to do with their students. In such in-service sessions teachers are often encouraged to think about analyzing, assessing, and guiding students' learning in some new and more appropriate ways, but they seldom deviate from thinking about their students and ways of enhancing the existing curricula. Radical change is not likely to happen if teachers are not being encouraged to think more openly about very different kinds of mathematics learning and teaching.

The continuing emphasis on pedagogy is important to the development of a professional teacher, but it cannot be the only component of an in-service program if we want teachers to have an opportunity to grow in entirely new directions as mathematicians. How can teachers find ways to spend time on the deeper, broader issues compatible with thinking about deep changes in classroom climate or teaching approach?

Reflective practice

In the September 1992 issue of the *Arithmetic Teacher*, Lyn Hart and her colleagues encourage teachers to become reflective practitioners—to analyze their teaching of mathematics, the students' response to that teaching, and the environment of their classroom. This kind of reflection is surely central to an analysis of teaching. Thinking about what you do and how it affects the mathematical environment in your classroom is a crucial part of making professional decisions. Learning as much as you can about alternative approaches to teaching and learning mathematics is an essential component of your own changes. Listening to students' ideas, learning about how students construct mathematical ideas, thinking about how to record and assess your students' progress—all these components are vital to reinventing practice. The missing element in this description is doing mathematics in a different way for yourself.

Learning mathematics differently

For most elementary school teachers, seeing mathematics as a way of thinking and analyzing—looking for patterns, making conjectures, analyzing examples and counterexamples, developing generalizations and definitions—requires a serious reorganization of beliefs about the nature of mathematics. Rachel would have a hard time considering mathematics as a way of thinking rather than a way of computing. She can sometimes identify ways in which students engage in these behaviors, but unless she learns to trust and understand mathematics as a way of thinking that may take many forms, she may prematurely cut off discussion or debate as her students work to make meaning of mathematics. We need to know in our bones that *mathematics makes meaning*. It isn't enough to think it; we need to have felt it. If we have not felt that mathematics does make sense, we cannot truly understand and support the point of view that doing mathematics helps students make sense of the world.

Why focus on content in professional development programs?

Teachers need mathematical experiences of their own that facilitate content knowledge. These experiences will help them invent images, metaphors, and principles on which to base mathematical investigation and talk in their classrooms. This involvement can furnish the "stuff" to help them reflect on learning from inside experience so that they can broaden "craft knowledge" as they reframe their teaching practice. If teachers can reflect not only on their own teaching and students' mathematics learning but also on how they have learned mathematics themselves, they will enrich their conversations with their students. A skilled, experienced practitioner of a craft enriches her encounters with novices in a special way because she knows the field from the inside out.

By doing their own mathematical thinking, teachers develop both content knowledge and pedagogical knowledge, knowledge *of* mathematics and knowledge *about* mathematics (Lampert 1988) that nurture their reflection on teaching and learning. Doing mathematics, reflecting on mathematics, and reinventing practice within a supportive community lead to an essential element of profound and lasting teacher growth.

What mathematics engages teachers' interest?

Teachers need to engage in mathematical inquiry in the domains of number and quantity, space and shape, and data. Engaging in investigations of polyhedra or prime numbers or data analysis and the construction of their own data representations, teachers not only experience important mathematical content but come to feel connected to the endeavor of mathematics as a living field constructed by humans. When teachers encounter classic mathematical problems, they can begin to feel connected to the larger enterprise of mathematics. By engaging with ideas and problems that have been pieces of mathematical thought over many centuries, teachers begin to feel that they are a part of a serious endeavor that has a history as well as a present day.

How is this outcome achieved in practice?

A group of twenty teachers recently worked on the classic problem of building the next larger square using only square patterning blocks as units. How many unit squares do you use for the smallest square? For the next larger square? And for the next larger square? Can you make a prediction about the number of unit squares that will be required to build the ninth square? Can you predict how many will be needed for any square? Teachers eagerly explored these patterns using the square patterning blocks.

In one group, members generated questions as they worked.

Ann: I don't understand this. I make the next bigger square and I get three squares.

Margarita: No, it's not three. It's four.

Jamela: Look at both your blocks! You've got the same blocks there. So how come you are saying different things?

Eleanor: Just tell me what to write down.

Ann: Well, I start with one and then there are three more. Oh, ... I see. It's a *total* of four. Oh, find the *total* number of blocks in the next bigger square.

Eleanor: So I'm writing down four.

(Later in the investigation)

Jamela: It goes 1, 4, 9, 16,... So what will be the tenth one?

Eleanor: I already figured that out because I don't like working with blocks. I get 100 for the tenth one.

Ann: How?

Eleanor: I made this list with just the numbers (shows the following table):

Sq.	1	2	3	4	5	6	7	8	9	10
Total	1	4	9	16	25	36	49	64	81	100

Ann: That's weird. Look, if you just multiply the number times itself, it comes out.

Jamela: Oh, no, it's the square numbers! They really are square!

Ann: Oh, ... no! ... (looks again at her original notes) If you go back to where I was at first, they get bigger each time by the next number. Like up by 3, up by 5, up by 7, up by 9, ... Does that pattern always work?

The group went on to make predictions, test them, and savor the fact that they could generate sentences in plain English words, numbers, and then even a formula, that captured that relationship. Not only could they make sense of their constructed formula, they could see that it both reflected and expressed their patterning-block model.

Next they asked more questions about the patterns of growth in the blocks. If square blocks produce the square numbers, then what patterns will evolve in building the next larger triangle from triangular blocks (will they be "triangle" numbers?)? Do related patterns occur for trapezoids? Rhombuses? Hexagons?

Even more important than their obvious enjoyment was the teachers' immersion in the process of constructing mathematics together. Because of this mental synthesis, they were truly engaged in many mathematical acts: posing questions; representing information; keeping track; expressing relationships; making and testing conjectures; and discussing, debating, and challenging one another's ideas. From this experience they learned much about doing engaging mathematics—the fits and starts of the process, the dead ends, the excitement of coming up with a conjecture, the dissonance of finding out that a conjecture is wrong, the satisfaction of keeping track of work so that it can be shared—and most important, about the messiness, nonlinearity, frustration, power, and beauty of doing mathematics together. As Ann put it later, "Together we are stronger, way stronger, than any one of us."

The process takes time

Developing a culture of mathematics with teachers takes time. It's important that everyone make a commitment to working together for some significant time. Too little time means that teachers will stay centered on their teaching and their students and so will be less likely to engage fully in the practice of building a mathematical community for themselves. As one teacher commented after an in-service experience:

> The most important thing [for me] is learning about pace.... I have a tendency to want to get things done and finished for the day and accomplish everything that I've set out to accomplish.

She found, however, in learning mathematics herself, that she needed more time, a flexible agenda, and less pressure to finish, to accomplish, to be done in a certain period. Her sense of what was needed in the classroom was irrevocably altered by her own learning experience.

The influence of membership in a mathematical community on classroom decisions

The connections between teachers' own mathematical work and their classroom practice are both obvious and subtle. Each teacher will take something different from an in-service experience, and most teachers will take something powerful from a mathematical culture. To feel the power of mathematics once, to enjoy working on a problem, to lose oneself in the magic of a mathematical investigation are to feel once again the thrill of first reading a book on one's own or having another person read aloud the story one has written. One's sense of empowerment is changed forever. Because responses to such experiences are so individual, the important issues are expressed very differently.

Mathematical language. One aspect of a mathematical community that changes teaching practice is the amount of language involved in the endeavor of doing mathematics. Teachers constantly talk, write, model, read, and comment. This focus on language is new for many teachers, and it often surprises them. For example, here are two teachers' reactions to making presentations of their work in a summer in-service mathematics experience. One woman focuses more on the fact that presenting her mathematics work increased her ownership:

> The whole importance of pulling something together, regardless of where you were, meant ... crystallizing more about what you were doing, and made you formulate something. And the whole business of standing up before other people and saying it made you have more self-confidence in what you've done. And it enabled you to raise more questions about it because other people helped articulate it. [I]t helped you own it, exploring it and being in love with it.

Another teacher emphasizes the role of talk as a catalyst for her growing mathematical understanding:

> One of the things I learned was that talking about it really helped to give me that understanding, because as I spoke about a problem it became clearer to me and that's one of the things I'm grateful for because I never knew how to *express* ideas. I'm learning!

Teachers' engagement in mathematics. Another feature of a mathematics community is the notion that everyone is genuinely engaged in constructing and creating mathematics. This is a subtle notion—many teachers have participated in professional development programs where they do mathematics but do not construct their own mathematics, follow their own questions, or generate their own conjectures. This sense of community is reflected in yet another teacher's comments:

> I also feel that I can identify myself as a mathematician now.... It took me a long time to identify myself as a writer because I liked writing a lot. I wanted to be a *writer*. [I can write] but can I identify myself as a writer? But here I am realizing that "Oh, I guess I can be a mathematician, too!"

How can teachers like these who feel the power and pull of mathematics fail to feel differently about their students' mathematical work?

It takes two

The author is convinced that teachers need to be liberated from the bonds of unhelpful past mathematics experiences so that they can empower their students. It is important that they learn as much as they can about teaching, learning, and materials and problems that are appealing and engaging for students. However, without some direct experience with the power and beauty of constructing and creating mathematics in a mathematics community, pedagogical reflection alone will not be enough for the profound levels of epistemological change we are hoping to engender. Even teachers who "know" how to teach mathematics and who are sensitive to how children learn take something powerful from direct experience with doing mathematics for themselves:

> It [was] really exciting: genuinely exciting, not just, "Well, that was interesting" but really exciting.... [L]evels of my own understanding of [mathematics] have just gone deeper and deeper and deeper. And the thing that I think about that is, I feel that when I came here I had these notions of "yes, it's great for kids to talk in groups, yes it's great for them to investigate, no I'm not really concerned with the right answer" ... those statements have an entirely other meaning for me now.

Mathematics Is Alive and Well

Experiencing mathematics as a living thing is exciting, empowering, and affirming. A supportive community that respects its participants, values their differences and their contributions, and enjoys their perceptions can go a long way toward empowering teachers to reflect on mathematics as well as their teaching and learning. Perhaps the best statement of the power of the experience comes from the words of a fifth-grade teacher who is a member of such a community:

> [W]hen I was in school … once somebody got the answer, it was dead. And if I didn't understand it, we, we just went on to the next dead body…. [O]n a lot of levels I don't feel like that any more…. I was able to work on two levels of self-esteem in asking—or saying, "I don't get it" at the same time…. [That] says a lot about people respecting each other to be in that place, to feel OK there.

How much we all need such reflective and empowering experiences in our professional lives! Moving toward the vision of a better mathematics environment put forward in the *Professional Teaching Standards* will require that teachers be able to think, talk, and learn about their pedagogy and about children's learning of mathematics and to engage in, reflect on, and construct mathematics *for themselves.*

Bibliography

California State Department of Education. *Mathematics Framework for California Public Schools, Kindergarten through Grade Eight.* Sacramento: California State Department of Education, 1991.

Corwin, Rebecca B., and May C. Reinhardt. *Mathematics Education: Learning from the Process Approach to Writing.* Proceedings of the National Educational Computing Conference, Boston, Mass., June 1989.

Hart, Lyn, Karen Schultz, Deborah Najee-Ullah, and Laura Nash. *Arithmetic Teacher* 40 (September 1992):40–42.

Lampert, Magdalene. "Connecting Mathematical Teaching and Learning." In *Integrating Research on Teaching and Learning Mathematics*, edited by Elizabeth Fennema, Thomas Carpenter, and Sharon Lamon. Madison, Wis.: Wisconsin Center for Education Research, 1988.

Mottershead, Lorraine. *Metamorphoses.* Palo Alto, Calif.: Dale Seymour Publications, 1977.

National Council of Teachers of Mathematics. *Professional Standards for Teaching Mathematics.* Reston, Va.: The Council, 1991.

Russell, Susan Jo, and Rebecca B. Corwin. "Going Slow" and "Letting Go," in *Proceedings of the Thirteenth Annual Meeting, North American Chapter of the International Group for the Psychology of Mathematics Education*, edited by Robert B. Underhill. Blacksburg, Va.: Christiansburg Printing Co., 16–19 October 1991.

Steen, Lynn Arthur, ed. *Everybody Counts: A Report to the Nation on the Future of Mathematics Education.* Washington, D.C.: National Academy Press, 1990.

Assessing Students' Beliefs about Mathematics

by

Denise A. Spangler

The beliefs that students and teachers hold about mathematics have been well documented in the research literature in recent years (e.g., Cooney 1985; Frank 1988, 1990; Garofalo 1989a, 1989b; Schoenfeld 1987; Thompson 1984, 1985, 1988). The research has shown that some beliefs are quite salient across various populations. These commonly held beliefs include the following (Frank 1988):

- Mathematics is computation.
- Mathematics problems should be solved in less than five minutes or else something is wrong with either the problem or the student.
- The goal of doing a mathematics problem is to obtain *the* correct answer.
- In the teaching-learning process, the student is passive and the teacher is active.

Educators generally agree that these beliefs are not conducive to the type of mathematics teaching and learning envisioned in the *Curriculum and Evaluation Standards for School Mathematics* (NCTM 1989).

A cyclic relationship appears to exist between beliefs and learning. Students' learning experiences are likely to contribute to their beliefs about what it means to learn mathe-

Denise Spangler is a doctoral student at the University of Georgia, Athens, GA 30602. Her research interests include students' and teachers' beliefs about mathematics and children's constructions of arithmetic.

This article is based on one by the same title that appeared in the winter 1992 issue of *Mathematics Educator,* the publication of the Mathematics Education Student Association at the University of Georgia, an affiliate of NCTM.

matics. In turn, their beliefs about mathematics are likely to influence how they approach new mathematical experiences. According to the *Standards* document, "[Students'] beliefs exert a powerful influence on students' evaluation of their own ability, on their willingness to engage in mathematical tasks, and on their ultimate mathematical disposition" (NCTM 1989, 233).

This apparent relationship between beliefs and learning raises the issue of how the cycle of influence can be used to reinforce positive attitudes. A rich collection of mathematical experiences in the spirit of the curriculum standards may help enrich students' beliefs. Another approach is to help students become aware of the beliefs that they hold about mathematics. The *Standards* document suggests that assessing students' beliefs about mathematics is an important component of the overall assessment of students' mathematical knowledge. Beliefs are addressed in the tenth standard of the evaluation section, which deals with assessing mathematical disposition. Mathematical disposition is defined to include students' beliefs about mathematics. The document recommends that teachers use informal discussions and observations to assess students' mathematical beliefs (NCTM 1989). Although teachers' awareness of students' mathematical beliefs is important, of equal importance may be students' awareness of their own beliefs about mathematics.

One medium for bringing students' beliefs to a conscious level is open-ended questions. As students ponder their responses to such questions, some of their beliefs about mathematics will be revealed. As groups of students discuss their responses to these questions, some students' beliefs will likely be challenged, leading to an examination of these beliefs and their origins and, possibly, to the modification of these beliefs.

This article presents some open-ended questions that have been used by the author with elementary, junior high, and senior high school students; preservice and in-service elementary, junior high, and senior high school teachers; and graduate students in mathematics education. The questions have been culled from a variety of sources and do not necessarily represent the author's original ideas. Each question is followed by a summary of typical responses. The responses from the various populations were quite similar, which is not surprising, since the research shows a striking similarity between the beliefs held by these groups. For some questions possible origins of the belief or possible avenues for further discussion are included.

These questions can be presented to students in various formats. Students can be given a question or series of questions to ponder for homework, or they can be assigned to gather responses to questions from an adult, an older student, and a younger student. Some questions can be posed as journal-writing entries, whereas others can be presented for class discussion with no prior preparation on the part of the students. Regardless of the manner of presentation of the questions, however, students should receive some response to their thinking. This important feedback may come in the form of a class or small-group discussion, or it may be in the form of questions or comments from the teacher in students' journals.

- If you and a friend got different answers to the same problem, what would you do?

The most common answer to this question is that the students would both rework the problem. When asked what reworking accomplishes, the students reply that one person might find an error in his or her work. Another popular answer is that it depends on who the other student is. If the other student is perceived to be "smarter," then the tendency is to accept that person's answer. If the student feels mathematically superior to the other person, though, he or she will stick with the original answer. Only on rare occasions do students suggest that both students could have a correct answer. When this option is presented to students, they tend to think of examples in which both students have represented the same numerical value in a different form (e.g., 1/2 and 3/6 or 0.5 or 1:2). Students rarely consider possibilities in which the two answers are completely different but equally correct, as often occurs in problem solving. These responses lend support for Frank's findings (1988) that students perceive mathematics as a search for *the* one right answer.

- If you were playing Password and you wanted a friend to guess the word *mathematics*, what clues would you give? (Password clues must be one word and may not contain any part of the word being guessed.)

The four most common answers are, predictably, "add," "subtract," "multiply," and "divide." Other clues include "numbers," "problems," "operations," "calculate," "hard," and "subject." These responses suggest that students tend to view mathematics as synonymous with arithmetic. This revelation can lead nicely into a discussion of other branches of mathematics, the types of problems that are posed in the branch, and the types of tools used, such as ruler, compass, graphing calculator, and so on. This discussion, along with some classroom activities in such other branches of mathematics as geometry, probability, and data analysis, can help dispel students' belief that mathematics is merely computation.

- If given a choice, when solving a problem would you prefer to have (*a*) one method that works all the time or (*b*) many methods that work all the time?

Most students indicate that they would prefer to have one method for solving a problem because they would not have to remember as much as if they had multiple methods. This response suggests that students perceive memorization as a major component of mathematics learning. Some students, however, indicate that they would prefer to have several methods from which to choose when solving a problem because they could check their answers using a different method. Other students point out that sometimes one method is more efficient for solving a particular problem than other methods. For example, many methods can be used to determine the center of a circle, including (*a*) folding paper or using a Mira to find the point of intersection of two diameters of the circle and (*b*) finding the point of intersection of the perpendicular bisectors of two chords of the circle. Sometimes the use of paper folding is impractical, so one of the other methods would be better. At other times, the perpendicular-bisector method may be cumbersome and time-consuming, so one of the other methods would be preferred. Also, some students will likely understand one method better than others, and all students are not likely to understand the same method. Students can debate this question among themselves, offering examples of mathematical situations that support their opinions.

- Is it possible to get the right answer to a mathematics problem and still not understand the problem? Explain.

Unfortunately, students are all too often able to obtain correct answers without understanding what they are doing. How many elementary school students can perform the invert-and-multiply algorithm for dividing fractions but cannot tell a story to go along with the number sentence? How often do students solve word problems by extracting the numbers and selecting an operation on the basis of relative sizes of the numbers without understanding how the mathematical operation relates to the action in the problem? After pondering the initial question for a while, many students admit that they often get an answer without understanding the problem. Students can generate examples of mathematical tasks that they perform by rote without understanding the reasons for the steps they perform. This reflection can present opportunities for meaningful reteaching of concepts by the teacher or for interesting research projects for individual students. This type of reteaching is often the focus of the first course in mathematics content taken by preservice elementary school teachers. This course typically consists of the conceptual underpinnings of the four basic operations on subsets of the real numbers. Class discussions are often punctuated by such comments as "So that is why the decimal point goes there!" Discussions of this nature can help students see that studying mathematics involves more than merely obtaining correct answers.

- How do you know when you have correctly solved a mathematics problem?

Reworking the problem, checking with the teacher or a classmate, looking in the back of the book, working backward (for arithmetic problems), or plugging in values (for algebra problems) are common answers to this question. Seldom do students suggest that they check to see if the answer makes sense in the context of the initial problem. This discussion offers an opportunity to introduce such a problem as the one given in the Third National Assessment of Educational Progress:

> An army bus holds 36 soldiers. If 1128 soldiers are being bused to their training site, how many buses are needed?

This problem was given to 45 000 high school students, and one-third of them responded that the answer was 31 remainder 12 without checking to see if such an answer made sense in the context of the problem (Schoenfeld 1987). All too often the check-back stage of the problem-solving process is neglected, either because students are in a hurry to finish the problem or because they do not perceive checking back as an essential component of problem solving. Many students equate checking back with checking numerical computations. They do not perceive looking for generalizable results, examining the efficiency of the method used, looking for additional answers, or identifying the underlying mathematical concepts as part of the problem-solving process. This limited view is likely due to their prevailing belief that the objective of working a mathematics problem is to obtain an answer.

- What subject or subjects is mathematics most like? Least like? Why?

The most popular answer to this question is that mathematics is most like science because it involves memorizing formulas and working with numbers. Virtually all other subject areas are nominated in the category of being least like mathematics. Nevertheless, during a class discussion, something interesting usually occurs. Someone may say that mathematics and music are not alike, but a student who has some musical background may reply, "Oh, yes

they are!" The student will go on to explain that music involves patterns, counting beats, using fractions to determine how long to hold a note, time signatures, and a variety of other mathematical concepts. A similar discussion usually ensues about art. This discussion furnishes a nice opportunity to talk about the golden ratio and its uses in art and architecture (see Billstein and Lott [1986]) or about visualization of abstract concepts of point, line, and plane (see Millman and Speranza [1991]). Some students will claim that mathematics is not similar to studying a foreign language, whereas other students will contend that mathematics *is* a foreign language! In both French and mathematics, it is necessary to adopt the conventions of the language, learn new vocabulary, and determine how isolated words or ideas connect to form meaningful sentences or concepts. And in both instances, practical experiences in the real world help to refine newly acquired skills and concepts.

For other subject areas, students are less likely to formulate an explanation of how the subject is similar to mathematics. This explanation usually has to be initiated by the teacher, and then students contribute their own ideas. For example, history and mathematics are alike because just as we cannot change history, we cannot alter certain mathematics facts (at least not without changing a great deal of mathematics). The Boston Tea Party occurred in Boston, not Orlando, and we cannot change that fact. Similarly, the probability of the occurrence of any given event must be between 0 and 1, inclusive, and we cannot change that fact. (The best tactic is to use an example that relates directly to the topic being studied when this discussion takes place.)

The frontiers of mathematical knowledge are being pushed farther every day.

Although a great deal of history is past and cannot be changed, history is being made right this very moment, just as new mathematical knowledge is constantly evolving (see Peitgen, Jurgens, and Saupe [1992] for a discussion of fractals and chaos). Students tend to perceive mathematics as a static discipline in which everything has already been created or discovered; however, the frontiers of mathematical knowledge are being pushed farther every day. Also, the knowledge we have about past historical events affects the way we live our lives today, just as the mathematics that has been known for several hundred years shapes the mathematics with which we work today. For example, the bombing of Pearl Harbor in 1941 affects the current location of the United States naval fleet, namely, that a majority of the fleet is not kept in the same harbor. Likewise, the fact that infinitely many prime numbers exist affects the modern-day work of cryptographers, who develop coding schemes using prime numbers.

Many similarities occur between mathematics and language arts, but they require some thoughtful consideration to uncover. Spelling, grammar, and mathematics are alike in that they have certain rules that must be memorized and followed. A key difference, however, is that rules in spelling and grammar are frequently broken, whereas rules in mathematics are generally universally applicable. Literature and mathematics are alike because two people may read the same story or poem and come away with entirely different messages. In mathematics, two people may interpret a problem differently and thus may get different answers or may take different approaches to the problem.

- Describe someone in your class or school who you think is mathematically talented.

This discussion needs to be handled with some tact so as not to hurt anyone's feelings. Encourage students not to use the name of an individual but rather to describe characteristics of that person that show evidence of mathematical talent. Many students, particularly elementary school students, will say that mathematically talented people can do mathematics quickly—those who raise their hand first to answer a question, finish a test first, or advance the farthest in the "around the world" flashcard game. This response likely stems from students' belief that mathematics problems should be done quickly. Older students often indicate that mathematically talented people are more logical and analytical and can do things in their heads. This view may explain some students' reluctance to draw diagrams or write down information to solve a problem. In addition to the aforementioned characteristics of mathematically talented people, students invariably mention stereotypical physical or personality characteristics of such people. The next question presents an opportunity to examine these stereotypes.

- Can you think of any television characters who are mathematically talented?

The first answers from students are usually characters who fit the archetypical "nerd" image. Such characters as Steve Urkel from "Family Matters" and Arvid from "Head of the Class" come readily to mind. These characters are equipped with pocket protectors, eyeglasses, briefcases, and white socks, and they are the intellectual giants of the situation comedies on which they appear. With a little bit of prompting, however, students can usually think of another popular, prime-time television character who is mathematically talented but who does not fit the "nerd" stereotype. Dwayne Wayne of "A Different World" is a college student majoring in mathematics who is good-looking, popular, fashionably dressed, and well respected by both his peers and his teachers. Several episodes of the show have dealt directly with mathematics, including episodes where Dwayne tutored students who were struggling with their mathematics classes. Another episode of the show found Dwayne enrolled in a poetry class in which he felt his intellectual talents were being wasted and could be better spent on coursework in his field. Once students begin thinking along these lines, they can think of other characters and nonfictional people who are mathematically talented but who do not fit the negative stereotype.

- Close your eyes and try to picture a mathematician at work. Where is the mathematician? What is the mathematician doing? What objects or instruments is the mathematician using? Open your eyes and draw a picture of what you imagined.

Ask students a variety of questions about the mathematician they imagined. Was their mathematician male or female? How old was their mathematician? What was their mathematician wearing? What did their mathematician look like? In what types of activities was the mathematician engaged? Were other people around?

This activity is used in science education to help students overcome stereotypes about scientists. The results of the activity are quite similar regardless of whether it is done using a scientist or a mathematician. In the instance of the mathematician, students generally picture an older male having gray Einstein-like hair, wearing glasses, and sitting at a desk. He is usually using pencil and paper, books, a calculator or computer, and sometimes a ruler. The mathematician is often in a nondescript room, and no other people are around. These observations suggest that students view mathematics as a solitary endeavor that is carried out in a place very different from their everyday surroundings. They also apparently view mathematics as a male-dominated discipline.

- Do you suppose McDonald's has a mathematician on its corporate staff? What might that person do for McDonald's?

"How does McDonald's decide where to build a new restaurant?"

The initial reaction of most students is that a mathematician is employed to help with inventory and accounting tasks. A common response from elementary school students is that a mathematician is needed to keep track of how many hamburgers have been sold so that the signs on the golden arches that proclaim "*x* billion hamburgers sold" will be accurate! These responses again suggest that students are considering only the computational aspect of mathematics. To stimulate additional thought, the teacher can pose such questions as "How does McDonald's decide where to build a new restaurant?" "How does McDonald's decide on new food products to offer?" and "How are the promotional games created?" These questions open the doors for discussions about data collection, probability, and decisions based on data.

- What businesses in our town might employ a mathematician? What would the mathematician do?

Responses to this question vary depending on the businesses in the town, but students generally have a limited view of the career opportunities for mathematicians. These questions can be used to initiate a discussion of careers in mathematics and careers that use mathematics. Students can interview townspeople who are mathematicians or who use mathematics in their jobs to gather information about various careers. Students can share their findings with the class or the entire school through oral reports, written reports compiled into a class book, pictures, murals, and videotapes or audiotapes. Carpenters, architects, nurses, engineers, scientists, actuaries, pharmacists, statisticians, and operations researchers are among the people who use a great deal of mathematics in their careers.

Conclusion

The preceding questions, individually or collectively, cannot supply teachers with definitive information about each student's beliefs about mathematics. However, such questions and discussions, coupled with observations of students' interactions in mathematical settings, can give teachers valuable information about the beliefs that influence their students' study of mathematics. Students' beliefs about mathematics are manifested in the classroom in whether and how they ask and answer questions, work on problems, and approach new mathematical tasks. The assessment of students' beliefs about mathematics can help teachers plan instruction and structure the classroom environment so as to help students develop more enlightened beliefs about mathematics and mathematics learning (NCTM 1989).

References

Billstein, Rick, and Johnny W. Lott. "Golden Rectangles and Ratios." *Student Math Notes* (September 1986):1–4.

Cooney, Thomas J. "A Beginning Teacher's View of Problem Solving." *Journal for Research in Mathematics Education* 16 (November 1985):324–36.

Frank, Martha L. "Problem Solving and Mathematical Beliefs." *Arithmetic Teacher* 35 (January 1988):32–34.

———. "What Myths about Mathematics Are Held and Conveyed by Teachers?" *Arithmetic Teacher* 37 (January 1990):10–12.

Garofalo, Joe. "Beliefs and Their Influence on Mathematical Performance." *Mathematics Teacher* 82 (October 1989a):502–5.

———. "Beliefs, Responses, and Mathematics Education: Observations from the Back of the Classroom." *School Science and Mathematics* 89 (October 1989b):451–55.

Millman, Richard S., and Ramona R. Speranza. "The Artist's View of Points and Lines." *Mathematics Teacher* 84 (February 1991):133–38.

National Council of Teachers of Mathematics. *Curriculum and Evaluation Standards for School Mathematics.* Reston, Va.: The Council, 1989.

Peitgen, Heinz-Otto, Hartmut Jurgens, and Dietmar Saupe. *Fractals for the Classroom, Part One: Introduction to Fractals and Chaos.* New York: Springer-Verlag New York and National Council of Teacher of Mathematics, 1992.

Schoenfeld, Alan H. "What's All the Fuss about Metacognition?" In *Cognitive Science and Mathematics Education,* edited by Alan H. Schoenfeld, 89–215. Hillsdale, N.J.: Lawrence Erlbaum Associates, 1987.

Thompson, Alba Gonzalez. "The Relationship of Teachers' Conceptions of Mathematics and Mathematics Teaching to Instructional Practice." *Educational Studies in Mathematics* 15 (1984):105–27.

Thompson, Alba G. "Teachers' Conceptions of Mathematics and the Teaching of Problem Solving." In *Teaching and Learning Mathematical Problem Solving: Multiple Research Perspectives,* edited by Edward A. Silver, 281–94. Hillsdale, N.J.: Lawrence Erlbaum Associates, 1985.

———. "Learning to Teach Mathematical Problem Solving: Changes in Teachers' Conceptions and Beliefs." In *The Teaching and Assessing of Mathematical Problem Solving,* edited by Randall I. Charles and Edward A. Silver, 232–43. Hillsdale, N.J.: Lawrence Erlbaum Associates, 1988.

On the Nature of Teaching and Assessing "Mathematical Power" and "Mathematical Thinking"

by

Jonathan Jay Greenwood

Two of the first three Standards for Teaching Mathematics begin with the following statements:

> The goal of teaching mathematics is to help all students develop *mathematical power* (emphasis added) and all students can learn to *think mathematically* (emphasis added) (NCTM 1991).

What exactly is "mathematical power" to someone who has always identified mathematics as being the mastery of facts, such as the multiplication tables, and procedures, such as the long division algorithm? What does it mean to "think mathematically" to a teacher who always struggled with story problems as a student? To those teachers who fit these descriptions, and a sizable number do, assessing students' mathematical power and mathematical thinking is even more bewildering.

Piaget refers to *mathematical power* as having to do with acquiring personal "autonomy" (Kamii 1984). In this context, mathematical power is the student's ability to think and function independently from the teacher. Mathematical power is attained by helping students develop thought processes that can he used to solve problems and to determine whether solutions are appropriate. Mathematical power is gained by minimizing the student's dependence on the teacher or answer key.

Mathematical thinking involves, among other things, the abilities to (*a*) recognize patterns, (*b*) generalize common problem situations, (*c*) identify errors, and (*d*) generate alternative strategies. Mathematical thinking implies a systematic approach to quantitative problems. It is a by-

Jay Greenwood teaches at Georgia Southwestern College, Americus, GA 31709, and also works with students at Sumter County Middle School.

product of learning and doing mathematics. At the same time, it can be the *focus* of learning rather than just a by-product. This focus suggests that all mathematics lessons could benefit by monitoring not only the content being studied but the actual growth in the student's ability to think and reason.

Until recently, the means by which teachers have assessed academic progress has been through the use of paper-and-pencil tests. The assumption has been that correct answers mean mastery; wrong answers mean learning deficiencies. Offered here are some ideas and alternatives to the more traditional methods of academic assessment. The suggested procedures, however, require a rethinking of the criteria for teaching and learning so that they are better aligned with the development of mathematical thinking and power. The article begins by offering seven such learning criteria. Included in the listing are suggestions for teaching and assessing students' progress that are compatible with each learning criterion. This discussion is followed with suggestions for assessing students' growth and grading it. Pedagogical foundations that support this approach and several content-specific applications of the methods outlined in this article can be found in Greenwood (1991, 1992).

Learning Criteria for Mathematical Thinking

The criteria found in table 1 are designed to be introduced to the students during the first class period to familiarize them with the notions of "mathematical thinking" and mathematical power." They can be written on large poster board and hung on the wall for the duration of the class. The idea is to refer to them often, daily if possible.

Table 1

Criteria for Mathematical Thinking

1. Everything you do in mathematics should make sense to you.

2. Whenever you get stuck, you should be able to use what you know to get yourself unstuck.

3. You should be able to identify errors in answers, in the use of materials, and in thinking.

4. Whenever you do a computation, you should use a minimum of counting.

5. You should be able to perform calculations with a minimum of rote pencil-paper computations.

6. When the strategy you are using isn't working, you should be willing to try another strategy instead of giving up.

7. You should be able to extend, or change, a problem situation by posing additional conditions or questions.

Introducing the criteria during the first week of school helps students anticipate probing questions throughout the year because they begin to see from the start that more will be expected of them than just correct answers.

In the discussion that follows, the learning criteria themselves are enumerated. The statement that follows each criterion is the rationale that is offered to the students during the first meeting. The accompanying lesson example is given to help convey ideas pertaining to teaching and monitoring each criterion. Before turning to the task of illustrating the criteria, a word is in order about the nature of the examples used. Care has been taken to depict scenarios that cover a wide range of instructional situations from basic computational exercises to more general problem solving. The intent of these examples is to show the applicability of the criteria across this range and to assist the audience most in need of these ideas.

1. *Everything you do in mathematics should make sense to you.*

You should be able to explain your strategies and thoughts so they are clearly understood by others, not just repeat the steps of what to do to get an answer. The only way I can determine whether something makes sense to you is by listening to you explain it to me or to others. My assumption is that you can't explain something unless you understand it yourself. Sometimes you will he asked to explain how you worked a problem by using manipulatives, diagrams, patterns, or other materials we will be using. Eventually you will be asked to describe your thoughts and the pictures you have in your mind. So you see, you will have many opportunities to show whether something makes sense to you.

Discussion and example. Imagine walking around the room as students are working on mathematics problems where they are asked to draw a rectangle with a perimeter of 18 and a length of 4. You stop to observe Doris, who seems to be progressing well. You interrupt her work quietly and ask her to explain how she arrived at the drawing of a 4×5 rectangle. Her first response is to erase the answer and proceed to work the problem over. Does this scenario sound familiar? In many classrooms, students have acquired the notion that the teacher asks for explanations only for incorrect answers (Kamii 1984). To develop thinking skills, we must begin to value students' explanations for *all* work, *all* thinking—correct and incorrect alike. When students begin to see that such questions as "Are you willing to show me how you got that answer?" "How do you know?" and "Why is that so?" apply to all the mathematics they do, they will develop more confidence in their original solutions and not feel compelled to erase them so quickly. Students who react to such questions with confidence illustrate growth in this criterion.

2. *Whenever you get stuck, you should he able to use what you know to get yourself unstuck.*

For you to learn to think for yourself, it is important that you learn how to answer your own questions. I'm asking you to learn how to build on what you know without asking the teacher or checking the answer key. To do so, it is important that you learn how to use what you know to straighten yourself out when you run into trouble. In the beginning, I will help you out by asking you some questions that will lead you to get unstuck. Later on, you will be able to ask the questions of yourself. When you start doing that, we will both know you are learning how to get unstuck.

Discussion and example. Rafael comes to you and asks, "What is '8×7'? I forgot." To supply the answer (56) is to get the student "unstuck." Often it is seen as the thing to do. Because of short-term gains, supplying the answer saves time, it keeps the student on task, it minimizes errors, and the student is more apt to seek you out for help when it is needed. However, the long-term effects of consistently giving answers can hinder students' ability to learn what is needed to get themselves unstuck (Bruner 1968). Therefore, this criterion suggests that students' questions be answered with *questions* that will lead to getting unstuck. In this example, an appropriate response might be, "Do you know what 8×8 is?" If the student answers "64," the teacher then asks, "Can you use that information to figure out what '8×7' is?" If the student doesn't know what 8×8 is or can't use the answer to figure out 8×7, try a follow-up question, such as "Do you know what '7×7' is, and if so can you use that information to figure out what '8×7' is?" As students anticipate your questions to their questions, they begin to ask the same kinds of questions of themselves. By the teacher's example they learn some strategies for getting unstuck. Students too can serve as "strategy teachers." They can share with the class difficulties they've encountered and tactics they've used to get unstuck. Sharing this information offers students alternatives and fosters independence in thinking.

3. *You should be able to identify errors in answers, in the use of materials, and in thinking.*

You can learn a great deal from your errors if you are willing to think about them once they've been spotted. At times I will ask whether you disagree with something and whether you can spot some mistake. If something is wrong and you can spot it, that will tell us both that you know how it is supposed to be. If nothing is wrong and you think there is, that will tell us something too. It will be important to listen to other students because I'm interested in how well you can help each other. We learn best when we take advantage of our mistakes because mistakes tell us a lot about what we need to work on. In a lot of ways, "mistakes" are stepping stones to learning.

Discussion and example. The class is using the fact that the sum of the measures of the three angles of any triangle is 180 degrees to find the sum of the measures of the four angles of any quadrilateral. Miguel has volunteered to come to the front of the class to demonstrate his answer of 720 degrees. He uses figure 1 to illustrate his thinking. He explains, "The quadrilateral *ABCD* is broken into four triangles, and each triangle has a total of 180 degrees. Therefore, the figure *ABCD* has 4 × 180° = 720° all together."

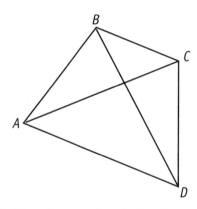

Fig. 1. Miguel's approach to finding the sum of the measures of the angles of quadrilateral *ABCD*

Several students nod approvingly, and several others look confused. The teacher asks if any students disagree, and although none signal the recognition of an error, Maria asks to share her result, which seems to suggest a different answer. She illustrates her answer with figure 2. She explains, "I broke *ABCD* into two triangles, and therefore the figure *ABCD* has 2 × 180° = 360° all together."

The discussion that ensues can go several ways. The teacher can, of course, point out that none of the angle measures *a, b, c, d* in figure 3 contribute to the sum of the measures of the angles of *ABCD*. This observation suggests that Miguel's answer needs to be decreased by 360

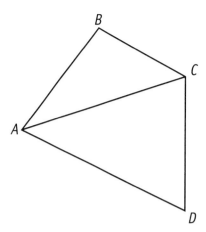

Fig. 2. Maria's approach to the same problem

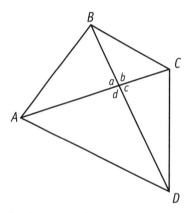

Fig. 3. The discrepancy between the work of Miguel and that of Maria lies in the four interior angles: *a, b, c, d*. The teaching question to consider is, How should the students be led to this fact?

degrees, and the adjusted answer of 720° − 360° = 360° agrees with Maria's. However, long-term advantages are gained by asking the students to discover the nature of the error in the first solution themselves (Bruner 1968; Wirtz 1976; Greenwood 1981). This criterion focuses on the importance of helping students develop the means and the confidence to question answers. Eventually, as students become more familiar with identifying errors, they also become more comfortable and articulate in demonstrating their thinking strategies.

4. *Whenever you do a computation, you should use a minimum of counting.*

I will be interested in how well you can learn to think about numbers and how you can picture them being added, subtracted, multiplied, and divided. To help you concentrate on *thinking*, I'm going to be asking you to try not to count. What I would like you to do, as much as possible, is think your way through a computation. By doing so, you'll actually find more and more patterns that will shorten your computations and make them easier for you to do. Every time you do a lot of counting, you actually stop thinking and begin to rely on the counting process itself. If you do this enough, you stop improving, you stop growing; you just fall back to counting. The more you count, the less you think. The more you think, the less you have to count. As we move along in our work together, I'm going to ask you to explain your work and your thinking in ways that minimize counting.

Discussion and example. This criterion is specifically meant to address the practice of counting on one's fingers to arrive at some addition or subtraction fact. Imagine the following situation occurring in a classroom. The teacher asks Marty, "What's eight plus five?" Marty is observed to use his fingers to count on from eight, moving a finger with each word, saying, "Nine, ten, eleven, twelve, thirteen. The answer is thirteen." Next imagine that twenty minutes have passed, and the teacher again asks Marty to find the answer to "eight plus five." It is not unusual to observe Marty repeat the earlier process in coming up with the answer of thirteen. In fact, when Marty is faced again with the same question, a day, week, or year later, it is not surprising that he employs the same process. The fact that counting always leads to the correct answer can actually hinder the student's learning anything permanent about the way numbers are combined and partitioned. This idea led Wirtz to conclude that "counting confounds thinking" and that "thinking is maximized when counting is minimized" (Wirtz 1976). It has also been shown that when students have already become dependent on counting as a means for producing addition and subtraction answers, it is counterproductive to demand that they discontinue the practice without helping them develop an alternative strategy with which to replace it (Newton 1985; Greenwood 1981). Therefore, whenever counting is observed, the teacher can wait until the student is finished before asking, "I noticed how you got your answer, Marty. Could you have found it without having to count?" Additional questions posed to the class to offer alternatives could also be framed in this way: "Can someone think of another way you could figure out the answer without having to count?" As these questions are asked over time and as alternative strategies are generated by their peers, students begin to value noncounting strategies and thus begin to generate and employ thinking processes to replace counting practices.

5. *You should be able to perform calculations with a minimum of rote pencil-paper computations.*

This criterion is very similar to item 4, but it is included to give extra emphasis to mental-computational strategies and the use of calculators and computers. It is important that we explore a lot of different ways of solving arithmetic computations and become comfortable with several that go beyond paper and pencil. Exploring alternatives will also help us learn to think mathematically because we'll be concentrating on how things fit together.

Discussion and example. Consider the following set of number sentences:

$$1 + 2 = 3$$

$$4 + 5 + 6 = 7 + 8$$

$$9 + 10 + 11 + 12 = 13 + 14 + 15$$

When each number sentence is presented one at a time, the teacher pauses and asks the class if each one is true. The first two sentences are easily judged by most classes as being true. The next sentence, however, oftentimes has students reaching for their pencils and calculators. In such situations, when students are asked to perform a computation in the context of solving a larger problem or investigating a pattern, it is important to take the opportunity to focus on mental-computational techniques. Thus, this criterion provides a forum around which the teacher can ask, "Can you determine whether the sentence is true by just using your mind?" Students will propose such strategies as "On the left side, '9 + 11 = 20,' and the other two numbers add up to '22,' and '20 + 22 = 42.' On the right side, add the three '10s' together and get '30,' and '3 + 4 + 5 = 12' and '30 + 12 = 42.' So the sentence is true." As other student-devised strategies are given, the point is made that many computations can be performed mentally and that a certain amount of "power" is gained by those who can learn to do so. The teacher can then ask if anyone can use the pattern of the first three sentences to describe the next sentence in this sequence. The class discussion, where students share their thinking, leads to the following:

$$1 + 2 = 3$$

$$4 + 5 + 6 = 7 + 8$$

$$9 + 10 + 11 + 12 = 13 + 14 + 15$$

$$16 + 17 + 18 + 19 + 20 = 21 + 22 + 23 + 24$$

The natural question at this point is whether this fourth sentence is true, and here again the students can be asked to try to determine the answer without using paper and pencil or a calculator. The author has witnessed several very clever techniques suggested by students. One favorite was given by a fifth-grade student who claimed that all such sentences formed in this way would be true. His reasoning went like this:

> The first sentence is easy, so I'll start with the next one. The second sentence starts off with 4, which is 2 twos. Give one of the 2s to the 5 and one of the 2s to the 6, and you get the right side (7 + 8).

$$4 + \underline{5 + 6} = 7 + 8$$

$$7 + 8 = 7 + 8$$

The third sentence starts off with 9, which is 3 threes. Give a 3 to the 10, a 3 to the 11, and a 3 to the 12, and you get the right side.

$$\begin{array}{ccc} 3 & 3 & 3 \end{array}$$
$$9 + 10 + 11 + 12 = 13 + 14 + 15$$
$$13 + 14 + 15 = 13 + 14 + 15$$

He continued in this way until he had shown that his method worked for the four sentences given. The class, and the author, were quite impressed. What would the next sentence in this sequence look like? Would it be a true sentence? Will this strategy be successful there too? This criterion is an attempt to help give value to these questions and these types of discussions.

6. *When the strategy you are using isn't working out, you should be willing to try another strategy instead of giving up.*

This criterion is probably the most important of all because it focuses on your learning how to think for yourself. It is also one of the hardest because it challenges you to work your way out of tight spots without the help of the teacher or the answer key. Learning how to think means you are learning how to take care of yourself. It means you don't always need someone else to solve your problems for you. Solving your own problems is the most important thing that school can teach you. It offers you a chance to develop a sort of independence and a sort of "power" that will help you learn on your own after school has taught you all it can. I want you to try to think about this criterion every time you get bogged down trying to solve a problem. Try to monitor your growth in this area and see whether you can minimize the number of times you "give up" on a problem. We will have a number of opportunities to talk about your progress throughout our work together.

Discussion and example. This criterion is similar to criterion 2, "getting unstuck," but like the earlier example of the relationship between criterion 4 and criterion 5, it too is more general than its earlier version because it refers to overall strategies rather than isolated facts or procedures. The intent of the criterion is to help students begin to think in terms of overall problem-solving strategies rather than just isolated answers to episodic problems. This example comes from an experience with a seventh-grade class that was working on geometric constructions. The class had been given a homework problem that asked them to construct a 75-degree angle. The next day, a class discussion showed that several students had solved the problem by constructing two perpendicular lines and bisecting the right angle forming a 45-degree angle. Then by constructing an equilateral triangle, they produced three 60-degree angles. Bisecting one of the angles of the

triangle formed a 30-degree angle. Copying adjacent 45-degree and 30-degree angles formed the desired 75-degree angle. See figure 4.

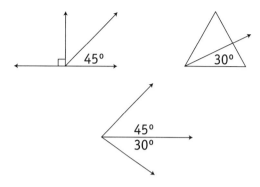

Fig. 4. Constructing a 75-degree angle by bisecting a right angle, bisecting a 60-degree angle, and copying the two angles as adjacent angles

One of the students, who had been unable to solve the problem the night it was assigned, came to class the day following the class discussion and shared the following solution (see fig. 5). He said that after he saw what other students had done, he had begun to think about the problem after class. When he figured out his solution, he was excited and wanted to share it with the class. This criterion creates a forum whereby secondary solutions and afterthoughts are an important component of mathematics.

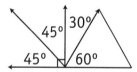

Fig. 5. Another approach requiring only one bisection and the construction of an equilateral triangle

7. *You should be able to extend a problem situation by posing additional conditions or questions.*

Every problem is determined by the specific conditions that it describes. By changing any of the conditions, you end up with a new and different problem. We will be trying to go beyond solving problems and coming up with answers. Part of our work will be about making up our own questions and problems. After we work a problem, we might ask, "What would happen if … ?" This question usually leads to a different problem, and I want you to pay attention to how often we explore it in class and how often you ask it yourself. Albert Einstein once said, "Imagination is more important than knowledge." This criterion is about imagination.

Discussion and example. Problem posing is the ultimate expression of mathematical growth (Bruner 1968; Wirtz

1976). Consider the following problem that was given to a fourth-grade class:

$$A$$
$$B$$
$$\underline{+\ C}$$
$$AB$$

Each letter represents a digit (0, 1, 2, ..., 9), and the students were to find the value of C. By trial and error, most students found that C = 9 and A = 1 and that B could be any other digit. The class discussion intrigued one student, Sophia. She continued to play around with the problem after class to the extent that she removed the restriction that C be a one-digit number. The next day, she shared her findings with the class. It seems that if A = 7 and B = 4, then

$$7$$
$$4$$
$$\underline{+\ C}$$
$$74$$

means that C = 63. Continuing in this vein, Sophia found that in each case, C would necessarily be a multiple of 9, and in fact would be 9 × A. By extending the problem she found another interesting property of numbers, and she was motivated to share her discovery with the class. More important in the long term, the class discussion that she prompted set a memorable example to the other students about the potential for posing one's own questions and problems.

These seven criteria, then, form the basis for establishing a classroom environment that advances the notion that "mathematics is a way of thinking." They lay a foundation whereby students can actually practice mathematical thinking while learning it themselves. The criteria go a long way in giving importance to the order and logic on which the field of mathematics is built. They depend on and support students' understandings and the ability to talk about their work in ways that will make sense to others. According to these criteria, mathematics is not seen as being just a chain of rules, each of which produces an answer. In fact, under these conditions, the student is meant to see that one's responsibility for doing a mathematics problem does not end when an answer is obtained. The process of explaining and defending one's strategy is of equal importance. Besides offering many valuable opportunities for students to learn from their own work, whether correct or incorrect, this process is also a critical diagnostic tool the teacher can use to see "inside the student's head" to determine the extent of understanding. The seven criteria support the notion that the strength of knowledge is in the ability not only to answer questions but also to have the sense and confidence to question answers.

Establishing these seven learning criteria alone will not automatically generate instant successful learning in all students. The teacher needs to see that establishing and referring to the learning criteria is an important first step. Given time and attention, the criteria can help students bring more thought and personal responsibility to their learning.

Assessing Students' Progress

We now shift our focus to assessing and grading students. In this area, the role of the teacher is to gather information that describes how students respond to each of these criteria; organize what is observed; and turn it into usable, accurate assessment data. The following discussion contains some ideas that have been found useful in this effort.

Whenever working or explaining finished work, the student supplies the teacher with information that can be used to gauge growth along at least one of the criteria. In the beginning, these observations can be recorded on the record sheet shown in table 2. After a while, as the assessment process is internalized by the teacher, most assessment data are more easily remembered and organized without having to record them. At any rate, in the beginning the recording sheet can be used as follows:

a. To keep an unmarked original record form, make a photocopy of it and refile the original for future use.

b. Write each student's name on the copy.

c. Make one copy of this record for each month assessment data are collected.

d. Equate each number at the top of the form with one of the criteria. For example:
   1 = Everything you do in mathematics should make sense to you. (Understands)
   2 = Whenever you get stuck, you should be able to use what you know to get yourself unstuck. (Gets unstuck)
   3 = You should be able to identify errors in answers in the use of materials and in thinking. (Spots errors)
   4 = Whenever you do a computation, you should use a minimum of counting. (Minimum of counting)
   5 = You should be able to perform calculations with a minimum of rote pencil-paper computations. (Minimum paper-pencil use)
   6 = When the strategy you are using isn't working out, you should be willing to try another strategy instead of giving up. (Perseverance)
   7 = You should be able to extend a problem situation by posing additional conditions or questions. (Problem posing)

e. Select a grading and recording system to use on the student data that will be collected.

Table 2
Student Record Form

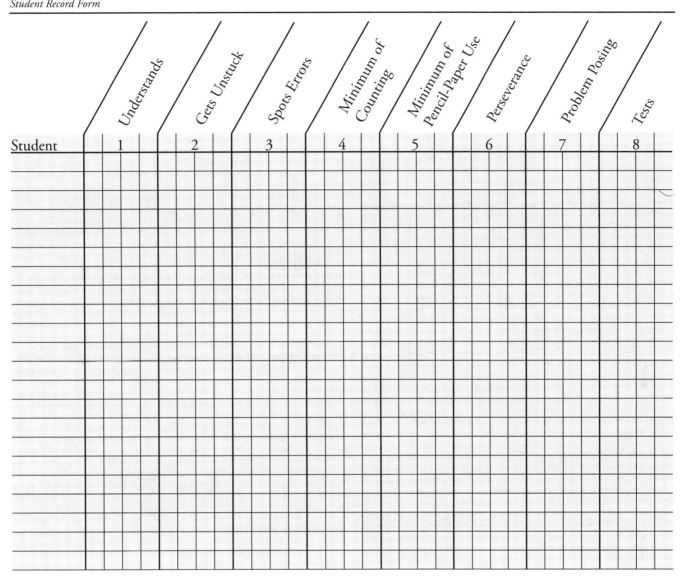

Student	Understands 1		Gets Unstuck 2		Spots Errors 3		Minimum of Counting 4		Minimum of Pencil-Paper Use 5		Perseverance 6		Problem Posing 7		Tests 8	

Letter grades, such as the traditional A–F, or others, such as the one offered here, can be used. If you prefer, the numbers 1–5 could be used in place of the letters and might be considered when a numerical average is desired. Several suggestions are given in table 3. Whichever code is selected, the teacher records the grade or score under the appropriate criterion when a student provides information to the teacher. For example, Su-Lin is observed working with another student, Hans. The teacher overhears the following conversation:

Su-Lin: Wait a minute, that's not right. Six times eight isn't fifty-six.

Hans: Yes it is.

Su-Lin: No, it's not. I'll bet you it's not.

Hans: Okay, let's get the grid and masks *(the materials being used at the time).*

They get the grid and masks, and Hans discovers that he's made a mistake. The teacher has gained valuable assessment information on both students. Su-Lin spotted an error and called it to Hans's attention, so the teacher can record an "E" or "V" under the number "3" next to her name (using the middle coding system). Hans was able to focus on the question raised by Su-Lin and had some sense of how to find the correct answer. In doing so, he found his error and corrected it. The teacher needs to decide whether this occurrence was an example of getting unstuck or finding an error, or both, but it is useful information no matter where it is recorded. It should also be noted that had Hans not suggested the grid and masks as a way of finding the correct answer, or if neither of them spotted the error, this information would also have been useful and could have been translated into a "B" or "N" for both. The situation given in the foregoing dialogue

Table 3

Grading Codes That Might Be Used for Each Criterion

Grade	Grade	Score	Interpretation
A	*E*	5	*Excellent.* A superior example of a clear explanation (use of materials, gets unstuck, spots errors, etc.)
B	*V*	4	*Very good.* Better-than-average explanation (use of materials, gets unstuck, spots errors, etc.)
C	*G*	3	*Good.* Satisfactory explanation but lacking in detail (use of materials, gets unstuck, spots errors, etc.)
D	*B*	2	*Below average.* Lacks detail and raises questions as to complete understanding (use of materials, gets unstuck, spots errors, etc.)
F	*N*	1	*Not satisfactory.* Not able to meet this criterion at this time

would be worthy of a class discussion to help students better understand how such interactions can be used to assess learning. It might be introduced to the class like this:

"While I was walking around during your work time, I saw Su-Lin and Hans discussing a difference of opinion about one of the problems. Su-Lin and Hans, are you willing to tell the class what happened?" After the situation is described, ask the class whether they can tell which of the learning criteria was demonstrated in that example, and then go on to tell Su-Lin and Hans that they need to think about taking credit for the way in which they handled it. (See Greenwood [1991, 1992] for more examples.)

The teacher should make an effort to collect information for each criterion on every student at least once per month. Therefore, copies of the record sheet are needed for each month of use. Often, if enough information hasn't been gathered for, say, Josef and the class is approaching the end of the month, the teacher may tell him that he will be asked to share some of his work at the front of the class the next day (or soon). It is important to give students advance notice when they will be asked to do something that involves personal risk (Newton 1985). It helps them prepare their focus, and they are not jolted with surprise when called on. In such situations, the teacher can also make a note to observe these students more closely. As time goes on, the teacher gets a lot better at pacing observations and spreading them around more evenly throughout the month.

At the end of each month the students can be asked to evaluate themselves according to the same seven criteria. By doing so, the students take an active part in monitoring their own growth and have a chance to compare their evaluative statements with the teacher's. Table 4 is a copy of the general form used with students.

On Monday or Tuesday of the last week of each month, the form is distributed to each student. The students are asked to consider each criterion carefully and to grade themselves, marking in the left column, according to how they think they've done over the course of the month. They are asked to use the same grading code that will be used by the teacher. The students can use the suggested code given previously in their self-evaluations. The code that follows has also been used with students because many find it easier to interpret:

A = Always
M = Most of the time
O = Occasionally
S = Seldom
N = Not at all

After sufficient time, students' self-evaluations are collected. The teacher then goes over each student's form carefully and evaluates it using the same grade codes, marking in the rightmost column. In the beginning, it is not unusual for students to be more critical of themselves and more negative with their own self-given scores than the assessments given by the teacher. Whenever these discrepancies occur, the student can be asked to try to describe how the *teacher's* grade was determined. That is, what information did the teacher use to assess the student's growth as being greater than that given by the student? The question is more than rhetorical, since it asks the student to reflect on how she or he is perceived by others; and since the teacher's grade is generally higher, it offers the student a chance to think about how she or he has grown. As time goes on, students develop a better sense for assessing themselves and seem to keep the criteria more in mind when they are working. Again over time, students lose the biting edge of self-criticism and become more kind to themselves. When the teacher finishes writing responses on the forms, they are returned to the students with the request that they be taken home and shown to their parents. They are to be returned the next day with the parent's signature and are kept until the end of the grading period. These informal assessments are intended to supplement the formal grades that are sent home at the end of each grading period. This type of monthly communication is vitally important in monitoring and reporting students' growth. It has been found that this total assessment program is effective for several reasons:

- It gives the students a chance to grade themselves, which is critical to developing a sense of personal involvement and personal responsibility in one's learning.

- It gives students an opportunity to compare their evaluative judgment with someone else's. This type of "reality check" helps solidify the student's "outside in" view of self.

Table 4
Studemt-Teacher Mathematics Evaluation Sheet

Student _____

What I'd give myself		What the teacher would give me
☐	1. I give clear and understandable explanations and can use the materials to show that the mathematics I do makes sense to me.	☐
☐	2. Whenever I get stuck, I can use what I know to get unstuck.	☐
☐	3. I am able to identify errors in answers, in the use of the mathematics materials, and in thinking.	☐
☐	4. When I do a computation, I do a minimum of counting.	☐
☐	5. When I do a computation, I don't always need paper and pencil.	☐
☐	6. When a srategy doesn't work, I try another one instead of giving up.	☐
☐	7. I can extend, or change, a problem by asking extra questions or posing different conditions.	☐
☐	8. I study and practice before tests and quizzes.	☐
☐	9. I am a helpful partner.	☐
☐	10. I take care of myself when learning mathematics.	☐

Use the following code to mark yourself in each criterion:

A = Always
M = Most of the time
O = Occasionally
S = Seldom
N = Not at all

- The learning criteria become more familiar, more important, and more useful to the students as they learn how to apply the criteria both to learning and to the assessment of learning.

- Students are not surprised when grades come out. They are much more a part of the grading process, and they begin to see it as a "consequence" of their efforts during the previous days and weeks.

Suggestions for Grading

The following discussion is difficult to broach because of the personally sensitive nature of grading students. It is also difficult because of the laudable work done recently to move assessment toward holistic parameters rather than reduce them to simplistic letter grades of the past (Stenmark 1989). The suggestions offered here are not intended in any way as a criticism of that work nor as implied support for letter grades and grade-point averages. The intent rather is to offer helpful suggestions to teachers who find themselves struggling with the problems of transition that will help broaden the concept of grades so that they better reflect students' growth in mathematical power and mathematical thinking and place less emphasis on procedural knowledge that is the domain of tests and quizzes.

With this intent in mind, the process of translating the foregoing discussion into recorded grades is the next step in expanding student assessment to reflect these new dimensions. It is important that students' grades reflect all the areas that have been the focus of the seven learning criteria given previously. Grades that are solely dependent on test scores and on the completion of homework assignments simply do not capture the quality of learning that is proposed and intended by the NCTM's *Curriculum and Evaluation Standards* (1989). The teacher can quantify each of the seven learning criteria by using numbers instead of letter grades, find their sum, and add the test scores to this total. Dividing this accumulated total by 8 (the seven criteria plus the average test score—see table 2) provides the teacher a meaningful, more complete measure of the student. When weighing each area somewhat equally, a composite grade might then be determined by averaging the eight criteria. Several alternatives in weighing are given in table 5.

Table 5

Suggestions for Weighting the Different Criteria

Ex. 1 Weight	Ex. 2 Weight	Ex. 3 Weight	Criterion
13%	15%	10%	Understanding
13%	10%	15%	Getting unstuck
12%	10%	10%	Spotting errors
12%	10%	15%	Using minimum of counting
13%	20%	15%	Using minimum of paper-pencil
12%	10%	15%	Perseverance
12%	10%	10%	Problem posing
13%	15%	10%	Tests and quizzes
100%	100%	100%	Total grade

Responses from parents, students, and administrators have shown that such a grade reflects a more total picture of the student's progress during the grading period. It also supplies valuable information for parents in their attempts to help students at home.

Summary

Implementing the NCTM's curriculum standards and professional teaching standards (1989, 1991) requires operational definitions for such terms as *mathematical power* and *mathematical thinking*. Without a workable process for defining our work in teaching and assessing these noble goals, we stand exposed to the close scrutiny of those more interested in test scores as a means of measuring students' growth. The ideas and experiences presented in this article are shared as an attempt to contribute to this effort. They are based on the use of seven learning criteria that help put into operation the concepts of mathematical power and mathematical thinking. The criteria can be used across grade levels and for all mathematical topics as a basis for planning, teaching, and assessing students' growth.

Bibliography

Bruner, Jerome S. *Toward a Theory of Instruction.* W. W. Norton & Co., 1968.

Greenwood, Jonathan Jay. *Developing Mathematical Thinking: A Complete Unit on the Addition and Subtraction Basic Facts.* Portland, Oreg.: Multnomah Education Service District, 1991.

————. *Developing Mathematical Thinking: A Complete Unit on the Multiplication and Division Basic Facts.* Portland, Oreg.: Multnomah Education Service District, 1992.

————. "The Effects of Student-conducted Error Analysis on Teacher Practices and Student Performance." Unpublished Ph.D diss., University of Oregon, June 1981.

Kamii, Constance. "Autonomy: The Aim of Education Envisioned by Piaget." *Phi Delta Kappan* 65 (February 1984):410–15.

National Council of Teachers of Mathematics. *Curriculum and Evaluation Standards for School Mathematics.* Reston, Va.: The Council, 1989.

————. *Professional Standards for Teaching Mathematics: Executive Summary.* Reston, Va.: The Council, 1991.

Newton, Fred E. *Alternatives to Failure: Resources for Improving Teaching: A Report of Two Alternative Classrooms.* Portland, Oreg.: Multnomah Education Service District, 1985.

Stenmark, Jean. *Assessment Alternatives in Mathematics.* Berkeley, Calif.: EQUALS Project, Lawrence Hall of Science, 1989.

Wirtz, Robert. *Banking on Problem Solving.* Monterey, Calif.: Curriculum Development Associates, 1976.

**Implementing the
Assessment
Standards for
School Mathematics**

Portfolios as Agents of Change

by

Karen S. Karp and DeAnn Huinker

I believe portfolios are very worthwhile. In fact, even though they are significantly more work, the benefits far outweigh any final exam, any day. The benefits include self-reflecting, re-examining activities, working through ideas that did not make sense and making sense of them. Plus, portfolios are so personal and individual—each one is a wonderful snapshot of us as future teachers.

—Elementary-mathematics-methods student

Utilizing portfolios this semester served me not only as a culmination tool, bringing concepts into clearer focus, but also as a means to both assess my own progress and bolster my self-confidence. Looking back, I see mistakes I have made, steps I have taken to address these errors, and I am given direction for further, even better, solutions to problems I encountered.

—Elementary-mathematics-methods student

As teachers in elementary classrooms examine the assessments they use in an effort to link the learning and evaluation process, so, too, must university education professors investigate the use of alternative-assessment techniques. In a recent survey of professors on their assessment practices in elementary mathematics methods and content courses, respondents frequently indicated

Karen Karp, kskarp01@ulkyvm.louisville.edu, teaches at the University of Louisville, Louisville, KY 40292. In her teaching and scholarly work, she has focused on equity issues in mathematics education. DeAnn Huinker, huinker@csd.uwm.edu, teaches at the University of Wisconsin—Milwaukee, Milwaukee, WI 53201-0413. She has a special interest in assessment issues and children's sense of whole numbers and fractions.

Edited by Jeane Joyner, North Carolina Department of Public Instruction, Raleigh, NC 27601-2825.

that portfolios were the assessment technique they would most like to try in the near future (Huinker and Karp 1995). Historically, portfolios have been used in university settings—sometimes by nontraditional students to translate life experiences into college credit or at other times by students in disciplines as diverse as art, writing, and business as a way to compile their accomplishments. Yet portfolio assessment is still considered a relatively new experience for many education students.

What Are Portfolios?

A portfolio is a purposeful collection of work that demonstrates a student's understanding, beliefs, attitudes, and growth. A portfolio might include such items as lesson plans, lesson reflections, journal entries, and case studies of children; these items are discussed further in this article. In preservice education the portfolio serves as an ongoing and evolving method of assessing students' progress in learning to teach mathematics. The portfolio gives preservice teachers an opportunity to document their own professional growth and development and to highlight some of the important ideas they have learned in their college courses about the teaching and learning of mathematics.

Why Use Portfolios in Mathematics Education?

We are currently seeing the expanded role of the portfolio in mathematics-education settings as a rich form of assessment. Initially it may have been a way to give preservice education students a firsthand opportunity to experience the portfolio assessment as a process that they will probably be using in their class. The key functions of a portfolio are to provide ways for students to self-assess their learning formally, gauge their growth on course objectives, and document their strengths. Also, as professors encourage students to develop the criteria used to organize and evaluate the portfolio, students can assume leadership roles in their own learning process.

Self-assessment

The NCTM's *Professional Standards for Teaching Mathematics* (1991) states that teachers are being asked to teach a subject in ways they have never experienced. One crucial variable in making lasting change in preservice teaching is the process of reflection (O'Loughlin 1990). Yet many current teacher-education programs do not involve students in a reflective approach; instead, classes are often driven by a model of the professor as the authority. The process of reflection needs to be built into the course on a regular basis, enabling students to evaluate their progress on the portfolio as they share with peers what they have learned and how they plan to prove that knowledge. During specified intervals throughout the semester, pieces of the portfolio can be shared in their embryonic state. For example, a midsemester activity involves students' sharing the draft of a portfolio item with a group of peers for early structural feedback. By making it an ongoing effort, the learner can begin to take charge of the learning process through looking at other students' work; discussing, rather than judging, how high-quality work should appear; and self-regulating through the use of what they themselves have set as a new standard. This format also encourages movement away from the professor as an authority figure through the use of colleagues to obtain feedback. Such a process not only models the experience that students will need when they move to the teaching profession but also allows them to learn about the challenges of giving constructive criticism to others, a skill necessary in their chosen profession.

Portfolios in the hiring process

Several states, as well as many individual school systems, currently use portfolios as part of the hiring process for both teachers and administrators. Although most portfolios at the university level communicate growth, professional portfolios incorporate examples of a student's *best* work. This form of documentation, more than the usual application snapshot, is instead a portrait of a candidate's strengths, accomplishments, and qualifications. It is much richer than a one-faceted product, such as a cumulative-grade-point-average record. Therefore, practice given in the university setting on how to develop such an in-depth self-assessment enhances a portfolio writer's chances in the hiring process.

Framework

A portfolio is not merely a resource file that contains every activity and assessment from the entire semester. Instead, the portfolio is a set of materials carefully chosen by the student and organized to tie individual pieces together meaningfully. Although goals are often established at the beginning of a course, the flexible format of the portfolio allows for structure as well as surprises and creativity. As the project becomes less professor directed, the students take more responsibility for their own learning. Some possible approaches that can be considered as frameworks include basing the evidence of growth on (1) meeting the established objectives of the course, (2) meeting the NCTM's Curriculum and Evaluation Standards (1989), (3) meeting the NCTM's Professional Standards for Teaching Mathematics (1991), or (4) presenting the five most meaningful pieces of work developed during the semester, which may include earlier, less successful attempts used for contrast.

Possible contents

Customarily the portfolio starts with a letter to the reader. In this narrative the reader should learn about the author's vision, the goals of the course, and the purposes for each piece of evidence used to illustrate growth (see fig. 1).

The next component is the documentation of growth, evidenced by various forms from various settings, such as projects done in class or activities conducted in elementary schools with children. Although no one required item must be included, the overriding variable in selecting items should be that they reveal in-depth information. The pieces used to substantiate this development can include lesson plans; lesson reflections and analyses; journal entries; assessments developed; case studies of children; detailed write-ups of solutions to problems; children's work with comments and feedback; mathematics autobiographies, which are personal histories of their experiences in mathematics; videotaped demonstrations of classroom teaching with self-assessment and peer-assessment; reactions to professional readings; and annotated class notes (see fig. 2). In each subcategory, students must include statements, often as a cover sheet, describing the item, linking the item's inclusion to ideas from class discussions or readings (i.e., Why is the item a worthwhile mathematics task?), and explaining why this particular item was selected and its significance in relation to the portfolio's objectives.

Making selections

As students decide which pieces of work are most persuasive, they often ask themselves essential questions about what is good teaching. The reflective nature of this

Dear Reader,

The development of my mathematical skills can best be described by the sequence of a spider building her web. The spider starts a new web by laying down some bridge lines as a frame upon which to build. At the beginning of the semester, I was starting "new" with math. With each class I developed a new insight, understanding, or perspective that I could use as part of my framework on which to build my skills.

Once the spider has built the frame, she puts in a temporary spiral, joining one spoke to the next; creating stability in the web. I perceive my skillls have developed to a point of stability. That is, I can more readily make connections betweeen mathematical concepts, and I am beginning to be able to apply mathematical concepts to other academic disciplines. I have an understanding of what is developmentally appropriate and the necessary methods and strategies to use to teach mathematics. I can see the "whole" and the interconnectedness of the parts. Each step, a part of the other, woven together. I am continuing to develop my skills, and like the spider, I build upon what I already know.

Lisa

Fig. 1. Portion of a letter to the reader

approach often fosters the evolution of metaphorical links to other disciplines and earlier experiences (see fig. 3). When students begin to write supportive pieces about why their evidence is relevant to the goals, they must explicitly state what they learned. Reflecting and writing about their learning pushes students to focus on where they can improve and helps them become leaders in their own learning.

Evaluating Portfolios

In many ways the process of evaluating a portfolio is similar to that of evaluating an essay. The decisions are subjective. Yet to clarify the procedure, a structure and an agreed-on set of criteria must be used to help define the quality of the work. Rubrics (see figs. 4 and 5) can constitute the evaluation framework and can be generated by the professor; the professor and students; or with additional assistance by others, such as cooperating teachers, local administrators, state-certification-agency staff, or other university educators. These external evaluators lend authenticity and credibility to the process while they learn how university-education classes develop prospective teachers as leaders in their own education. Of course, each of these groups can appropriately use the rubric to assess the final portfolio.

When the portfolios are complete, students are frequently asked to bring them to class with a completed self-assessment rubric. The students then meet with peers and exchange portfolios. Peers read the portfolio and use the rubric to score their classmate's work. Later, local cooperating teachers, administrators in a position to hire, districtwide curriculum coordinators, or other professors can visit the class and examine the portfolios, thereby becoming a part of an assessment team. In this model, assessment conducted by the professor of the course becomes an evaluation of the student's ability to self-assess. Feedback to the student on this criterion can lead to additional growth.

Conclusions

Portfolios are not only powerful assessment tools that can develop a student's own reflection and responsibility for the learning process but can also augment elementary teachers' lessons and can help professors examine their own instruction. Portfolios can become a valuable component of the course assessment. Trends emerge as students select significant moments and events from either the course or classroom experiences with children. Professors can then use this information to redefine the course and better meet students' needs. As well, students' identifying struggles they have had with confusing or difficult concepts will enable the professor to elaborate on these topics in the future.

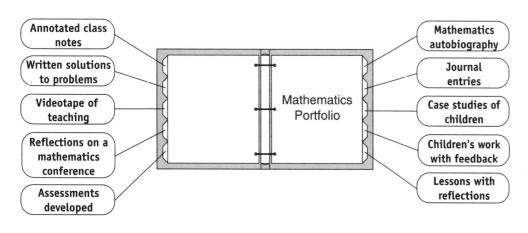

Fig. 2. What's in a portfolio?

Dear Reader,

I begin this letter under much duress. The thought of ever doing a portfolio for mathematics has never entered my frail human mind. I find myself in a position that is foreign to my social science loving heart. I am convinced that to understand my view of math is to come to grips with the mathematical beast in my past. Hence, I have chosen to take you on a journey through my mathematical inferno. Dante wrote concerning the fears of the darkness from a strictly medieval mind-set. As a sixth grader in the midwest, I imagined purgatory as a never ending math class. The instructor played the part of the tormentor using the dreaded ditto.

Teaching mathematics was not high on my list of priorities as a prospective educator. The thought of becoming one of the tormentors made me sad. I was determined that teaching mathematics would be a time of pain for student and teacher. We would suffer together and I would exhibit sympathy for those under my ditto master. Then came the mathematics methods course and my hopes were raised from the pits of purgatory to the joys of paradise. I invite you, the reader, to sail with me as we travel to paradise. However, like Dante of old, although we will see my growth, the real challenge lies in my future.

Richard "Dante"

Fig. 3. Portion of a letter to a reader

The NCTM's *Assessment Standards for School Mathematics* (1995, 3) describes assessment as the "process of gathering evidence about a student's knowledge of, ability to use, and disposition toward, mathematics and of making inferences from that evidence for a variety of purposes." The professor can use the following six questions, based on the assessment standards, to reflect on the process of using portfolios for assessment purposes in mathematics-methods courses.

♦ What *significant mathematics* is reflected in the portfolios?

♦ What evidence contained in the portfolio represents how the students' *mathematics teaching and learning* was enhanced?

♦ How has the portfolio process promoted *equity* by enabling all students to exhibit what they know and can do as future teachers of mathematics?

♦ In what ways has the process of developing and reviewing the portfolios been *open* to the students?

Justify your response in the space below each item or on another page.

	Low			High
The letter to the reader is free of grammatical and mechanical errors and is well written.	1	2	3	4
The letter defines individual goals of the course. The definitions are meaningful and detailed.	1	2	3	4
The letter explains the purpose of each piece of evidence included in the table of contents and how each item relates to one of the defined course goals.	1	2	3	4
The letter is interesting and personalized: it passes the "so what" test.	1	2	3	4
Each defined goal is addressed by one or more rich and meaningful portfolio items.	1	2	3	4
The evidence in the portfolio is significant and compelling.	1	2	3	4
The portfolio is well organized and is pleasing in appearance.	1	2	3	4
The portfolio demonstrates growth on the stated objectives.	1	2	3	4
The portfolio demonstrates knowledge of methods to teach mathematics to elementary school students.	1	2	3	4
The portfolio demonstrates creativity.	1	2	3	4
The portfolio shows evidence of reflection.	1	2	3	4
Overall assessment	1	2	3	4

Fig. 4. Sample rubric

Organization and Presentation

5 Creative, very clear, easy to follow
4 Clear
3 Mostly clear
2 Some clear parts
1 Unclear

Cover Letter

7 Includes synthesis, reflection, quality writing, and all components
5 Connections made to readings and class
3 Some connections made, some components
2 Lists items, makes basic observations
1 Inaccurate statement, poor writing

Knowledge of Worthwhile Mathematical Tasks

5 Extended, generalized connections made, inquiry based
4 Clear understanding
3 Understood most of the time
2 Partially understood
1 Misunderstood

Knowledge of Assessment Techniques

5 Extended, generalized, child centered
4 Clear understanding
3 Understood most of the time
2 Partially understood
1 Misunderstood

Reflection on Teaching and Learning Mathematics

8 Includes synthesis and extensions
6 Connections made to readings and class
4 Some connections made, not consistent
2 Some observations included
0 No reflections and descriptions included

Knowledge of Tools for Learning Mathematics

5 Extended, generalized
4 Clear understanding
3 Understood most of the time
2 Partially understood
1 Misunderstood

General Quality and Completion

5 High-quality writing, completed on time, all required components present
4 Quality writing for the most part, completed on time, all components
3 Some errors, some late components, or some components missing
2 Many errors, late, or some components missing
1 Poor writing, very late, components missing

Fig. 5. Portfolio rubric

♦ How have you ensured that the portfolios will allow you to make valid *inferences* about the students' developing knowledge of mathematics teaching and learning?

♦ How have the portfolios contributed to a *coherent* assessment process?

The inclusion of portfolios can be a powerful component in the process of evaluating students and encouraging change. By shifting the responsibility for the construction of knowledge to preservice education students, the use of portfolios can become a model of lifelong learning that will, it is hoped, be passed to their own students for years to come.

Bibliography

Dewey, John. *How We Think: A Restatement of the Relation of Reflective Thinking to the Educative Process.* Boston: D. C. Heath & Co., 1933.

Huinker, DeAnn, and Karen Karp. "Assessment Practices in Elementary Mathematics Teacher Preparation." *AMTE News—Newsletter of the Association of Mathematics Teacher Educators* 4 (Fall 1995): 8–10.

National Council of Teachers of Mathematics. *Curriculum and Evaluation Standards for School Mathematics.* Reston, Va.: The Council, 1989.

———. *Professional Standards for Teaching Mathematics.* Reston, Va.: The Council, 1991.

———. *Assessment Standards for School Mathematics.* Reston, Va.: The Council, 1995.

O'Loughlin, Michael. "Teachers' Ways of Knowing: A Journal Study of Teachers Learning in a Dialogical and Constructivist Learning Environment." Paper presented at the annual meeting of the American Educational Research Association, Boston, April 1990.

Activities

The Reflective Learner

Corwin, "Doing Mathematics Together: Creating a Mathematics Culture"

Select a group problem-solving activity in which you have participated. Write a reflective account of the processes that your group went through to reach a solution.

(*a*) Identify and discuss the mathematical acts that you used from the following list: posing questions; representing information; keeping track; expressing relationships; making and testing conjectures; and discussing, debating, and challenging one another's ideas.

(*b*) What implications does this awareness of processes have for you as a teacher of mathematics?

Spangler, "Assessing Students' Beliefs about Mathematics"

Spangler poses eleven open-ended questions (denoted by bullets) in her article.

(*a*) Select at least two of these questions and write out your personal responses to them.

(*b*) Describe how your responses relate to the discussion of the questions provided by the author.

Greenwood, "On the Nature of Teaching and Assessing 'Mathematical Power' and 'Mathematical Thinking' "

1. Using the evaluation sheet in table 4, rate your performance on mathematical tasks over the past month.

2. Discuss the value of using the self-evaluation form in table 4. If applicable, reword items or suggest other items that should be added to the list.

3. Discuss the usefulness of the self-evaluation sheet for your classroom.

Karp and Huinker, "Portfolios as Agents of Change"

Use the guidelines given in the article to design and implement a portfolio component for your class. Explain why you chose your particular design. (This activity may be done as an individual, group, or whole-class project.)

Section 4
Creating a Different Kind of Classroom

Implementing the Standards will require new roles for both the teacher and the student as they work together to create more-effective learning environments. The *Professional Standards for Teaching Mathematics* (NCTM 1991) has developed a vision of "what a teacher at any level of schooling must know and be able to do"(p. 5). This vision is organized as a set of standards that include the following (NCTM 1991, p. 5):

- Setting goals and selecting or creating mathematical *tasks* to help students achieve these goals
- Stimulating and managing classroom *discourse* so that both the students and the teacher are clearer about what is being learned
- Creating a classroom *environment* to support teaching and learning mathematics
- *Analyzing* student learning, the mathematical tasks, and the environment in order to make ongoing instructional decisions.

The articles in this section focus primarily on the teacher's role in creating mathematical tasks and stimulating discourse. Classrooms, however, exist as a complex whole, and each article also presents information related to the overall environment and the ways that teachers continually assess students. The classroom vignettes and examples of students' work that the authors report vividly show these NCTM Standards in action. As you read through the articles, reflect on your own past and present learning experiences and compare them with the images of a different kind of classroom described by each author.

Reys and Long describe six criteria that characterize good mathematical tasks and illustrate each with an example taken from a classroom problem-solving situation. Such tasks provide for skill development as well as encourage mathematical thinking, exploring, and making and validating conjectures. Teachers must play an active role in the creation of worthwhile tasks, since they are the ones who decide how the prescribed curriculum is to be taught. The authors point out that many effective tasks evolve out of the classroom environment, which provides meaningful contexts for studying new ideas.

Teaching Standards 2 and 3 from the *Professional Standards for Teaching Mathematics* (NCTM 1991) outline the teacher's and students' roles in classroom discourse and provide short elaborations of each outline. These descriptions of discourse paint a picture of an active classroom in which students and teachers are engaged in doing mathematics—writing about and representing ideas, asking questions, discussing problems, and explaining their reasoning.

Two aspects of discourse—talking and writing about mathematics—are illustrated by the next two articles. Andrews describes six aspects of children's natural use of language that can be drawn on to enhance their mathematics lessons. Classroom vignettes illustrating the six aspects demonstrate the quality of mathematical talk engaged in by kindergarten children. Scheibelhut presents examples of children's work to illustrate how writing can be used to help children clarify their understandings as well as provide teachers with assessment information. The article describes the growth of preservice teachers' appreciation of writing as a tool for learning in mathematics as they experimented with various classroom activities.

The *NCTM Xchange* article and the Farivar and Webb article examine how cooperative groups can be used to facilitate mathematics learning. In the *Xchange,* teachers give examples of how they have interpreted, within their own classrooms, the NCTM *Standards* recommendations for individual, small-group, and whole-class work. Different groupings reflect the goals of particular tasks, assessment requirements, and the types of students in each classroom. Farivar and Webb outline a sequence of steps for developing effective group behavior. These steps include communication skills, team building, and helping skills. The authors include charts listing helping behaviors, illustrated with examples of appropriate forms of communication.

The final article in this section, by Campbell and Langrall, addresses the issue of equity in the mathematics classroom. The authors describe eight criteria, implemented in three predominately minority urban schools, that are designed to support equal achievement and encourage participation by all students. This article illustrates the teachers' and students' roles in creating effective learning environments.

Reference

National Council of Teachers of Mathematics. *Professional Standards for Teaching Mathematics.* Reston, Va.: National Council of Teachers of Mathematics, 1991.

Implementing the *Professional Standards for Teaching Mathematics*

Teacher as Architect of Mathematical Tasks

by

Barbara J. Reys and Vena M. Long

No other decision that teachers make has greater impact on students' opportunity to learn and on their perceptions about what mathematics is than the selection or creation of the tasks with which the teacher engages the students in studying mathematics. Here the teacher is the architect, the designer of the curriculum.

—Lappan 1993, 524

The first Standard presented in the *Professional Standards for Teaching Mathematics* (NCTM 1991) highlights the importance of choosing and using *worthwhile mathematical tasks.* Teachers are curriculum architects charged with ensuring the quality of the mathematical tasks in which their students engage. Although *what* is taught may be a state, province, or district decision, *how* it is taught is a decision the classroom teacher makes daily. Embedding curriculum in worthwhile mathematical tasks increases the likelihood of success and enjoyment for both students and teacher. Monitoring students' work during the task, as well as during students' presentation and defense of their solutions, gives teachers invaluable information about what the students know and are comfortable doing.

Barbara Reys reaches at the University of Missouri, Columbia, MO 65211. Vena Long teaches at the University of Missouri, Kansas City, MO 64110.

Edited by Nancy Nesbitt Vacc, University of North Carolina at Greensboro, Greensboro, NC 27412.

What Are Good Mathematical Tasks?

Good mathematical tasks capture students' curiosity and do not separate mathematical thinking from mathematical concepts or skills (NCTM 1991). They offer ample opportunity for skill development within the context of an experience meaningful to students. They evolve from a classroom environment that invites students to explore and discover mathematical relationships and connections and to pursue and validate mathematical hunches. Teachers capitalize on good tasks by being perceptive and flexible, looking ahead and steering students to appropriate follow-up explorations. On the one hand, good tasks are easy neither to design and describe nor to replicate because they depend on specific students and on the classroom environment in which they evolve. On the other hand, good tasks are easy to recognize in progress and share some characteristics.

Good tasks are often authentic in that they come from the students' environment. Recently in a first-grade class, a teaching aide was talking about her baby. One student asked her how old the baby was. The aide replied, "Fourteen months." The student quickly asked, "Is that over one?" The teacher capitalized on the question by asking the students to work on this problem. Several went to the calendar and carefully counted the months. Others sat down and began making marks to represent months. Once the students had convinced themselves that the baby was more than one year old, the teacher asked them to think about how old, in months, they were. This question, or mathematical task, launched a new investigation that was both challenging and rich in mathematical discoveries. Students used a variety of tools—calendars, counters, and calculators—and strategies—counting, charting, adding, and multiplying—and found that their ages ranged from eighty to eighty-eight months.

Finally, the teacher asked students to think about who might be 100 months old. She asked if the school might have such a student. If so, in what grade would that student be? Could they find such a person? Another rich investigation was launched.

Good tasks are challenging yet within the reach of the students. Mrs. Almond, a second-grade teacher, recently visited the fifth-grade class of her friend, Mrs. Heinke. During the visit, students were asked to think about the following problem:

> If every citizen, both adults and children, in our state were asked to line up around the state border to defend our state, could we hold hands? Could we see each other? How close would we need to stand to each other?

The students responded with insightful and interesting questions:

Tony: What's the population of our state?

Nathan: What about the river? The state line is in the middle!

Amanda: How do we measure the state's border?

After some general discussion, during which the teacher evaded answering the students' questions, the class quickly settled into their working groups to determine a reasonable estimate of the state's population and the length of the border. After a time, the teacher asked each group to present and defend its solution. A variety of methods were used to reach answers that were remarkably similar. Figure 1 presents the solution of one group.

Later, the teacher extended the problem by asking students to name states whose population could defend the border and others that could not.

"Why didn't you give them the population and the boundary length so they could use the right numbers?" asked Mrs. Almond after the class.

The teacher explained that the students needed some encouragement to develop better number sense and confidence in their own mathematical power.

"I didn't want to spoil the adventure!" she replied. "I wanted the students to see that with a map and some brainstorming, they could come up with some very good estimates on their own."

Good tasks pique the curiosity of the students. They often evolve from a simple question posed by students or the teacher. They are characterized by searching for solutions and sharing ideas.

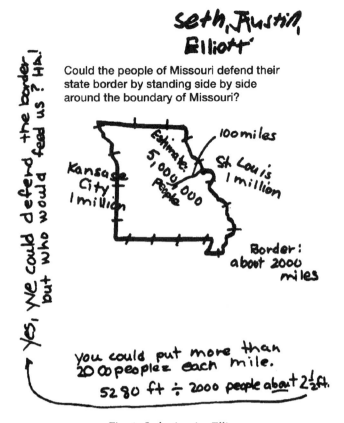

Fig. 1. Seth, Austin, Elliott

Recently in Mrs. Summers's second-grade classroom, a visiting soldier was sharing his experiences as an airplane service technician. He talked about getting very big planes airborne. He mentioned that the B-52 aircraft is so big that it cannot be completely fueled until after it is airborne. He was about to tell how the refueling was accomplished when the teacher, seeing an opportunity to engage the children in problem solving, stepped in and posed this question to the second graders: "How do you suppose the plane can be fueled once it is flying?" The children took the problem and "flew" with it. They brainstormed and posed a variety of solutions ranging from making the fuel on board the plane to "slurping" up the fuel with a very long, airplane-sized drinking straw. During this activity, the children engaged in problem solving not often found in the traditional mathematics curriculum yet very valuable to their development as critical thinkers.

Similarly, in a kindergarten class, students were using a calculator to skip-count. Whitney had chosen to count by tens and was amazed at "how high the numbers" were. Her teacher gave her a piece of adding-machine tape and asked her to write down the numbers the calculator displayed and to be alert for patterns. Whitney went to work and soon returned with a half-filled tape. She showed the teacher that she was already at 470 (see photograph on page 86). The teacher asked Whitney how far she thought she would be when she reached the end of the tape.

Whitney's eyes got very large, and she said, "Maybe a thousand. That's a very large number!" Although these children do not typically encounter very large numbers or a skip-count past 50, they were very excited about seeing and handling numbers so big. The calculator and the teacher's questions constituted a rich discovery for Whitney.

Good tasks encourage students to make sense of mathematical ideas. Students are naturally interested in learning new things. By taking advantage of their present knowledge and their expanding interests with tasks that are authentic and challenging and elicit curiosity, teachers help mathematics emerge as a sense-making activity. The effectiveness of a problem task is not judged on the basis of students' involvement alone. Rather, it is judged on how well it elicits investigation, exploration, thoughtful justification, and discussion of solutions and on how well it promotes mathematical reasoning, student ownership, and making connections (Thornton and Bley 1994, 51).

First graders were asked how they could show one-third on a circle. Various students posed possible solutions. See figure 2 for a sample of one group's work. Other students judged the fairness of each model and helped suggest other solutions. One first grader remarked, "You know, thirds is much harder than halves and fourths or even some others [fractions]." The teacher asked her to think about why this might be so. She later explained that "anything with twos was easy, 'cause you just keep cutting the pieces in half, but the others are trickier."

Whitney displays the results of her skip-counting activity.

Good tasks encourage multiple perspectives and interrelated mathematical ideas. Students' working together, sharing ideas and perspectives, is often a hallmark of a good task.

A fifth-grade class, working in small groups, was given a set of seven fraction cards, with each card containing one of the following fractions: 3/8, 4/5, 1/3, 2/20, 5/9, 3/4, or 11/12. They were asked to work on three tasks:

- By estimating, sort the fraction cards into two piles, one set with fractions less than 1/2

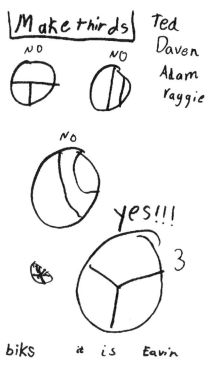

Fig. 2. Ted, Daven, Adam, Vaggie

and the other with fractions greater than 1/2. Convince your partners of the placement of each card.

- Order all the fraction cards from least to greatest. Justify your thinking. Tell which cards were the most difficult to order by estimating. What benchmarks did you use?

- Each person in the group is to make a new card showing a fraction not already represented. Place this fraction card in the ordered list. Tell how you decided where it should be placed.

The tasks stimulated much thinking and conversation about fractions. In particular, students had an opportunity to look for and use benchmarks and patterns to judge the size of various fractions (see fig. 3). They also justified their ideas and listened to others explain their thinking, making the experience richer for each child. Having students critique other students' possible solutions helps underscore the point that if the solution does not make sense to others, it is not good enough—or at least the explanation is not good enough.

Good tasks nest skill development in the context of problem solving. Rich mathematical tasks do not separate mathematical thinking from mathematical concepts and skills. They furnish ample opportunity for skills development within the context of an experience meaningful to students. In selecting, adapting, or designing mathematical tasks, the *Professional Teaching Standards* (NCTM 1991) suggests that teachers evaluate the mathematical content of a task from three perspectives: First, does the task

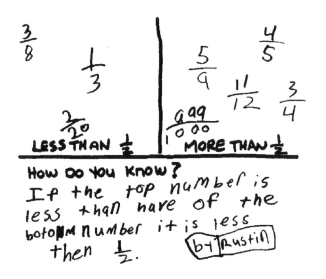

Fig. 3. Rustin

A student writes a new fraction to place in an ordered list.

appropriately represent the concepts and procedures desired? What "big ideas" are embedded in the task, and which mandated objectives are present? Will the students naturally encounter the desired mathematics? Second, does the task accurately portray what it means to do mathematics? Is the experience richer than just arriving at correct answers? Third, to what extent does the task promote developing appropriate skill and automaticity? The ideal is to create situations that promote skill development as the students explore, reason, solve problems, and communicate solutions and thinking (NCTM 1991).

Where Are Good Mathematical Tasks Found?

The most successful tasks often evolve from students and the situations they encounter. However, good tasks can also be initiated by the teacher from textbooks, resource materials, prior years' experiences, and situations shared among colleagues. Be alert to the potential mathematics in what students are saying, and do not discount their interests because they do not look "mathy" enough. Students' interests, dispositions, and experiences are critical filters through which mathematics is processed and learned or discarded. Within most classrooms can be found a range of intellectual capability, interest, and learning needs as well as an uneven landscape of concept formation, attitudes, and learning habits (Thornton and Bley 1994, 50). Not every task will reach every student, but, over time with

variety and persistence, every student can be involved in doing worthwhile mathematics.

Summary

As the *Professional Standards for Teaching Mathematics* (NCTM 1991) states, "Each student is worthy of being challenged intellectually" (p. 27). Whereas once the curriculum and student activities came directly and with little alteration from the textbook, the *Professional Teaching Standards* states that the best curriculum comes from the teacher, the students, and the environment of the classroom. This message does not mean that all mathematics lessons are spontaneous or that structured mathematics lessons have no place. Certainly, teachers are the architects who design and support opportunities for children to explore ideas in ways that invite them into the world of mathematics and capture and sustain their curiosity to learn more.

References

Lappan, Glenda. "What Do We Have and Where Do We Go from Here?" *Arithmetic Teacher* 40 (May 1993):524–26.

National Council of Teachers of Mathematics. *Professional Standards for Teaching Mathematics*. Reston, Va.: The Council, 1991.

Thornton, Carol A., and Nancy S. Bley, eds. *Windows of Opportunity: Mathematics for Students with Special Needs*. Reston, Va.: National Council of Teachers of Mathematics, 1994.

Discourse

The discourse of a classroom—the ways of representing, thinking, talking, agreeing and disagreeing—is central to what students learn about mathematics as a domain of human inquiry with characteristic ways of knowing. Discourse is both the way ideas are exchanged and what the ideas entail: Who talks? About what? In what ways? What do people write, what do they record and why? What questions are important? How do ideas change? Whose ideas and ways of thinking are valued? Who determines when to end a discussion? The discourse is shaped by the tasks in which students engage and the nature of the learning environment; it also influences them.

Discourse entails fundamental issues about knowledge: What makes something true or reasonable in mathematics? How can we figure out whether or not something makes sense? That something is true because the teacher or the book says so is the basis for much traditional classroom discourse. Another view, the one put forth here, centers on mathematical reasoning and evidence as the basis for the discourse. In order for students to develop the ability to formulate problems, to explore, conjecture, and reason logically, to evaluate whether something makes sense, classroom discourse must be founded on mathematical evidence.

Students must talk, with one another as well as in response to the teacher. When the teacher talks most, the flow of ideas and knowledge is primarily from teacher to student. When students make public conjectures and reason with others about mathematics, ideas and knowledge are developed collaboratively, revealing mathematics as constructed by human beings within an intellectual community. Writing is another important component of the discourse. Students learn to use, in a meaningful context, the tools of mathematical discourse—special terms, diagrams, graphs, sketches, analogies, and physical models, as well as symbols.

The teacher's role is to initiate and orchestrate this kind of discourse and to use it skillfully to foster student learning. In order to facilitate learning by all students, teachers must also be perceptive and skillful in analyzing the culture of the classroom, looking out for patterns of inequality, dominance, and low expectations that are primary causes of nonparticipation by many students. Engaging every student in the discourse of the class requires considerable skill as well as an appreciation of, and respect for, students' diversity.

Standard 2: The Teacher's Role in Discourse

The teacher of mathematics should orchestrate discourse by—

♦ posing questions and tasks that elicit, engage, and challenge each student's thinking;

♦ listening carefully to students' ideas;

♦ asking students to clarify and justify their ideas orally and in writing;

♦ deciding what to pursue in depth from among the ideas that students bring up during a discussion;

♦ deciding when and how to attach mathematical notation and language to students' ideas;

♦ deciding when to provide information, when to clarify an issue, when to model, when to lead, and when to let a student struggle with a difficulty;

♦ monitoring students' participation in discussions and deciding when and how to encourage each student to participate.

Elaboration

Like a piece of music, the classroom discourse has themes that pull together to create a whole that has meaning. The teacher has a central role in orchestrating the oral and written discourse in ways that contribute to students' understanding of mathematics.

The kind of mathematical discourse described above does not occur spontaneously in most classrooms. It requires an environment in which everyone's thinking is respected and in which reasoning and arguing about mathematical meanings is the norm. Students, used to the teacher doing most of the talking while they remain passive, need guidance and encouragement in order to participate actively in the discourse of a collaborative community. Some students, particularly those who have been successful in more traditional mathematics classrooms, may be resistant to talking, writing, and reasoning together about mathematics.

One aspect of the teacher's role is to provoke students' reasoning about mathematics. Teachers must do this through the tasks they provide and the questions they ask. For example, teachers should regularly follow students' statements with, "Why?" or by asking them to explain. Doing this consistently, irrespective of the correctness of students' statements, is an important part of establishing a discourse centered on mathematical reasoning. Cultivating a tone of interest when asking a student to explain or elaborate on an idea helps to establish norms of civility and respect rather than criticism and doubt. Teachers also stimulate discourse by asking students to write explanations for their solutions and provide justifications for their ideas.

Emphasizing tasks that focus on thinking and reasoning serves to provide the teacher with ongoing assessment information. Well-posed questions can simultaneously elicit and extend students' thinking. The teacher's skill at formulating questions to orchestrate the oral and written discourse in the direction of mathematical reasoning is crucial.

A second feature of the teacher's role is to be active in a different way from that in traditional classroom discourse. Instead of doing virtually all the talking, modeling, and explaining themselves, teachers must encourage and expect students to do so. Teachers must do more listening, students more reasoning. For the discourse to promote students' learning, teachers must orchestrate it carefully. Because many more ideas will come up than are fruitful to pursue at the moment, teachers must filter and direct the students' explorations by picking up on some points and by leaving others behind. Doing this prevents student activity and talk from becoming too diffuse and unfo-

cused. Knowledge of mathematics, of the curriculum, and of students should guide the teacher's decisions about the path of the discourse. Other key decisions concern the teacher's role in contributing to the discourse. Beyond asking clarifying or provocative questions, teachers should also, at times, provide information and lead students. Decisions about when to let students struggle to make sense of an idea or a problem without direct teacher input, when to ask leading questions, and when to tell students something directly are crucial to orchestrating productive mathematical discourse in the classroom. Such decisions depend on teachers' understandings of mathematics and of their students—on judgments about the things that students can figure out on their own or collectively and those for which they will need input.

A third aspect of the teacher's role in orchestrating classroom discourse is to monitor and organize students' participation. Who is volunteering comments and who is not? How are students responding to one another? What are different students able to record or represent on paper about their thinking? What are they able to put into words, in what kinds of contexts? Teachers must be committed to engaging every student in contributing to the thinking of the class. Teachers must judge when students should work and talk in small groups and when the whole group is the most useful context. They must make sensitive decisions about how turns to speak are shared in the large group—for example, whom to call on when and whether to call on particular students who do not volunteer. Substantively, if the discourse is to focus on making sense of mathematics, on learning to reason mathematically, teachers must refrain from calling only on students who seem to have right answers or valid ideas to allow a broader spectrum of thinking to be explored in the discourse. By modeling respect for students' thinking and conveying the assumption that students make sense, teachers can encourage students to participate within a norm that expects group members to justify their ideas. Teachers must think broadly about a variety of ways for students to contribute to the class's thinking—using means that are written or pictorial, concrete or representational, as well as oral.

Standard 3: Students' Role in Discourse

The teacher of mathematics should promote classroom discourse in which students—

♦ listen to, respond to, and question the teacher and one another;
♦ use a variety of tools to reason, make connections, solve problems, and communicate;
♦ initiate problems and questions;
♦ make conjectures and present solutions;

- explore examples and counterexamples to investigate a conjecture;
- try to convince themselves and one another of the validity of particular representations, solutions, conjectures, and answers;
- rely on mathematical evidence and argument to determine validity.

Elaboration

The nature of classroom discourse is a major influence on what students learn about mathematics. Students should engage in making conjectures, proposing approaches and solutions to problems, and arguing about the validity of particular claims. They should learn to verify, revise, and discard claims on the basis of mathematical evidence and use a variety of mathematical tools. Whether working in small or large groups, they should be the audience for one another's comments—that is, they should speak to one another, aiming to convince or to question their peers. Above all, the discourse should be focused on making sense of mathematical ideas, on using mathematical ideas sensibly in setting up and solving problems.

Doing What Comes Naturally
Talking about Mathematics

By

Angela Giglio Andrews

How did you figure out how to divide these cookies equally?" I asked the kindergarten children seated at the red table.

"Oh, we just talked it out!" said Eric, going on to explain the process that classmates at his table had used to share a plate of cookies fairly.

Early childhood teachers would probably agree that talking comes naturally to most young children. Their informal learning and exploration of their environment during free-choice time is usually accompanied and illuminated by an unceasing flow of talk. Children use their growing language skills to report observations, recall past events, and predict future ones. They talk when collaborating; dis-

Angela Giglio Andrews, agandrews@aol.com, teachers kindergarten at Scott Elementary School, Naperville, IL 60565, and takes undergraduate and graduate mathematics-education courses at National-Louis University in Wheaton, Illinois. She is strongly committed to making mathematics meaningful to young learners. She is a coeditor of this department with Christina Myren. John Noe, an early childhood educator from Wheaton, Illinois, helped prepare this article.

Edited by Christina Myren, 73720.1725@compuserv.com, Acacia Elementary School, Thousand Oaks, CA 91360.

cussing alternatives; explaining phenomena; focusing attention; imagining and creating fantasy; justifying their reasoning; and reflecting on, and dealing with, problems.

Photo by Angela Giglio Andrews; all rights reserved

Students learn mathematics by discussing mathematics.

Talking also plays a key role in learning about mathematics, as recognized by the NCTM's *Curriculum and Evaluation Standards for School Mathematics*, particularly Standard 2: Mathematics as Communication (1989). When children talk about mathematical concepts, they are actually increasing their understanding of that concept. Language allows them to reflect on and revise their thoughts. In other words, the child who talks about what she or he knows can change it or expand on it. "Thus when children and adults talk together, they are not only receiving knowledge, but remaking it for themselves" (Barnes).

The National Council of Teachers of English (NCTE 1991) agrees that the skills of spoken language are as important in mathematics as in other areas of the curriculum. Its position is that "No matter what the subject, those who read it, write it and *talk about it* [emphasis added] are the ones who learn it best." The NCTE cites research indicating that *those who do the most talking learn the most.*

If talking comes naturally to most young learners and if talking about mathematics has proved to be important, then it would seem that one of the best ways to foster pattern recognition, purposeful learning, and pleasure in doing mathematics is to encourage the genuine give and take of talking in the classroom. To do so, the teacher must believe and expect that when children open their mouths, they have something important to say. Teachers with this expectation will be pleasantly surprised at the quantity and quality of children's ideas about mathematics. In our local kindergarten classrooms, for example, teachers try to focus the children's thinking, listening, and speaking on the relevant mathematics occurring daily. The following vignettes from our classrooms illustrate children's *natural uses of language*, as described in *A Language for Life* (Bullock 1975), and reveal how their language is, or can be, directed toward mathematics.

Children naturally use language to report on present and recalled experiences (Bullock 1975). Eric comments, "Yesterday we had one boy and two girls absent, but today we have only one girl absent." "How do you know that?" asks the teacher. "I just counted the name tags that are left on the table. Then I noticed that Lindsay isn't here, so I knew," explains Eric. A discussion ensues, and Carl mentions a day when seven children were absent. The class decides it must have been on the day of the terrible snowstorm. "It was a below temperature that day," comments Ellen. The teacher then shows the children how to collect data to back up their hypothesis that "When the temperature is below zero, we will have lots of children absent."

Children naturally use language to collaborate toward agreed ends (Bullock 1975). Daniel is late to school because he had to take his dog to the veterinarian. The children begin to talk, all at the same time, about the pets they have and their experiences with the veterinarian. The teacher allows the children to go to their tables for "Math Talk." After a few minutes, the children come back to the group. The teacher tells the children that she would be interested in knowing what pets the children have but that she is sure she will forget if everyone just tells her. Ronnie suggests using a chalkboard to add up tally marks. Akash wants to know how they will know when everybody has been asked. The children develop a plan to solve this problem. The captain at each table will be in charge of polling children at that table and will report back to the "helper of the day." Later these data will be organized into a graph by the children, with some help from the teacher.

Children naturally use language to project into the future, anticipate results, predict events, and discuss possible alternatives (Bullock 1975). The children are discussing the point to which the number line on the wall will stretch on the 100th day of school. Rebecca predicts it will stretch to the door. Bryan disagrees. "It will be even further, because look where it was on the 50th day. That is more than halfway to the door. I think it will be almost to the sink." Later Rebecca and Bryan are observed using their arm spans to measure these distances and talking about their results.

"Are we older than the morning kids?" asks Arturo. This question leads to an interesting discussion on how to find out. Ronya suggests that they make linking-cube trains with as many cubes as years for each child in class. "This way we'll know how old we are all together." After much debate, the class decides not to count "halves." As the children build their "age trains" and connect them, Karen wants to add the teacher's age. "This way, we will beat the afternoonies!" she explains. However, Barbara thinks it will not be fair unless the teacher adds her age to the afternoon class train, too. Ben remarks, "Then we might as well not do it because it will just be the same." The other children are not clear about what he means, so he has to explain. He uses the cubes to prove his point. "See, if the teacher was ten, we'd have to add ten to both piles. So it would be the same." Some children are still not convinced. "But the teacher is *not* ten," argues Claire. The class finally decides to leave the teacher out. "It will be easier to count this way," says Mark. "Teacher is very old."

The children go to their tables for "Math Talk."

Children naturally use language to focus on causal and dependent relationships and how and why things happen (Bullock 1975). At the beginning of each day, the children sit in an A-B horseshoe arrangement at the front of the room. Juan says that he has noticed that each day, if a boy starts the pattern, a boy is at the end as well. He wants to see what happens if a girl starts the pattern. He thinks a girl will be at the end. The class decides to try his idea. Juan is surprised to discover that this situation continues to yield a boy at the end. Some discussion occurs and Claire thinks they should try it again tomorrow. "It only works if everybody is here," says Amos. The children want to talk about this situation, so the teacher allows them to go to their tables to discuss it further. Most children conclude that it happens because the class has one more boy than it has girls, but all are not convinced. They continue to talk each day as they form the horseshoe.

David and Dan work in the block area, trying to build a part of a "chain-reaction machine" like they saw in *I Spy School Days* (Walter and Marzollo 1995) in which one block falls over and causes the next block to fall, and so on. "I think we have to make them closer together because they aren't bumping each other now," says Dan. They try, but it does not work. "Not that close!" David says. 'Cause look, they are jamming up." They decide to put blocks in between to keep the upright blocks from jamming, which does not work either. They experiment further, talking the whole time. The teacher does not interrupt this discussion but is ready with the camera to record their progress and eventual success.

Children naturally use language to create and discuss imaginative problems and visualize possible solutions (Bullock 1975). The teacher overhears a conversation in the housekeeping area about the dolls being "picky eaters." Later the teacher tells the children a story about what a picky eater she was as a girl. She recalls the time when she had to drink all her orange juice. She told her mother, who was always nagging her to drink more juice, that she would drink half the juice that was left in the glass every minute if she (her mother) would promise not to refill the glass until it was completely empty. Her mother agreed. The teacher asks the children how long they think it took her to finish her juice. A lively discussion ensues with varying answers. "It's hard to drink half of a tiny bit!" remarks Rachel. "I'm not sure teacher will ever finish her juice," remarks Alex. "Of course she did!" counters Samir. "She'd still be sitting there if she didn't!" This problem is the subject of heated debate for several weeks afterward, with groups of children doing experiments at the water table with calibrated jars and others talking as they sketch the problem in their mathematics journals.

Photo by Angela Giglio Andrews; all rights reserved

Students play the attribute-train game.

The children are very familiar with Eric Carle's story of *The Very Hungry Caterpillar* (1979). One day the teacher asks the children to think about what would happen if the caterpillar had eaten some different things than in the story. They are challenged to change the story, which the class enjoys. Later Mark tells of the *Not So Hungry Caterpillar*, who on Monday ate five grapes and continued eating smaller foods in smaller amounts, ending on Friday when it ate one crumb. Later when the teacher asks the children to work on the problem "How many things were eaten from Monday through Friday?" some children are surprised that the same number of items had been eaten by the caterpillar in both stories! "How can that be?" asks the teacher. A lively discussion about constancy of number ensues. Even when some children attempt to prove that the answer is the same by using manipulatives or drawing

pictures, some children are still not convinced. This concept is confusing for preoperational children who are distracted by size.

Children naturally use language to justify their reasoning and reflect on events, actions, and feelings (Bullock 1975). The teacher is playing the attribute-train game with the class. She has asked Daniel to find an attribute shape that is different in only one way from the large, yellow, thin circle. Daniel begins to look for a shape. "I'm going to find the small one like that," he mutters as he searches. "You can't use that one because I have it," crows Elle. "Just change something else!" encourages Marjani. After some deliberation, Daniel chooses a shape. "See I got the large, red, thin circle. It is the same size and shape and fatness but it's a different color!" "Does everybody agree?" asks the teacher.

"While we were working on that problem I got a little confused," says the teacher. "Did anyone else?" Anton agrees. "Yeah. I got *fuzzy*," referring to the term the teacher uses often to describe not understanding. "I didn't! It was easy!" says Melissa. "It's easy when you know how!" corrects Sara. "That's right, Sara," says the teacher. "When I don't understand, I get a little nervous inside." The teacher continues. "It's important to know that even the best mathematicians get fuzzy sometimes. If it happens to you, it helps to let the teacher or a friend know. Can anybody figure out what part confused me?" Several children have different ideas. "I think it was because when we counted, we didn't have a plan where to start counting, so we got different answers," suggests Abe. "Maybe we could do that problem again," asks Martin, "and let Anton count this time?"

From the previous examples, it is obvious that many of the children in these classrooms are comfortable talking about mathematics. However, every classroom contains a few children who, for various reasons, are reluctant to talk about their ideas, especially to the teacher. How can teachers help these more reticent children talk? Asking leading questions is one of the best ways to encourage children to talk, not only to the teacher but with one another, about their ideas.

Some questions that help elicit this talk might include these:

- "Do you have any ideas about Chris's part? Will you tell her?"
- "How do you think she or he figured that out?"
- "Which do you think was the most challenging part of this task for Annie?"
- "Will you tell Joyce how it works, what you are doing, and why you used that part?"
- "Why do you agree with John?"
- "How did you two work this part out?"
- "Why do you think that happens?"

- "What do you think would happen if Barbara had …?"
- "What will you do next? Have you discussed your plan with …?"
- "Can you tell me how Andrea did that part?"
- "How did Leah do it differently?" "Ask Cassi about that. What did she say? What do you think about what she said?"

Comments that place the emphasis on the children's thinking and problem-solving strategies can also extend the mathematical talking and thinking process. Phrases that encourage this thinking process include these:

- "I wonder …"
- "Do you suppose …?"
- "I hadn't thought of that. Tell me more."
- "Did it work the same way when you did it?"
- "What made you think that?"
- "Did you make any discoveries or see any patterns?"
- "Could you help me understand this part?"
- "I wonder if you could change this part and make it work the same way."
- "What would happen if you had started over here instead?"

Some students think about mathematics in intuitive ways but have great difficulty explaining their thinking. Often these students shrug and say, "I don't know," "I guessed," or even "I just knowed!" when the teacher questions them. Intuitive mathematicians need help in learning to communicate their reasoning. For example, a teacher reported to the kindergarten children gathered around his chair that the morning class had cleaned the block corner in five minutes.

"How many minutes did we take?" asked Ben.

"You took three minutes," the teacher responded.

"How much faster did we do it?" Ben questioned.

"Two."

This answer came from Robert. The teacher knew from past experience that Robert would not be able to elaborate or explain his thinking, so the teacher turned to Claire, a more verbal student.

"Claire, will you tell Robert how you think he figured it out?"

"Well," said Claire, thoughtfully, turning toward Robert. "You could have done it like this. See. Here is five minutes, and here are three fingers for our minutes"

[rubbing three fingers with her other hand]. "That leaves two fingers, so we were two minutes quicker!"

Asking leading questions encourages children to talk.

Robert usually listened and agreed when other children tried to give possible ways that he could have figured out a solution. The teacher knew that it was valuable for Robert to hear his solutions verbalized, even if he could not yet do the verbalizing. Today, however, Robert's response was surprising.

"No, that's not how I did it. I think I took the three minutes we cleaned up in" [showing three fingers of his hand], "then I counted from three to five. I saw I counted two fingers, so I knowed it was two."

"Right on!" crowed Ben.

Such incidents should remind us that the genuine give and take of talking about mathematics is important to the lives of children to maximize their mathematical understanding and power. As early-childhood teachers, we must make sure that our mathematics curriculum places major emphasis on allowing children to talk with, and listen to, one another.

Bibliography

Bullock, Alan. "The Bullock Report." In *A Language for Life*. London: H.M.S.O., 1975.

Carle, Eric. *The Very Hungry Caterpillar*. New York: Collins Publishers, 1979.

Elliott, Portia C., ed. *Communication in Mathematics, K–12 and Beyond*. 1996 Yearbook of the National Council of Teachers of Mathematics. Reston, Va.: The Council, 1996.

The Mathematical Association (United Kingdom). *Math Talk*. Portsmouth, N.H.: Heinemann, 1987.

National Council of Teachers of English. *NCTE's Position on the Teaching of English: Assumptions and Practices*. Urbana, Ill.: The Council, 1991.

National Council of Teachers of Mathematics. *Curriculum and Evaluation Standards for School Mathematics*. Reston, Va.: The Council, 1989.

———. *Professional Standards For Teaching Mathematics*. Reston, Va.: The Council, 1991.

Schwartz, Sydney L. "Hidden Messages in Teacher Talk: Praise and Empowerment." *Teaching Children Mathematics* (March 1996): 396–401.

Wick, Walter, and Jean Marzollo. *I Spy School Days: A Book of Picture Riddles*. New York: Scholastic Books, 1995.

I Do and I Understand, I Reflect and I Improve

by

Carolyn Scheibelhut

I hear and I forget. I see and I remember. I do and I understand. "In my college methods course on teaching and learning mathematics, my goal is to prepare prospective elementary teachers to meet the challenge of implementing the *Curriculum and Evaluation Standards for School Mathematics* (NCTM 1989). My colleagues agree that it is important for our students majoring in education to develop understanding by "doing," so our students are given the opportunity to plan and teach lessons in a clinical classroom during the semester in which they take their methods courses.

When I observed my students teaching in their classrooms, I was pleased to see them using manipulative materials in activity-based mathematics lessons. But I noticed a glaring omission. Even though they had heard me emphasize the importance of integrating writing with mathematics, and they had seen me exhibit examples of children's writing, the majority still were not using writing as a tool for teaching mathematics. Something had to change. In designing my next course, I restructured the requirements to help them appreciate the value of making writing a regular part of the mathematics curriculum. To ensure that they actually experience writing, my students are required to incorporate the activity into at least one mathematics lesson that they teach in their clinical classroom and to reflect on how the information they gained from this experience could be used to improve future lessons.

Carolyn Scheibelhut teaches at Concordia College, Moorhead, MN 56562. She also presents workshops for elementary school teachers on implementing NCTM's Curriculum and Evaluation Standards.

Reflective Practice

Teaching a mathematics lesson in which they integrated writing was an essential first step for my students, but the crucial component was reflection. NCTM's *Professional Standards for Teaching Mathematics* suggests that preservice teachers of mathematics should have opportunities to "analyze and evaluate the appropriateness and effectiveness of their teaching," (NCTM 1991, 160). After teaching their lesson, my students were asked to consider whether their intended objective for having the children write was met, what insights into the children they gained from the experience, and how this information could be used to improve instruction. They submitted these reflections to me along with the children's writing.

> ## Students' writing tells us more than viewing single answers on worksheets.

In a recent *Arithmetic Teacher* article, Hart and her colleagues encourage teachers to become reflective practitioners and use the information they gain "to guide and change their instructional practices so they can be more effective" (Hart et al. 1992, 40). Reflection is a powerful change agent because it enables teachers to recognize how their actions affect the classroom environment. By reflecting on the teaching and learning process, they gain insight into how better to meet the instructional needs of their pupils.

Incorporating Writing into Mathematics

To familiarize my students with the numerous ways to incorporate writing into mathematics, I suggested that they read Countryman's (1992) *Writing to Learn Mathematics*. In addition to describing various writing activities, her book indicates several reasons for having children write about mathematics. By forcing a slowdown in the thought process, writing enables the mind to clarify ideas and more fully integrate new knowledge. Each child is actively involved in reflecting on what she or he has been doing and thus has the opportunity to formulate and rethink her or his ideas. Learning becomes an active process of knowledge construction and sense making by the student. This writing also helps the teacher evaluate students' understanding and thus make better instructional decisions.

Several of my students asked their pupils to write how they felt about mathematics and what they liked or did not like about learning it. Typical responses from children who disliked mathematics were similar to those of a fifth-grade boy who wrote, "I hate math because it is my worst subject. I do bad in it. I do not understand some things." Reflecting on the children's replies, my students gained insight into the importance of making assessment an integral part of teaching. As one of my students wrote, "No wonder some kids don't like math! It's up to me to continually check and make sure that each child understands and is successful." When asked what he liked most and least about mathematics, a sixth-grade boy wrote, "My favorite part is when we get out of class. The hardest part is remembering all the stuff." My student observed, "These kids view math as a collection of arbitrary rules to memorize. I need to help them see that math makes sense and get them actively involved in the learning process. If we fail to build conceptual understanding and only teach children how to do the procedures by rote memory, many are going to be confused and alienated."

Sometimes we learn as much about ourselves and our teaching from the children's responses as we do about them. When asked to write "what math means to you," almost every child in a fourth-grade classroom identified mathematics with number: "Math is numbers, decimal points, adding, subtracting, multiplying, and all that stuff." The NCTM's *Curriculum and Evaluation Standards* (1989) recommends that computation be only one facet of the mathematics program, but for these children, as shown by their written responses, computation is the entire program. In her reflection, my student commented, "I want to show these kids that math is far more than pencil-and-paper computation. I want them to experience the excitement of data collection, the beauty of geometry, the exhilaration of solving a nontraditional problem."

We can design more effective lessons by reflecting on students' writing.

Children's writing can give much more insight into what they actually know about a topic than can their responses on a worksheet. One of my students was teaching a fraction unit in a first-grade classroom. To evaluate the children's understanding of the concept, he asked them to write about and depict a situation in which they might use fractions in everyday life. Their pictures showed whether the child could represent the fraction accurately. To facilitate reading, some spelling and punctuation of the children's texts have been corrected. Jared wrote, "Me and my friend are eating pizza at my house and having fun together, and we divided it into eight pieces"; he drew eight equal-sized pieces (fig. l). Katie's reply, "I share a bar of chocolate with my friend. I cut the chocolate bar with a knife. We each got 15," showed that she realized that 15/30 was equivalent to 1/2, but the thirty pieces in her drawing are not equal in size (fig. 2). This information allowed for more individualized subsequent instruction. As my student commented, "I'll need to do some follow-up work with Katie to make sure she understands that fractional parts have to be the same size." He also discovered the value of an open-ended assignment, which enables each child to contribute. "All of the children were able to think of something in their lives that gets divided

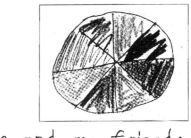

Me and my friends are eating pissa at my house and having fun together. and we devided it into eight pises.
by Jared

Fig. 1. Jared's writing

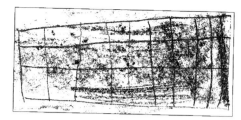

Katie

I sheare a bare
of chockelit with
my fireand I
cut the chockelit
bare with a nife
we each got 15

Fig. 2. Katie's writing

Name Brian   Date 4/19/93

1. With out using numbers, explain what 4×8 means.
you pluss four eight times.

2. Now draw a picture of 4×8.
||||| ||||| |||||/||||/|||||/|||||| ||||/|||||/ |||||

3. what does multiplication mean?
you take the first number and ad it how ever many times the second number is.
4. when do you use multiplication?
When you see this sign, ×.

5. What advice would you give next years third graders, about Multiplication?
Its fun and it gets you farther In your math book

Fig. 3. Brian's writing

into equal parts and to write about it. Everyone was successful. If I had just given them a worksheet, some of the less capable students might have struggled."

Several of my students learned through experience that the writing assignment needs to be structured carefully if it is to yield useful information. To pretest her fourth graders' knowledge before a unit on geometry, one student asked her class to define geometry. Greg wrote, "Geometry is different kinds of shapes like squares and stuff." Sarah's trusting answer was "I don't know what it is, but if you say it is fun, then I'm sure I'll like it." My student found that it was "hard to gauge from their responses how much they actually knew about geometry" and concluded that if she were to try this activity again, she would need to ask specific questions about the geometric concepts she intended to teach.

By asking more focused questions, another student found writing to be a valuable diagnostic tool in evaluating her third graders' understanding of multiplication. As seen from his explanation, Brian understood multiplication as repeated addition but viewed "4 × 8" as eight sets of four rather than four sets of eight (fig. 3). My student planned further instruction for Brian to have him use the more accepted convention, as well as a review of the array model of multiplication, which he did not mention. Although most of her class understood the process of multiplication, their answers to "When do you use multiplication?" showed that they were unable to apply the concept in real life. Brian was prompted to use the operation only when he saw the multiplication sign in a problem. Many other students replied that multiplication is used "when you have a worksheet to do" or "in math." My student observed, "[M]ost of the children don't know when they would use multiplication other than in math class. This

showed me that I need to incorporate lots of real-life examples into my lessons."

To help her children see this connection between the mathematics they learn in school and its application to everyday life, another of my students asked her third graders to write story problems that used multiplication. The children were all successful, but most were not as fanciful as Dan, who wrote, "I went to a Christmas party, and there was a mistletoe right by the door. I was kissed by 16 girls 2 times each." My student reflected, "This lesson helped the children bridge the gap and apply mathematics to their own personal lives. It is evident from their stories that they know how to use multiplication in a meaningful way."

When another student discovered that her fifth graders were "confused about geometry and didn't really like it," she had them cut from magazines pictures of rays, points, planes, and line segments. Then they wrote about what they had learned. She hoped to "give them a better understanding of the terms they were studying, and a better attitude toward geometry." From the class's responses, it was evident that this objective was met. Kim, whose response was representative, wrote, "Today I learned that a simple fence was a pair of parallel lines! A sky is a plane! And spotlights hitting each other are rays! I think it's really cool, because I didn't know that in my backyard there are lots of lines of geometry! Miss C. makes it fun to do math! I can't wait till tomorrow!" My student, Miss C., reflected, "I gained a lot of insight into the students from this project. They really liked being involved and a part of learning, rather than just taking notes on terms. I think the writing really helped them pinpoint exactly what they had learned, and it allowed me to see what the students understood."

Conclusion

The preservice teachers from my classes said that this project convinced them that incorporating writing into mathematics had many advantages. They saw it as a tool for helping children understand and communicate mathematics. Through writing, the children were able to make sense out of mathematics and recognize its relationship to their everyday lives. Every mathematics class presents opportunities for writing. Writing about how they feel about mathematics helps the students focus on what works or does not work for them. This type of writing gives the teacher insight into the attitudes and needs of the individual student and may uncover mathematics anxiety or parental pressure. When negative attitudes toward mathematics are revealed, teachers can identify the causes and help change them.

At the beginning of a new unit, asking the children to write what they know about the topic and what they think they will learn can be a useful diagnostic tool to determine students' current level of knowledge. This rich information base will allow the teacher to tailor lessons to meet the individual instructional needs of the class. Writing at the beginning of a unit also develops a mind-set for studying the topic and helps students form connections between what they already know and the new material.

Open-ended writing as a follow-up to a lesson helps students mentally reconstruct what has gone on during the lesson. The last few minutes of the class period can be used to have the children write about what they do or do not understand about what they did in class. By writing about what they have just learned, they reframe the knowledge into their own words, extending and deepening their understanding. Being able to glimpse the children's thinking through their writing enables teachers to diagnose misconceptions and problems more clearly, correcting errors as they arise.

Many students do not understand routine textbook word problems. Having them formulate their own problems, either individually or as part of a cooperative group, empowers them to connect mathematics with real-life situations that make sense to them.

Writing helps pinpoint exactly what students have and have not learned.

A student mathematics journal also might be used. This journal can be a collection of freewriting comments about the material, their progress, or the mathematics period in general. To gain specific information, teachers might ask students to complete a sentence stem, such as "I think calculators ..." or "To study for a math test, I usually...." Such journals are especially valuable if they become dialogue journals in which the teacher writes replies to the students' entries.

The preservice teachers who participated in this project commented that they believed that one of the biggest assets of having their students write was that it furnished information about the children that could be used to improve teaching. By analyzing their students' needs, they could structure more-effective lessons. Reflection helped them to see what was working and what needed to be changed. I hope that when they have classrooms of their own, they will become reflective practitioners who will continue to grow and improve throughout their careers.

References

Countryman, Joan. *Writing to Learn Mathematics*. Portsmouth. N.H.: Heinemann Educational Books, 1992.

Hart, Lynn, Karen Schultz, Deborah Najee-ullah, and Linda Nash. "The Role of Reflection in Teaching." *Arithmetic Teacher* 40 (September 1992):40–42.

National Council of Teachers of Mathematics. *Curriculum and Evaluation Standards for School Mathematics*. Reston, Va.: The Council, 1998.

———. *Professional Standards for Teaching Mathematics*. Reston, Va.: The Council, 1991.

Cooperative Groups
What Role Do They Play in the Teaching and Learning of Mathematics?

When do the NCTM *Standards* call for the use of cooperative groups in mathematics classes?

- ○ Always
- ○ Sometimes
- ○ Never
- ○ I don't know.

Suppose that you found the multiple-choice question above on the final exam of your mathematics methods course. How would you respond?

Members of many groups are reviewing and reacting to the NCTM *Standards* documents as part of the process for developing the next edition of them. When comments from these groups and individuals are reviewed, it becomes clear that no consensus has been reached regarding the need for, the use of, and the recommended frequency of cooperative groups as a classroom strategy.

In the overview of the *Curriculum and Evaluation Standards* (p. 10), the following passage addresses instructional strategies.

[The] constructive, active view of the learning process must be reflected in the way much of mathematics is taught. Thus, instruction should vary and include opportunities for—

- appropriate project work;
- group and individual assignments;
- discussion between teacher and students and among students;
- practice on mathematical methods;
- exposition by the teacher.

From this passage, it seems clear that the NCTM's vision of mathematics teaching and learning is one of varied organizational patterns. But ...

- How do teachers decide which strategy to use?
- How can individual students' work be monitored and assessed in group situations?
- Can the expected material be covered when students work in groups?
- Is additional guidance available in the *Standards* to help teachers plan for effective learning?
- Is group work always preferable to exposition?

One place to look for answers to these questions lies in the Curriculum Standards themselves. As an example, consider the following statement from K–4 Standard 8: Whole Number Computation, which urges students to—

- use a variety of mental computation and estimation techniques.

As I think about helping my students achieve this standard, I realize that students need to share their own invented strategies for mental arithmetic. That leads me to create both large- and small-group opportunities for students to share, try out, and refine mental arithmetic techniques. But I also know that I should create opportunities to observe and listen to individual students as they apply their techniques.

On the following pages, classroom teachers express their views on this issue.

Vince O'Connor
Milwaukee, Wisconsin

Teachers "Talk" about Cooperative Learning

High School

Selected comments from

Carlos Cabana
San Lorenzo High School
San Lorenzo, California

Susan McMillan and
Carole Ann Theesfeld
Addison Trail High School
Addison, Illinois

Linda Steiner
Orange Glen High School
Escondido, California

Linda: Because I know that straight rows of desks and silence do not make a very productive classroom and because the best students always use study groups, I have been using cooperative learning groups for several years. At first the groups were informal; we reviewed textbook chapters in groups, made and played games to review for finals, and arranged group presentations of math problems.

Susan: My students begin their cooperative learning experience by working in pairs. We discuss the roles of partner and coach: what they should and should not do. The coach provides assistance in many ways: she gives feedback, asks questions, and above all is patient and never negative. A coach does not do the work for her partner.

Linda: At first I purposely arranged the groups to have one A and one F student and two C students in each group. Now, I have the students arrange themselves across the front of my classroom, using such categories as height, address, initials, and—one of their favorites—shoe size. Sometimes I use playing cards and have all the 2s sit together, and so on. I change groups frequently; that way everyone's happy.

Carole: Because our student population has shifted to one that is multicultural and of varied racial and ethnic groups, I now must form groups not randomly but heterogeneously so that they can begin to respect one another's backgrounds. This is difficult to do and still form positive, working, cooperative groups. If the groups are not properly put together, there will be no honest help, no caring for one another's success, and no pride for each member on the team.

Linda: Since working with groups can sometimes be a classroom nightmare, I have occasionally issued group grades to help maintain a positive learning environment. If a specific group is using its time to "visit," I place a card on that group's table with a C, D, or F on it, indicating how well they are working. When they begin to work together better, I change that card. The immediate recognition of better study skills changes their behavior. I rarely record these grades.

Susan: Students understand the concepts better when they are called on to answer questions from their peers. They learn to pose more specific, directed questions to find out what it is they need to know in order to continue working, instead of the more general "I don't get this!"

Carlos: We focus on process standards, simply because we've found them necessary for students' future success. In later courses, we want to be able to rely on group collaboration as the normal mode of operation. This commitment to group work comes from the belief that by finding tasks that are *worthy* of groups, we can both ask harder questions *and* increase the level of access. It sounds contradictory, but it is not.

Linda: The power of cooperative activities does not lie solely in accomplishing a mathematical task but rather in the quality of the mathematics you will hear the students discuss. Major arguments erupt in my classroom about topics and methods needed to solve a problem.

Carlos: By posing hard questions with little guidance, students talk to one another out of necessity, and different kids get to be smart in different ways.

Carole: As teachers, we must find the level of ability of each student to handle cooperative learning and then start from that point in our organization of the classroom. All students can succeed at some level in a cooperative learning setting.

Susan: They enjoy working with one another!

Middle School

Selected comments from

Debra Coggins
Walnut Creek Intermediate School
Walnut Creek, California

Judy Vandermeulen
Wheaton Warrenville South
Wheaton, Illinois

Barbara Nimerovsky
Louis Armstrong Middle School
East Elmhust, New York

Ava Taylor
Woodford County Middle School
Versailles, Kentucky

Debra: We begin the school year by having our sixth-grade students work in groups on a task from each of the strands in our curriculum. We want students to begin to see mathematics as something more than arithmetic. We want them to practice what it means to be a good group member: being on task, making helpful comments, taking care of one another, and putting materials away. We want to challenge some ideas they have about what it means to be good in mathematics.

Judy: I sometimes group students by their strengths. I might put a divergent thinker with someone who is good at computing, with another who is well organized and can keep a group on task. I put students in small groups when we are working on a relatively new concept. It helps them clarify their own understanding when they talk with others about their thinking. I also give "pair quizzes," which allows me to pose more in-depth questions and forces students to justify their thinking to their partners. And there is a practical consideration: I grade only half as many quiz papers.

Ava: I use small groups when we are doing a discovery lesson or an investigation. We recently worked on a problem from a Marilyn Burns book where students investigate six different methods of finding the area of a circle. In this problem, students worked in pairs.

Barbara: I have a routine in my fifth-grade class called "triangle"— I create three centers, each with an activity where students have different experiences with the same topic. I make three groups, and over three days the groups move among the centers. We begin the study of fractions with a "triangle." In one activity students investigate naming fractions using pattern blocks. In a second activity they use a template to cut sectors of a circle and give the fraction name, assuming the whole circle is the unit. In a third activity they use a red and an orange Cuisenaire rod as the unit and then give fractional names to rods.

Ava: Often the groups' size depends on how many sets of materials I have to support the investigation. But if I want students to practice skills, like using formulas to find the volume of different solids, then they work individually.

Barbara: I spend about fifteen minutes with each group, listening, posing questions to push their thinking, and noting what they seem to understand and where they are having some difficulties. On the fourth day, we have a whole-group discussion: What did these center activities have in common? How were they different? It is important to help them extract the mathematics from the activities. Then they write in their journals what they know about this idea. By observing and by reading their journal entries, I get a good sense of where each individual student is in her or his mathematical thinking.

Judy: The challenge is finding tasks that are motivating enough or at the right level of difficulty to keep everyone in the group on task. During group work, I observe their efforts. If I hear the same frustration from several groups, I

may decide that we need some additional whole-group instruction or clarification. One way I hold each student accountable is to assign parts of a project to individuals. There is a group grade, but each student is also graded on his or her specific contribution.

Debra: We pose problems where it is unlikely that an individual student will have a solution but where the efforts of the group can lead to a solution. One of our favorite geometry problems has students use Cuisenaire rods to investigate which three rods will make a triangle and which ones will not. They try to generalize with a statement about the lengths of the three segments that make a triangle. Each student writes up the results of the investigation. Problems of this kind seem to provide access to students who may have been low achieving in mathematics in the elementary grades. And they often prove to be challenging to those who have been high achieving. The problems are at the edge of what they are capable of individually, and the group efforts are always "greater than the sum of the parts."

Elementary School

Selected comments from

Donna Droge
Tecumseh North Elementary School
Tecumseh, Kansas

Paula McLean
Thoreau and Grantosa Elementary Schools
Milwaukee, Wisconsin

Sharon Zagorski
Garfield and Hartford Elementary Schools
Milwaukee, Wisconsin

Donna: In nineteen years of teaching, my instruction practices have changed dramatically. I began with desks in straight lines, children working individually, and my time spent helping endless lines of questioning students—with no guarantee that I would be able to satisfy all their different learning styles with answers. After attending conferences, workshops, and other training sessions, I began to see many different strategies and ideas for teaching and organizing students that would provide more-productive learning environments.

Paula: The connection between mathematics and science is evident, both in cooperative groups and in individual settings. An activity I have used as a science/math topic is graphing the data we have collected. Students are introduced to the concept of plant diversity. I take my students to a wooded area, where they work in groups to count the number of species and the number of plants within the species. Each group is given a specific area in which to work, and they record the data as a group. Back in the classroom, we resume in a large group. A class graph is created and results are shared.

Sharon: When working with first-grade students on the concept of number, I often use whole-group time coupled with individual time as a model for effective teaching. I begin by having the entire group sit on the carpet in front of me and talk about numbers. I might ask the group how they can show me the number five. Individual students might jump up and down five times, clap five times, or find five objects. I am letting them show one another that numbers have many meanings.

Paula: Once their group results are shared, students are given their individual task—to repeat the activity at home and bring samples of the species with the graph they have developed. I find this gives me an opportunity to assess each student's understanding. I can do this from their individual graphs and from their comments as I interview them on the project.

Sharon: I might ask students to show me different ways to make "five" using two colors of Unifix cubes in a bowl. After demonstrating different ways to show the number, I give each child a sheet of paper with a number on it and send them to their seats. The children are free to get whatever materials they need, build their number, and record their work.

Donna: Although cooperative grouping is my favorite strategy for teaching mathematics, I do use other strategies. Large-group instruction is effective when I am introducing fractions, for example. The class works as a group cutting and making fraction strips to use in game-like situations. Discussion is a very important aspect of large-group instruction. By listening to discussion, I can assess how well students are understanding important concepts before I move on to more-difficult ones. Peer tutoring is another strategy I use extensively in my classes. Often after large-group instruction, I find that (1) many students understand the concept and are ready to take off on their own, (2) a majority of students have a basis for going further but need further direction, and (3) some are still not sure what has been taught. I then pair volunteers who are confident of the concepts with those who need more help understanding. Today, I focus on finding the best possible learning environment for each of my students. I like to introduce new topics with hands-on lessons where children are working in cooperative groups. The children find that there are a variety of ways to solve problems, not just "my way."

Helping and Getting Help—Essential Skills for Effective Group Problem Solving

by

Sydney Farivar and Noreen M. Webb

Seventh-grade teacher: "My students have been working together in groups for a while now. They're getting along fine. But I'm finding that a lot of them still don't understand the work. I tell them to 'work together' and that it is all right to help each other. Sometimes I worry that they are only giving each other the answers. How can I get them to focus on problem solving and not just putting down the right answer?"

Mathematics educators are increasingly placing high priority on developing reasoning and problem-solving skills and have come to recognize the importance of small-group work as a context for developing and communicating mathematical ideas. As explained in the NCTM's *Curriculum and Evaluation Standards for School Mathematics* (1989) for grades 5 to 8 (p. 78), "opportunities to explain, conjecture, and defend one's ideas orally and in writing can stimulate deeper understandings of concepts and principles." Curricular

Photo by Joanne Wald; all rights reserved

In healthy, interactive groups, leadership is shared and participation is equal.

frameworks for many states are also increasingly calling for collaborative small-group work to help students persist at, and succeed on, difficult and sophisticated problems (see, e.g., California State Department of Education [1992]). But as the concerned seventh-grade teacher pointed out, copying a fellow student's answers clearly does not help students learn to become independent problem solvers. Simply putting students in small groups will not guarantee that they will interact with each other in ways that are beneficial to learning. What can teachers do to teach students how to help one another learn to solve problems? A good place to start is to look at the research on helping behavior in small groups giving help and receiving help (Webb 1985a, 1985b, 1991). Knowing more about helping behavior gives teachers important information that they can use to enable students to help each other learn without giving answers.

In this article we outline the steps necessary for students to learn how to use one another as resources for doing mathematics. These steps were used in an urban, predominantly minority (Hispanic and African American) middle school. The activities, explained in the *Helping Behavior Activities Handbook* (Farivar and Webb 1991), were based on research showing which kinds of helping behaviors in small groups are effective for learning and which ones are not. Although research on cooperative learning has shown that working collaboratively with others can increase

Sydney Farivar teaches at California State University—Northridge, Northridge, CA 91328-1277. She studies students' relationships with one another in small groups and is particularly interested in preparing students for group work. Noreen Webb teaches at the University of California—Los Angeles, Los Angeles, CA 90024. Her work focuses on the relationship between small-group dynamics and learning in mathematics classrooms.

achievement (see, e.g., Slavin [1990]), research on helping behaviors in small groups shows that not all behavior is equally effective for learning. *Explaining* is more effective for learning than sharing the answer for both the helper and the student who receives the help (Webb 1985a, 1985b, 1991).

Thorough preparation for working in groups can take as long as one-half the period each day for three weeks. To many, this time will seem very long, perhaps too long. To those who already use groups on a regular basis, it will seem normal. Because both preparation for group work and mathematics instruction can be fit into each class period, the pressure on the curricular time schedule is not great.

Preparation for Group Work

Much of the preparation involves developing basic communication and social skills. These skills apply to any subject matter, not just to mathematics, so many of the activities described here are presented in a general, nonmathematical context (see also Gibbs [1987]; Kagan [1992]; and Johnson et al. [1988] for additional activities to teach small-group skills). In contrast to the earlier steps, the final step—helping skills—*is* specific to mathematics and is illustrated using mathematical content. The final step depends on completion of the earlier steps; the process of developing effective group-work skills in mathematics is sequential and cumulative.

It is very important that teachers not skimp on the time it takes to lay the groundwork for group work. Even among students who have worked in groups, many may have had experiences in which one student did most of the work or told all the answers. Or one student, appointed (usually by the teacher) to be the "leader," may have "bossed" everyone around. Students may think that this model is representative of working and learning in groups. It is not. In healthy, interactive groups, leadership is shared and participation is equal. Students help one another by asking for and giving help as needed. They use one another as important resources in their learning.

The first step in preparing students for group work is *class building*. Do your students know one another? Do they know one another's names? Are they comfortable in class? We used four "class building" activities to help students become acquainted with one another. Students wore name tags so that they could learn their classmates' names. They also played such games as "people shuffle," in which six or seven students stand in front of the class and as the teacher introduces them, the class practices saying their names. The students at their seats close their eyes, and the students in front change places. The seated students must then call the students by name to rearrange them in the order in which they were originally standing. In another activity, students leave their seats to interact with one another, for instance, to find classmates who like the same season or activities they like. Finally, students can interview another student and introduce this partner to the small group at their table.

The second step in preparation for group work is *learning how to work with others*. Students have not necessarily learned this skill. We taught three kinds of communication skills, which students then practiced before we assigned them to groups.

1. *Basic communication skills.* Do your students know how to listen attentively? Can they work with fellow classmates without putting them down? When they work in groups do all group members participate equally? Do they know the differences among competition, cooperation, and working individually? Have they ever created something as a group? Certain class and group rules, which we call "norms," need to be introduced to students who work in groups. *Class norms*, especially attentive listening and elimination of put-downs, stress the importance of positive interaction (Gibbs 1987). *Group norms*, such as "twelve-inch voices" (low voices that cannot be heard more than 12 inches away) and equal participation, are intended (*a*) to encourage students to use one another as resources, to work with one another using voices that are just loud enough for group members to hear, and to ask group mates when they have a question before they ask the teacher and (*b*) to discourage "hitch hikers"—people in the group who sit back and do nothing. Everyone in the group is to be active and involved. Discussion of these norms is very important. Students need to understand that these rules make it possible for their group to be effective. In addition, students discuss examples of different ways of interacting—cooperation, competition, and working individually—and the rules for each.

2. *Team building.* Once students are assigned to heterogeneous groups of no more than four students, what can the teacher do to help them get to know their teammates and establish a group identity? Students can select a group name; they should make a sign displaying their name so that the teacher can use the group's name instead of students' names. Students can also list things that they all have in common. Procedures for group work need to be identified and explained. For example, each student in the group might take responsibility for a certain task, such as recording the homework, getting the group's folder, or putting up the group's sign. These tasks must be explained so that everyone knows what is expected. Students should take turns performing different roles so that all students know that they are valuable members of the group.

3. *Small-group social skills.* How are your students' social skills? Can the students articulate ideas? Talk about the work? Get the group back on task? Encourage others to talk? Without previous practice in classroom social skills, many students are socially incompetent. Such simple skills

as giving ideas, asking questions, inviting others to talk, and saying "thank you" are, for many, new and different ways of interacting with others. We identified social skills that are particularly important for group problem solving, such as checking for understanding and sharing information and ideas. We also identified skills to keep the groups working well together, such as encouraging each other and checking for agreement. Students brainstormed what using each skill would look like and sound like. Students were told that when they were working in groups, the teacher would walk around to listen and look for their use of these social skills.

Fine-Tuning Communication and Cooperation Skills

Have you found some students doing most of the talking and directing when they work in groups? Do some students who are good thinkers and problem solvers sometimes make careless computational mistakes? Would some students prefer your help to that of a capable classmate whose judgment they don't trust because he or she is a peer? It's important that students practice their emerging group skills of cooperation with nonacademic activities. Such practice gives them a chance to cooperate, solve problems, be creative, have fun, and become aware of teammates' nonacademic skills without fear of being "wrong" or "stupid." For example, students may work together to make kitchen utensils out of index cards, pencils, toothpicks, and paper clips. Without talking, they can cooperate and build towers out of paper and tape. They can practice explaining and listening by making designs on a grid and calling out the coordinates for teammates to fill in. Students can try, without asking questions, to draw a figure described by another student. Then when they are permitted to ask questions, they discover how much more successful they can be.

Developing Helping Skills

Do your students help each other? Do they wait to give help until they are asked? Do they give "terminal help," that is, just the answer? Do they watch while the person they are helping works through a problem, to make sure he or she is doing it correctly?

To be really effective participants in small-group problem solving, students need helping skills. On the basis of research findings about giving and seeking help (Nelson-Le Gall 1981; Webb 1985b), we developed and used charts that outlined what students should say when they do not understand and what to say when giving help (simplified examples of the charts appear in tables 1 and 2).

We used an overhead projector to project the charts and taught the students appropriate ways to give and seek help. The charts were also posted on the walls of the classroom. Furthermore, several students performed skits to demonstrate "good" helping and "unhelpful" helping (adapted from Swing and Peterson [1982]). The skits for good helping showed one student explaining to another student the steps in solving a problem, giving the other student a chance to try to solve the problem, correcting the other student's errors with explanations of what should have been done and why, asking follow-up questions to make sure that the other student truly understands, and giving praise for work well done. Skits for "unhelpful" helping showed a student giving another student only the answer to the problem without describing the solution process, telling the other student to hurry up, and telling the other student to concentrate on getting the answer rather than on understanding how to solve the problem. The class then discussed the skits. We also developed "good helper" and "good help receiver" checklists for students to evaluate their developing helping skills (see fig. l). The last five minutes of each class period was used for small-group and whole-class discussion about helping.

Table 1

Chart of Behaviors for Students Who Do Not Understand How to Solve the Problem

Behavior	Example
Problem: Groups design their own restaurant menus with prices for entrées, desserts, and drinks. They each select a meal and estimate the total cost for their entire group, including 8.5 percent sales tax and 15 percent tip.	
1. Recognize that you need help.	"I don't understand how to calculate the sales tax."
2. Decide to get help from another student.	"I'm going to ask someone for help."
3. Choose someone to help you.	"I think Maria could help me."
4. Ask for help.	"Could you help me with the sales tax?"
5. Ask clear and precise questions.	"Our group's bill is $24.00. Why don't we just add $0.85 to $24.00 for the sales tax?"
6. Keep asking until you understand.	"So if the bill was $50.00, are you saying that the sales tax would be 8.5 percent of $50.00?"

Table 2
Chart of Behaviors for Students Who Do Understand How to Solve the Problem

Behavior	Example
1. Notice when other students need help.	Look around your group to see if anyone needs help.
2. Tell other students to ask you if they need help.	"If you need help, ask me."
3. When someone asks for help, help him or her.	"Sure I'll help you. What don't you understand?"
4. Be a good listener.	"Let your teammate explain what he or she doesn't understand."
5. Give explanations instead of the answer.	"8.5 percent is not the same as $0.85. The sales tax is not the same amount of money for every bill. The bigger the bill is, the bigger the tax will be. So here we have to figure out 8.5 percent of $24.00. Since 10 percent of $24.00 is $2.40, the sales tax will be a little less than that.
6. Watch how your teammate solves the problem.	
7. Give specific feedback on how your teammate solved the problem.	"You multiplied the numbers OK, but you have to be careful of the decimal point. If the bill is $24.00, it doesn't make sense that the sales tax is $204.00."
8. Check for understanding.	"Tell me again why you think the sales tax is $2.04 instead of $204.00."
9. Praise your teammate for doing a good job.	"Good job!" "Nice work!" "You've got it!"

How good a helper are you?	YES	NO
When you are helping, do you—		
1. tell other students to ask for help when they need it?	___	___
2. notice when other students need help?	___	___
3. respond to requests for help?	___	___
4. listen when you're told the specific kind of help needed?	___	___
5. give *explanations* of how or why to do the problem?	___	___
6. watch how your teammate solves the problem?	___	___
7. give specific feedback on how your teammate solved the problem?	___	___
8. check that your teammate understands how to do the problem?	___	___
9. praise your teammate for doing a good job?	___	___

How good are you at asking for help?		
When you need help, do you—		
1. recognize that you need help?	___	___
2. decide to ask a classmate for help?	___	___
3. choose someone to ask for help?	___	___
4. ask for help?	___	___
5. ask clear and precise questions?	___	___
6. keep asking until you are sure you understand?	___	___

Fig. 1. "Good helper" and "good help receiver" checklists

The program is cumulative, and the steps must be carried out sequentially. Later steps cannot be covered effectively before the completion of earlier steps. For example, the development of specific helping skills depends on the prior development of communication skills, team building, and class inclusion. Before they can be effective help givers, students need to be able to communicate positively with other students without putting them down, to understand the importance of cooperation and two-way communication, and to be receptive to other students' questions and difficulties. Before they will seek help and be receptive to help offered, students must feel comfortable in their groups, believe that other students value their efforts, and be able to communicate freely their misconceptions and difficulties.

Conclusions

The program described here for developing students' communication and helping skills will help students feel included and comfortable in their groups and classroom. It also helps them develop many skills needed for effective group work in mathematics, including communicating with others in positive and effective ways, recognizing and using others' mathematical skills, and explaining the processes in conceptualizing and solving mathematical problems.

Research using the program described here has shown multiple benefits for students. The program had positive effects on students' ability to obtain explanations from their teammates about how to solve problems and on their achievement, particularly among Hispanic and African American students (Webb and Farivar, in review). Furthermore, students' regard for one another increased for those in either ethnic groups or achievement groups and for female students (Farivar 1991, 1992). Most important, the activities described here help students take responsibility for their own behavior and their own learning in mathematics. By cooperating with other students in solving problems, they learn how to communicate their mathematical ideas, share intellectual resources, and develop a greater understanding of mathematics.

References

California State Department of Education. *Mathematics Framework for California Public Schools, Kindergarten through Grade Twelve.* Sacramento, Calif.: California Department of Education, 1992.

Gibbs, Jeanne. *Tribes: A Process for Social Development and Cooperative Learning.* Santa Rosa, Calif: Center Source Publications, 1987.

Farivar, Sydney H. *Intergroup Relations in Cooperative Learning Groups.* Paper presented at the annual meeting of the American Educational Research Association, Chicago, April 1991.

———. *Middle School Math Students' Reactions to Heterogeneous Small Group Work: They Like It!* Paper presented at the annual meeting of the American Educational Research Association, San Francisco, April 1992.

Farivar, Sydney H., and Noreen M. Webb. *Helping Behavior Activities Handbook.* Los Angeles: Graduate School of Education, University of California, 1991. Available from Dr. Noreen Webb, Graduate School of Education, UCLA, Los Angeles, CA 90024.

Johnson, David W., Roger T. Johnson, Judy K. Bartlett, and Linda M. Johnson. *Our Cooperative Classroom.* Edina, Minn.: Interaction Book Co., 1988.

Kagan, Spencer. *Cooperative Learning.* San Juan Capistrano, Calif.: Resources for Teachers, 1992.

National Council of Teachers of Mathematics. *Curriculum and Evaluation Standards for School Mathematics.* Reston, Va.: The Council, 1989.

Nelson-Le Gall, Sharon. "Help-Seeking: An Understudied Problem-solving Skill in Children." *Developmental Review* 1 (September 1981):224–46.

Slavin, Robert E. *Cooperative Learning: Theory, Research and Practice.* Englewood Cliffs, N.J.: Prentice Hall, 1990.

Swing, Susan R., and Penelope L. Peterson. "The Relationship of Student Ability and Small-Group Interaction to Student Achievement." *American Educational Research Journal* 19 (Summer 1982):259–74.

Webb, Noreen M. "Student Interaction and Learning in Small Groups: A Research Summary." In *Learning to Cooperate, Cooperating to Learn,* edited by Robert E. Slavin, Shlomo Sharan, Spencer Kagan, Rachel Hertz-Lazarowitz, Noreen M. Webb, and Richard Schumck, 147–72. New York: Plenum Press, 1985a.

———. "Verbal Interaction and Learning in Peer-Directed Groups." *Theory into Practice* 24 (Winter 1985b):32–39.

———. "Task-related Verbal Interaction and Mathematics Learning in Small Groups." *Journal for Research in Mathematics Education* 22 (November 1991):366–89.

Research into Practice

Making Equity a Reality in Classrooms

by
Patricia F. Campbell and Cynthia Langrall

The NCTM's *Curriculum and Evaluation Standards for School Mathematics* (1989) speaks of the necessity of providing effective mathematics education for all students. Noting that "the social injustices of past schooling practices can no longer be tolerated" (p. 4), the *Standards* document calls for a mathematics content that is "what we believe all students will need if they are to be productive citizens in the twenty-first century. If all students do not have the opportunity to learn this mathematics, we face the danger of creating an intellectual elite and polarized society" (p. 9). Similarly, the National Research Council's Mathematical Sciences Education Board noted that two themes underlie current analysis of American education: "equity in opportunity and ... excellence in results" (1989, 28–29). Although the NCTM's *Standards* and other reform documents have been critiqued as addressing the issue of equity in terms of "enlightened self-interest" as opposed to seeking justice (Secada 1989), these documents have called attention to educational disparity. The issue today is how to make the goal of equity a reality in classrooms. To do otherwise would be to assign "mathematics for all" to the status of a slogan, a catchy phrase but having no meaning in practice.

Prepared by Patricia F. Campbell
University of Maryland
College Park, MD 20742

Cynthia Langrall
Illinois State University
Normal, IL 61671

Pat Campbell and Cindy Langrall have been associated with Project IMPACT since 1989–90. They also teach graduate and undergraduate mathematics education courses at their respective universities, Campbell at the University of Maryland, College Park, MD 20742, and Langrall at Illinois State University, Normal, IL 61671.

The preparation of this material was supported in part by a grant from the National Science Foundation under Grant no. MDR-8954652. Any opinions, findings, and conclusions or recommendations expressed in this material are those of the authors and do not necessarily reflect the views of the National Science Foundation.

What Is Equity?

Although historically and legally the definition of equity has revolved around equal opportunity, today one finds more widespread acceptance of stronger criteria: equal treatment and equal outcomes (Fennema and Meyer 1989). The standard is that educational experiences in the classroom support equal achievement and future participation in mathematics for all students regardless of their gender, ethnicity and race, or socioeconomic background. Within this perspective, equity refers to justice (Secada 1989). The criteria for opportunity move beyond availability of instruction to taking steps "to ensure that students have a real chance to become engaged in and to learn from the academic core that they encounter" (Secada 1989, 40).

Research offers no formulas or checklists to guarantee equity in mathematics classrooms. However, research does offer an indication about what approaches seem to be ineffective and what approaches may hold promise. Consider the evidence of ineffective practice.

An examination of national entry and achievement data indicates that those students who are academically disadvantaged at the beginning of the school year are likely to show "progressive retardation" as they continue in school (Walberg 1988). An examination of educational practice in these classrooms often reveals different expectations. For example, students deemed as being less capable are taught less mathematics or are presented with skill-oriented, direct instruction and practice as opposed to conceptually focused instruction promoting problem solving and understanding. The premise is that the students are deficient and therefore need remediation directed at the root of their problem, their lack of basic or prerequisite skills. This deficit model of policy has been critiqued for many years (e.g., Bronfenbrenner 1979), although it remains the basis of many state and federal programs.

What other approach can be used? The alternative to the deficit model is to change the environment of the students' instruction, to focus on the character of the instruction as opposed to the perceived deficiencies of the student. This approach requires a nonthreatening classroom environment, an environment marked by an atmosphere of trust and respect, respect between the teacher and each student as well as respect among the students (Baptiste 1992). Applying the principles suggested in research on students' learning of mathematics, as well as the vision offered in both the *Curriculum and Evaluation Standards* (NCTM 1989) and the *Professional Teaching Standards* (NCTM 1991), the intent is to organize mathematics instruction around the notion of each student's "making sense" of mathematics. Recently, an National Science Foundation–funded project has been attempting to implement this approach to mathematics equity in three predominantly minority urban public schools outside Washington, D.C. These schools reflect diversity, both in minority racial-ethnic groups and in language.

Supporting Each Child's Engagement in the Classroom

Build on prior knowledge

Project IMPACT (Increasing the Mathematical Power of All Children and Teachers) is a school-based project wherein all kindergarten through third-grade teachers work together as grade-level teams with a mathematics specialist to establish a mathematical culture in each classroom. These classrooms are becoming places where ideas are accepted, where suggestions are investigated, and where meaningful problems are solved. Teachers in Project IMPACT have come to recognize that every student, no matter what economic or social conditions he or she endures outside school, has mathematical knowledge. This knowledge may not be the formal mathematical

knowledge of school curricula. In fact, it may be understood by students only in the context of a particular setting or application. Nevertheless, it is knowledge. The emphasis in IMPACT is to teach students mathematics by building on their existing knowledge. Teachers focus on students' thinking and direct attention to that thinking, as opposed to focusing on the correctness of their answer. These principles are firmly grounded in research on mathematical learning.

Use meaningful, shared contexts

When students are presented mathematical ideas, or even realistic problems, in contexts or phrasings that are not meaningful or relevant to them, it may limit some students' potential to connect or use their informal knowledge with the mathematics or problem under discussion. This lack of connection in turn may discourage a student from attempting a solution or suggesting an approach. However, if the mathematical idea is set in a meaningful context, either because it is a common experience in the community outside of school or because it is a problem that is set in the shared culture of the school or classroom, all students are more likely to offer information or suggest approaches. In IMPACT classrooms, teachers attempt to propose mathematical investigations in context. Then they will frequently say or ask, "What do you see? … Tell us something else about this problem…. What do you know? … What else do you know? … Tell us your thinking…. So what is the problem? … What could we try? … Someone else tell the class what you are thinking about…. Does anyone else notice something else about this problem? … Does anyone have another idea?" These questions serve to legitimize students' thoughts and to encourage students to verbalize or show their ideas. They also give teachers a sense of the meanings that students are attributing to the problem or situation presented.

Celebrate each student's thinking

Just as important, all responses are valued; questioning does not stop when an expected response is offered; no responses are judged. The intent is to celebrate each student's thinking, whether that thinking is a solution process, a recognition of a relationship, or simply a statement of fact about the problem. The expectation in IMPACT is that all students can learn to communicate mathematical ideas and to participate actively in mathematical inquiry. Teachers continue to solicit responses as long as different ideas continue to be offered by the students.

In many of IMPACT's urban classrooms are students who did not initially respond to questions. Either their prior perception was that mathematics instruction meant waiting for the teacher to tell you what to do or they did not yet trust either their teacher or their classmates sufficiently. We must recognize that students take a risk when they expose their thinking or approaches. However, IMPACT teachers resist the impulse to excuse any student from participation. Instead they might note almost parenthetically to the class that the student is certainly thinking and that the class will wait quietly to hear what he or she is thinking about. The difficult step for IMPACT teachers and students is actually to wait at this point. But waiting has a reward. Even the reluctant student eventually responds in some form, and when that response is accepted and valued by the teacher, that student learns to persevere and participate in the class.

Permit sufficient time for investigation

In IMPACT classrooms, following the discussion of a problem or a topic, time is permitted for the students to solve mathematics problems with the expectation that the students will express and explain their thinking. This thinking might occur in cooperative pairs or groups with the group charged with the responsibility of figuring out a solution for a problem. At other times, students work on problems individually. But eventually, either during the same class period or the next day, students express and justify their approach, either in writing or in classroom discussion.

Value explanation without judgment

IMPACT teachers attempt to refrain from evaluating an approach as being correct or incorrect; however, this nonjudgmental pose can be very difficult. At first, the tendency of many IMPACT teachers was to praise correct responses and to accept incorrect responses by either offering no comment or by tendering the refrain, "Good thinking." Their intent was to encourage problem-solving attempts, but instead they were implicitly communicating a judgment without explanation and simultaneously generating confusion. Eventually the IMPACT teachers decided that they still did not want to be the authority passing judgment but that any student should be expected to explain or justify his or her approach. Thus the classroom routine now promotes questioning of *all* responses within classroom discourse: "I'm not sure I understand. Explain that again.... Did anyone think of that in a different way? ... So that is Darrell's idea. What do you think? Does anyone want to ask Darrell a question? ... Does everyone agree that you could think about this idea that way? Or does someone disagree or have a question? ... Wait a minute. I'm not sure I follow this. How did you know ...? In this way, students are encouraged to reflect on their thinking as they verbalize or demonstrate their strategy. They learn to disagree without insult. They also learn to ask questions without losing esteem. Sometimes,

as a result of discussion, a student may realize that his or her initial thinking was erroneous or that he or she prefers another student's approach. In IMPACT classrooms, students are told that it is OK at any time to change one's mind, that even teachers sometimes change their mind. The venture "I changed my mind" permits a student to modify or reverse an opinion without losing respect. The positive classroom atmosphere generated in this manner fosters motivation and responsibility.

Encourage listening and participation

Teachers use two approaches to encourage listening and participation. The teacher might ask if anyone else had solved a problem in the same way and then ask clarifying questions of *any* of those students. Or the teacher might ask if anyone had solved a problem in a different way. Following explanation, students might be asked to compare those two approaches. Or, if a student offered a previously described approach, that student would be challenged to explain how it was similar to, or different from, the prior strategy. Thus, a classroom norm is established wherein knowing what has already been discussed is significant if one wants to share one's ideas.

Integrate mathematical ideas

When asked how their mathematics teaching has changed, IMPACT teachers are unanimous in their reports that they have extended the time spent on mathematics. They not only have extended the length of time for mathematics lessons, they have related mathematics to other subject areas. Graphing and data collection are standard approaches for investigating science and social studies, even in kindergarten. Through a calendar center with full-class sharing, some topics are continually examined (e.g., revisiting place value in second grade by bundling tongue depressors, one tongue depressor for each day of school all year long) and other topics are anticipated (e.g., expressing completed and future days of school in a week or until a vacation or celebration as a fraction in third grade). The result is that students' access to mathematics is maximized and revisited.

Raise expectations

Experience in IMPACT classrooms demonstrates that generally preexisting assumptions regarding expectations for urban students and mathematics are low expectations. The phenomenon of "But not *my* students! *My* students can't do that" is all too alive and well in the primary classrooms of predominantly urban public schools. The intent must be to offer challenging, but not frustrating, mathematics, often using meaningful problem contexts. The determination of what is "challenging, but not frustrating" comes from aiming a little higher than one would expect and then honestly reflecting on the strengths of, and ideas offered by, the students.

Implications from Research

Researchers hypothesize that this approach to teaching has two benefits. First, because the perspective of each student is valued and the involvement of each student is expected in the problem-solving investigation, the classroom environment may encourage students to question and construct mathematical relationships. This atmosphere, in turn, promotes mathematical understanding. Second, because students express their ideas, teachers are able to reflect on their students' understandings, to ask questions to foster further thinking, and to recognize that instruction needs to be modified in some way to support a student's learning. This reflection assists teachers' decision making. The result is an equitable classroom (Carey et al., in press).

Research indicates that ability grouping in elementary school mathematics can exaggerate differences between students and lead to differentiated outcomes (Oakes 1985, 1990). Goodlad (1984, 141) noted that after first grade, ability groupings tend to become established and foster limited opportunities for learning:

> One of the reasons for this stability in group membership is that the work of upper and lower groups becomes more sharply differentiated with each passing day. Since those comprising each group are taught as a group most of the time, it is difficult for any one child to move ahead and catch up with children in a more advanced group, especially in mathematics. It is not uncommon for a child in the most advanced group to have progressed five times as fast as a child in the least advanced group over the course of the year.

IMPACT classrooms do not implement homogeneous mathematics groups. Frequently, whole-class instruction is used, but sometimes students are grouped, either to permit more teacher observation and interaction or to vary the rigor of the mathematics problems being solved. However, even when grouping is used to vary problems, the mathematical topic being addressed remains constant across the groups. Further, the whole-class sharing still occurs.

Concern is voiced that current efforts toward reform in mathematics education will widen the differential achievement gap because the potential exists that those students "who are situated to take advantage of educational innovations receive a disproportionate amount of their benefits" (Secada 1989, 40). But this situation need not happen. The challenge is for teachers to "emancipate, empower and transform both themselves and their students" (Ladson-Billings 1992, 109), recognizing that teaching cannot be relegated to "prescriptive steps and techniques to be learned and demonstrated, ... that the way social interaction takes place in the classroom is important to student success, ... [and that] knowledge is continuously recreated, recycled and shared" (pp. 113–14). Teachers in IMPACT have taken up this challenge. We urge the reader to do the same.

References

Baptiste, H. Prentice, Jr. "Conceptual and Theoretical Issues." In *Students at Risk in At-Risk Schools: Improving Environments for Learning*, edited by Hersholt C. Waxman, Judith W. de Felix, James E. Anderson, and H. Prentice Baptiste, Jr., 11–16. Newbury Park, Calif.: Corwin Press, 1992.

Bronfenbrenner, Uri. "Beyond the Deficit Model in Child and Family Policy." *Teachers College Press* 81 (Fall 1979):95–104.

Carey, Deborah A., Elizabeth Fennema, Thomas P. Carpenter, and Megan L. Franke. *Cognitively Guided Instruction: Towards Equitable Classrooms*. In press.

Fennema, Elizabeth, and Margaret R. Meyer. "Gender, Equity, and Mathematics." In *Equity in Education*, edited by Walter G. Secada, 146–57. Bristol, Pa.: Falmer Press, 1989.

Goodlad, John J. *A Place Called School: Prospects for the Future*. New York: McGraw-Hill, 1984.

Ladson-Billings, Gloria. "Culturally Relevant Teaching: The Key to Making Multicultural Education Work." In *Research and Multicultural Education: From the Margins to the Mainstream*, edited by Carl A. Grant, 106–21. Bristol, Pa.: Falmer Press, 1992.

National Council of Teachers of Mathematics. *Curriculum and Evaluation Standards for School Mathematics*. Reston, Va.: The Council, 1989.

———. *Professional Standards for Teaching Mathematics*. Reston, Va.: The Council, 1991.

National Research Council. Mathematical Sciences Education Board. *Everybody Counts: A Report to the Nation on the Future of Mathematics Education*. Washington, D.C.: National Academy Press, 1989.

Oakes, Jeannie. *Keeping Track: How Schools Structure Inequality*. New Haven: Yale University Press, 1985.

———. *Multiplying Inequalities: The Effects of Race, Social Class, and Tracking on Opportunities to Learn Mathematics and Science*. Santa Monica, Calif.: Rand Corp., 1990.

Secada, Walter G. "Agenda Setting, Enlightened Self-Interest, and Equity in Mathematics Education." *Peabody Journal of Education* 66 (Winter 1989):22–56.

Walberg, Herbert J. "Synthesis of Research on Time and Learning." *Educational Leadership* 45 (March 1988):76–85.

Activities

Creating a Different Kind of Classroom

Reys and Long, "Teacher as Architect of Mathematical Tasks"

1. Individual or class project

   (a) Find the answer for your state for the problem of lining up the total population along the border of the state.

   (b) Using one sheet of paper, write up a description of the strategy you used so it can be clearly understood. Post all write-ups so the rest of the class can read them.

   (c) Find two of the posted strategies that are different from yours. Write an explanation of how they are different. Rate the difficulty of understanding each strategy (easy, just right, or difficult), and explain your reasons for this rating.

2. Choose three tasks you have done in your class this year and discuss how they fit the six criteria for a good mathematical task.

Discourse Standards from *Professional Standards for Teaching Mathematics*

Select two activities from your classroom that illustrate the ideas of discourse—one that illustrates the teacher's role and one that illustrates the students' role. Give details about the classroom examples, and clearly explain how they illustrate specific aspects of discourse.

Scheibelhut, "I Do and I Understand, I Reflect and I Improve"

Write a reaction paper to this article. Reflect on your own (or your students') use of writing and its effect, if any, on learning. Provide specific examples of activities to clarify your discussion.

NCTM Xchange, "Cooperative Groups: What Role Do They Play in the Teaching and Learning of Mathematics?"

Select three mathematics tasks: one that is appropriate for individual work, one for small-group work, and one for whole-class work. Use the comments of the teachers in the article to explain why each task is appropriate for that configuration of students.

Section 5
Developing Mathematical Thinking

This section looks at what is meant by "mathematical thinking skills." We use the phrase all the time, yet it is a very general expression that can refer to a wide range of mental activities. The four authors included here focus on different aspects of these skills and provide examples of problems and children's work to flesh out their use of the words *thinking* and *reasoning*. As you read the articles, reflect on what attributes of these processes make them inherently mathematical and what it is about the nature of the discipline that requires these specialized skills.

Rathmell provides a general discussion of the importance of developing children's thinking and reasoning rather than focusing on rote learning skills. His examples of children's strategies illustrate the importance of such skills in the development of mathematical power. Andrews picks up on the theme of mathematical power with her discussion of "taking the magic" out of mathematics. She presents a reflective account of how she changed her teaching to encourage students to engage in systematic thinking rather than wild guessing. Her insightful interpretations of the children's

behavior show how their attitudes changed from anxiety to enjoyment as a result of the different instructional emphasis.

Bushman presents the results of a classroom experiment that examined the effects of providing a worked example to students engaged in a series of problem-solving tasks. He found that the second-grade students took more ownership of the problems, engaged in more-relevant thinking strategies, and reached more correct solutions when worked examples were not included. This article highlights the importance of helping students develop higher-order-thinking skills rather than allowing them to rely on external help when solving problems that have no immediately apparent answer.

Krulik and Rudnick discuss how reflecting at the end of the problem-solving process can stimulate critical- and creative-thinking skills. They describe five steps that students can use to reflect on their problem solving. Solutions to different problems are analyzed and extended by the authors in interesting ways to illustrate each step and its pedagogical implications.

One Point of View

Planning for Instruction Involves Focusing on Children's Thinking

by

Edward C. Rathmell

Too often when teachers plan for instruction, such mathematical skills as two-digit subtraction, multiplication facts, and equivalent fractions take precedence over thinking-and-reasoning strategies. Planning for instruction that promotes the development of children's thinking and reasoning about mathematics not only helps them make sense of the content they are studying but also helps them learn ways of thinking that later will enable them to make sense of *new* content. Consider some of the following examples:

- Children who have learned to "count on" as a way to solve addition facts (count on from 8—9, 10, 11—to solve 3 + 8) have learned a thinking strategy that will help them solve problems with larger numbers, read a clock, count a set of coins, and make change.

- Children who have learned to make 10 as a way to solve addition and subtraction facts (9 and 1 is 10, 4 more is 14) have learned a thinking strategy they might use to solve mental-computation and estimation problems with larger numbers.

- Children who have learned part-to-whole relationships (3 and 5 are the parts and 8 is the whole) have learned a thinking strategy that will aid in solving subtraction problems involving numbers they can easily add; deciding when to add and when to subtract; and beginning to understand fractions, ratio, proportion, and percent.

- Children who have learned to use the distributive property to solve multiplication facts (five 8s is 40, so six 8s is just 40 plus one more 8) have learned a thinking strategy that will help them solve mental-

computation and estimation problems with larger numbers and rename numbers and algebraic expressions. They also have learned a problem-solving strategy that breaks a problem into manageable parts, works with the parts, and integrates those partial solutions into a meaningful whole.

New thinking strategies are encouraged.

As teachers begin to focus their instructional planning on children's thinking, they begin to shift the content emphasis from proficiency with skills to using thinking and reasoning to solve problems in context and to make thoughtful decisions about real situations. They shift the emphasis in instruction from an individual student's memorizing facts, rules, and procedures to developing a student-centered classroom that can hold intellectual discussions about solution strategies and reasonableness.

A mathematics classroom that focuses on developing thinking and reasoning differs from most current mathematics classrooms. The curriculum usually is problem driven. These problems can stem from real situations, children's literature, and problems posed by the children and the teacher. However, time is available every day for children in these settings to make their own sense of mathematics. They are given the opportunity to ask questions, make conjectures, or pose problems. They decide what thinking strategies and reasoning patterns they will use or invent to solve problems. They have the opportunity to explain their thinking and listen to others' strategies and

Edward Rathmell teaches at the University of Northern Iowa, Cedar Falls, IA 50614.

points of view. They have the chance to reflect on their solution strategies and the reasonableness of solutions they have generated.

Problems posed by students often involve large numbers and are more complicated than typical textbook problems. However, because the problems are presented in the context of a real or imagined situation, students are able to make sense of them. New thinking strategies and reasoning patterns are encouraged because of these complex situations. For example, students who might automatically count to find an answer when using small numbers will often invent a more sophisticated procedure with larger numbers in the context of a familiar setting. When the numbers are greater than the comfort level of their paper-and-pencil computational skills, they are almost forced to invent new strategies to solve these problems.

One teacher often begins her mathematics class by describing a situation. She then asks children to pose problems about that setting. For example, after creating a setting that encouraged children to pose problems about counting by twos, fives, tens, and so on, one of the students suggested that they count by fours to find the number of wheels on the cars in the school parking lot. These second-grade children, who had not yet been introduced to multiplication, spent valuable time determining the number of wheels on twenty-one cars.

When students play an active role in determining the curriculum, the interest in mathematics and problem solving is apparent. One first-grade girl wrote, "It's hard to do hard things like this. But I feel grown-up and we're getting into the big stuff." (See fig. 1.)

Mathematics teachers who focus on thinking and reasoning rather than rote-learning skills naturally integrate assessment and instruction. These teachers create situations where children have the opportunity to express various ways of thinking about a topic. Observing group work informally, listening to explanations of solutions and the reasonableness of answers, and interpreting written reports contribute to a teacher's learning about the thinking and reasoning levels of the students. Providing opportunities for children to pose problems also affords teachers the opportunity to check the limits of an individual student's thinking and understanding.

Everyone can develop mathematical power.

The positive attitudes that schoolchildren develop toward mathematics and learning are the most important outcomes of a classroom that focuses on thinking and reasoning. As students pose, discuss, and solve problems, they develop confidence in their ability to make sense of mathematics and to use their reasoning skills to solve problems. As their thinking strategies and reasoning skills expand, they begin to develop true mathematical power.

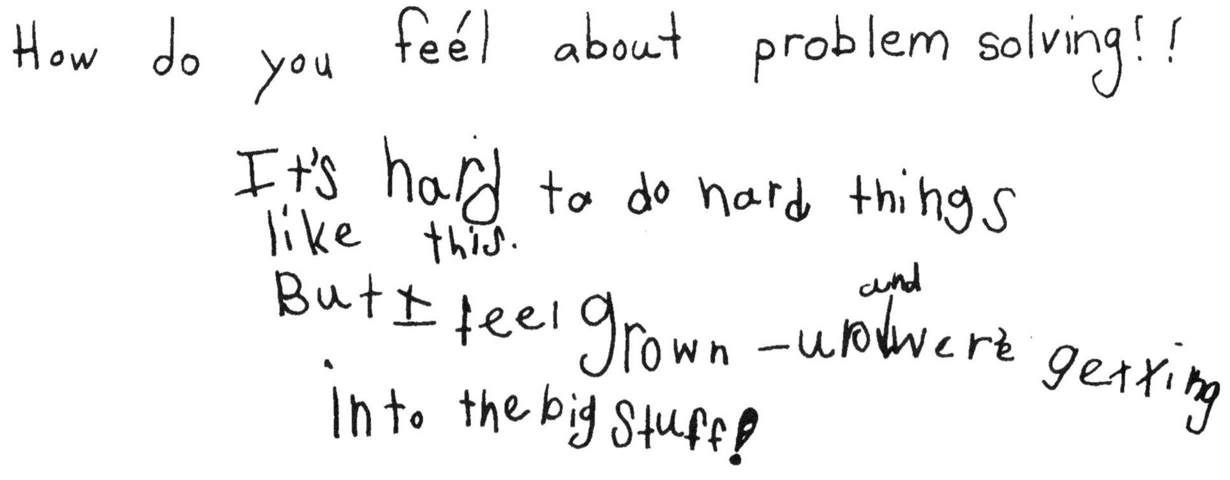

How do you feel about problem solving!!

It's hard to do hard things like this.
But I feel grown-up and we're getting
into the big stuff!

Fig. 1. Student expressing feelings about problem solving

Early Childhood Corner

Take the Magic out of Your Classroom!

by

Angela Giglio Andrews

From ancient times, people have attributed phenomena that they do not fully comprehend to the supernatural and to magic, which is "the production of results through mysterious influences or unexplained powers" according to the 1984 *Random House College Dictionary*. Even in this day and time, to many children and adults, mathematics and magic seem to be interchangeable terms; after all, magicians and mathematicians both seem to be expert at producing baffling effects and extraordinary results through some seemingly inexplicable power. For many of us, success at either mathematics or magic still seems to lie in knowing the tricks. I know I held this belief for many years.

I remember attending my first magic show at age four. The magician always chose a child from the audience as an assistant and said to each young helper, "Now, you aren't going to tell anyone how we did this trick, are you?" When I was chosen to assist, I eagerly promised not to tell the secret of the trick. I held two glasses while the magi-

Children will meaningfully discuss estimates if the proper conditions are maintained.

Photo by Angela Giglio Andrews; all rights reserved

cian poured water into one of them. Then I was to pour the water from one glass to the other. Before my amazed eyes, each time I poured the water, it changed colors! My head began spinning. I was doing something that was amazing, but I did not know how it worked! I felt so bewildered that I hardly heard the magician's banter or the audience's applause. At the trick's end, the magician whisked the glasses away and asked me the dreaded question, "Now, you aren't going to reveal the secret of this trick, are you?" I desperately wanted to ask, "How did you do that?" but I was too embarrassed. The truth was that I had no idea what had just transpired, but I thought I was supposed to know. I could not let the magician or my parents see that I did not know, so I smiled and said, "Oh, no, Sir!" and returned to my seat.

This memory returned to haunt me many times in school, where I began to perceive mathematics as a collection of magic tricks and secrets to which I was not privy. How I dreaded my reluctant trips to the chalkboard "stage" to pretend that I understood these elusive "mathematics tricks" that I was being asked by my teacher to perform.

Like many others, I entered the field of early childhood teaching, still unconsciously believing that mathematics was a subject full of tricks that I could neither understand nor use to my benefit. Unfortunately, I often communicated this belief to the youngsters in my class in subtle, unintentional, and well-meaning ways.

Angela Giglio Andrews, agandrews@aol.com, is a kindergarten teacher at Scott Elementary School, Naperville, IL 60565, who has for years been active in mathematics education. She is coeditor of this department with Sydney Schwartz, slsqc@qcvaxa.acc.qc.edu, Queens College of the City University of New York, Flushing, NY 11367.

Demystifying an Estimation Activity

One typical way I unconsciously passed along the idea that mathematics was "magical" was by introducing the activity of "guessing" how many jelly beans were contained in a jar. I viewed this activity as a motivational way to develop estimating skills, in keeping with NCTM's Standard 5 (1989), which states that "the curriculum should include opportunities to explore estimation strategies." Each week at whole-group time, I put a small number of items in a jar and passed it around, encouraging each child to have a "guess." After doing this weekly estimating activity for a while, I began to sense that although some children certainly seemed to enjoy the activity, others seemed to be experiencing "anticipatory anxiety" and were reluctant to make a guess. They held the jar for long periods of time, turning it over and over nervously in their hands, remaining very silent. These children often attempted to count the items in the jar and became very frustrated when they could not do so. I was shocked to hear one impatient student urging his friend, "It doesn't matter—just make a guess!"

Two things about the students' behavior bothered me. Why were some of them unable to take the risk of naming a number that might not be correct? Did they think this task involved a "trick" for which they did not know the secret? Equally important, I wondered why some other children thought that the number given did not "matter"—did they think that this activity was magic and so they had little control over the answer? Other children would take the jar and pass it quickly like a "hot potato," naming the number said by the previous "guesser." Sometimes five or six children in a row would repeat the same number, often without even looking at the contents. It seemed to me that these students were eager to end their turn and visibly relaxed when they were able to pass the jar. Most disturbing to me, however, was the *unreasonableness* of the answers some children gave. Although I never put more than 10 or 20 objects in the jar, some children would make "wild guesses," such as 1000 or even 0, when they could see that the jar contained some objects! What aspect of this activity led my usually thoughtful students to such illogical responses? Finally, it disturbed me that when we would open the jar and count the actual number, many children would insist that they had "guessed" that number, even though I knew this statement to be untrue. What feature of this activity led young children to value the "right" answer so much that they would "suspend reality" like that?

As I began to reflect on this activity, it occurred to me that the fault was not with the activity itself but with my presentation of it. I was teaching estimation as if it were a magic trick, and as presented, it actually had little to do

with estimation. By encouraging random answers, I was trivializing the mathematical process of estimation. Skillful estimation is based on making a reasonable, accurate numerical inference based on facts and prior knowledge. By using the word *guess*, I was suggesting to my students that no information was available form which to draw a logical conclusion. I was communicating to them that no other route to the answer existed other than "pretending to know" (making a random guess) or, even worse, "knowing the trick" (unscrewing the jar lid in secret and counting, which I observed several children doing).

I then made two changes to eliminate the illusion of magic. First, I no longer asked the children to guess. Instead I asked them to estimate, to figure out *about* how many when the opportunity to count is not offered. Second, I gave them more information to use for estimating by adding a referent jar. This jar was identical in size and shape, with only ten objects inside. I invited the children to verify this number by counting. They could then use this information to make a comparison and figure out a reasonable estimation. This approach increased the children's spontaneous discussions about the reasonableness of one another's answers. I heard such comments as "It couldn't be fourteen because the jar with ten beans only comes to here and the other jar goes all the way to the top! It needs to be a bigger number!" These changes seemed to demystify the activity and encourage the children to bear down intellectually on the mathematical task at hand.

My modifications to the process promoted changes in the way the children pursued the activity. I found that my students made much more reasonable estimates of the contents of the jar. I seldom got "out of the ballpark" estimates. I heard more meaningful conversation among the students as the jar was passed around. The students seemed more comfortable with their own estimates and also more comfortable with the idea of what constitutes an estimate. They were less preoccupied with checking their estimate against the "actual" amount than they had been in the past. When we did check, I heard such remarks as "I was a little too low again" or "I estimated too high, but my answer was still reasonable." One of my favorite remarks, however, came from a little boy as he said goodbye to me at the end of a day. "Teacher," he said, "I just love this estimating!"

Focusing the Twenty-Questions Game

With this small success under my belt, I began to look around my kindergarten class to see whether I needed to take the *guess* word and *guesswork* out of other mathematical experiences. I focused on a classification activity that I had learned in a summer class called "What's in the Box?" In this activity children ask up to twenty questions to which the teacher answers only "yes" or "no." The children are then expected to use the information gained from this questioning to "guess" what is in the large treasure box. If they are unable to do so, they can try again the next day because, in theory, increased experience improves children's questions.

Photo by Angela Giglio Andrews; all rights reserved

Students enjoy playing "What's in the Box," even when they know the answer.

Once I initiated this activity, I began to have those same concerns about "guessing" that I had had with the estimating-jar-contents activity. Specific questions, such as "Is it a truck?" dominated the activity. Despite my best efforts to explain how to ask a question that narrowed the search, the children's reasoning took them to guessing "the last item identified"; echoing the "guess" of the previous person; or guessing any noun that came into their head, such as *dog*. When the children did not "guess" the contents on one day, I found it difficult to engage them in playing the game again the next day. In addition, I did not notice any improvement in their use of questions to figure out what was inside the box.

I believed the game had the potential to foster the use and refinement of classification and mathematical skills, so what aspects of the game had led my students to ask illogical, irrelevant, and repetitive questions? By suggesting to my students that they "guess" what was in the box, was I inferring that they had no information they could use to come to logical conclusions about its contents? How could I focus the children's attention on the process rather than the product?

As in the estimating activity, the first thing I did was take the word *guess* out of the game. The next time I presented the "treasure box," containing a tricorn hat, I told the children that we would be playing the game differently today. Instead of "guessing," I would expect them to think about what might be in the box before the questions started. I modeled this approach by asking the children, "Would it be reasonable for a teacher to be inside this box?" Using mental-measurement thinking, the children quickly decided that it would be unreasonable because a teacher would be too big to fit inside. Then I asked them to think of other things that would be unreasonable. One student suggested that it would be unreasonable for an ant to be in the box "because it would be so small that it could crawl out the cracks while we weren't watching." After a lengthy discussion, the class concluded that knowing the size would be important and also knowing if the object were alive. I then encouraged the children to think about other kinds of questions that might help them figure out what could be in the box. This approach generated lots of discussion and seemed to help the children bear down intellectually on the task at hand. I decided to forget the "twenty questions" challenge and see what would happen.

The first child asked, "Is it blueberries?"

"No," I answered, discouraged. A pint of blueberries had been placed in the box the last time, when we were reading *Blueberries for Sal* by Robert McClosky (New York: Puffin Books, 1976). What was this child telling me with her question? I decided who better to ask than the children? I departed from the regular game format to ask, "Why do you suppose JoAnne asked me if it was blueberries?" Hands shot up.

Kelly: Maybe because you put stuff we are learning in the box—like the pumpkin when we went to the pumpkin farm.

Lamont: And the 100-dollar bill on 100 day!

Teacher: Oh, so you think we might be studying about the object in the box because this has happened before? What other questions does this make you think of?

The children continued to discuss among themselves the recent topics of study. I heard "teethbrushing," "Abraham Lincoln," "Valentine's Day," "*Abiyoyo*" (a book we were studying).... Again, this talk went counter to the manner in which I thought the game should be played. I wondered if I should allow this discussion, but the continuing pattern of questions assured me that the children were on the right track.

Ben: Does it have anything to do with something we are studying?

Grace: About how many would fit in the box?

At this point I had to make a teaching decision. Was it more important to stick to the game as designed, with its "yes or no" rule, or to feed the children's quantitative and classification thinking. I opted for the latter.

"About six would fit in this box," I replied.

Mathematical thinking ensued as Justin confidently stated, "Then it can't be toothbrushes. More than that would fit inside. Probably more than a hundred!"

I wanted to capitalize on Justin's estimating to extend the children's thinking. "Does Justin's estimation give us any more information or make us think of another question?"

The children posed several more questions, some typical of those they had asked in previous games. "Is it red?" led to a string of color questions until black was asked. At this point I decided the children needed to review what information they had already gathered.

"Let's see, now, what do we know for sure?" I restated that we knew that the object was somehow connected to something we were studying, that six would fit inside the box, and that it was black.

"And we know it's not a toothbrush!" Justin reminded me.

Following his lead, I said, "What else do we know it could not be?"

This question brought a new rush of discussion from the group. A magic wand (from the story *Abiyoyo*) was eliminated because of size, a log cabin was eliminated because of size and color, a teddy bear was eliminated because we were not studying bears, and so on. After a few more questions, some being more focused than in previous games, Marisa asked, "Is it a square?"

The children were closing in now. After they had determined it was triangular in shape, one child asked confidently, "Is it a pirate hat?" As soon as I confirmed it was indeed a tricorn, George Washington's headgear, the children said, "Let's do it again!"

Since I had not previously heard this response while playing this game, I was somewhat confused and asked, "You mean, with something different in the box?"

"No. Let's do it again with the hat!" And so they did. At playtime that day and for several days afterward, small groups of children would put the hat into the box, choose a "teacher," and play the game. It was surprising that no one named the tricorn immediately, even though they knew it was in the box. Instead, they asked different questions each day that helped them focus on the physical and mathematical attributes of the hat. They returned to size

("Is it larger than Abraham Lincoln's hat?") and shape ("Is it shaped like a coat hanger?") over and over again. They considered weight ("Is it heavier than a book?") and experimented with set thinking ("Is it something you wear?"). It was as if when the emphasis was off the "product" (the correct answer), they were more empowered to concentrate on the "process" of asking logical questions. This activity continues to be a favorite, both at our more structured circle time and at free-choice time. Often the children will bring a sack containing an object from home and "orchestrate" a game themselves.

Conclusion

I have made other gradual changes in my kindergarten classroom and believe that I need to make even more modifications so that my presentation of mathematical ideas and concepts encourages my students to believe that mathematics is not mysterious or "magic." By being allowed to use number and volume comparisons to estimate and by being encouraged to develop set thinking and size, capacity, and weight comparisons during classification games, my students, I believe, will begin to view mathematics as a sense-making discipline, something about which to think rather than to guess.

Bibliography

Baratta-Lorton, Mary. *Mathematics Their Way*. Reading, Mass.: Addison-Wesley Publishing Co., 1976.

Harte, Sandra W., and Matthew J. Glover. "Estimation Is Mathematical Thinking." *Arithmetic Teacher* 41 (October 1993):75–77.

Hyde, Arthur, and Pamela Hyde. *Mathwise*. Portsmouth, N.H.: Heinemann Educational Books, 1991.

National Council of Teachers of Mathematics. *Curriculum and Evaluation Standards for School Mathematics*. Reston, Va.: The Council, 1989.

———. *Professional Standards for Teaching Mathematics*. Reston, Va.: The Council, 1991.

Nelson, Joane. "Exact Answer about Estimation." In *Making the Case for Math*. Lexington, Mass.: D. C. Heath & Co., 1992.

Sometimes Less Is More

by

Larry Buschman

This is a true story. Not long ago, on a chilly day in November, a teacher named Mr. B. gave his second-grade students some problems similar to those found in most mathematics textbooks (fig. 1). Since these students would be "problem solving," Mr. B. reminded them that they could use the classroom calculators and would be working in cooperative learning pairs.

Although the students had not been introduced to multiplication, Mr. B. was confident that they could complete this activity successfully. His confidence was based on the fact that all the students had participated in the school's problem-a-day program since the beginning of the school year. This program supplemented the mathematics textbook used in the classroom. Daily problem-solving activities required students to solve problems that required a solution and that had no apparent or immediate answer. To ensure that the students practiced their problem-solving skills and strategies, Mr. B. decided not to include a solution example for the first problem.

The students completed the paper with little difficulty after engaging in long and exuberant discussions over how to solve the problems and the accuracy of their solutions. Mr. B. was pleased with the students' performance during the activity and with their scores. These scores are summarized in table 1.

Later in the school year, as part of the regular textbook curriculum on multiplication, Mr. B. again passed out the same paper previously given to the students in November. However, this time he followed the practice of most textbook publishers and included a solution example for the first problem.

Larry Buschman teaches second grade at Jefferson Elementary School, Jefferson, OR 97352. He is interested in developing students' problem-solving skills.

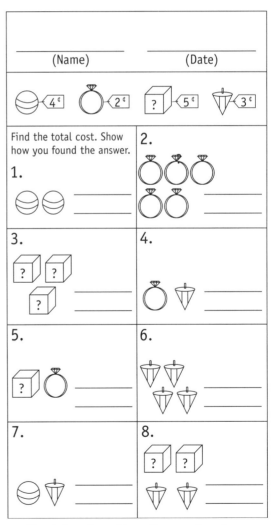

Fig. 1. Sample problems for second graders

Table 1

Number of Students to Answer Incorrectly without a Solution Example

0–1 problem	2–3 problems	4–5 problems
23	3	1

Since many of the students completed the paper in record time without the usual noisy discussions that accompanied most classroom problem-solving activities, Mr. B. assumed that students had remembered the solutions to the problems from their previous exposure. Expecting the students' performance to be even higher, Mr. B. was shocked to learn that their scores were actually lower. The scores appear in table 2.

Table 2

Number of Students to Answer Incorrectly with a Solution Example

0–1 problem	2–3 problems	4–5 problems
7	17	3

Including a solution to the first problem had a profound impact on the students' performance. When they were given an example to follow, that is exactly what these second-grade students did. After seeing the solution example, it was as if the students no longer felt the need to apply higher-order-thinking skills to the solution of the problems and instead relied on lower-order thinking by simply following directions. Perhaps they had come to the conclusion that the solution example indicated that someone else had done their thinking for them and they were free to fill in the blanks and perform the calculations mechanically.

Determined to unravel this mystery, Mr. B. performed an experiment the following school year. He selected four pages from the second-grade mathematics textbook that could be used as problem-solving activities. The students completed each page twice: first with the solution example *removed* from the paper and second with the solution example *included* on the paper, one to two months later. When given the paper the second time, most students did not recognize it as a paper they had completed two months before. The results of this experiment are summarized in table 3.

Although these scores indicate that including a solution to the first problem on each paper influenced students' performance, the scores do not indicate *why* student performance was affected so dramatically. Better to understand this question, the classroom observations conducted by Mr. B. lent some insight into the thinking processes used by these students. These observations were documented through (1) tape recordings of students' conversa-

Table 3

Number of Students to Answer Incorrectly

	0–1 problem	2–3 problems	4–5 problems
Page A			
Without example	23	5	0
With example	11	15	2
Page B			
Without example	18	7	3
With example	9	16	3
Page C			
Without example	13	11	4
With example	5	19	4
***Page D**			
Without example	6	5	2
With example	3	6	4

*The results for page D represent the students' scores for a slightly different version of the experiment conducted by Mr. B. In this version, the class was divided into two groups, each with comparable ability levels. Both groups solved the problems at the same time; half the students completed the page with examples, and the other half completed the page without examples.

tions as they worked in cooperative learning pairs, (2) notes kept by Mr. B. of questions students asked during the activity, and (3) notes kept by Mr. B. of interviews conducted with students after the activity. The following summaries are results of these classroom observations.

When a solution example was not provided, the following behavior occurred:

- Students seemed to assume more ownership for solving the problems and actively explored various solution strategies.

- Students' thinking was generally more divergent in nature and focused on all aspects of the process they used to arrive at an answer.

- Discussions within and between pairs of students were more numerous and lasted longer. These discussions centered on figuring out what to do, clarifying and organizing information, determining a strategy for solving the problem, and checking to make sure the solution was correct and reasonable. (The tone of these discussions was, for the most part, accepting in nature and avoided sharp criticism of other students' ideas, problem solutions, or answers.)

- The most frequently used phrase by students during the activity was "I think...."

- Although the students initially seemed confused by the lack of an example to follow, they displayed a great deal of confidence in their solution strategies.

- Students checked their problem-solving strategies and answers with other groups.

- Students adopted a more individualized and flexible approach to the activity. They had a legitimate problem and searched for a solution.

When a solution example was provided, students exhibited the following behavior:

- Many students relied on the example as "the" correct solution to all the problems on the paper.
- Students' thinking was generally more convergent in nature and focused almost entirely on the answers produced using the example as a guide.
- Discussions within and between pairs were infrequent and brief. They centered primarily on how to apply the solution example to each of the problems and whether the answers themselves were correct. (Of greatest concern to Mr. B. was the tone in which these discussions were carried out. Exchanges between students were often very critical and harsh, especially when anyone was chastised for straying from "the way" shown in the example.)
- The most frequently used phrase by students during the activity was "But the paper [the example solution] says...."
- Although the solution example allowed the students to begin working on the problems immediately, they gradually became more confused and started to distrust their own thinking when it became evident that applying the example was yielding some very questionable answers.

Students thought more creatively when no examples were given.

- Students rarely checked their answers with other groups or attempted to validate their thinking process by consulting with others.

- Students tended to impose on the activity a rigid structure that they seemed obligated to follow. They had a legitimate solution and searched for ways to make it fit the problems on the paper.

These results can be represented by the following axiom: *When learning how to solve problems having no apparent or immediate answer, it is often better not to supply students with solution examples but rather to encourage them to develop their own solutions through applying higher-order-thinking skills and problem-solving strategies.* This procedure will help to ensure that students do their own thinking instead of relying on the thinking of someone else as represented by the solution example. It also helps ensure that students will think more about the problem and their solution, since they have no preconceived "right way" of doing the problems. In a shortened version, this axiom can be stated thus: *Less can be more because sometimes the less information you give students, the more thinking you get from them.* When examples are not included, students are required to take full responsibility for their own thinking, which is a necessary and essential ingredient for successful problem solving.

As more problem-solving activities are incorporated into the mathematics curriculum, it is our responsibility to ensure that these activities promote the development of students' thinking skills rather than direction-following skills. When students are learning how to solve problems, we need to examine carefully how and when solution examples are included on students' assignments. We also need to be aware of the possible negative effects that these examples can have on students' creativity, thinking processes, and performance.

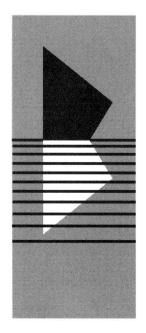

Reflect ... for Better Problem Solving and Reasoning

by

Stephen Krulik and Jesse A. Rudnick

During the past decade, many articles have been written and many speeches have been delivered about using the heuristic method in the mathematics classroom to improve the problem-solving skills of students. Pólya's plan for problem solving, whether in its original four-step model or in one of the modified versions found in contemporary textbooks, has proved to be an effective pedagogical way to improve students' problem-solving performance (Pólya 1980).

Teachers have been encouraged to use this method in their classrooms, and directions to do so have been given by many authors and speakers. Some researchers have suggested that teachers present the heuristic teaching method in its entirety, or "holistically," whereas others have suggested that teachers follow separately the individual steps of *read, plan, solve,* and *look back.* In this article, we carefully examine the final step in the plan—Pólya's "look back," or "examine the solution obtained." The authors were moved in this direction by the emphasis being placed on developing reasoning skills in the *Curriculum and Evaluation Standards for School Mathematics* (NCTM 1989). We are convinced that improving higher-order thinking skills, particularly creative thinking, can be achieved by expanding the "reflect" category, which is the final step of the heuristic method. The choice of the word *reflect* occurred after spending a considerable amount of

time developing classroom strategies that would enable students to improve their thinking skills. The authors are convinced that extended effort in this final stage can greatly contribute to this development.

To many people, this final step of the heuristic method means examine the answer—to determine if it is mathematically correct, see if it makes sense, and check how well it answers the question. These all-important questions, however, do not go far enough. In other words, they are necessary but not sufficient. Much more can be done, as shall be suggested. These additional tasks will allow our students to develop their thinking skills further, as well as improve their problem-solving skills. The problem does not end when an answer has been found and checked for correctness, plausibility, and appropriateness. Rather, this time can be used to expand the critical and creative thinking of the student, allow metacognition to take place, and further self-assessment. It is an opportunity for the teacher and students to create a series of new problems, some more or less difficult than the original and others at the same difficulty level. The word *reflect* indicates the students' actions that should occur at this point in the problem-solving process.

After the answer has been found and checked for computational errors, at least five steps should occur:

1. Test the reasonableness and practicality of the answer.

2. Write a summary paragraph about the problem and its solution.

3. Find other solutions.

4. Change the conditions of the problem.

5. Extend the problem to a mathematical formula, concept, or generalization.

Stephen Krulik teaches at Temple University, Philadelphia, PA 19122, where Jesse Rudnick is an emeritus professor. Together they have coauthored numerous books on problem solving and reasoning for students as well as for teachers at all grade levels from K through 12.

REFLECTING ON PRACTICE IN ELEMENTARY SCHOOL MATHEMATICS

Test the Reasonableness and Practicality of the Answer

Once the students' answer has been checked for mathematical completeness and accuracy, it should be examined to see if it is reasonable. For example, a weight of 517 pounds is hardly reasonable for a seven-year-old (51.7 pounds makes more sense).

> *Problem:* A total of 615 members of the student body are going to the championship football game. Each bus will hold 42 students. How many buses are needed to transport all the students?

A calculator reveals that 14.64 buses are needed. Here, the arithmetic is correct, yet the answer is not practical. Students must interpret the answer to see if it makes sense and if it is reasonable. The answer should be 15 buses. Sometimes even correct arithmetic must be adjusted to make sense.

Write a Summary Paragraph

When the student has found the answer and checked whether it is accurate, practical, and reasonable, a brief paragraph should be written to explain the method used, the reason it was chosen, and the results that were obtained. This paragraph should reveal not only successful attempts but also attempts that led to blind alleys.

The paragraph forces students to examine their thought processes from the beginning of the solution process. It clarifies ideas and presents a running account of the method of attack. This form of metacognition, thinking about one's own thinking, helps the students clarify their thought processes and reflect on their ideas and reasoning skills. Seeing their notes at a later date, students can review the way in which they approached the problem, the manner in which they solved it, and the results that occurred. This approach is far more valuable to students than merely supplying an answer.

From the teacher's point of view, the summary paragraph permits a look inside the student's head to examine the thought processes in which he or she was engaged at the time. It is a part of the assessment process that will be helpful as the school year progresses.

Some teachers have their students keep a journal of their reasoning as they attempt to solve the problem. The authors recommend a summary paragraph instead. The summary paragraph will not disturb the continuous flow of the creativity as students work but will force them to examine the complete thought process.

Find Other Solutions

To allow creative thinking to occur, teachers should ask students who have solved a problem to try it again in a completely different way. No conditions of the problem are changed; everything remains the same as before, but students try to find as many different solutions as possible. It is hoped that all the solutions generate the same answer.

The problem does not end when the answer has been found.

The following problem has appeared in numerous publications. We include it here because it offers several interesting, alternative solutions.

> *Problem:* A farmer sends his son and daughter out into the barnyard to count the number of chickens and the number of pigs. When they return, the son says that he counted a total of 200 legs. The daughter says that she counted 70 heads. How many pigs and how many chickens does the farmer actually have?

Solution 1. For those who have a background in algebra, the solution is straightforward. By representing the number of pigs by p and the number of chickens by c, we obtain the following equations:

$$p + c = 70$$
$$4p + 2c = 200$$

(Of course this setup assumes 1 head per animal, 4 legs per pig, and 2 legs per chicken.) The equations can be solved to obtain the answer of 30 pigs and 40 chickens.

Solution 2. For those not versed in algebra, the answer can be found by using the guess-and-test procedure, accompanied by a carefully drawn table (see table 1). Again, the answer is 30 pigs and 40 chickens. Notice, too, that other guesses might have been made, producing numbers of legs either greater or smaller than the required 200.

Solution 3. Use logic with a guess. Suppose the first guess was 50 pigs and 20 chickens. This guess gives the required 70 heads but also 240 legs. This guess is 40 legs too many! We must reduce the number of legs by 40. Every time we replace a pig with a chicken, we lose 2 legs but keep the number of heads the same. Therefore, we must replace 20 pigs with 20 chickens. The farmer has 30 pigs and 40 chickens.

Solution 4. Draw the animals! Of course, drawing 70 animals might take too long, so simplify the problem:

Table 1
Guess-and-test solutions

	Pigs		Chickens		
	Heads	Legs	Heads	Legs	Total Legs
Guess 1	60	240	10	20	260 (too many)
Guess 2	10	40	60	120	160 (too few)
Guess 3	40	160	30	60	220 (still too many)
Guess 4	35	140	35	70	210 (closer)
Guess 5	30	120	40	80	200 (correct)

Reduce the given numbers by a factor of 10. We'll multiply by 10 at the end. Use 7 animals having 20 legs. Regardless of the kind of animal, legs occur in pairs (see fig. 1), so seven animals have a minimum of 14 legs. Add the remaining 6 legs, which are also in pairs (see fig. 2), to arrive at the answer of 3 four-legged animals and 4 two-legged animals. Multiply these results by 10 to obtain the answer of 30 pigs and 40 chickens.

Fig. 1. Seven animals each with 2 legs

Fig. 2. Seven animals, three with 4 legs

Solution 5. Use the concept of a one-to-one correspondence. Assume all chickens stand on one leg and all pigs stand on their two hind legs. Then we have 70 heads and only 100 legs on the ground. Since the chickens have only 1 leg on the ground and 1 head in the air, the extra 30 legs must belong to the pigs. Thus, again we obtain the answer 30 pigs and 40 chickens.

Students try other approaches after they find the answer.

In each of these solutions, the original problem was not changed. The same conditions were given and the same question was asked; only the solution was different.

What has been achieved by generating five solutions to the same problem as opposed to a single solution to each of five different problems? A great deal! By finding alternative solutions, the original task of analysis and understanding is removed, allowing the students to stretch and think creatively. Students see that problems can be attacked and resolved in more than one way. They should be given time to share their solutions with classmates so that all can profit from the experience. This approach adds to the students' communication skills.

Change the Conditions of the Problem

We call this activity the *what if* phase. In this reflection, the teacher or student makes some changes in the given conditions, such as in the numbers given in the problem. For example, *what if* we use odd numbers instead of even numbers—how will the answer change? Or we might change the given conditions of the problem. For example, *what if* the price of bananas were raised to 69 cents a pound? *What if* the figure were a rhombus instead of a rectangle? This approach permits students to examine the cause-and-effect relationships that exist between the given conditions and the results. Of course, the answer will probably change as well.

Problem: Sarita hit the dart board with exactly 4 darts and scored 55 points. How might she have done it? (See fig. 3.)

Solution. Notice that more than one answer is possible. For example, 31-10-7-7 and 15-15-15-10 are just two possibilities. (This fact in itself is often confusing to many students.) Next, let's change the given conditions (fig. 4).

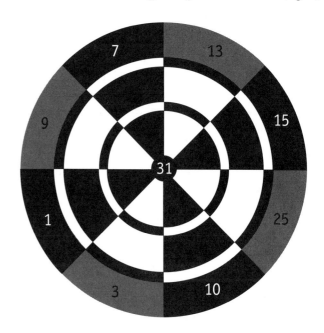

Fig. 3. Dart board used in the original problem

REFLECTING ON PRACTICE IN ELEMENTARY SCHOOL MATHEMATICS

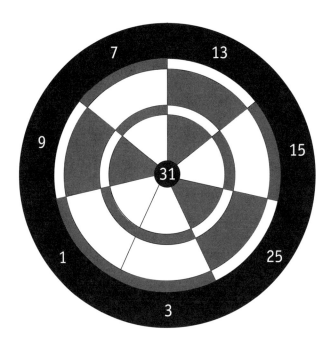

Fig. 4. Dart board used for the *what-if* problem

What if we remove the number 10 from the dart board? How might Sarita have scored 55 points? The students will again use the guess-and-test strategy to find a set of 4 numbers whose sum is 55. It may take a while until someone realizes that all the numbers on the changed dart board are odd numbers, and the sum of four odd numbers can never be an odd number. Thus, this change in the given conditions created a problem whose answer is that no set of numbers exists to satisfy the given condition.

Although this problem as originally presented was of little interest other than for drill and practice and did not require much thought, applying the *what-if* reflection yielded some high-quality mathematics.

Extend the problem

After the student has found the correct answer to the particular problem, he or she should attempt to determine the mathematical formula, concept, or generalization that underlies the problem. The ultimate goal of our work is, of course, to find the mathematics that underlies what we have done. This extension may lead to a formula, a generalization, or a statement about the kinds of numbers reflected in the answer, such as prime numbers, perfect squares, or even numbers.

> *Problem:* At the end of the seventh inning, the score of the championship baseball game was 8-8. How many scores were possible at the end of the sixth inning?

Solution. This problem is an excellent example because any of several solutions are possible. For example, one could write out all the possible scores beginning with 0-0 and ending with 8-8 and reason as follows: The first team could have had any one of 9 scores, 0 through 8. Similarly, the second team could have had any one of 9 scores, 0 through 8. Thus, 9×9, or 81, scores are possible. We could also use the strategy of reduction and expansion (see table 2). We could continue in this manner until we have all the possible scores for an 8-8 game. However, a pattern is revealed. The number of possible scores seems to be related to perfect squares (1, 4, 9, 16, ...). Thus, we might conclude that for a score of 8-8, a total of 9^2, or 81, different scores were possible. Notice that the number of scores is the square of one more than the numerical score.

Table 2
Scores Possible Before the Seventh Inning Is Played

Score at the End of the Seventh Inning	Possible Scores Before the Seventh Inning Is Played	Number of Possible Scores
0-0	0-0	1
1-1	0-0, 1-0, 0-1, 1-1	4
2-2	0-0, 1-0, 2-0, 1-1, 2-1, 0-1, 0-2, 2-2, 1-2	9
3-3	0-0, 1-0, 2-0, 3-0, 0-1, 0-2, 0-3, 1-1, 1-2, 1-3, 2-1, 2-2, 2-3, 3-1, 3-2, 3-3	16

We next extend the problem to a tie score of *n-n*. Examining the pattern that was discovered leads to the formula for the number of scores possible: $(n + 1)^2$. To extend the problem, we ask *what if* the score had not been a tie but had been, say, *a-b*? Similar reasoning will lead to the formula for the number of possible scores as $(a + 1)(b + 1)$. Once the formula is known, the scores for any games can be changed and the answer found.

Each step of the heuristic method is important and plays a key role in the problem-solving process. However, the final heuristic—reflect—affords a magnificent opportunity to stimulate and enhance students' creative-thinking skills. The authors have found not only that reflecting on the problem and its solutions improves creative thinking but that students are motivated by, and enjoy the challenge of, finding alternative solutions, asking *what if,* and finding a mathematical expression or concept that describes the situation.

It is suggested that teachers try "reflecting" in their classrooms. The authors believe that it will produce the desirable outcomes we are all seeking: to make students better problem solvers and reasoners.

Bibliography

Brown, Stephen I., and Marion Walter. *The Art of Problem Posing*. Hillsdale, N.J.: Lawrence Erlbaum Associates, 1990.

Dolan, Daniel, and James Williamson. *Teaching Problem Solving Strategies*. Menlo Park, Calif: Addison-Wesley Publishing Co., 1983.

Krulik, Stephen, ed. *Problem Solving in School Mathematics*. 1980 Yearbook of the National Council of Teachers of Mathematics. Reston, Va.: The Council, 1980.

Krulik, Stephen, and Jesse A. Rudnick. *Reasoning and Problem Solving: A Handbook for Elementary School Teachers*. Needham Heights, Mass.: Allyn & Bacon, 1993.

National Council of Teachers of Mathematics. *Curriculum and Evaluation Standards for School Mathematics*. Reston, Va.: The Council, 1989.

———. *Professional Standards for Teaching Mathematics*. Reston, Va.: The Council, 1991.

Pólya, George. *How to Solve It*. Princeton, N.J.: Princeton University Press, 1973.

Activities

Developing Mathematical Thinking

Krulik and Rudnick, "Reflect … for Better Problem Solving and Reasoning"

As an individual or as a group, use the guidelines in the article to complete the following activities:

(*a*) Select a problem that you have solved recently that was difficult for you, and write a summary paragraph. Describe your solution strategy and results and analyze the difficult aspects of this problem.

(*b*) In your group, select a problem you have done recently and find and write down as many other solutions or solution strategies as possible.

(*c*) Select a problem you have done and change the conditions of the problem. Create one problem that is easier to solve and one that is harder. Write an explanation of why the second problem is harder.

(*d*) In your group, select a problem you have done and extend the problem. Write a group report explaining the mathematical formula, concept, or generalization that underlies the problem. Summarize the processes you used to reach your final mathematical formula or generalization.

General questions on entire Section 5

1. Read the articles in this section and reflect on them.

   (*a*) Develop your own definition of "mathematical thinking."

   (*b*) Compare this definition with the definition of "mathematical power" presented in the discussion of the NCTM Standards documents in Section 1 and with the ideas of mathematical thinking and reasoning in the discussion of discourse in Section 4.

   (*c*) Find other examples of mathematical thinking in the articles presented in other sections of this collection and compare them with your definition.

2. Class Project

   (*a*) Compile a class definition of "mathematical thinking." Brainstorm the attributes of this concept in small groups and combine ideas through a whole-class discussion.

   (*b*) Ask other classes or professional educators to review your definition.

Section 6
Tools and Technology

Calculators and computer technology have changed the nature of the workforce by reducing many jobs to automation and creating new jobs in the support of information technology. Technology has also opened up new ways of looking at, and thinking about, the world. An obvious impact of the pervasiveness of calculators and computers in the larger community is the need for education to prepare students to use technologies effectively as occupational tools.

Calculators and computers serve not only as means to an end (e.g., performing calculations or managing information) but also as pedagogical tools. That is, they can be used to help students reflect on their actions, pose problems, and investigate the structure of ideas. Thus technology provides powerful tools for thinking. The authors in this section discuss the nature of this thinking and furnish examples of how calculators and specific computer software, including databases and spreadsheets, play an important role in NCTM Standards-based mathematics education.

The first two articles in this section focus on the role of calculators in the classroom. Reys and Smith discuss some of the barriers that exist to integrating calculators and describe the changes in how this integration has been carried out over the last twenty years. Higgins points out that the question should be not *whether* but *how* calculators are used in schools. His examples illustrate how calculators can serve as tools to encourage exploration and thought.

The article by Ploger, Klingler, and Rooney describes the power of computer spreadsheets for promoting mathematical exploration and for developing algebraic thinking. Specific activities are presented that enable students to investigate powerful mathematical ideas by posing "what if"

questions and receiving immediate feedback on the reasonableness of their conjectures.

The short "interview" with the Logo turtle by Clements and Meredith sets the stage for the following, longer article (also coauthored by Clements). The authors discuss the software program Logo, emphasizing the pedagogical value of its tool-like environment. This program encourages students to become autonomous and self-motivated as they actively build ideas and solve problems.

The article by Clements and McMillen discusses how manipulatives, both as physical objects and as computer representations, serve as important thinking tools. The authors emphasize that manipulatives do not embody a mathematical idea. Rather, students must build these ideas by working with the tools in effective ways and by reflecting on their activity. Examples of specific computer programs such as Logo illustrate how computer manipulatives can enhance the teaching and learning of mathematics. The range of programs described—from visual representations of base-ten blocks and geoboards to spreadsheets and database software—highlights the variety of educational software available for different kinds of mathematical thinking.

The article by the Cognition and Technology Group at Vanderbilt University presents a different use of technology. Instead of providing tools for computation or the manipulation and investigation of mathematical relationships, the videodisc of The Adventures of Jasper Woodbury creates an environment for in-depth, open-ended problem solving. The article uses one of Jasper's adventures to illustrate the important aspects of mathematical power that students develop as they participate in the program.

In My Opinion

Integrating Calculators
How Far Have We Come?

by

Barbara J. Reys and Nancy L. Smith

Barbara J. Reys   Nancy L. Smith

The mathematics education community has been recommending the integration of calculators into mathematics curriculum and instruction for nearly twenty years. One early statement appeared in the National Advisory Committee on Mathematics Education (NACOME) report (1975, 138):

> At *benchmark 1975* [emphasis added] the National Advisory Committee on Mathematics Education sees the following recommendations as reasonable and essential features of a contemporary mathematics curriculum … that beginning no later than the end of the eighth grade, a calculator should be available for each mathematics student during each mathematics class. Each student should be permitted to use the calculator during all of his or her mathematical work including tests.

Since 1975, every major reform document in mathematics education has stressed and further elaborated the

Barbara Reys teaches at the University of Missouri—Columbia, Columbia, MO 65211. Her interests include the use of calculators and the development of number sense. Nancy Smith teaches at Emporia State University, Emporia, KS 66801. She shares an interest in using calculators and teaching meaningful mathematics.

need for reforming curriculum, materials, teacher preparation, and assessment to integrate calculators in school mathematics. For example, NCTM's *Agenda for Action* (1980, 8–9) extended the recommendation to all grades and stressed the need for integrating technology into instructional materials:

> Mathematics programs must take full advantage of the power of calculators and computers at all grade levels…. Curriculum materials that integrate and require the use of the calculator and computer in diverse and imaginative ways should be developed and made available.

So, why have we not heeded the recommendation? We believe that several barriers exist to integrating calculators as envisioned by the recommendations, including (*a*) teachers' understanding of the role of various computation tools, (*b*) a clearly delineated computation curriculum that offers guidelines for proficiency in various computation methods, (*c*) availability of curriculum materials designed with the assumption that various computation tools are available, and (*d*) assessments that accurately measure the new curriculum.

Alerting Textbook Publishers

To a large extent, the burden of curriculum reform has fallen on textbook publishers. Curriculum frameworks have stressed the importance of incorporating calculators and have demanded redesigned programs and materials. Publishers have responded in varying ways over the past fifteen years.

The first generation of calculator-integrated mathematics textbooks were published in the early to mid-1980s and were characterized by a calculator page or a technology lesson added to the end of each chapter. These activities were generally entertaining, having no real tie to the mathematical content of the chapter. A classic example was this activity: "Do this, then turn your calculator over and read the word on the display." In short, the lesson emphasized making calculators visible but not altering the mathematical content or instructional emphasis of the text.

The second generation of textbooks appeared in the middle to late 1980s. During this time, integrating the calculator meant making the calculator *more* visible but not changing the mathematical content of the textbook. Calculator activities were expanded from the technology page in the back of the chapter to ancillary pages for calculators, features on the bottom of the right-hand page of the typical two-page-lesson spread, and an occasional sprinkling of calculator logos in the exercise set. The logos were meant to signal students that they were to use a calculator.

During this time, one publisher inserted a calculator into the binding of each elementary school textbook in its series. Although the idea had potential, the folly of the approach was quickly recognized as reviewers realized that students would ultimately be asked to compute by hand while a calculator lay literally inches from the exercises. This approach underscored the necessity to rethink the role of computation in the curriculum when alternative computational tools are available to students.

The third generation of textbooks, the ones currently used, appeared in the late 1980s and early 1990s. For the first time, some mathematics content has been significantly modified. Integrating the calculator has eliminated some traditional content and features. For example, in some series, the use of two-digit divisors has been moved from the fourth grade to the fifth grade. Division with three digits has practically disappeared. Calculator features located at the end of the book or at the end of a lesson and calculator-targeted exercises appear less frequently.

Current textbooks also present alternative computational procedures including mental computation and estimation. Philosophy statements currently appear in many teachers' editions describing the important role that calculators play in teaching and learning mathematics.

An Essential Tool

Progress has been made; however, more progress is needed if we are to realize the vision outlined in reform documents. The next generation needs textbook materials in which the calculator is regarded as an essential tool, along with the many other tools we consider essential in a modern classroom. These materials must also address the main obstacle to true integration of calculators—the traditional emphasis on paper-and-pencil computation. What computational tools, procedures, and skill levels do we value at the elementary level? Should students learn standard written algorithms? If so, which ones, when, and to what level of difficulty?

The curriculum materials advocated by reform documents will more likely evolve if leadership deals with these fundamental issues. Curriculum developers, textbook publishers, and teachers should demand that the professional community address these questions so that at benchmark 2000 we are closer to the vision.

References

Conference Board of the Mathematical Sciences, National Advisory Committee on Mathematics Education (NACOME). *Overview and Analysis of School Mathematics, Grades K–12.* Reston, Va.: National Council of Teachers of Mathematics, 1975.

National Council of Teachers of Mathematics. *An Agenda for Action.* Reston, Va.: The Council, 1980.

One Point of View

Calculators and Common Sense

by

Jon L. Higgins

When NCTM released its *Curriculum and Evaluation Standards for School Mathematics* in March 1989, I looked for the reaction of the press to this very important document. In almost every newspaper the headline or the thrust of the article related to the *Standards* was that NCTM now recommended that calculators be used in mathematics classrooms. How discouraging! NCTM members know that in March 1989 that recommendation was very old news. Even worse was the fact that the more substantial recommendations of the *Standards* were generally ignored.

Because they are tangible, calculators will probably always be more newsworthy than abstract ideas, such as a mathematics core curriculum. Rather than wish that the calculator issue would go away, it is time to try to bring some common sense to the topic. Despite the publicity given to arguments about using calculators in the mathematics classroom, I believe that we are devoting time and energy to a nonissue. The real issue is not *whether* calculators should be used in mathematics classrooms; it is *how* calculators should be used in classrooms. We ignore this important distinction when, as a profession, we proclaim that the use of calculators should be required. Requiring the use of calculators by mathematics students is a dramatic attention grabber, but I believe that it is a professional

Jon Higgins works with preservice teachers and teaches graduate courses in mathematics education at Ohio State University, Columbus, OH 43210. He is interested in relating learning theories to the teaching of mathematics.

blunder. We need to focus on how the teacher guides students in the use of the calculator, and in some situations we should require that unimaginative mathematics teachers not use calculators.

In many instances, those who are against the use of calculators in the classroom and those who are for the use of calculators seem to be talking past each other. These camps seem not to realize that they are talking about very different ways to use calculators. As a result, both sides can point to appropriate "horror stories" to bolster their positions. I recently visited a general mathematics classroom in which some of my undergraduate students had been observing. One of them decried the fact that some of the general mathematics students could not find 10 percent of a number without using a calculator. What a wonderful example for those who believe that calculators "rot the mind"! If calculators are used as a substitute for thinking, of course they rot the mind! It is only human nature to try to minimize difficult thinking, and in today's stressful workplace such strategies may be vital survival skills. Nevertheless, the avoidance of thinking in classrooms is not appropriate for learning. The use of calculators to avoid thinking is inappropriate. Simply keying a problem from a mathematics textbook into a calculator and pressing the equals key may very well be a way to avoid thinking. Teachers who cannot imagine any other ways to use calculators in classrooms should be required to stop using calculators in mathematics classrooms at once!

But of course, calculators can be used in other ways. One of my students told me that she had never successfully taught the concept of pi until she started using calculators. Oh yes, she had had students measure lots of circumferences and lots of diameters, but in the process of doing the long division with paper and pencil everyone got bogged down and lost the idea of ratio. If calculators are used, the time usually required for division is freed for other things. One exciting introductory activity is to show students cross sections of various circular objects—a pill bottle, a soft-drink can, and a wastebasket might be examples. Then ask them to predict the relative sizes of the quotients if one were to measure each circumference and divide by the corresponding diameter. Most children, and many adults, will agree that the wastebasket should give a division answer much bigger than the pill bottle, for example. By measuring with string and using calculators to divide, students can very quickly focus on the fact that the differences are not evident until the first or second decimal place. Using the calculator has shifted the focus from the calculation to the idea behind the calculation. But it has not served as a substitute for thinking.

Consider the calculation of 10 percent. The matter of "taking a percent" seems very much like an operation, and if one uses a calculator that has a percent key, the process does seem like a new operation. But is "taking a percent" related to other operations? If 50 percent is half of something and 33 1/3 percent is one-third of something, is 20 percent, or 10 percent, also related to dividing? Does one really need a calculator to divide or multiply by 10? If a calculator is used to help answer a series of questions like these, then I would maintain that the calculator is not being used as a substitute for thinking. It is used once again to shift the focus from the calculation to the idea behind the calculation.

How, in general, is this shifting accomplished? The two foregoing examples, as well as the hundreds more that readers can generate, have one thing in common. They use the calculator to *explore*. The key to exploration in the classroom is finding the necessary time. And time is exactly what can be saved by using calculators—time for searching, conjecturing, and testing—in short, time for thinking. If calculators are used to explore and to encourage thought, then and only then should calculators be required in mathematics classrooms. But if calculators are used to avoid thinking about mathematics problems, then of course they should be banned. Perhaps NCTM should issue licenses that would permit mathematics teachers to use calculators in classrooms; teachers who could not give examples of mathematical explorations with calculators should be forbidden to use them in teaching.

Finally, I have suspected for some time now that one of the things that sets good teachers apart from ordinary teachers is that the good ones don't take anything for granted! As a profession, we tend to take for granted that students can judge when calculator use is appropriate and when it is inappropriate. This assumption is almost certainly false. We need explicitly to teach students when mental arithmetic and paper-and-pencil calculations have an advantage over calculators. Several years ago I had the good fortune to participate in a contest between ten fourth graders with paper and pencil and me with a calculator on twenty simple subtraction problems. Because the subtraction problems could all be done by mental arithmetic (e.g., $18 - 7 = ?$), all ten of the fourth graders beat the professor, who laboriously had to key every number and operation into his calculator. Every student learned something that day about appropriate and inappropriate uses of calculators! We need to build a lot of these lessons into our curriculum and have explicit discussions with students about the best use of calculators. Knowing how to use a calculator should also include knowing when to use a calculator.

"Should calculators be required in every mathematics classroom?" I believe that that question misses the point and is inappropriate. "How should calculators be used in mathematics classrooms?" is the appropriate question. When one looks at the appropriate question, common sense suggests that some uses of calculators are appropriate and that other uses of calculators are inappropriate. Instead of globally mandating the use of calculators or globally banishing them from the classroom, it's time to use common sense.

Reference

National Council of Teachers of Mathematics. *Curriculum and Evaluation Standards for School Mathematics.* Reston, Va.: The Council, 1989.

Spreadsheets, Patterns, and Algebraic Thinking

by

Don Ploger, Lee Klingler, and Michael Rooney

What is the first Fibonacci number greater than a million? Can elementary teachers use a challenging problem, such as this, to enhance the algebraic thinking of their students? Even with a calculator, the computations are quite tedious. The computer is certainly the right tool for the job; the problem is to find appropriate software. We have found that elementary school students can productively explore such questions using a computer spreadsheet.

Children display a tremendous intellectual curiosity about number patterns. Computer spreadsheets provide a vehicle for students to express that curiosity, allowing them to explore number patterns algebraically while the computer performs the tedious calculations. In the very act of telling the computer what to do, students must think algebraically, expressing themselves using algebraic formulas in an intuitively meaningful way. Moreover, instantaneous feedback from the computer allows the students to see immediately whether their reasoning is correct. They can decide if the answer is reasonable, ask what further results might be obtained, and then pose problems based on those results.

Don Ploger, ploger@acc.fau.edu, teaches at Florida Atlantic University in Davie, FL 33314. He is interested in using technology to help students learn mathematics. Lee Klingler, klingler@acc.fau.edu, teaches at the Boca Raton campus of Florida Atlantic University, Boca Raton, FL 33431. In addition to his research interest in abstract algebra, he is interested in the mathematical preparation of future teachers. Michael Rooney teaches at Welleby Elementary School, Sunrise, FL 33352. In addition to teaching mathematics to children in grades K–5, he offers workshops for in-service teachers.

This article describes the results of a fifth-grade class using spreadsheets to investigate challenging mathematical topics. Consistent with the *Curriculum and Evaluation Standards for School Mathematics*, children are encouraged to "recognize, describe, extend, and create a wide variety of patterns" (NCTM 1989, 60). After a few weeks of guided exploration, many children can, with just a few minutes of effort, set up a spreadsheet to list the Fibonacci numbers. They can also program spreadsheets to generate odd and even numbers, a multiplication table, squares, square roots, and exponential growth.

We outline an intuitive approach for introducing the concepts of functions and sequences through investigating the topics just discussed. We also provide guidelines to help teachers use this powerful technology to enhance the algebraic thinking of their students. Recent NCTM publications have recognized the power of spreadsheets for high school mathematics teachers (Masalski 1990) and middle school teachers (Russell 1992). Our aim is to describe a set of specific learning activities to help elementary school children use almost any commercially available package to create their own spreadsheet models. (The instructions can be applied directly to ClarisWorks, Excel, Lotus for Windows, and Great Works; with other spreadsheet packages, slight modifications might be required.) Our discussion applies most directly to the fifth grade, but the ideas can easily be applied to the fourth or even third grades.

Introducing Spreadsheets

Computer spreadsheets display a grid of rows and columns, and the resulting rectangular cells can contain numbers. Spreadsheets will perform arithmetic in a straightforward manner. Furthermore, spreadsheets will repeat calculations, as will a constant key on a calculator.

However, unlike a calculator, a spreadsheet can display a long list of calculations, and the resulting numerical data can readily be used in further calculations. Furthermore, spreadsheets can also contain text, making it easy to arrange and label the data.

Begin by telling students to open the spreadsheet icon on any Macintosh or any computer that supports Windows. Each computer screen will show something that resembles figure 1. Notice that the example spreadsheet has four columns, labeled A, B, C, and D, and ten rows, labeled 1 through 10. The cursor is located in row 1 of column A, referred to as cell A1. All cells follow this notation: the lower-right cell, for example, is D10.

After explaining how to name the rows, columns, and cells of a spreadsheet, explain that spreadsheets will do arithmetic. You can also mention that spreadsheets will repeat calculations and show you a long list of calculations all at once. To achieve these benefits, students need to know how to (1) enter a value, (2) calculate a value, and (3) extend a pattern. The following example will illustrate how to generate the first ten even numbers.

	A	B	C	D
1				
2				
3				
4				
5				
6				
7				
8				
9				
10				

Fig. 1. A blank spreadsheet

The Even Numbers

To produce the even numbers (2, 4, 6, 8, …) in column A, begin by entering the first value of the sequence: Put your cursor in cell A1 and type "2." When you press the ENTER key, the value of 2 will appear in cell A1.

To assign the next value in the sequence, increment the first value: Put your cursor in cell A2 and type "=A1+2." When you press the ENTER key, the value of 4 will appear in cell A2.

Finally, to extend the pattern, click your mouse on cell A2, and drag down to cell A10. Go to the "Calculate" window and select "Fill down." The first ten even numbers will appear in the first ten cells of column A (fig. 2a).

	A
1	2
2	4
3	6
4	8
5	10
6	12
7	14
8	16
9	18
10	20

(a) The even numbers

	A
1	1
2	3
3	5
4	7
5	9
6	11
7	13
8	15
9	17
10	19

(b) The odd numbers

	A	B	C
1	1	2	3
2	2	4	6
3	3	6	9
4	4	8	12
5	5	10	15
6	6	12	18
7	7	14	21
8	8	16	24
9	9	18	27
10	10	20	30

(c) The first three columns of Elena's times table

Fig. 2

Encouraging "What If" Thinking

Computer spreadsheets provide excellent opportunities for students to explore mathematical possibilities. For example, students asked, "What if we change the first number?" They found that no matter what number they selected, a pattern was present: counting by twos. Furthermore, if the first number is even, all the numbers are even; if the first number is odd, all are odd. Figure 2b shows the odd numbers. Note that all that is needed is to change a single value (typing "1" in cell A1) to get these numbers.

At this point, the teacher suggested, "What if we change the number in our assignment statement?" Robert changed the assignment statement in cell A2 to "=A1+10." Then he changed the value of A1 to 10, and he produced the multiples of ten. Following Robert's discovery, other students produced the multiples of other numbers.

After students had explored the idea, the teacher asked whether they could make a multiplication table. No one solved the problem during that session. The next day, Elena arranged the first column with multiples of 1; the second, with multiples of 2; and so on, up to 10. Part of her result is shown in figure 2c.

As these examples illustrate, spreadsheets can generate considerable interest among students who are exploring number patterns. Often students pose their own "what if" questions spontaneously. At other times, the teacher poses a what-if question as a prompt, allowing students to complete the solution. On occasion the teacher illustrates what-if thinking by showing an example *and* the solution.

The "Penny Doubling" Problem

Some students noted that they had seen the "penny doubling" problem: You have the choice of receiving $1 000 per day for a month or a penny the first day, two pennies the second day, four the third day, and so on, always doubling the previous day's amount until the end of the month. Jennifer remembered that the penny-doubling method resulted in more money, but none of the students could recall the precise details.

The students wanted to put "penny doubling" into a spreadsheet. They placed the numbers 1 through 31 in column A, using the assignment statement "=A1+1." Then we began to enter the values of the pennies in column B. On day 1 a single penny was received, so the students entered 1 in cell B1. On day 2, two pennies were received, so the students entered 2 in cell B2. The teacher asked, "What would be a good assignment statement for cell B3?" One student suggested "=B2+2." When this pattern was continued down column B, the result was 60 cents on day 31. The children saw immediately that this statement was not the correct answer. When they correctly changed the assignment statement to "=B2*2," over a billion pennies were received on day 31 (see fig. 3). The asterisk indicates multiplication.

Children display a tremendous intellectual curiosity about number patterns.

Once they saw the pattern, students spent time wondering what they would do with $10 million. When they finished their discussion, the teacher asked, "What is the sum of all the money on all thirty-one days?" At first, the students said that the problem was too difficult.

The teacher showed how to record the sums. In cell C1, the sum of the first day was entered by typing "=B1." The sum of the first two days was the sum of the previous day plus the total of the second day, which was entered in cell C2 as "=C1+B2." When this pattern was continued, the sums for each day appeared in column C.

After a few minutes, the students began to see a pattern: the sum is one penny less than twice the amount for any given day and, therefore, a penny less than the amount for the following day. For example, on day 4, the amount received is 8 and the total is 15, or one less than the amount received on day 5, which is 16 (see fig. 4).

A	B
1	1
2	2
3	4
4	8
5	16
6	32
7	64
8	128
9	256
10	512
11	1024
12	2048
13	4096
14	8192
15	16384
16	32768
17	65536
18	131072
19	262144
20	524288
21	1048576
22	2097152
23	4194304
24	8388608
25	16777216
26	33554432
27	67108864
28	134217728
29	268435456
30	536870912
31	1073741824

Fig. 3. The results of the penny-doubling problem

A	B	C
1	1	1
2	2	3
3	4	7
4	8	15
5	16	31
6	32	63
7	64	127
8	128	255
9	256	511
10	512	1023

Fig. 4. The sum of the penny doubling

Exploring Powers

Students became interested in raising numbers to various powers. They quickly saw how easy it was to construct a table that raised each of the first ten counting numbers to the powers 1 through 6.

The students spontaneously invented the following method. First, they put headers as shown in row 1 of figure 5. Then, in

n	n^2	n^3	n^4	n^5	n^6
1	1	1	1	1	1
2	4	8	16	32	64
3	9	27	81	243	729
4	16	64	256	1024	4096
5	25	125	625	3125	15625
6	36	216	1296	7776	46656
7	49	343	2401	16807	117649
8	64	512	4096	32768	262144
9	81	729	6561	59049	531441
10	100	1000	10000	100000	1000000

Fig. 5. The first ten counting numbers raised to powers

column A, they numbered cells A2 through A11 from 1 through 10; note that the header was in cell A1. In cell B2, they entered "=A2*1" and continued that pattern across the second row. In cell B3, they entered "=A3*2" and continued the pattern of doubling the neighboring cell across the third row. They continued this pattern for each of the numbers in column A, tripling the numbers in succession across the fourth row, and so on. The result is shown in figure 5.

They noted a pattern. The first six powers of 2 are 2, 4, 8, 16, 32, and 64. The first three powers of 4 are 4, 16, and 64. This pattern can be extended to show the powers of 8 and 16 (see fig. 6).

A	B	C	D
2	4	8	16
4	16	64	256
8	64	512	4096
16	256	4096	65536
32	1024	32768	1048576
64	4096	262144	16777216
128	16384	2097152	
256	65536	16777216	
512	262144		
1024	1048576		
2048	4194304		
4096	16777216		
8192			

Fig. 6. The first few powers of 2, 4, 8, and 16

Note that the powers of 4 consist of every other power of 2, the powers of 8 are every third power of 2, and the powers of 16 are every fourth power of 2. If a number is found anywhere in the powers of 4, 8, or 16, then it will be found in the powers of 2. Every number in the powers of 16 is found in both the powers of 4 and 2.

A similar pattern was found for the powers of 3 (3, 9, 27, 81, 243, and 729) and nine (9, 81, and 729). You

might ask students whether all of the powers of 9 would be found in the powers of 3. Suggest that they predict a pattern, such as that every other power of 3 is a power of 9, and then test their prediction by extending both sequences. Ask them what other number patterns might fit this relationship.

This activity is a starting point for a deep intuitive understanding of the laws of exponents. For example, the idea that every power of 4 is found as every second power of 2 can be expressed formally as $4^n = 2^{2n}$. Students do not, however, need to use complicated terminology. Instead, they notice patterns in sequences of numbers.

Fibonacci Numbers

The teacher showed the students how to create the Fibonacci numbers. They entered 1 in cell A1 and 1 in cell A2. In cell A3, the teacher told them to enter "=A1+A2." Then the students extended the pattern down column A to display the first ten.

After the students had the first ten Fibonacci numbers in the spreadsheet, the teacher asked, "When do you think the Fibonacci number will be greater than one million?" Although most of their guesses were relatively high, such as the 1 000th term, Edgar guessed 30. He reasoned that this guess is similar to the repeated-doubling pattern, and so 30 seemed to be reasonable. As it turns out, the 31st Fibonacci number is the first to be greater than one million. The student's reasoning is only approximate, 2^{30} is approximately one billion, so, to a certain degree, Edgar made a lucky guess. But he correctly realized that the Fibonacci sequence would become very large in relatively few terms. Most important, he was speculating about ways to extend patterns to include very large numbers, and we encouraged such attempts. Edgar's spreadsheet version of the Fibonacci sequence is shown in figure 7.

Spreadsheets provide a medium for the development of what-if thinking.

It is extremely easy to modify the Fibonacci sequence, and students can see the interesting patterns that result, such as those shown in figure 8. Column A shows the standard sequence; column B shows a variation where the first two numbers have been changed from 1, 1 to 2, 2. In column C, the first two numbers are 10.

	A
1	1
2	1
3	2
4	3
5	5
6	8
7	13
8	21
9	34
10	55
11	89
12	144
13	233
14	377
15	610
16	987
17	1597
18	2584
19	4181
20	6765
21	10946
22	17711
23	28657
24	46368
25	75025
26	121393
27	196418
28	317811
29	514229
30	832040
31	1346269

Fig. 7. The Fibonacci numbers

Note that every number in column B is twice the corresponding number in column A and that every number in column C is ten times the corresponding number in column A.

From Patterns to Functions

The sequence of even numbers can be examined from a different perspective. Show students figure 9 and ask them to create it on their spreadsheet. Most students will make the numbers in column B by entering 2 in cell B1, and typing "=B1+2" in cell B2, which is of course true. The even numbers can be thought of as being a sequence in which each term is 2 more than the previous term.

Once the students were familiar with this method, the teacher showed another way to get the values in column B: The value of B1 can be assigned "=A1*2"; this assignment statement can then be filled down. Students have found the entry in B5, for example, in two different ways: 5*2 and also 2+2+2+2+2. Because these two calculations yield the same result, students get experimental confirmation that multiplication is repeated addition.

Each approach has advantages. On the one hand, repeated addition is much more intuitive to elementary school children. On the other hand, simple multiplication by 2 lets the students directly find the 100th even number. (The last row in fig. 9 shows this result.) To get the 100th value using the repeated-addition approach, it is necessary to extend the pattern to see the 100th term.

	A	B	C
1	1	2	10
2	1	2	10
3	2	4	20
4	3	6	30
5	5	10	50
6	8	16	80
7	13	26	130
8	21	42	210
9	34	68	340
10	55	110	550

Fig. 8. Patterns with the Fibonacci numbers

A	B
1	2
2	4
3	6
4	8
5	10
6	12
7	14
8	16
9	18
10	20
100	200

Fig. 9. Some integral values of the function $f(x) = 2x$

This activity provides an intuitive preparation for understanding linear functions. Although it would be premature to introduce the function notation, $f(x) = 2x$, to fifth-grade students, they are nevertheless readily able to create spreadsheet models of the number patterns. Consequently, these students have developed a rich set of intuitive ideas that can serve as the basis of a deep understanding of the concept of a mathematical function.

(Note that the students were developing an informal understanding of recursive functions. A formal definition of a recursive function is beyond this level. However, it intuitively means that one starts with the first term(s) of a sequence and then defines each "next term" from previous term(s). For example, to find out the tenth term of a sequence, one would have to know about the previous term(s). This recursive process explains, basically, the way computer spreadsheets work and is a powerful way of thinking mathematically.)

Conclusion

This study has a number of practical implications. We have shown how computer tools can bring powerful ideas into the elementary school classroom. Children learn how to use spreadsheets to explore powerful ideas in mathematics. They learn how to generate patterns, create a running total, and create a pattern using a formula. Most significant, students learn to pose problems and to create explorations of their own.

Furthermore, students can use spreadsheets to explore patterns that they have learned previously or that occur to them during their explorations. Spreadsheets supply a rich representation that can be examined for patterns, as in the comparison of the powers of 2 with the powers of 4.

This use of technology is a good way to help prepare children for algebra. They see the effects of algebraic transformations on familiar numbers. As a result, they are relieved of the tedious burden of arithmetic calculations, and they can use algebra without being confused by unfamiliar symbols. Students used formulas in a meaningful way, and they received immediate feedback in the change of the number pattern.

In introducing functions, we look at number patterns from two points of view. On the one hand, we look for patterns in a sequence of numbers, asking the question "How do we get from one member of the sequence to the next?" For example, in the sequence of even numbers, we get from one even number to the next by adding 2. On the other hand, we look for patterns in functions, asking the question "How do we get a particular member of the sequence directly?" For example, in the sequence of even numbers, we get the nth even number by multiplying n by 2. Spreadsheets allow students to discover both of these powerful ideas and in so doing, help them relate their ideas of number patterns to the mathematical concept of a function.

Computer spreadsheets provide a medium for the development of what-if thinking. Students can ask, "What if we change the first number?" and a single keystroke can change the pattern in a systematic way. In a similar fashion, students can modify assignment statements and assemble similar patterns to build mathematical tables. In this study, students began with simple elements and then progressively created the multiplication table and their own version of a table of powers. The students generated many powerful what-if questions, and they gained increasing skill in the art of problem posing.

References

Masalski, William J. *How to Use the Spreadsheet as a Tool in the Secondary Mathematics Classroom.* Reston, Va.: The Council, 1990.

National Council of Teachers of Mathematics. *Curriculum and Evaluation Standards for School Mathematics.* Reston, Va.: The Council, 1989.

Russell, John C. *Spreadsheet Activities in Middle School Mathematics.* Reston, Va.: The Council, 1992.

One Point of View

My Turn
A Talk with the Logo Turtle

by
Douglas H. Clements and Julie Sarama Meredith

What might be the role of using Logo in mathematics education, given the information in the *Curriculum and Evaluation Standards* (NCTM 1989) and the appearance of numerous new software packages? A recent rare interview with the Logo turtle may dispel some rumors and offer new insights into this question.

Interviewer: Start us off with the big picture. Can computers be used effectively in school?

Turtle: Research shows that students make significant learning gains using computers, especially in mathematics (Clements and Nastasi 1992; Roblyer, Castine, and King 1988). These

Douglas Clements teaches at the State University of New York at Buffalo, Buffalo, NY 14260. He is interested in students' learning of geometry, especially in computer environments. Julie Meredith is a research assistant currently working on a new version of Logo with Clements.

Portions of this article were originally published by the International Society for Technology in Education (ISTE) in Clements, D. H. "Logo: Search and Research, Turtle Talk." *Logo Exchange* 10 (Fall 1991):43–47. Funding for this material was partially provided by the National Science Foundation under grants no. MDR-8651668, MDR-9050210, and MDR-8954664. Any opinions, findings, conclusions, and recommendations expressed in this publication are those of the authors and do not necessarily reflect the views of the National Science Foundation.

gains are consistent across schools and grades.

I: So, computers are effective.

T: Yes, but this research doesn't imply that using *any* software in *any* way guarantees automatic learning.

I: The Logo language has been around for decades. Shouldn't we be looking at what's new?

T: This issue really gets under my shell. Logo is not "old" software; it is evolving. I've heard people say that newer software is easier to use. One consultant said, "I don't suggest Logo anymore, now that we have Dazzle Draw." The point is not the drawing, it's thinking about doing the drawing (Clements and Battista 1992). A lot more thought has to go into deciding what should be "easy" and what should remain a struggle, in the positive sense of the word. Sometimes you have to stick your neck out.

Programs must become tools for thinking.

I: But shouldn't students use a lot of different types of programs?

T: Yes, except that the programs they use should become tools for thinking. We need to be wary of serving a potpourri of applications with no internal coherence. Research comparing Logo with a set of utility and problem-solving programs demonstrated that stronger feelings of control and mastery emerged with Logo (Clements and Nastasi 1992).

I: Well, how about good drill and practice? Did you say that it doesn't matter whether you use drill-and-practice software or Logo, as long as it's a good-quality product?

T: No! I agree that research indicates that both approaches, done right, can raise achievement scores. But that's just the beginning. You have to consider *your* goals. Recent recommendations for school reform, such as those in the *Curriculum and Evaluation Standards* (NCTM 1989) demand that certain approaches be emphasized.

The turtle went on to further discuss the connection between Logo and the Curriculum Standards. The *Standards* document discusses Logo specifically:

> Computer microworlds such as Logo turtle graphics and the topics of constructions and loci provide opportunities for a great deal of student involvement. In particular, the first two contexts serve as excellent vehicles for students to develop, compare, and apply algorithms (p. 159).

However, other excerpts from the *Curriculum Standards* that do not mention Logo better exemplify its full power.

> In learning geometry, children need to investigate, experiment, and explore ... (p. 48).

> When mathematics evolves naturally from problem situations that have meaning to children and are regularly related to their environment, it becomes relevant and helps children link their knowledge to many kinds of situations (p. 23).

> A major goal of mathematics instruction is to help children develop the belief that they have the power to do mathematics and that they have control over their own success or failure (p. 29).

What should be "easy" and what should remain a struggle?

The Logo philosophy and the constructivist philosophy of the Curriculum Standards have the same two major goals (Clements and Battista 1990). First, students should actively experience building ideas and solving personally meaningful problems. Second, students should become autonomous and self-motivated.

I: So, Logo fits the philosophy of the Curriculum Standards.

T: I don't mean to be too hard-shelled, but I remember when some mathematics educators called the Logo philosophy "romantic" and "unrealistic." Now that the

Standards document expresses a similar point of view, Logo should be increasingly discussed at professional conferences. But it's not nearly enough.

I: But I've heard that students don't always do mathematics when they use Logo.

T: I never intended to work alone. I talk mathematics. But students don't always listen (Leron 1985). I need teachers' help. To produce successful Logo projects, teachers don't load Logo and then withdraw into their shells. They think about the Logo tasks. They help students enrich their intuitive, visual strategies ("It looks like about FD 30") by presenting problems that also require *analytic* solutions, such as drawing figures with the turtle (see fig. 1).

Students reflect on their work.

Successful teachers talk to students about their work and encourage them to talk to each other. They are responsible for guiding and supporting students' viable ideas rather than transmitting "correct" adult knowledge. As a result, their students reflect on their individual work and *link* what they know in and out of the Logo environment (Clements and Battista 1992). (A bibliography of teaching resources is listed at the end of this article.)

Surprising research results from using Logo appear in its social and emotional benefits to students. Students cooperate more while working in Logo environments, and they concentrate on learning. They may disagree more about ideas, but they are more likely to resolve these disagreements successfully by synthesizing their ideas (Clements and Nastasi 1992; Nastasi, Clements, and Battista 1990).

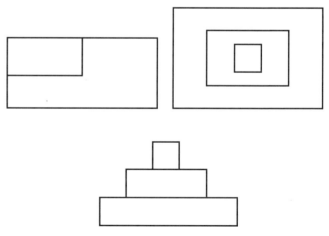

Fig. 1. Figures drawn using the Logo turtle

I: I know you must leave to make a screen appearance. Can you summarize your thoughts for us?

T: I don't mean to "repeat" myself, but research suggests that if you want a safe and relatively easy path, choose drill-and-practice software. You'll probably increase achievement. If instead you want to effect substantive change in the quality of your students' educational experiences, use Logo software, but be ready to work hard at it. But, as my grandfather told me, slow but steady wins the race.

References

Clements, Douglas H., and Michael T. Battista. "Research into Practice: Constructivist Learning and Teaching." *Arithmetic Teacher* 38 (September 1990):34–35.

———. "Geometry and Spatial Reasoning." In *Handbook of Research on Mathematics Teaching and Learning*, edited by D. A. Grouws, 420–64. New York: Macmillan Publishing, 1992.

Clements, Douglas H., and Bonnie K. Nastasi. "Computers and Early Childhood Education." In *Advances in School Psychology: Preschool and Early Childhood Treatment Directions*, edited by M. Gettinger, S. N. Elliott, and T. R. Kratochwill, 187–246. Hillsdale, N.J.: Lawrence Erlbaum Associates, 1992.

Leron, Uri. "Logo Today: Vision and Reality." *Computing Teacher* 12 (February 1985):26–32.

Nastasi, Bonnie K., Douglas H. Clements, and Michael T. Battista. "Social-Cognitive Interactions, Motivation, and Cognitive Growth in Logo Programming and CAI Problem-solving Environments." *Journal of Educational Psychology* 82 (March 1990):150–58.

National Council of Teachers of Mathematics. *Curriculum and Evaluation Standards for School Mathematics*. Reston, Va.: The Council, 1989.

Roblyer, M. D., W. H. Castine, and F. J. King. *Assessing the Impact of Computer-based Instruction: A Review of Recent Research*. New York: Haworth Press, 1988.

Bibliography

Battista, Michael T., and Douglas H. Clements. "Research into Practice: Constructing Geometric Concepts in Logo." *Arithmetic Teacher* 38 (November 1990):15–17.

———. *Logo Geometry*. Morristown, N.J.: Silver Burdett & Ginn, 1991.

Clarke, Valerie A., and Susan M. Chambers. *Thinking with Logo*. New York: McGraw-Hill, 1985.

Goldenberg, E. Paul. "Learning to Think Algebraically." *Logo Exchange* 5 (October 1986): 16–20.

Harper, Dennis. *Logo: Theory and Practice*. Pacific Grove, Calif.: Brooks/Cole Publishing Co., 1989.

Hoyles, Celia, and Richard Noss. *Learning Mathematics and Logo*. Cambridge, Mass.: MIT Press, 1992.

Logo Exchange. Eugene, Oreg.: SIGLogo/ISTE.

Nevile, Liddy, and Carolyn Dowling. *Let's Talk Apple Turtle*. Reston, Va.: Prentice-Hall, 1983.

Ryoti, Don E. "Computer Corner: Using the Computer and Logo to Investigate Symmetry." *Arithmetic Teacher* 34 (November 1986):36–37.

Shimabukuro, Bini. *Thinking in Logo: A Sourcebook for Teachers of Primary Students*. Menlo Park, Calif.: Addison-Wesley Publishing Co., 1988.

Shumway, Richard J. "Why Logo?" *Arithmetic Teacher* 32 (May 1985):18–19.

Thomas, Eleanor M., and Rex A. Thomas. "Exploring Geometry with Logo." *Arithmetic Teacher* 32 (September 1984):16–18.

Watt, Molly, and Daniel Watt. *Teaching with Logo*. Menlo Park, Calif.: Addison-Wesley Publishing Co., 1986.

Rethinking "Concrete" Manipulatives

by
Douglas H. Clements and Sue McMillen

Close your eyes and picture students doing mathematics. Like many educators, the mental pictures may include manipulative objects, such as cubes, geoboards, or colored rods. Does the use of such concrete objects really help students learn mathematics? What is meant by "concrete"? Are computer displays concrete and can they play an important role in learning? By addressing these questions, the authors hope to change the mental picture of what manipulatives are and how they might be used effectively.

Douglas Clements teaches and conducts research at the State University of New York at Buffalo, Amherst, NY 14260; clements@ubvms.cc.buffalo.edu. He develops educational software and elementary curriculum materials. Sue McMillen teaches at D'Youville College, Buffalo, NY 14201; vo62jb72@ubvms.cc.buffalo.edu. Her current research interests are graphing calculators, educational software, and eduction for mathematically gifted students.

Time to prepare this material was funded in part by the National Science Foundation under grants no. MDR-9050210 and MDR-8954664. Any opinions, findings, and conclusions or recommendations expressed in this publication are those of the authors and do not necessarily reflect the views of the National Science Foundation.

The authors extend their appreciation to Arthur J. Baroody and several anonymous reviewers for their insightful comments and suggestions on earlier drafts of this article.

Are Manipulatives Helpful?

Helpful, yes ... Students who use manipulatives in their mathematics classes usually outperform those who do not (Driscoll 1983; Sowell 1989; Suydam 1986). This benefit holds across grade level, ability level, and topic, given that using a manipulative makes sense for the topic. Manipulative use also increases scores on retention and problem-solving tests. Finally, attitudes toward mathematics are improved when students are instructed with concrete materials by teachers knowledgeable about their use (Sowell 1989).

... but no guarantee. Manipulatives, however, do not guarantee success (Baroody 1989). One study showed that classes not using manipulatives outperformed classes using manipulatives on a test of transfer (Fennema 1972). In this study, all teachers emphasized learning with understanding.

In contrast, students sometimes learn to use manipulatives only in a rote manner. They perform the correct steps but have learned little more. For example, a student working on place value with beans and bean sticks used the beans as 10 and the bean stick as 1 (Hiebert and Wearne 1992).

Similarly, students often fail to link their actions on base-ten blocks with the notation system used to describe the actions (Thompson and Thompson 1990). For example, when asked to select a block to stand for 1 then put blocks out to represent 3.41, one fourth grader put out three flats, four longs, and one single after reading the decimal as "three hundred forty-one."

Although research suggests that instruction begin concretely, it also warns that concrete manipulatives are not sufficient to guarantee meaningful learning. This conclusion leads to the next question.

What Is Concrete?

Manipulatives are supposed to be good for students because they are concrete. The first question to consider might be, What does *concrete* mean? Does it mean something that students can grasp with their hands? Does this sensory character itself make manipulatives helpful? This view presents several problems.

First, it cannot be assumed that when children mentally close their eyes and picture manipulative-based concepts, they "see" the same picture that the teacher sees. Holt (1982, 138–39) said that he and his fellow teacher "were excited about the rods because we could see strong connections between the world of rods and the world of numbers. We therefore assumed that children, looking at rods and doing things with them, could *see* how the world of numbers and numerical operations worked. The trouble with this theory is that [my colleague] and I *already* knew how the numbers worked. We could say, 'Oh, the rods behaved just the way numbers do.' But if we *hadn't* known how numbers behaved, would looking at the rods enable us to find out? Maybe so, maybe not."

Photo by Charleen Herrick of Bell Park Portrait Studio; all rights reserved

Second, physical actions with certain manipulatives may suggest mental actions different from those that teachers wish students to learn. For example, researchers found a mismatch when students used the number line to perform addition. When adding 5 and 4, the students located 5, counted "one, two, three, four," and read the answer. This procedure did not help them solve the problem mentally, for to do so they must count "six, seven, eight, nine" and at the same time count the counts—6 is 1, 7 is 2, and so on. These actions are quite different (Gravemeijer 1991, 59). These researchers also found that students' external

actions on an abacus did not always match the mental activity intended by the teacher.

Although manipulatives have an important place in learning, they do not carry the meaning of the mathematical idea. They can even be used in a rote manner. Students may need concrete materials to build meaning initially, but they must reflect on their *actions* with manipulatives to do so. Later, they are expected to have a "concrete" understanding that goes beyond these physical manipulatives. For example, teachers like to see that numbers as mental objects—"I can think of 13 + 10 in my head"-—are "concrete" for sixth graders. It appears that "concrete" can be defined in different ways.

Types of concrete knowledge

Students demonstrate *sensory-concrete* knowledge when they use sensory material to make sense of an idea. For example, at early stages, children cannot count, add, or subtract meaningfully unless they have actual objects to touch.

Integrated-concrete knowledge is built through learning. It is knowledge that is connected in special ways. This concept is the root of the word *concrete*—"to grow together." Sidewalk concrete derives its strength from the combination of separate particles in an interconnected mass. Integrated-concrete thinking derives its strength from the combination of many separate ideas in an interconnected structure of knowledge. While still in primary school, Jacob read a problem on a restaurant place mat asking for the answer to 3/4 + 3/4. He solved the problem by thinking about the fractions in terms of money: 75¢ plus 75¢ is $1.50, so 3/4 + 3/4 is 1 1/2. When children have this type of interconnected knowledge, the physical objects, the actions they perform on the objects, and the abstractions they make are all interrelated in a strong mental structure. Ideas such as "four," "3/4," and "rectangle" become as real and tangible as a concrete sidewalk. Each idea is as concrete to a student as a ratchet wrench is to a plumber—an accessible and useful tool. Jacob's knowledge of money was such a tool.

An idea, therefore, is not simply concrete or not concrete. Depending on what kind of relationship the student has with it (Wilensky 1991), an idea might be sensory-concrete, abstract, or integrated-concrete. The catch, however, is that mathematics cannot be packaged into sensory-concrete materials, no matter how clever our attempts are, because ideas such as number are not "out there." As Piaget has shown, they are constructions—reinventions—of each human mind. "Fourness" is no more "in" four blocks than it is "in" a picture of four blocks. The child creates "four" by building a representation of number and connecting it with either real or pictured blocks (Clements 1989; Clements and Battista 1990; Kamii 1973, 1985, 1986).

Mathematical ideas are ultimately made integrated-concrete not by their physical or real-world characteristics but rather by how "meaningful"—connected to other ideas and situations—they are. Holt (1982, 219) found that children who already understood numbers could perform the tasks with or without the blocks. "But children who could not do these problems without the blocks didn't have a clue about how to do them with the blocks …. They found the blocks … as abstract, as disconnected from reality, mysterious, arbitrary, and capricious as the numbers that these blocks were supposed to bring to life."

Are Computer Manipulatives Concrete?

The reader's earlier mental picture of students using manipulatives probably did not feature computer technology. But as has been shown, "concrete" cannot be equated simply with physical manipulatives. Computers might supply representations that are just as personally meaningful to students as are real objects; that is, they might help develop integrated-concrete knowledge. These representations may also be more manageable, "clean," flexible, and extensible. For example, one group of young students learned number concepts with a computer-felt-board environment. They constructed "bean stick pictures" by selecting and arranging beans, sticks, and number symbols. Compared with a real bean-stick environment, this computer environment offered equal, and sometimes greater, control and flexibility to students (Char 1989). The computer manipulatives were just as meaningful and were easier to use for learning. Both computer and physical bean sticks were worthwhile, but work with one did not need to precede work with the other.

The important point is that "concrete" is, quite literally, in the mind of the beholder. Ironically, Piaget's period of concrete operations is often used, incorrectly, as a rationalization for objects-for-objects'-sake activities in elementary school. Good concrete activity is good *mental* activity (Clements 1989; Kamii 1989).

This idea can be made more concrete. Several computer programs allow children to manipulate on-screen base-ten blocks. These blocks are not physically concrete. However, no base-ten blocks "contain" place-value ideas (Kamii 1986). Students must build these ideas from working with the blocks and thinking about their actions.

Actual base-ten blocks can be so clumsy and the manipulations so disconnected one from the other that students may see only the trees—manipulations of many pieces—and miss the forest—place-value ideas. The computer blocks can be more manageable and "clean."

In addition, students can break computer base-ten blocks into ones or glue ones together to form tens. Such

actions are more in line with the mental actions that students are expected to learn. The computer also links the blocks to the symbols. For example, the number represented by the base-ten blocks is usually dynamically linked to the students' actions on the blocks; when the student changes the blocks, the number displayed is automatically changed as well. This process can help students make sense of their activity and the numbers. Computers encourage students to make their knowledge explicit, which helps them build integrated-concrete knowledge. A summary of specific advantages follows.

Computers offer a manageable, clean manipulative. They avoid distractions often present when students use physical manipulatives. They can also mirror the desired mental actions more closely.

Computers afford flexibility. Some computer manipulatives offer more flexibility than do their noncomputer counterparts. For example, Elastic Lines (Harvey, McHugh, and McGlathery 1989) allows the student to change instantly both the size, that is, the number of pegs per row, and the shape of a computer-generated geoboard (fig. 1). The ease of accessing these computer geoboards allows the software user many more experiences on a wider variety of geoboards. Eventually, these quantitative differences become qualitative differences.

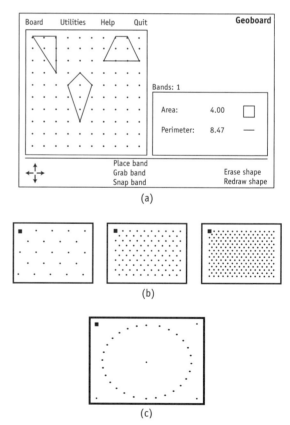

Fig. 1. Elastic Lines (Harvey, McHugh, and McGlathery 1989) allows a variety of arrangements of "nails" on its electronic geoboard: size can also be altered.

Computer manipulatives allow for changing the arrangement or representation. Another aspect of the flexibility afforded by many computer manipulatives is the ability to change an arrangement of the data. Most spreadsheet and database software will sort and reorder the data in numerous different ways. Primary Graphing and Probability Workshop (Clements, Crown, and Kantowski 1991) allows the user to convert a picture graph to a bar graph with a single keystroke (fig. 2).

Computers store and later retrieve configurations. Students and teachers can save and later retrieve any arrangement of computer manipulatives. Students who had partially solved a problem can pick up immediately where they left off. They can save a spreadsheet or database created for one project and use it for other projects.

Computers record and replay students' actions. Computers allow the storage of more than static configurations. Once a series of actions is finished, it is often difficult to reflect on it. But computers have the power to record and replay *sequences* of actions on manipulatives. The computer-programming commands can be recorded and later replayed, changed, and viewed. This ability encourages real mathematical exploration. Computer games such as Tetris allow students to replay the same game. In one version, Tumbling Tetrominoes, which is included in Clements, Russell et al. (1995), students try to cover a region with a random sequence of tetrominoes (fig. 3). If students believe that they can improve their strategy, they can elect to receive the same tetrominoes in the same order and try a new approach.

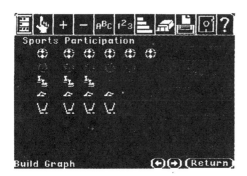

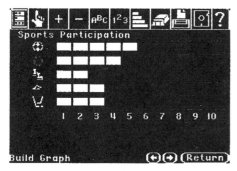

Fig. 2. Primary Graphing and Probability Workshop (Clements, Crown, Kantowski 1991) converts a picture graph to a bar graph with a single keystroke.

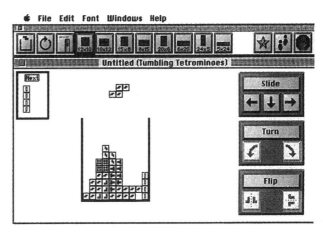

Fig. 3. When playing Tumbling Tetrominoes (Clements, Russell, et al. 1995), students attempt to tile tetrominoes—shapes that are like dominoes except that four squares are connected with full sides touching. Research indicates that playing such games involves conceptual and spatial reasoning (Bright, Usnick, and Williams 1992). Students can elect to replay a game to improve their strategy.

Computer manipulatives link the concrete and the symbolic by means of feedback. Other benefits go beyond convenience. For example, a major advantage of the computer is the ability to associate active experience with manipulatives to symbolic representations. The computer connects manipulatives that students make, move, and change with numbers and words. Many students fail to relate their actions on manipulatives with the notation system used to describe these actions. The computer links the two.

For example, students can draw rectangles by hand but never go further to think about them in a mathematical way. In Logo, however, students must analyze the figure to construct a sequence of commands, or a procedure, to draw a rectangle (see fig. 4). They have to apply numbers to the measures of the sides and angles, or turns. This process helps them become explicitly aware of such characteristics as "opposite sides equal in length." If instead of fd 75 they enter fd 90, the figure will not be a

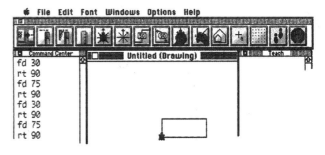

Fig. 4. Students use a new version of Logo, Turtle Math (Clements and Meredith 1994), to construct a rectangle. The commands are listed in the command center on the left (Clements, Battista, et al. 1995; Clements and Meredith 1994).

rectangle. The link between the symbols and the figure is direct and immediate. Studies confirm that students' ideas about shapes are more mathematical and precise after using Logo (Clements and Battista 1989; Clements and Battista 1992).

Some students understand certain ideas, such as angle measure, for the first time only after they have used Logo. They have to make sense of what is being controlled by the numbers they give to right- and left-turn commands. The turtle immediately links the symbolic command to a sensory-concrete turning action. Receiving feedback from their explorations over several tasks, they develop an awareness of these quantities and the geometric ideas of angle and rotation (Kieran and Hillel 1990).

Fortunately, students are not surprised that the computer does not understand natural language and that they must formalize their ideas to communicate them. Students formalize about fives times more often using computers than they do using paper (Hoyles, Healy, and Sutherland 1991). For example, students struggled to express the number pattern that had they explored on spreadsheets. They used such phrases as "this cell equals the next one plus 2; and then that result plus this cell plus 3 equals this." Their use of the structure of the spreadsheet's rows and columns, and their incorporation of formulas in the cells of the spreadsheet, helped them more formally express the generalized pattern they had invented.

But is it too restrictive or too hard to operate on symbols rather than to operate directly on the manipulatives? Ironically, less "freedom" might be more helpful. In a study of place value, one group of students worked with a computer base-ten manipulative. The students could not move the computer blocks directly. Instead, they had to operate on symbols—digits—as shown in figure 5 (Thompson 1992; Thompson and Thompson 1990). Another group of students used physical base-ten blocks. Although teachers frequently guided students to see the connection between what they did with the blocks and what they wrote on paper, the physical-blocks group did not feel constrained to write something that represented what they did with blocks. Instead, they appeared to look at the two as separate activities. In comparison, the computer group used symbols more meaningfully, tending to connect them to the base-ten blocks.

In computer environments, such as computer base-ten blocks or computer programming, students cannot overlook the consequences of their actions, which is possible to do with physical manipulatives. Computer manipulatives, therefore, can help students build on their physical experiences, tying them tightly to symbolic representations. In this way, computers help students link sensory-concrete and abstract knowledge so they can build integrated-concrete knowledge.

Computer manipulatives dynamically link multiple representations. Such computer links can help students connect many types of representations, such as pictures, tables, graphs, and equations. For example, many programs allow students to see immediately the changes in a graph as they change data in a table.

These links can also be dynamic. Students might stretch a computer geoboard's rectangle and see the measures of the sides, perimeter, and area change with their actions.

Computers change the very nature of the manipulative. Students can do things that they cannot do with physical manipulatives. Instead of trading one hundred-block for ten ten-blocks, students can break the hundred-block pictured on the screen into ten ten-blocks, a procedure that mirrors the mathematical action closely. Students can expand computer geoboards to any size or shape. They can command the computer to draw automatically a figure symmetrical to any they create on the geoboard.

Advantages of Computer Manipulatives for Teaching and Learning

In addition to the aforementioned advantages, computers and computer manipulatives possess other characteristics that enhance teaching and learning mathematics. Descriptions of these features follow.

Computer manipulatives link the specific to the general. Certain computer manipulatives help students view a mathematical object not just as one instance but as a representative of an entire class of objects. For example, in Geometric Supposer (Schwartz and Yerushalmy 1986) or Logo, students are more likely to see a given rectangle as one of many that could be made rather than as just one rectangle.

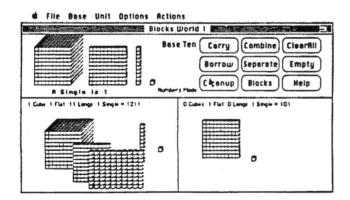

Fig. 5. A screen display of the base-ten-blocks computer microworld (Thompson 1992)

REFLECTING ON PRACTICE IN ELEMENTARY SCHOOL MATHEMATICS

This effect even extends to problem-solving strategies. In a series of studies, fourth-grade through high school students who used Logo learned problem-solving strategies better than those who were taught the same strategies with noncomputer manipulatives (Swan and Black 1989). Logo provided malleable representations of the strategies that students could inspect, manipulate, and test through practice. For example, in Logo, students broke a problem into parts by disembedding, planning, and programming each piece of a complex picture separately. They then generalized this strategy to other mathematics problems.

Computer manipulatives encourage problem posing and conjecturing. This ability to link the specific to the general also encourages students to make their own conjectures. "The essence of mathematical creativity lies in the making and exploring of mathematical conjectures" (Schwartz 1989). Computer manipulatives can furnish tools that allow students to explore their own conjectures while also decreasing the psychological cost of making incorrect conjectures.

Because students may themselves test their ideas on the computer, they can more easily move from naive to empirical to logical thinking as they make and test conjectures. In addition, the environments appear conducive not only to posing problems but to wondering and to playing with ideas. In early phases of problem solving, the environments help students explore possibilities, not become "stuck" when no solution path presents itself. Overall, research suggests that computer manipulatives can enable "teaching children to be mathematicians vs. teaching about mathematics" (Papert 1980, 177).

For example, consider the following dialogue in which a teacher was overheard discussing students' Logo procedures for drawing equilateral triangles.

Teacher: Great. We got the turtle to draw bigger and smaller equilateral triangles. Who can summarize how we did it?

Monica: We changed all the forward numbers with a different number—but all the same. But the turns had to stay 120, 'cause they're all the same in equilateral triangles. (See fig. 6.)

Chris: We didn't make the biggest triangle.

Teacher: What do you mean?

Chris: What's the biggest one you could make?

Teacher: What do people think?

Rashad: Let's try 300.

The class did (see fig. 7).

Monica: It didn't fit on the screen. All we see is an angle.

Teacher: Where's the rest?

Beth: Off here [gesturing]. The turtle doesn't wrap around the screen.

Tanisha: Let's try 900!

The student typing made a mistake and changed the command to fd 3900.

Teacher: Whoa! Keep it! Before you try it, class, tell me what it will look like!

Ryan: It'll be bigger. Totally off the screen! You won't see it at all!

Jacob: No, two lines will still be there, but they'll be way far apart.

The children were surprised when it turned out the same! (See fig. 8.)

Teacher: Is that what you predicted?

Rashad: No! We made a mistake.

Monica: Oh, I get it. It's right. It's just farther off the

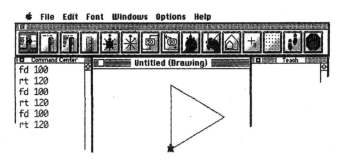

Fig. 6. Students use Turtle Math (Clements and Meredith 1994) to construct an equilateral triangle.

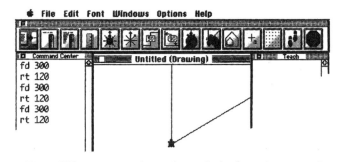

Fig. 7. When commands are changed, the figure is automatically changed—here, to an equilateral triangle with sides of length 300 turtle steps.

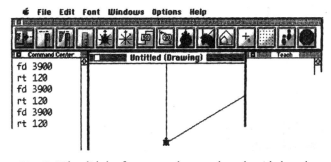

Fig. 8. Why did the figure not change when the side lengths were changed to 3900 turtle steps?

screen. See, it goes way off, there, like about past the ceiling.

The teacher challenged them to explore this and other problems they could think of.

> *Jacob:* I'm going to find the smallest equilateral triangle.
>
> *Rashad:* We're going to try to get all the sizes inside one another.

Computer manipulatives build scaffolding for problem solving. Computer environments may be unique in furnishing problem-solving scaffolding that allows students to build on their initial intuitive visual approaches and construct more analytic approaches. In this way, early concepts and strategies may be precursors of more sophisticated mathematics. In the realm of turtle geometry, research supports Papert's (1980) contention that ideas of turtle geometry are based on personal, intuitive knowledge (Clements and Battista 1991; Kynigos 1992). One boy, for example, wrote a procedure to draw a rectangle. He created a different variable for the length of each of the four sides. He gradually saw that he needed only two variables, since the lengths of the opposite sides are equal. In this way, he recognized that the variables could represent *values* rather than specific sides of the rectangle. No teacher intervened; Logo supplied the scaffolding by requiring a symbolic representation and by allowing the boy to link the symbols to the figure.

Computer manipulatives may also build scaffolding by assisting students in getting started on a solution. For example, in a spreadsheet environment, typing headings or entering fixed numbers might help students organize their ideas.

Computer manipulatives focus attention and increase motivation. One group of researchers studied pairs of students as they worked on computers and found that the computer "somehow draws the attention of the pupils and becomes a focus for discussion," thus resulting in very little off-task talk (Hoyles, Healy, and Sutherland 1991). Although most children seem to enjoy working on the computer, such activity can be especially motivating for some students who have been unsuccessful with mathematics. For example, two such third graders were observed as they eagerly worked in a Logo environment. They had gone forward twenty-three turtle steps but then figured out that they needed to go forward sixty turtle steps in all. They were so involved that both of them wanted to do the necessary subtraction. One grabbed the paper from the other so he could compute the difference.

Computer manipulatives encourage and facilitate complete, precise explanations. Compared with students using paper and pencil, students using computers work with more precision and exactness (Butler and Close 1989; Clements and Battista 1991; Gallou-Dumiel 1989). For example,

students can use physical manipulatives to perform such motions as slides, flips, and turns. However, they make intuitive movements and corrections without being aware of these geometric motions. Even young children can move puzzle pieces into place without a conscious awareness of the geometric motions that can describe these physical movements. In one study, researchers attempted to help a group of students using noncomputer manipulatives become aware of these motions. However, descriptions of the motions were generated from, and interpreted by, physical motions of students who understood the task. In contrast, students using the computer specified motions to the computer, which does not "already understand." The specification had to be thorough and detailed. The results of these commands were observed, reflected on, and corrected. This effort led to more discussion of the motions themselves, not just the shapes (Butler and Close 1989).

Firming Up Ideas about the Concrete

Manipulatives can play a role in students' construction of meaningful ideas. They should be used before formal instruction, such as teaching algorithms. However, teachers and students should avoid using manipulatives as an end—without careful thought—rather than as a means to that end.

The appropriate use of representations is important to mathematics learning. In certain topics, such as early number concepts, geometry, measurement, and fractions, the proper use of manipulatives is especially crucial. However, manipulatives alone are not sufficient—they must be used to actively engage children's thinking with teacher guidance— and definitions of what constitute a "manipulative" may need to be expanded. Research offers specific guidelines for selecting and using manipulatives.

How Should Manipulatives Be Selected?

The following guidelines are offered to assist teachers in selecting appropriate and effective manipulatives.

Select manipulatives primarily for children's use. Teacher demonstrations with manipulatives can be valuable; however, children themselves should use the manipulatives to solve a variety of problems.

Select manipulatives that allow children to use their informal methods. Manipulatives should not prescribe or unnecessarily limit students' solutions or ways of making sense of mathematical ideas. Students should be in control.

Use caution in selecting "prestructured" manipulatives in which the mathematics is built in by the manufacturer, such as base-ten blocks as opposed to interlocking cubes. They can become what the colored rods were for Holt's students—"another kind of numeral, symbols made of colored wood rather than marks on paper" (1982, 170). Sometimes the simpler, the better. For example, educators from the Netherlands found that students did not learn well using base-ten blocks and other structured base-ten materials. A mismatch may have occurred between trading one base-ten block for other and the actions of mentally separating a ten to ten ones or thinking of the same quantity simultaneously as "one ten" and "ten ones." The Netherlands students were more successful after hearing a story of a sultan who often wants to count his gold. The setting of the story gave students a reason for counting and grouping: the gold had to be counted, packed, and sometimes unwrapped—and an inventory had to be constantly maintained (Gravemeijer 1991). Students, therefore, might best start by using manipulatives with which they create and break up groups of tens into ones, such as interlocking cubes, instead of base-ten blocks (Baroody 1990). Settings that give reasons for grouping are ideal.

Select manipulatives that can serve many purposes. Some manipulatives, such as interlocking cubes, can be used for counting, place value, arithmetic, patterning, and many other topics. This versatility allows students to find many different uses. However, a few single-purpose devices, such as mirrors or Miras, make a significant contribution.

Choose particular representations of mathematical ideas with care. Perhaps the most important criteria are that the experience be meaningful to students and that they become actively engaged in thinking about it.

To introduce a topic, use a single manipulative instead of many different manipulatives. One theory held that students had to see an idea presented by several different manipulatives to abstract the essence of this idea. However, in some circumstances, using the same material consistently is advantageous. "Using the tool metaphor for representations, perhaps a representation becomes useful for students as they handle it and work with it repeatedly" (Hiebert and Wearne 1992, 114). If the tool is to become useful, perhaps an advantage accrues in using the same tool in different situations rather than in using different tools in the same situation. Students gain expertise through using a tool over and over on different projects.

Should only one manipulative be used, then? No, different children may find different models meaningful (Baroody 1990). Further, reflecting on and discussing different models may indeed help students abstract the mathematical idea. Brief and trivial use, however, will not help; each manipulative should become a tool for thinking. Different manipulatives allow, and even encourage, students to choose their own representations. New material can

also be used to assess whether students understand the idea or just have learned to use the previous material in a rote manner.

Select computer manipulatives when appropriate. Certain computer manipulatives may be more beneficial than any physical manipulative. Some are just the sort of tools that can lead to mathematical expertise. The following recommendations and special considerations pertain to computer manipulatives. Select programs that—

- have uncomplicated changing, repeating, and undoing actions;
- allow students to save configurations and sequences of actions;
- dynamically link different representations and maintain a tight connection between pictured objects and symbols;
- allow students and teachers to pose and solve their own problems; and
- allow students to develop increasing control of a flexible, extensible, mathematical tool. Such programs also serve many purposes and help form connections among mathematical ideas.

Select computer manipulatives that—

- encourage easy alterations of scale and arrangement,
- go beyond what can be done with physical manipulatives, and
- demand increasingly complete and precise specifications.

How Should Manipulatives Be Used?

The following suggestions are offered to assist teachers in effectively using manipulatives in their classrooms.

Increase the students' use of manipulatives. Most students do not use manipulatives as often as needed. Thoughtful use can enhance almost every topic. Also, short sessions do not significantly enhance learning. Students must learn to use manipulatives as tools for thinking about mathematics.

Recognize that students may differ in their need for manipulatives. Teachers should be cautious about requiring all students to use the same manipulative. Many students might be better off if allowed to choose their manipulatives or to use just paper and pencil. Some students in the Netherlands were more successful when they drew pictures of the sultan's gold pieces than when they used any physical manipulative. Others may need manipulatives for different lengths of time (Suydam 1986).

Encourage students to use manipulatives to solve a variety of problems and then to reflect on and justify their solutions. Such varied experience and justification help students build and maintain understanding. Ask students to explain what each step in their solution means and to analyze any errors that occurred as they use manipulatives—some of which may have resulted from using the manipulative.

Become experienced with manipulatives. Attitudes toward mathematics, as well as concepts, are improved when students have instruction with manipulatives, but only if their teachers are knowledgeable about their use (Sowell 1989).

Some recommendations are specific to computer manipulatives.

- Use computer manipulatives for assessment as mirrors of students' thinking.
- Guide students to alter and reflect on their actions, always predicting and explaining.
- Create tasks that cause students to see conflicts or gaps in their thinking.
- Have students work cooperatively in pairs.
- If possible, use one computer and a large-screen display to focus and extend follow-up discussions with the class.
- Recognize that much information may have to be introduced before moving to work on computers, including the purpose of the software, ways to operate the hardware and software, mathematics content and problem-solving strategies, and so on.
- Use extensible programs for long periods across topics when possible.

Final Words

With both physical and computer manipulatives, teachers should choose meaningful representations and then guide students to make connections between these representations. No one yet knows what modes of presentations are crucial and what sequence of representations should be used before symbols are introduced (Baroody 1989; Clements 1989). Teachers should be careful about adhering blindly to an unproved, concrete-pictorial-abstract sequence, especially when more than one way of thinking about "concrete" is possible. It is known that students' knowledge is strongest when they connect realworld situations, manipulatives, pictures, and spoken and written symbols (Lesh 1990). They should relate manipulative models to their intuitive, informal understanding of concepts and translate between representations at all points of their learning. This process builds integrated-concrete ideas.

Now when teachers close their eyes and picture children doing mathematics, manipulatives should still be in the picture, but the mental image should include a new perspective on how to use them.

References

Baroody, Arthur J. "One Point of View: Manipulatives Don't Come with Guarantees." *Arithmetic Teacher* 37 (October 1989):4–5.

———. "How and When Should Place-Value Concepts and Skills Be Taught?" *Journal for Research in Mathematics Education* 21 (July 1990):281–86.

Bright, George, Virginia E. Usnick, and Susan Williams. *Orientation of Shapes in a Video Game.* Hilton Head, S.C.: Eastern Educational Research Association, 1992.

Butler, Deirdre, and Sean Close. "Assessing the Benefits of a; Logo Problem-Solving Course." *Irish Educational Studies* 8 (1989): 168–90.

Char, Cynthia A. *Computer Graphics Feltboards: New Software Approaches for Young Children's Mathematical Exploration.* San Francisco: American Educational Research Association, 1989.

Clements, Douglas H. *Computers in Elementary Mathematics Education.* Englewood Cliffs, N.J.: Prentice Hall, 1989.

Clements, Douglas H., and Michael T. Battista. "Learning of Geometric Concepts in a Logo Environment." *Journal for Research in Mathematics Education* 20 (November 1989):450–67,

———. "Research into Practice: Constructivist Learning and Teaching." *Arithmetic Teacher* 38 (September 1990):34–35.

———. "The Development of a Logo-Based Elementary School Geometry Curriculum." Final report for NSF grant no. MDR-8651668. Buffalo, N.Y.: State University of New York at Buffalo, and Kent, Ohio: Kent State University, 1991.

———. "Geometry and Spatial Reasoning." In *Handbook of Research on Mathematics Teaching and Learning,* edited by Douglas A. Grouws, 420–64. New York: Maemillan Publishing Co., 1992.

Clements, Douglas H., Michael T. Battista, Joan Akers, Virginia Woolley, Julie Sarama Meredith, and Sue McMillen. *Turtle Paths.* Cambridge, Mass.: Dale Seymour Publications, 1995. (Includes software.)

Clements, Douglas H., Warren D. Crown, and Mary Grace Kantowski. Primary Graphing and Probability Workshop. Glenview, Ill.: Scott, Foresman & Co., 1991. (Software.)

Clements, Douglas H., and Julie Sarama Meredith.Turtle Math. Montreal: Logo Computer Systems (LCSI), 1994. (Software.)

Clements, Douglas H., Susan Jo Russell, Cornelia Tierney, Michael T. Battista, and Julie Sarama Meredith. *Flips, Turns, and Area.* Cambridge, Mass.: Dale Seymour Publications, 1995. (Includes software.)

Driscoll, Mark J. *Research within Reach: Elementary School Mathematics and Reading.* St. Louis: CEMREL, 1983.

Fennema, Elizabeth. "The Relative Effectiveness of a Symbolic and a Concrete Model in Learning a Selected Mathematical Principle." *Journal for Research in Mathematics Education* 3 (November 1972):233–38.

Gallou-Dumiel, Elisabeth. "Reflections, Point Symmetry and Logo." In *Proceedings of the Eleventh Annual Meeting, North American Chapter of the International Group for the Psychology of Mathematics Education*, edited by C. A. Maher, G. A. Goldin, and R. B. Davis, 140–57. New Brunswick, N.J.: Rutgers University Press, 1989.

Gravemeijer, K. P. E. "An Instruction-Theoretical Reflection on the Use of Manipulatives." In *Realistic Mathematics Education in Primary School*, edited by L. Streefland, 57–76. Utrecht, the Netherlands: Freudenthal Institute, Utrecht University, 1991.

Harvey, Wayne, Robert McHugh, and Douglas McGlathery. Elastic Lines. Pleasantville, N.Y.: Sunburst Communications, 1989. (Software.)

Hiebert, James, and Diana Wearne. "Links between Teaching and Learning Place Value with Understanding in First Grade." *Journal for Research in Mathematics Education* 23 (March 1992):98–122.

Holt, John. *How Children Fail.* New York: Dell Publishing Co., 1982.

Hoyles, Celia, Lulu Healy, and Rosamund Sutherland. "Patterns of Discussion between Pupil Pairs in Computer and Non-Computer Environments." *Journal of Computer Assisted Learning* 7 (1991):210–28.

Kamii, Constance. "Pedagogical Principles Derived from Piaget's Theory: Relevance for Educational Practice." In *Piaget in the Classroom*, edited by M. Schwebel and J. Raph, 199–215. New York: Basic Books, 1973.

————. *Young Children Reinvent Arithmetic: Implications of Piaget's Theory.* New York: Teachers College Press, 1985.

————. "Place Value: An Explanation of Its Difficulty and Educational Implications for the Primary Grades." *Journal of Research in Childhood Education* 1 (August 1986):75–86.

————. *Young Children Continue to Reinvent Arithmetic: 2nd Grade. Implications of Piaget's Theory.* New York: Teachers College Press, 1989.

Kieran, Carolyn, and Joel Hillel. "'It's Tough When You Have to Make the Triangles Angles': Insights from a Computer-Based Geometry Environment." *Journal of Mathematical Behavior* 9 (October 1990):99–127.

Kynigos, Chronis. "The Turtle Metaphor as a Tool for Children's Geometry." In *Learning Mathematics and Logo*, edited by C. Hoyles and R. Noss, 97–126. Cambridge, Mass.: MIT Press, 1992.

Lesh, Richard. "Computer-Based Assessment of Higher Order Understandings and Processes in Elementary Mathematics." In *Assessing Higher Order Thinking in Mathematics*, edited by G. Kulm, 81–110. Washington, D.C.: American Association for the Advancement of Science, 1990.

Papert, Seymour. *Mindstorms: Children, Computers, and Powerful Ideas.* New York: Basic Books, 1980.

Schwartz, Judah L. "Intellectual Mirrors: A Step in the Direction of Making Schools Knowledge-Making Places." *Harvard Educational Review* 59 (February 1989):51–61.

Schwartz, Judah L., and Michal Yerushalmy. The Geometric Supposer Series. Pleasantville, N.Y.: Sunburst Communications, 1986. (Software.)

Sowell, Evelyn J. "Effects of Manipulative Materials in Mathematics Instruction." *Journal for Research in Mathematics Education* 20 (November 1989):498–505.

Suydam, Marilyn N. "Research Report: Manipulative Materials and Achievement." *Arithmetic Teacher* 33 (February 1986):10, 32.

Swan, Karen, and John B. Black. "Logo Programming, Problem Solving, and Knowledge-Based Instruction." University of Albany, Albany, N.Y., 1989. (Manuscript.)

Thompson, Patrick W. "Notations, Conventions, and Constraints: Contributions to Effective Uses of Concrete Materials in Elementary Mathematics." *Journal for Research in Mathematics Education* 23 (March 1992):123–47.

Thompson, Patrick W., and Alba G. Thompson. *Salient Aspects of Experience with Concrete Manipulatives.* Mexico City: International Group for the Psychology of Mathematics Education, 1990.

Wilensky, Uri. "Abstract Mediations on the Concrete and Concrete Implications for Mathematics Education." In *Constructionism*, edited by I. Harel and S. Papert, 193–99. Norwood, N.J.: Ablex Publishing Corp., 1991.

The Jasper Experiment

Using Video to Furnish Real-World Problem-Solving Contexts

by

**The Cognition and Technology Group
at Vanderbilt University**

Photo by David Crenshaw, Vanderbilt University, Nashville, Tennessee; all rights reserved

The safe rescue of the wounded bald eagle becomes the students' problem for group solutions.

The Cognition and Technology Group at Vanderbilt (CTGV) University is and interdisciplinary team associated with the Vanderbilt Learning Technology Center, Box 45, Peabody College, Vanderbilt University, Nashville, TN 37203. Members of the CTGV who contributed to this article are Linda Barron, John Bransford, Laura Goin, Elizabeth Goldman, Susan Goldman, Ted Hasselbring, James Pellegrino, Kirsten Rewey, Robert Sherwood, and Nancy Vye.

This work has been supported in part by grants form the National Science Foundation (#MDR-9050191) and the James S. McDonnell Foundation (#91-6). Any opinions, findings, or conclusions expressed in this article are those of the authors and do not necessarily reflect the views of these foundations. For further information about the Jasper research, contact the Learning Technology Center, Box 45, Peabody College, Vanderbilt University, Nashville, TN 37203; e-mail: PoeFT@ctrvax.vanderbilt.edu. For further information about the Jasper materials, contact Optical Data Corporation, 30 Technology Drive, Warren, NJ 07059; or call 1-800-524-2481.

The music quickens, suggesting urgency, and the video focuses on Jasper, who is frantically trying to contact Hilda on his radio:

> Come in Hilda! This is Jasper. I have an emergency. Come in Hilda—or anyone. Repeat, this is an emergency!
>
> I read you Jasper. This is Hilda. What's the matter?
>
> I'm at Boone's Meadow. Some idiot shot a bald eagle up here; it's hurt pretty bad.
>
> I copy, Jasper. What do you want me to do about it?
>
> Call Emily Johnson; she'll think of something.

Emily and Doctor Ramirez study a map as they consider the dilemma: Jasper is approximately 65 miles from the veterinarian, in a remote area that is not accessible by an automobile. Hilda's gas station is closer to Boone's Meadow but is still a five-hour hike from Jasper's campsite. Larry Peterson's ultralight aircraft is a potential solution because Boone's Meadow has an open area that is long enough for the aircraft to land. What is the quickest way to get the eagle to Ramirez for treatment and how long will the trip take?

Up to this point, the sixth-grade class watching the video has been absorbed by the story. Now Emily and Jasper's problem becomes their problem as they divide into groups to try to decide if Larry can fly in to the wooded area to bring the eagle out. Information about fuel capacity and the payload of the aircraft will be important considerations. One by one, the groups conclude that Larry's weight, which was revealed earlier, combined with the weight of the eagle and the extra fuel he will need to use to get from Cumberland City to Boone's Meadow and back again, exceeds the maximum weight that the ultralight aircraft can safely carry. This weight calculation is one of the subproblems that must be identified and solved to decide if the rescue is possible.

Since the video story is on a laserdisc rather than on videotape, students can search the disc quickly with a hand-held remote control to retrieve information that they may not have noticed while first watching the story. Someone in the group can usually remember where in the story the information was presented to speed the process along. The teacher has supplied the groups with maps that are facsimiles of the one Emily and Ramirez use in the video, and students can diagram the possible routes. Students are free to search the videodisc player equipment to look for information and then discuss among themselves the merits of different approaches.

Not all groups come up with the same solution. During the group presentations, alternative solutions are debated, argued, and defended. Most of the class agree that the optimum solution is to have Emily fly in with one extra gallon of gasoline and bring the eagle to Hilda's, where Larry will meet them in the truck, since the truck can make better time than the aircraft. One group argues that the aircraft should be loaded onto the truck where it can be taken to Hilda's and flown the short distance in and out of the meadow. This possibility is accepted, although nobody is sure if the ultralight aircraft can be transported by truck or how long it will take to load and unload it.

Theoretical Basis for the Video Materials

Rescue at Boone's Meadow is one of a series of four problem-solving videodisc adventure stories known collectively as The Adventures of Jasper Woodbury, which we developed for research purposes and which are being field-tested in a number of fifth- and sixth-grade classrooms around the country. Our use of the video technology to furnish a context for school mathematics is based on a theoretical framework that emphasizes the importance of anchoring or situating instruction in meaningful, problem-solving contexts (Brown, Collins, and Duguid 1989; Cognition and Technology Group at Vanderbilt 1990, 1991). This cognitive theory is reflected in the NCTM's *Curriculum and Evaluation Standards* (1989) recommendation that classroom activities should include more emphasis on complex, open-ended problem solving that connects mathematics to other subjects and to the world outside the classroom.

Students are free to use the videodisc equipment to search for information.

[T]he mathematics curriculum should engage students in some problems that demand extended effort to solve. Some might be group projects that require students to use available technology and to engage in cooperative problem solving and discussion. For grades 5–8, an important criterion of problems is that they be interesting to students (p. 75).

Commercial television has been criticized because it distracts children from more worthwhile and intellectually stimulating activities. Using a video that is produced for educational purposes usually shows "experts" delivering information. We created the Jasper series to see if it is possible, through careful design, to use the engaging power of video to create an *active* instead of a passive learning

Jasper uses the radio to call for help.

environment, and to determine if the use of video improves a student's ability to solve complex problems.

Design Principles for the Jasper Series

Contributors to the design of the Jasper series and the associated research studies include university faculty from mathematics and science education; mathematics, physics, chemistry, computer science, cognitive psychology, and instructional technology; video production specialists; school administrators; and teachers. The video adventures have the following design characteristics (Cognition and Technology Group at Vanderbilt 1991, 1992).

1. *Video-based-presentation format.* The videodisc format offers several advantages over problem-solving materials that are supplied orally or in writing. First, and most obvious, is the high interest level of video. A second reason for using the video medium is that the problems can be more complex and interconnected than if they were written—this is especially important for students who are poor readers or when English is a second language. Students may be more able to imagine the problem situation when dynamic images rather than text are displayed (McNamara, Miller, and Bransford 1991). Finally, the videodisc format aids the search for information, and students enjoy using the hand-held remote control to find information that is realistically embedded in the story. Most teachers have students work in groups during part of the exercise, and teachers report that searching and analyzing clues encourages mathematical discussion and debate.

2. *Generative-learning format.* Generative knowledge, including the ability to construct mathematical argu-

Larry teaches Emily how to fly the ultralight aircraft.

ments, plan strategy, and formulate and solve problems, is an important aspect of what NCTM's *Professional Standards* document (1991) calls "mathematical power." Each story series has a complex problem or challenge that students are asked to help solve. Although the mathematics required for solving the challenge is easily within reach of middle school students, generating the subproblems that supply information necessary for the solution is not trivial. In a traditional word problem, the question is usually presented to the students; in a Jasper format, the students must ask the questions.

Some teachers who use these materials show the video once and then engage the class in a discussion where students suggest, and the teacher or a student records, what they need to know to solve the challenge. Other teachers leave it to groups or individuals to identify and solve their own subproblems. In either approach, students are active participants in identifying and solving problems.

3. *Embedded data.* All the information the students need to solve the problem is contained in the video. The challenge is not revealed at the beginning of the story; in fact, many teachers showing the first Jasper episode do not tell the class that they will be solving a mathematics problem. Recalling and finding information in the story motivates students to contribute to the group, sometimes unexpectedly.

4. *Problem complexity.* The NCTM (1991) has argued that students need an opportunity to engage in the kind of sustained mathematical thinking that is needed to solve problems in the real world, where often no single answer is right. The adventures in Jasper present complex real-world problems. For example, the solution to the first adventure requires at least fifteen interrelated calculations. Other adventures, such as *Rescue at Boone's Meadow*, have multiple solutions, just as in real life; and part of the task is to select the *best* one.

Lower-achieving students and students from groups that are traditionally underrepresented in mathematics have often been denied the opportunity to participate in complex problem-solving activities (Cole and Griffin 1987, NCTM 1989). One reason may be the difficulties teachers face in offering problems that are complex, yet motivating to these students. Another reason is the assumption that the "basics" must first be mastered. Computational deficiencies have not appeared to deter students working on Jasper challenges, and teachers report that students will ask or look up mathematical procedures or information they need. We encourage teachers to furnish calculators for the students to use when working on the adventures.

5. *Mathematics topics consistent with NCTM's curriculum standards.* Jasper is organized around pairs of episodes,

each pair representing a mathematical topic or set of related topics that are recommended by the curriculum standards for the grades 5–8 mathematics curriculum. The first two episodes involve trip planning, map reading, estimating, and calculating using decimals, ratios, and integers. The second pair uses topics from statistics and probability. The third pair, which we are now producing, will focus on geometry. Each completed episode is accompanied by additional video and print materials that extend the mathematical ideas contained in the main story.

6. *Connections to other content areas.* Each narrative episode contains opportunities to connect to such areas of the curriculum as literature, history, and science. Aerodynamics, history of flight, endangered species, and conservation of natural resources can all logically connect to the *Rescue at Boone's Meadow.*

Jasper Research Results

Jasper has been evaluated in two major ways. The first was a yearlong implementation of the series in classrooms across nine states in the Southeast. Teachers in these areas used four Jasper videos during a school year and periodically administered tests over the materials. The tests were also completed by students who did not receive Jasper instruction. The findings indicate that the Jasper-instructed students outperformed students receiving regular mathematics instruction in several tested areas. At the end of the year, Jasper students were better at solving one-, two-, and multiple-step word problems and more successful at formulating or generating problems to be solved. In addition, the Jasper instruction had significant effects on students' attitudes toward mathematics. At the end of the year, Jasper students liked mathematics better than before,

Emily plans the rescue.

were likelier to want to work on challenging problems, and considered mathematics to be more useful than they had previously thought. These changes in learning and attitude were observed in both low- and high-achieving students. (For additional information on Jasper evaluation studies, see Goodman et al. [1991]; Pellegrino et al. [1991]; and van Haneghan et al. [1992].)

A major emphasis of the ongoing research on Jasper is to study different ways to use the videos in mathematics instruction, for example, small-group compared with large-group formats. The NCTM recommends the use of small-group learning where students engage in mathematical dialogue while assuming primary responsibility for guiding the course of problem solving. As a consequence, current Jasper research examines the nature of the discussions that take place as students solve problems in groups and the effects of group problem solving on later individual performance.

The Teacher's Role

Teachers have been involved with Jasper research and development from the early prototype videos to the current materials produced by professionals in the video field. Teachers have reviewed scripts, suggested instructional approaches and design modifications, and have been valuable partners in the research effort. Some have also appeared in the videos.

Ultimately, the generative nature of the materials depends on the way the classroom teacher chooses to use them. Teachers using Jasper for the first time may want to structure the subproblems to keep students from going off in the wrong direction or becoming frustrated. Most teachers who have experience using the materials tell us that students do not need as much coaching as teachers had originally thought. Students do periodically head off into blind alleys when generating their own subproblems, but minimal guidance from the teacher is usually enough to get them back on course. Teachers often report that after a class has solved one of the Jasper problems, subsequent stories require less teacher intervention. One of the important goals of the instructional design is to help students develop the skills and the inclination to monitor their own progress toward the final solution. For this reason, we think it is important that when possible, students organize and direct their own problem solving.

Technology Issues

The Jasper series is produced on videodisc for two important reasons: random-access capability and computer control. One side of a videodisc contains up to 54 000 frames, each of which can be accessed almost instantly by using a numeric keypad on the remote control. Scanning a videodisc is faster than searching a videotape, and segments can be played in slow motion or frozen for closer examination. Videotaped versions of the episodes have been used, but this medium tends to inhibit the kind of active and generative activity important to solving the problem because searching the videotape can be laborious. When teachers adapt by having students jot down important facts while playing the tape, problem solving is tedious. We recommend against this use of the video.

Videodisc access can also be controlled by a computer. Specifically designed multimedia software, created with programs such as Hyper-Card, can be used to access and organize video scenes and to associate additional data with videos. For example, the computer program that accompanies *Rescue at Boone's Meadow* contains a copy of Emily's map (fig. 1). In addition to having the map readily available to study or print, students can access different scenes of the video by pointing the cursor to the spot on the map where the scene took place and clicking the mouse.

Students can also use this software to create their own multimedia products, such as a research report on the reason the bald eagle is an endangered species. Pictures from the video can be imported into documents to be displayed on the computer screen. The scenes from *Rescue at Boone's Meadow* that accompany this article, for example, are computer-generated images captured from the videodisc. Classes can produce their own databases to accompany the videos or can pose additional problems using the existing video. (Suppose, for example, that Emily must consider a head wind on her trip to Boone's Meadow.)

This use of the computer is somewhat different from most of the examples of technology applications to mathematics instruction described in NCTM's *Curriculum Standards*. Students working on Jasper problems routinely use calculators for computation, but our existing multimedia software is used neither as a computational device nor as a tool for manipulating or investigating mathematical relationships, although one of our goals is to develop such applications in the future. The major function of our current software is to enable teachers and students to integrate learning across different curricular areas. The potential of multimedia software as an information organizer and communication device is only beginning to be explored (see, e.g., Kozma [1991] or Nix and Spiro [1990]),

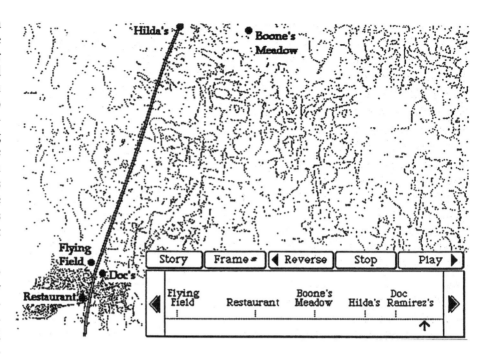

Fig. 1. Emily's map from the HyperCard program used for controlling the videodisc player

and we plan to collect more information on the use of the Jasper videos in further research.

Concluding Remarks

Can a video-presentation format make a long-term difference in a student's willingness and ability to engage in complex problem solving, and can we develop materials to assess this effect? Are teachers and school administrators willing to spend multiple class periods working on a single problem? Can teachers use, and schools afford, the technology needed to make use of the materials? Will parents accept the fact that their children spend time in mathematics class watching television? All these are legitimate questions that have not been fully answered, although the preliminary indications are positive. We talk about the need to make connections between mathematics and the real world, but in an important sense, the video medium is the world of today's youth. Our goal is to turn it into an instructional advantage.

References

Brown, John Seely, Allan Collins, and Paul Duguid. "Situated Cognition and the Culture of Learning." *Educational Researcher* 18 (January/February 1989):32–42.

Cognition and Technology Group at Vanderbilt. "Anchored Instruction and Its Relationship to Situated Cognition." *Educational Researcher* 19 (August/September 1990):2–10.

———. "Technology and the Design of Generative Learning Environments." *Educational Technology* 31 (May 1991):34–40.

————. "The Jasper Experiment: An Exploration of Issues in Learning and Instructional Design." *Educational Technology Research and Development* 40 (First Quarter 1992):179–211.

Cole, Michael, and Peg Griffin. *Contextual Factors in Education.* Madison, Wis.: Wisconsin Center for Educational Research, University of Wisconsin, 1987.

Goldman, Susan, Nancy Vye, Susan Williams, Kirsten Rewey, James Pellegrino, and the Cognition and Technology Group at Vanderbilt. "Solution Space Analysis of the Jasper Problems and Students' Attempts to Solve Them." Paper presented at the annual conference of the American Educational Research Association, Chicago, April 1991.

Kozma, Robert. "Learning with Media." *Review of Educational Research* 61 (Summer 1991):179–211.

McNamara, Tim, Diana Miller, and John Bransford. "Mental Models and Reading Comprehension." In *Handbook of Reading Research*, vol. 2, edited by Rebecca Barr, Michael Kamil, Peter Mosenthal, and P. David Pearson, 490–511. New York: Longman Publishing Group, 1991.

National Council of Teachers of Mathematics. *Curriculum and Evaluation Standards for School Mathematics.* Reston, Va.: The Council, 1989.

————. *Professional Standards for Teaching Mathematics.* Reston, Va.: The Council, 1991.

Nix, Don, and Rand Spiro. *Cognition, Education, Multimedia: Exploring Ideas in High Technology.* Hillsdale, N.J.: Lawrence Erlbaum Associates, 1990.

Pellegrino, James, Allison Heath, Susan Warren, and the Cognition and Technology Group at Vanderbilt. "Collaboration at a Distance: A Jasper Implementation Experiment in Nine States." Paper presented at the annual conference of the American Educational Research Association, Chicago, April 1991.

Van Haneghan, James, Linda Barron, Michael Young, Susan Williams, Nancy Vye, and John Bransford. "The Jasper Series: An Experiment with New Ways to Enhance Mathematical Thinking." In *Enhancing Thinking Skills in the Sciences and Mathematics*, edited by Diane Halpern, 15–38. Hillsdale, N.J.: Lawrence Erlbaum Associates, 1992.

Activities

Tools and Technology

Reys and Smith, "Integrating Calculators: How Far Have We Come?"

The authors pose three questions at the end of their article:

(1) What computational tools, procedures, and skill levels do we value at the elementary level?

(2) Should students learn standard written algorithms?

(3) If students should learn standard written algorithms, which ones, when, and to what level of difficulty?

Write a reaction paper to this article, specifically addressing the three questions. Include your position on using calculators in the mathematics classroom in your answers.

Ploger, Klingler, and Rooney, "Spreadsheets, Patterns, and Algebraic Thinking"

As a connection to literature, read The King's Chessboard by David Birch (New York: Dial Books for Young Readers, 1988). Use a spreadsheet to check the Chief Mathematician's calculations for the total amount of rice sent to the wise man.

Clements and Meredith, "My Turn: A Talk with the Logo Turtle"

Clements and McMillen, "Rethinking 'Concrete' Manipulatives"

1. Computer Activity

   (a) Use Logo software with a partner to create procedures to draw each of the following shapes: square, rectangle, triangle, parallelogram, hexagon, pentagon.

   (b) Using at least four of your procedures for drawing shapes, create a new procedure that will draw a house. Be creative.

2. The authors claim that using Logo builds scaffolding for problem solving, helps students actively build ideas, and facilitates the development of complete, precise explanations.

   (a) Explain how your participation in the Logo activity did or did not produce any or all of these results. Identify other characteristics of the computer environment that enhanced your learning.

   (b) Discuss how changing the Logo activity might improve your experience according to the pedagogical criteria listed in the two articles.

Part 2
Mathematical Content

Section 7
The Real-Number System

The NCTM *Standards* documents present a vision, rather than a specific prescription, of the mathematics students should know and be able to do. How this vision should be implemented in actual practice, however, is open to interpretation. (See Section 1.) Important questions to consider include the following (Davis 1994):

- What specific content or topics should be covered?
- What kind of knowledge should students develop about each topic?
- What kinds of experiences should students have in order to reach a school's educational goals?

The articles in this section can be used to think about the preceding questions. The various authors present specific mathematics content developed through activities that encourage students to probe for meaning beyond the procedural level. As you read through the articles, reflect on your own understandings of each concept and think about how the activities might help you view these concepts in new and richer ways; then think about how you might answer the three questions posed above.

The first four articles (by Graeber, Çemen, Cooke, and Lobato) focus on the operations of addition, subtraction, multiplication, and division with whole numbers, integers, decimal numbers, and fractions. The next three articles (by Fitzgerald and Boyd, Whitin, and Juraschek and Evans) step back and examine the properties of whole numbers. These authors describe activities that encourage students to ask questions and look for the answers to these question in patterns that they create.

The articles by Wentworth and Monroe and by Warrington describe activities that help students think deeply about the nature of fractions and their behavior under the operations of multiplication and division. These authors illustrate that given appropriate opportunities, students can construct meaningful mathematics about the often confusing topic of fractions. The article by Goldberg presents a set of activities that explore other number bases, another area of mathematics that students find confusing. Next, Krusen's article describes how students' attempts at developing a number system for a "primitive society" led them to deeper insights into their own base-ten system.

The article by Reys highlights the properties of both "number sense" and "operation sense" related to whole numbers, integers, rational numbers, and decimal numbers. The activities that are described provide useful tools for assessing students' intuitive understanding of number.

The final two articles in this section discuss the need for mathematics educators to rethink their traditional definitions of school algebra. Instead of providing a new definition, Yackel invites the reader to join her in considering the nature of thinking that should be foundational to algebraic reasoning. Examples of one type of reasoning are illustrated with activities that refocus thinking away from numerical results to generalizations about mathematical relationships. The article by Ruopp et al. presents problems that focus on algebraic thinking across grades. Solution strategies used by elementary through high school in-service teachers illustrate how algebraic thinking fits naturally into the grades K–12 curriculum.

The mathematics classroom is a complex entity made up of complicated interactions among teacher, students, subject matter, and pedagogy. Even though the focus of this section is on mathematical content, each article can also be read from the perspective of one or more of the preceding sections. The articles in this section illustrate how good mathematical tasks, classroom discourse, the encouragement of invented strategies, mathematical thinking, and new ways to conceptualize mathematics combine to create powerful learning experiences. The articles also illustrate the need for teachers to reconceptualize both what is meant by mathematics and what it means for students to learn the subject in school.

Reference

Davis, Robert B. "What Mathematics Should Students Learn?" *Journal of Mathematical Behavior* 13 (March 1994): 3–33.

Research into Practice

Misconceptions about Multiplication and Division

by

Anna O. Graeber

Multiply your options—*divide and conquer*—these and many other everyday expressions imply that multiplication always makes larger and division always makes smaller. In fact, these two ideas are so self-evident and so pervasive in many people's thinking that they are among the most notorious *mis*conceptions about mathematics. Misconceptions or naive conceptions are commonly held ideas or beliefs that are contrary to what is formally acknowledged to be correct. Mathematics educators study misconceptions because if we can understand how students are apt to see mathematical ideas, we may be better prepared to offer instructional experiences that help them develop accepted conceptions. The two misconceptions just described have been the subject of many research investigations (see, e.g., Bell, Fischbein, and Greer [1984]; Fischbein, Deri, Nello, and Marino [1985]; Greer [1987]).

The two misconceptions "multiplication makes bigger" and "division makes smaller" are often noticed only when students attempt to solve multiplication or division word problems involving rational numbers less than 1. Faced with a word problem, students realize from the contextual clues in the problem that the answer should be greater than or less than one of the numbers in the problem. Students multiply if they are looking for a larger number and divide if they are looking for a smaller number. For example, consider the problem "If a car travels 30 miles on 1

Prepared by Anna O. Graeber
University of Maryland
College Park, MD 20742

Edited by Patricia F. Campbell
University of Maryland
College Park, MD 20742

gallon of gasoline, how far will it travel on 1/2 gallon?" Students influenced by the misconception will reason that since they have less than one gallon, the car will travel *less* than 30 miles, so the answer must be 30 *divided* by 1/2 rather than 30 multiplied by 1/2. Similar reasoning may be applied to a problem such as "If cookies are to be packaged 0.65 pounds to a box, how many boxes can be filled with 5 pounds of cookies?" Here students offer the alternative argument: Since they are putting less than 1 pound in each box, they will have *more* than 5 boxes, so the answer must be 5 *multiplied* by 0.65 rather than 5 divided by 0.65.

Why do students believe that "multiplication makes bigger"? First, everyday language suggests it is so. Consider such expressions as "I'm going to multiply my options" or "Rabbits multiply quickly." Another reason for the misconception is the permanence of first impressions. Except for problems involving 0 or 1, students' first contact with multiplication involves problems with whole numbers wherein the product is greater than either factor. Further, multiplication is often defined as repeated addition. The repeated-addition definition, although a useful link between multiplication and addition, is limiting if it is the students' *only* concept of multiplication. With the repeated-addition model, multiplication with mixed numbers, common fractions, or decimal fractions is not easily interpreted. Why? First, because addition with fractions is difficult. In terms of the repeated-addition model, 3 × 4/5 = 4/5 + 4/5 + 4/5. But 4/5 + 4/5 + 4/5 is not trivial. Second, what does repeated addition mean if both factors are common or decimal fractions? Consider 2/3 × 1 3/4. What does it mean to a student to add 1 3/4 to itself 2/3 time? Or in 0.5 × 0.5, what does it mean to add 0.5 to itself 1/2 time? Students' hesitancy to accept 0.25 as the product of 0.5 × 0.5 is logical in light of the fact that until faced with decimals and fractions, multiplication (by factors other than 0 or 1) has always "made bigger."

Helping students make sense of "multiplication making smaller." Upper elementary and middle school teachers are expected to extend multiplication to the rational numbers in a meaningful way. The area model of multiplication is a useful device to use with rational numbers, but students must first understand this interpretation of multiplication with whole numbers. Then the area model can be used to make sense of expressions like 9 × 2/3, 1/2 × 1/10, or 0.5 × 0.5 (see fig. 1). However, to increase the chance that students will use the area model as an aid in seeing that the product of two numbers less than 1 is a number smaller than either of the two factors, first be sure that the area model is a familiar way for students to interpret multiplication of whole numbers.

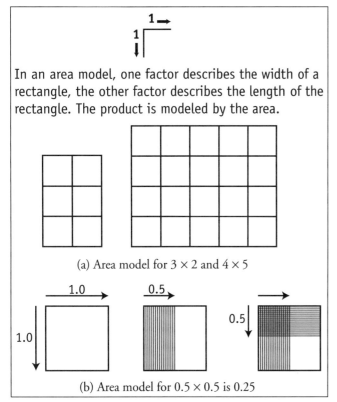

In an area model, one factor describes the width of a rectangle, the other factor describes the length of the rectangle. The product is modeled by the area.

(a) Area model for 3 × 2 and 4 × 5

(b) Area model for 0.5 × 0.5 is 0.25

Fig. 1

Other activities can also help to lay the foundation for accepting that multiplication does not always "make bigger." For example, explorations of products in such patterns as 5 × 20 = ❏, 4 × 20 = ❏, ..., 1 × 20 = ❏, 0 × 20 = ❏ may establish an estimate of the product of 1/2 × 20 as being between 0 × 20 and 1 × 20, that is, as less than 20. If this work is done with real-world problems involving size changes or expansions and contractions of objects, the reasonableness of the results of the calculations may be even more evident (see fig. 2). Once students have devel-

---

Grasshoppers sometimes jump almost twenty times their body length. In the picture below, the body length of some grasshoppers is given in centimeters. Find out how far each grasshopper would jump if it were to jump twenty times its body length.

A 4-centimeter-long grasshopper can jump 4 × 20, or ❏, cm.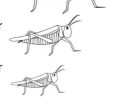

A 3-centimeter-long grasshopper can jump 3 × 20, or ❏, cm.

A 2-centimeter-long grasshopper can jump 2 × 20, or ❏, cm.

A 1-centimeter-long grasshopper can jump 1 × 20, or ❏, cm.

How far can a 3.5-cm-long grasshopper jump?

_____

How far can a 2.4-cm-long grasshopper jump?

_____

How far can a 0.6-cm-long grasshopper jump?

_____

*Using whole-number factors to estimate the product of a whole number and a decimal fraction can help you check the reasonableness of an answer.

Fig. 2. Finding the length of jumps made by grasshoppers of various sizes*

oped some number sense with decimals, fractions, and mixed numbers, students can connect their knowledge of the relative size of the decimal, fraction, or mixed number and the information they have gained from the set of products, 5 × 20, 4 × 20, and so on, to estimate boundaries for such products as 3.5 × 20, 2.4 × 20, 1.7 × 20, and eventually 0.6 × 20. Products involving decimals can also be found using a calculator (calculators such as the TI Explorer™ are now available that will allow students to enter fractions and mixed numbers). The class discussion should focus on the pattern in the size of the factors and in the size of the product. Students could also be encouraged to write about the pattern. For example, they could be charged with describing it for another student, noting anything they consider to be strange or unexpected and telling why they consider this result strange.

Why do students believe that "division makes smaller"? Students' early experiences with division are also limited to whole-number divisors and whole-number quotients. This limitation leads students to place restrictions on division that are not necessarily true with rational-number divisors and quotients. For example, students often believe that the divisor must be less than the dividend (see Graeber and

Baker [1992]); many students will argue that the quotient for $0.25\overline{)2}$ could certainly *never* be 8 because "division always makes smaller." Furthermore, everyday language reinforces the notion that division means cutting into parts, that is, making smaller.

Isolated numerical examples such as $0.25\overline{)2}$ offer no context that a student can use to make sense of the expression. Many students have difficulty bringing meaning to such examples as $0.25\overline{)2}$ because they have no interpretation of division other than that it is the opposite of multiplication. If they do attempt to give meaning to such an example, they will likely attempt to use the partitive, or sharing, interpretation of division rather than the measurement interpretation (see fig. 3). Unfortunately, in these types of problems the measurement interpretation would be more helpful. On the one hand, the partitive interpretation asks the question "How many are in 1 group if there are 2 in 0.25 of a group?" This situation is not particularly easy to imagine or draw. On the other hand, the measurement interpretation asks the question" How many 0.25s are in 2?" Conceptually this situation is a bit easier to decipher. It can be modeled with fraction pieces or with a drawing. It can also be restated as a related question about money—"How many quarters are in two dollars?"

Partitive model for 6 ÷ 2

Two people share six cookies. How many cookies does each get if they share fairly?

In partitive situations, a total is known and the number of sets to be made is known. The question asks how large each of these sets will be, or how many individual items will be in each of these sets.

In this example, the total is six and we know we are to make two equal sets. We are trying to find out how many cookies will be in each of the two sets.

Measurement model for 6 ÷ 2

Two cookies are to be given out to each person. There are six cookies. How many people will get cookies?

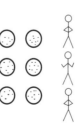

In measurment situations, a total is known and the size of each set is given. The question asks how many such sets can be made.

In this example, the total is six, the set size is two, and we are trying to find how many sets of two cookies each can be made.

Fig. 3. Contrast between the partitive and measurement models of division

Most elementary-level textbooks introduce division as repeated subtraction: 12 ÷ 3 means "How many times can 3 be subtracted from 12?" This interpretation leads directly to the measurement interpretation of division: "How many 3s are in 12?" However, once the partitive interpretation of division is introduced, the use of measurement word problems in textbooks frequently declines, reinforcing the partitive model. Although this partitive model is certainly important, it is not the model that is most helpful in giving meaning to division by mixed numbers or fractions.

Helping students make sense of "division making bigger." Before investigating formal algorithms for division by decimals or fractions, students can use the measurement interpretation of division with fraction pieces, drawings, or their knowledge of the monetary system to solve simple division problems including divisors less than 1. Familiarity with the measurement model can help students realize that the operation being performed is division. Examples of problems that can be explored with fraction pieces are shown in figure 4.

How many bags can I fill with 1/4 pound of peanuts if I buy 2 1/2 pounds of peanuts in the bulk-foods section of the store? (2 1/2 ÷ 1/4)

How many nickels are in a quarter? (1/4 ÷ 1/20)

We will take some first graders with us on Billy Goat Trail, and we estimate that we can cover only 3/4 mile each hour. If the trail is 2 miles long, how long will it take us to complete the hike? (2 ÷ 3/4)

Fig. 4. Examples of division-by-a-fraction problems (division that makes bigger) that can be modeled with fraction pieces

Patterns resulting from the division of a constant number by a decreasing divisor can also be explored, for example, 24 ÷ 24 = ❑, 24 ÷ 12 = ❑, 24 ÷ 8 = ❑, 24 ÷ 6 = ❑, ..., 24 ÷ 1 = ❑, 24 ÷ 1/2 = ❑. Again these examples should be drawn from a context. If I have 24 pounds of candy and I package it 24 pounds (12, 8, 6, 4, 3, 2, 1, 1/2, or 1/4 pound) to a bag, how many bags of candy will I get? A discussion of the results; a look at the divisors that "make smaller, don't change, make larger"; and a discussion of the reasons for the common belief that division makes smaller are important parts of such experiences.

Conclusions

• As teachers we should not reinforce students' tendencies to think that when a problem calls for a bigger answer, it means add or multiply; or that when a problem is thought to need a smaller answer, it means subtract or divide (see Sowder [1989]). Although this strategy "works" in lower grades, it does not help students understand the various interpretations of the operations and can lead learners into trouble when confronting such problems as the following:

A pound of cheese costs $5.59. If one package is marked to show that it holds 0.33 pounds of this cheese, how much will this package of cheese cost?

I wish to tile the bottom 4 feet of my bathroom walls. If the tiles are squares 1/3 foot × 1/3 foot, how many rows of tiles will I need to fix the walls?

• Develop and make use of the area model of multiplication and the measurement model of division. Include some word problems that are examples of the partitive model of division and some that are examples of the measurement model of division.

• Introduce students to counterintuitive notions as soon as possible. Word problems leading to such calculations as 4 × 1/2, 1/2 × 1/2, 2 ÷ 1/4, or 1 1/2 ÷ 1/4 can be solved with understanding as early as fourth or fifth grade. The use of manipulatives or drawings, not standard algorithms, will facilitate understanding. A firm understanding of the meaning of fractions and much discussion about the apparent "strange" results are needed. Why are the answers unexpected? Why is it reasonable to think that multiplication makes bigger and division makes smaller? When does multiplication make bigger and division make smaller? When does multiplication make smaller and division make larger?

• Neither elementary school students nor adults easily "get rid of" misconceptions. Some researchers even argue that adults never really overcome their misconceptions. They argue that, at best, we come to recognize that we have these misconceptions and learn to be on guard against the faulty thinking that some intuitive notions support. Thus it is important for the teacher to help students realize that checking answers is more than checking computation. "Checking one's work" also involves looking at the reasonableness of an answer in light of the context from which the calculation was derived. Prior to attempting a problem, intuition often plays an important role in estimating the size of the answer. But "checking work" can help all of us catch those times when our intuition about the size of the answer leads us to make an incorrect assumption in planning how to solve the problem.

Bibliography

Bell, Alan, Efraim Fischbein, and Brian Greer. "Choice of Operation in Verbal Arithmetic Problems: The Effects of Number Size, Problem Structure, and Content." *Educational Studies in Mathematics* 15 (February 1984):129–47.

Fischbein, Efraim, Maria Deri, Maria Nello, and Maria S. Marino. "The Role of Implicit Models in Solving Problems in Multiplication and Division." *Journal for Research in Mathematics Education* 16 (January 1985):3–17.

Graeber, Anna, and Kay Baker. "Little into Big Is the Way It Always Is." *Arithmetic Teacher* 39 (April 1992):19–21.

Graeber, Anna, and Elaine Tanenhaus. "Multiplication and Division: From Whole Numbers to Rational Numbers." In *Interpreting Research for the Mathematics Classroom: Middle Grades,* edited by Douglas Owens. New York: Macmillan, in press.

Greer, Brian. "Nonconservation of Multiplication and Division Involving Decimals." *Journal for Research in Mathematics Education* 18 (January 1987):37–45.

Kouba, Vicky, and Kathy Franklin. "Multiplication and Division." In *Interpreting Research for the Mathematics Classroom: Early Childhood,* edited by Robert Jensen. New York: Macmillan, in press.

Sowder, Larry. "Story Problems and Students' Strategies." *Arithmetic Teacher* 36 (May 1989):25–26.

Teacher to Teacher

Adding and Subtracting Integers on the Number Line

by

Pamala Byrd Çemen

Various models have been proposed for teaching addition and subtraction of integers (e.g., Grady [1978]; Dirks [1984]; and Chang [1985]), including money, two-color tiles, and the number line. The money model involves giving and receiving money owed but does not make a clear distinction between negatives and subtraction. The two-color-tiles model involves one color for positive numbers and one for negatives. Subtraction is illustrated by taking away appropriate color tiles, thus "−2 − −5" involves taking away five negatives, whereas "−2 + 5" involves adding five positives. In this way, the two-color-tiles model aids in distinguishing between negatives and subtraction. However, the model remains abstract in explaining why taking away five negatives will always have the same result as adding five positives.

This article presents a method for showing addition and subtraction of integers on the number line in a way that clearly distinguishes between subtraction and negative numbers. The method also clarifies why subtracting an integer has the same effect as adding its inverse.

Addition and Subtraction of Integers on the Number Line

Table 1 lists the rules for adding integers on the number line and includes some examples. Notice that the actions of moving either forward or backward are tied to the number, since the sign is part of the number. For example, we illustrate −5 by walking backward five steps. The model

Pamala Byrd Çemen
Oklahoma State University
Stillwater, OK 74078-0613

Table 1

Rules for Adding Integers on the Number Lne and Some Examples

Rules for Adding Integers on the Number Line

1. Always start at zero, facing toward the positive numbers.
2. Move forward for positive numbers.
3. Move backward for negative numbers.

−3 + −6 = −9.
Take three steps backward for the −3, then six steps backward for the −6. We end up at −9.

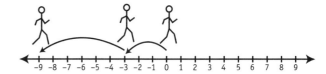

−4 + 7 = 3.
Take four steps backward for the −4, then seven steps forward for the +7. We end up at +3.

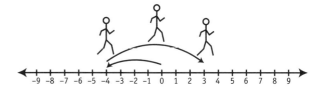

5 + −9 = −4.
Take five steps forward for the +5, then nine steps backward for the −9. We end up at −4.

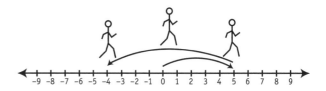

also illustrates the computational rules as well. When adding two integers with the same sign, we are moving in the same direction, thus we add the absolute values. The sign is determined by which direction we are moving. When the signs are different, we move in opposite directions. The two numbers "pull" against each other, as in a tug-of-war; thus we subtract absolute values. The sign of the sum is the sign of the one that pulls harder.

Subtraction is illustrated with an action that is totally independent of the numbers: turning around. The rules for subtracting integers on the number line are presented in table 2 with some examples. The model distinguishes between the negative sign as part of a number and the subtraction sign as an operation. Also, students can see why subtracting a negative (turning around and walking backward) always yields the same result as adding a positive (not turning around and walking forward). Similarly, subtracting a positive (turning around and walking forward) always yields the same result as adding a negative (not turning around and walking backward). These two results can be combined into the traditional rule, Add the inverse.

Teaching a Unit

To introduce the number-line rules, a large number line can be made on brown paper or computer printer paper. The number line should be large enough for all students to see when it is taped to the chalkboard. A number line can also be drawn directly on the chalkboard. Either the teacher or a student can work out problems in front of the class. For individual student work or groups, a smaller number line can be used with a cutout person to move around, or the brown paper can be taped to the floor.

Start by introducing addition, with examples. Once the rules for using the number line are established, students can be guided to discover the computational rules. After students have practiced and mastered addition, a similar process can be used for subtraction.

References

Chang, Lisa. "Multiple Methods of Teaching Addition and Subtraction of Integers." *Arithmetic Teacher* 33 (December 1985):14–19.

Dirks, Michael. "The Integer Abacus." *Arithmetic Teacher* 31 (March 1984):50–54.

Table 2

Rules for Subtracting Integers on the Number Line and Some Examples

Rules for Subtracting Integers on the Number Line

1. Always start at 0, facing toward the positive numbers.
2. Move forward, that is, in the direction you are facing, for positive numbers.
3. Move backward, that is, in the opposite of the direction you are facing, for negative numbers.
4. Turn around for the subtraction sign.

$2 - 8 = {}^-6$.

Take two steps forward for the ⁺2. Turn around for the subtraction. Take eight steps forward in the direction you are facing for the ⁺8. We end up at ⁻6.

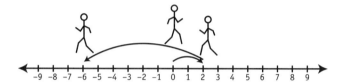

$4 - {}^-2 = 6$.

Take four steps forward for the +4. Turn around for the subtraction. Then take two steps backward for the ⁻2. We end up at +6.

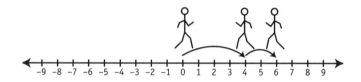

${}^-5 - {}^-2 = {}^-3$.

Take five steps backward for the ⁻5. Turn around for the subtraction. Then take two steps backward for the ⁻2. We end up at ⁻3.

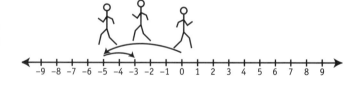

Teacher to Teacher

A Videotaping Project to Explore the Multiplication of Integers

by

Marcia B. Cooke

My eighth-grade mathematics class was having some of the usual difficulties with beginning-algebra concepts. Because the students were becoming somewhat frustrated, I was looking for a way to present the multiplication of integers so that students could readily understand the concept. Relating this idea to the distance formula, which we had already studied, would not only help put this idea into a more familiar context but also would review a formula that the students would often be using the next year in first-year algebra.

I began our class discussion by saying, "Today we are going to explore both positive and negative rates. Imagine a rate that is positive when a person moves from left to right in front of the number line and negative when he or she moves right to left." Students' comments indicated that they understood the idea. I continued, "Next, imagine continuing the rate for one minute, two minutes, and so forth." We did some examples at the chalkboard of such rates as +10 yards per minute × 1 minute, 2 minutes, 3 minutes, and so on. We repeated the same examples for -10 yards per minute × 1 minute, 2 minutes, 3 minutes, and so on. Left-to-right movement in front of the number line was the model for forward rates; right-to-left movement denoted negative rates.

Marcia Cooke runs the mathematics laboratory at Saint George's Episcopal School, New Orleans, LA 70115. She is certified in both mathematics and science, and her interests are in mathematics connections across the curriculum and hands-on mathematics.

The author wishes to thank Jim Hobbs, a reference librarian at Loyola University in New Orleans, and Edward Haspel, a generous volunteer videographer, who helped with the article.

Photo by Paul Brou; all rights reserved

With signs in hand, students will later view themselves walking forward and backward, as technology assists teaching positive and negative rates.

Quite frankly, I had intended to present this motion model for only the two situations of

positive time × positive rate = positive distance

and

positive time × negative rate = negative distance.

I would then present the other two situations as opposites of the former two:

negative time × negative rate = positive distance

and

negative time × positive rate = negative distance.

This neat plan derailed when a student named Alex asked, "How could you have a negative time?" Not having anticipated this question, I was stumped. Ashley interjected, "Time moves only forward." Clearly, the students were discomfited by my use of a model that accounted for only half the multiplication products. And I was discomfited at not having a ready answer! After a collective pause, Gloria suggested a model for negative time: "Maybe it's like a film that is rewinding."

The foregoing discussion was the impetus for an experiment that we carried out several days later. A parent volunteer used a videocamera to tape the students walking forward and backward in front of the school's cafeteria. Each student was filmed walking approximately fifteen yards forward carrying a green "I am walking forward" sign. After that, each student was filmed walking backward carrying a pink "backward" sign.

Before watching the videotape, we discussed the motions we thought we would be seeing on the video monitor. Students were given a copy of figure 1 and asked to predict the apparent motion. Students had little difficulty correctly and confidently predicting the outcomes of the first three situations. When the tape of a student walking forward is rewound, *she* appears to be walking backward, just as the tape of a student walking backward operated in the play-forward mode appears to be walking backward. Despite the logical symmetry, the class could not commit to an outcome if the tape of a student walking backward is played in "rewind" mode. Students argued, and the class was equally divided on the *apparent* motion. When the tape was played, jubilant relief was evident. The outcome that had been logical yet counterintuitive actually happened on the screen. Yes, a negative rate times a negative time yielded a positive distance! We played the tape over and over to reassure ourselves, double-checking that we saw the pink backward sign in the rewind mode.

Thus, my skeptical eighth graders became convinced, by their own design and efforts, that a negative rate times a negative time yields a positive product. I hope that when they encounter a formal proof of this situation in high school or study the motion of objects in physics, our activity will help the results seem inevitable and natural to them.

1. Walk forward; play video forward.

   Prediction: _____

   _____

   Actual: _____

   _____

2. Walk forward; play video backward.

   Prediction: _____

   _____

   Actual: _____

   _____

3. Walk backward; play video forward.

   Prediction: _____

   _____

   Actual: _____

   _____

4. Walk backward; play video backward.

   Prediction: _____

   _____

   Actual: _____

   _____

Fig. 1. Student worksheet

Bibliography

Annett, William G. "Products of Signed Numbers: An Inductive Approach." *Mathematics Teacher* 54 (March 1961):169–70.

Battista, Michael T. "A Complete Model for Operations on Integers." *Arithmetic Teacher* 30 (May 1983):26–31.

Crowley, Mary L., and Kenneth A. Dunn. "On Multiplying Negative Numbers." *Mathematics Teacher* 78 (April 1985):252–56.

Dirks, Michael K. "The Integer Abacus." *Arithmetic Teacher* 31 (March 1984):50–54.

Fulkerson, Elbert. "Teaching the Law of Signs in Multiplication." *Mathematics Teacher* 32 (January 1939):27–29.

Kline, Morris. *Mathematics and the Physical World.* New York: Dover Publications, 1981.

Phillips, E. Ray. "Negative Number Times Negative Number Gives Positive Number: An Understandable Proof for High School Students." *School Science and Mathematics* 71 (December 1971):797–800.

Sarrer, Vernon. "Why Does a Negative Times a Negative Produce a Positive?" *Mathematics Teacher* 79 (March 1986):178–83.

Making Connections with Estimation

by
Joanne E. Lobato

During a recent visit to a sixth-grade classroom, students were observed estimating the sums of columns of multidigit numbers by first painstakingly computing the exact sum of each column of numbers on paper, then rounding the answers to obtain estimates. Apparently the students were not bothered by the fact that it didn't make much sense to round the numbers after already finding an exact sum. Furthermore, they seemed unaware that the power of estimating lies in the speed with which a person can obtain an amount that is close enough for the purpose at hand. Instead, estimation had been turned into a cumbersome process intended, at most, to satisfy the directions on a work sheet.

The logic of the students is more understandable when considered in light of the students' experience with estimation. The topic had been taught separately as an algorithm; for example, round each number and operate. This

Photograph of students from Saint Mark's School in San Rafael, California, was taken by Christopher Ritter. All rights reserved.

Estimating flag-color percents connects mathematic, art, and geography.

principle was to be used on problems that looked just like the items in the textbook requiring exact computation; however, no explanation of the purpose of estimating had been given. Far from being an isolated instance, this estimating situation has frequently been noted by teachers and researchers (Trafton 1986, Sowder and Wheeler 1989). When estimation is taught as an arbitrary set of rules, even when several procedures are presented, students are not likely to see unifying ideas, connections, or the relevance and usefulness of estimation.

One purpose of this article is to describe ways to structure estimation activities so that students can make connections between their understanding of numbers and extensions of those concepts to estimating. Another purpose is to illustrate how estimation activities can reinforce connections with mathematical topics, other subjects being studied, and the real world. When estimation makes use of the way that students construct problem-solving strategies and apply knowledge of numbers, it can offer a rich opportunity to make *many* types of connections.

Joanne Lobato is a textbook author for D. C. Heath and Company, 95 Hayden Avenue, Lexington, MA 02173. Her main interest is the development of number sense, particularly at the middle-grades level.

Making the Learning Connection

The "learning connection" refers to making connections between a student's understanding of a concept and extensions or applications of that knowledge. Rather than teach each new topic as if it were unconnected to other topics, it is important to use previous experiences that students bring to the new material. According to the *Curriculum and Evaluation Standards for School Mathematics* (NCTM 1989), the mathematics curriculum should include the "investigation of mathematical connections so that students can … use a mathematical idea to further their understanding of other mathematical ideas" (p. 84).

To illustrate how to support learning connections in the classroom, consider the topic of estimating sums. The conventional approach has been to teach an estimation strategy directly, followed by individual student practice. Traditionally this strategy has been to round the number, but more recently such other strategies as front-end estimation have found their way into classrooms (see fig. 1).

An alternative approach is to begin with a problem that can be solved using estimation and to allow the students to invent strategies based on what they know about numbers and operations. Figure 2 puts the problem in figure 1 into a real-life context. Many students develop such strategies as front-end estimation on their own if given engaging, sensible tasks. The strategies shown in figure 3 were invented by three fifth graders who had had no formal instruction in estimation other than having learned the rounding strategy. Notice the richness and inventiveness of the strategies. Since students can combine numbers in many ways to construct their own strategies, it is important that students share their estimation methods with each other during classroom instruction.

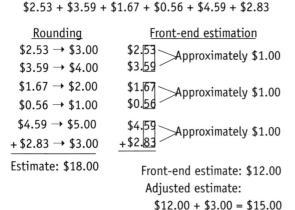

$2.53 + $3.59 + $1.67 + $0.56 + $4.59 + $2.83

Rounding	Front-end estimation
$2.53 → $3.00	$2.53 ⎱
$3.59 → $4.00	$3.59 ⎰ Approximately $1.00
$1.67 → $2.00	$1.67 ⎱
$0.56 → $1.00	$0.56 ⎰ Approximately $1.00
$4.59 → $5.00	$4.59 ⎱
+ $2.83 → $3.00	+ $2.83 ⎰ Approximately $1.00
Estimate: $18.00	Front-end estimate: $12.00
	Adjusted estimate: $12.00 + $3.00 = $15.00

Fig. 1. Two typical strategies for estimating a sum

Suppose you walk up to the cash register in a grocery store with six items having these price tags. The clerk says, "That will be $18.37." Do you think that total is reasonable, or could the clerk have made a mistake?

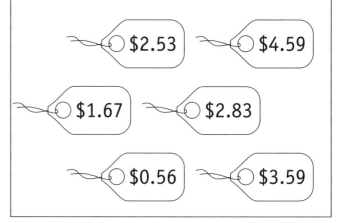

Fig. 2. Using the previous example in a real-life situation

Sheena's method: The dollar amounts add up to $12.00. The largest cents amount is 83¢. Since each cents amount is less than 83¢, which is 17¢ less than $1.00, then together the cents amounts of the six items won't add up to $6.00. So, the total is less than $18.00 and $18.37 is unreasonable.

Joel's method: Since there are six price tags, each should be about $3.00 if the total was really about $18.00. The $3.59 and the $4.59 are about $2.00 total over the $3.00; but the others are much less than $2.00 under. So the total won't make it up to $18.00. The $18.37 is not reasonable

David's method: The total of the dollar bills is $12.00. The $0.56 and the $0.59 make about another dollar; $0.53 and $0.59 is a dollar; and $0.83 plus $0.67 is about $1.40. $12.00 + $1.00 + $1.00 + $1.40 = $15.40. Then, the pennies not included so far will probably make another dollar, but you still need $3.00. So, the total wouldn't be $18.37.

Fig. 3. Three strategies used by fifth graders to solve the estimating problem in figure 2

Other key features of this alternative approach are described in the following *teaching suggestions:*

1. *Help students make problems come alive.* One way to present the problem in figure 2 is to cut out price tags and then have the students pretend that they are in a store. At other times, use real items, such as cans of soup or erasers with price tags. This approach will help take the problem from the worksheet and make it real for the students so that they can use previous experience to solve it.

2. *Present problems that illustrate the purposes of estimation.* Estimation strategies often don't make much sense to students unless they understand why they are estimating in the first place. When students realize that some problems can be solved more efficiently by estimating than by using paper and pencil or even a calculator, then it will make more sense to use approximate numbers to obtain an estimate.

3. *Include problems that involve decision making.* Most of the estimation tasks that students see in school are of the type shown in figure 1. If the problem's level of required precision is not spelled out, students have to guess how close their answers should be. In contrast, students will experience far less frustration with problems that require decision making, such as the one shown in figure 2, since the appropriate level of precision is naturally determined by the context of the problem. Using problems requiring decision making can be particularly effective at the beginning of the year when students are learning to become tolerant of imprecision. Once students are more comfortable with estimation, open-ended problems that require students to estimate "about how much" can be used. However, whenever open-ended problems arc used, students should be allowed to help determine how close is close enough rather than rely on the teacher to determine a range of acceptable estimates.

4. *Use class discussions to establish reasonable estimates.* Unlike the traditional approach in which estimates are checked to see if they fall within a range of acceptable numbers determined by the textbook or teacher, this alternative approach uses student discussion to determine a reasonable estimate. Students have to convince each other of the reasonableness of their estimates. Also, through hearing other explanations, students often locate flaws in their own reasoning and refine their strategies.

The remainder of this article includes more examples to illustrate the points listed previously. The following examples will also demonstrate how estimation activities can connect with other subjects, mathematical topics, and the real world. Throughout these examples, the underlying theme is to build on students' number knowledge by using situations that make sense.

Connections with Other Curricular Areas

The following two activities illustrate connections between estimation and social studies, geography, science, and art.

Activity 1: Making sense of numbers in the world around you, a social studies and science connection. Several years ago, during a social studies lesson about the Great Pyramid of Cheops, a group of students seemed unimpressed to learn that the Egyptian pyramid originally stood 481 feet high. The teacher thought that the students did not really realize how *high* that is and decided to use estimation to compare the height with some reference point that the students understood. Together they chose the height of an average sixth grader as the reference point and created the problem "About how many 5-foot-tall students standing head to toe will equal the height of the Great Pyramid?" They arrived at the estimate of "between 90 and 100 students." (see fig. 4).

Problem: About how many 5-foot-tall students standing head to toe will equal the height of the pyramid, which is 481 feet tall?

Solutions:

$$5\overline{)481}^{\,?}$$

481 is close to 450, and 5 × 90 is 450.

481 is close to 500, and 5 goes into 500 100 times.

$$5\overline{)450}^{\,90}$$

$$5\overline{)500}^{\,100}$$

Since 481 is between 450 and 500, then the actual number of students needed is between 90 and 100.

Fig. 4. Estimating the height of the Great Pyramid of Cheops

To drive the point home even further, the students figured out that it would take about three classes of fellow students standing head to toe to equal the height of the pyramid. Suddenly they were impressed! The figure of 481 feet finally had some meaning.

Reference points and estimation can be used to make sense of numbers that students learn in other subjects. Estimation can come into play in science when studying the height of the tallest tree, the weight of an elephant, and the length of the migratory routes of whales.

Activity 2: Flags, a geography and art connection. In this activity, students use pictures of flags to estimate what percent of a flag is devoted to a particular color, as shown in figure 5. They can use flags pictured in an encyclopedia or poster or construct a class set of flags using poster board and construction paper. If laminated, the flags can be used year after year, and students can use grease pencils to highlight important regions directly on the flags.

Geography is naturally integrated into this activity, even though the initial question is a mathematical rather than a geographical problem. Questions such as "Where is Jamaica?" arise naturally and can be addressed by having students locate Jamaica on a world map. Students might also want to learn more about these countries.

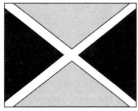

About what percent of the flag is black?

Jamaica

Typical solution: If you cut the flag into fourths, then each black part is a little less than 1/4, or 25%. Together the two black areas are a little less than 50%. So 45% is a reasonable estimate.

Fig. 5. An estimation problem connecting mathematics with social studies

A nice extension to this activity is to have students create their own flags. One way to integrate mathematics into this art activity is to have students work in pairs and place constraints on each other. For example, one student might require that his or her partner make a flag that is 55 percent yellow, 18 percent red, 25 percent blue, and 2 percent black. The partner must then create a flag that meets these specifications.

Connections with Other Mathematical Topics

In the flag activity, students need to be able to move back and forth between fractions and percents. However, students often see decimals, percents, and fractions as three separate number systems rather than as three different representations of a single number. Estimation can connect these three forms by establishing and using quantities such as 25% = 1/4 = 0.25.

Such mathematical connections do not always come easily. Students frequently make mistakes, such as thinking that 1/4 equals 0.4. When such errors occur, it is important to remind students of the meaning of each symbol. For example, use grids like the ones shown in figure 6. Also, one can refer to the money metaphor, reminding students, for example, that 1/4 of a dollar is written as $0.25.

Once students have been introduced to number systems in a meaningful way, it is important to ask them to solve problems that use these systems in the solution process, for example, estimating a 15 percent tip when the bill is $82.97. It is not necessary to teach an algorithm for computing 15 percent of an amount. Instead, students can make progress on this problem once they know that 10% = 1/10 = 0.10. Figure 7 illustrates various strategies that some sixth and seventh graders have used through class discussion to solve this tipping problem.

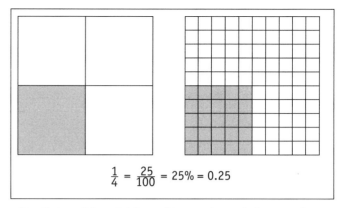

$$\frac{1}{4} = \frac{25}{100} = 25\% = 0.25$$

Fig. 6. A useful model for making mathematical connections

Problem: In a restaurant, it is customary to leave a 15 percent tip. How much money should you leave as a tip if the bill for your party comes to $82.97?

Latasha's method: 10 percent of $80.00 is 1/10 of $80.00, which is $8.00. 20 percent is double $8.00, which is $16.00. So 15 percent of $80.00 is halfway between $8.00 and $16.00, which is $12.00. The tip should be $12.00.

Segio's method: 25 percent of $80.00 is $20.00, since 25 percent is 1/4. Half of 25 percent is about 12 percent, which is close to 15 percent. Half of $20.00 is $10.00. That means that 12 percent of $80.00 is $10.00. To make a 15 percent tip, I'll add a little bit more to make a tip of $11.00 or $12.00.

Korey's method: $82.97 is close t $80.00. 10 percent is around 0.1, and 0.1 × $80.00 is $8.00, since I just move the decimal point one place to the left. 5 percent is half of 10 percent, so 5 percent is $4.00. Then add $8.00 and $4.00 to get $12.00, which is 15 percent of $80.00.

Fig. 7. Students' solutions to a tipping problem

Connecting with the Real World

Making connections with the real world helps students see the usefulness of mathematics and understand how particular topics are applied. Thus, it is important to present real problems in various contexts. In addition to the problems already described, a few other real-world problems involving estimation are given in figure 8.

Conclusion

Making connections between students' number knowledge and the applications of that knowledge will more likely produce estimators who have more ways to find solutions than simply presenting and practicing estimation

- The school cook looks at today's attendance at the middle school: grade 6 has 656 students, grade 7 has 538 students, and grade 8 has 557 students. The cook has enough food to serve 1500 people and estimates that about 75 of these students will bring lunches from home. Does the cook have enough food for today's lunch?

- Your family is driving to your grandmother's house. The last road sign indicated that you have 185 miles left to go. The time is 1:55 P.M. Will you get to your grandmother's house before 6:00 P.M., which is when dinner will be served?

- Latasha swims laps in a pool in which thirty-six laps equals 1 mile. She has already swum ten laps. About what part of a mile has she swum?

- The Last Ditch Deli charges $3.65 per pound for Swiss cheese. Camilla only wants to spend about $2.00 on cheese. About how much of a pound should she ask the deli clerk to slice for her?

Fig. 8. Some real-world estimation problem

strategies. Approaching estimation as a problem-solving skill rather than as an isolated skill has greater potential for developing the types of connections we would like students to make. As one student once remarked, "Estimation is guessing with a little bit of *problem solving.*"

References

National Council of Teachers of Mathematics. *Curriculum and Evaluation Standards for School Mathematics.* Reston, Va.: The Council, 1989.

Sowder, Judith T., and Margariete M. Wheeler. "The Development of Concepts and Strategies Used in Computational Estimation." *Journal for Research in Mathematics Education* 20 (March 1989):130–46.

Trafton, Paul R. "Teaching Computational Estimation: Establishing an Estimation Mind-Set." In *Estimation and Mental Computation*, 1986 Yearbook of the National Council of Teachers of Mathematics, edited by Harold L. Schoen and Marilyn J. Zweng, 16–30. Reston, Va.: The Council, 1986.

Teacher to Teacher

A Number Line with Character

by

William M. Fitzgerald and Jane U. Boyd

Vince and Sarah are playing the Factor Game, a two-person game in which the first player selects a number from 1 to 30 (see game board in fig. 1). The second player then selects all the divisors of the first number that are less than that number. If Vince begins the game by choosing 13, Sarah would select 1 because the divisors of 13 are 1 and 13 and Vince has already selected 13. The score is then 13 to 1 in favor of Vince. During the second round of play it is Sarah's turn to go first. She chooses 24 and has a total of 1 + 24 = 25 points. However, next Vince can select 2, 3, 4, 6, 8, and 12 (the remaining divisors of 24), which, added to his previous score of 13, will give a total of 48 points. Once a number is chosen, it is out of play and can be marked off or covered up. A play is legal only if a divisor remains on the board for the opponent to select. A player making an illegal move gets to keep the number chosen, but loses his or her next turn. The game ends when no more legal moves are possible. The highest sum wins. The Factor Game is the first activity in *Factors and Multiples*, a unit of the Middle Grades

Students saw the visual representation of numbers from 1 to 30 become more vivid.

© 1993, Debbie Boyd

Mathematics Project (Fitzgerald et al. 1986).

When this game was introduced to a fourth-grade class, students very quickly evidenced that they didn't understand the *multiplicative* nature of the numbers they were being asked to think about. The teachers then set about the task of helping the students focus on the divisors of the numbers by constructing a new kind of number line. It was called a "number line with character" because the individual numbers began to develop a unique "spatial" personality (see fig. 2).

The students were working in groups of three, so each group was assigned the task of representing particular numbers as areas of rectangles made from paper squares.

1	2	3	4	5
6	7	8	9	10
11	12	13	14	15
16	17	18	19	20
21	22	23	24	25
26	27	28	29	30

Fig. 1. Playing board for the Factor Game

William Fitzgerald teaches at Michigan State University, East Lansing, MI 48823-1050. Jane Boyd teaches at Averill School, Lansing, MI 48911.

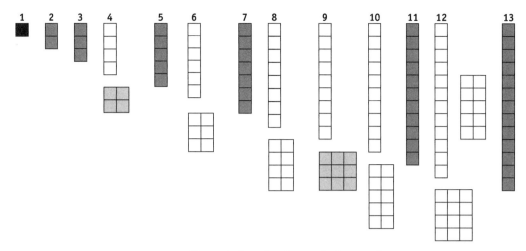

Fig. 2. A "number line with character"

Each number was first represented by a strip 1 unit wide and as many units long as needed and then in other ways by as many rectangular regions as could be found with units greater than 1 unit. Seven groups were involved, so the first group represented the numbers 1, 8, 15, 22, …; the second group represented 2, 9, 16, 23, …; and so on.

"Hey, look! I made another region for '12,' '3 times 4.' That makes three ways now. But I only found one way to make '13.' Thirteen is bigger than '12'—I don't get it!" questioned Jimmy. His cutting rectangles of the squared paper led him to grapple with the puzzle of why a number could have only one representation and yet be larger than one with three representations.

The representations were displayed in order on the chalkboard at the back of the room. During the first day, numbers up into the 20s were fairly complete, as were other larger isolated numbers. The second day found us with reasonable representations up to 40, but the chalkboard was getting quite messy as the numbers got larger. Because of the size of the "factor game" that we wanted to play, we trimmed the display back to 30.

"You know—I just saw—some are squares. Is that OK?" "Yeah—squares are special rectangles—but that's neat!"

This interchange between Joshua and Audra led to our suggestion that they cut new squares out of different-colored paper. This suggestion, in turn, led Corey and Chantel to want to cut new "singly represented" numbers out of paper of another color. Students saw the visual representation of numbers from 1 to 30 become more vivid. The numbers 2, 3, 5, 7, 11, 13, 17, 19, 23, and 29 were all represented by pink strips. The numbers 4, 9, 16, and 25 were white

strips with yellow squares below them. The number 1 was a problem. They finally decided that 1 was a square but had only one representation, so they made it black. Those numbers that were neither prime nor squares remained white. The pink numbers were identified as *prime* numbers, and the others were identified as *composite* numbers because they were composed of prime numbers.

Rob noticed, "Hey, look. The squares get farther apart as they go up. You start at '1,' then skip three numbers to '4,' then skip five numbers to '9,' then skip seven to '16,' then skip nine to '25.' Does this pattern always work?"

The class added 11 to 25 and got 36—the next square! Then they added 13 to 36 and got 49. At this point, the fourth graders were convinced that Rob had found a secret about square numbers.

The impetus for creating the "number line with character" was to help the students play the Factor Game. But many other ideas occurred as the students wrestled with such things as primes, composites, squares, and the beginnings of their learning about fractions. The new number line remained on the back chalkboard for the remainder of the year and was referred to repeatedly when questions about these ideas occurred. Before the end of the year we again introduced the Factor Game, and the students experienced a reasonable degree of success.

Reference

Fitzgerald, William, Mary Winter, Glenda Lappan, and Elizabeth Phillips. *Factors and Multiples*. The Middle Grades Mathematics Project. Reading, Mass.: Addison-Wesley Publishing Co., 1986.

Becca's Investigation

by

David J. Whitin

As my eleven-year-old daughter, Becca, was doing her mathematics homework one night, she called me into her room. "Dad, do you think '36 × 8' is the same as '48 × 6'?"

"Well, I'm not sure," I said. And before I could do any further figuring, she announced, "Well, it is. See," pointing to these two problems on her worksheet. Becca had just solved 36 × 8, and then when she encountered 48 × 6 about eight problems later, the product of 288 seemed familiar. The coincidence intrigued her, and so she had called me into her room to share this observation.

"Why does that work?" she asked. I paused to look at the problems again, but she proceeded to answer her own question. "Oh, I see," she said and recorded the multiplicative similarities in this way:

$$
\begin{array}{cc}
36 & 48 \\
\times 8 & \times 6 \\
\hline
6 \times 8 = 48 & 8 \times 6 = 48 \\
\\
8 \times 3 = 24 & 6 \times 4 = 24
\end{array}
$$

David Whitin teaches at the University of South Carolina, Columbia, SC 29208. He works regularly in an elementary classroom to create a curriculum that supports mathematical learning through inquiry.

"You see, there's two ways to multiply to get '48' and two ways to multiply to get '24,'" she explained. When she could not find other answers on her worksheet that were the same, she asked, "Are there other numbers that work that way?" This question started her on the mathematical journey described in this article. It is important to note that *she* raised the question. If the NCTM's *Curriculum and Evaluation Standards* (1989) are to become a living reality in the classrooms of this country, then one of the first questions we must ask ourselves is "Where are the questions in my mathematics class coming from?" It is crucial that students live in a classroom that supports them in generating and pursuing their own questions. Only then can we build a learning community that continues to extend and outgrow itself through a spirit of collaboration and inquiry.

The Investigation Continues

Becca next tried to create other pairs of multiplication problems that looked different but still had the same product. She realized that she needed to find numbers with different factors, and she tried out various possibilities. "You could take another number, like '36,' because you can multiply it by '6 × 6' and '9 × 4.'" She then recorded the following on paper:

$$\begin{array}{r} 6\ \Box \\ \times\ 6 \end{array} \qquad \begin{array}{r} 4\ \Box \\ \times\ 9 \end{array}$$

She figured that the same number she had put in the tens column of the multiplicand must also be put in the ones column, and so she recorded her final answer as follows:

$$\begin{array}{r} 6\ \boxed{6} \\ \times\ 6 \\ \hline 396 \end{array} \qquad \begin{array}{r} 4\ \boxed{4} \\ \times\ 9 \\ \hline 396 \end{array}$$

She continued to try out other numbers to see which ones might work. "Let's see, '49,' there's '7 × 7,' but what else?" I continued to listen as she set out to solve her own questions. She divided 49 by 2 and found a remainder. "No, it has to come out even," she reasoned and continued to search for other factors. It is interesting to note here that Becca actually divided 49 by 2 on her paper and found 24r1.

From other conversations I have had with her, I know that she can distinguish between odd and even numbers. Why did she not use her knowledge of odd and even numbers here and not bother with this unnecessary long division? First, I think there is a difference between recognizing odd and even numbers in the abstract and putting that understanding to use in a problem-solving situation. This kind of distinction lies at the heart of the NCTM's *Curriculum Standards*. Relationships are a crucial part of the Standards, and certainly the relationship of odd and even numbers is important for learners to understand. However, merely coming to recognize that relationship is not sufficient. Only when learners come to use that relationship to solve other problems can they really come to value mathematics.

Tolerance for ambiguity is an important part of problem solving.

Although Becca knew how to distinguish between odd and even numbers, she was so preoccupied with the newness of this mathematical investigation, and so intent on uncovering other numerical factors, that she did not draw on her knowledge of odd and even numbers at this time. In this respect Becca demonstrated that learners cannot attend to all the significant features of a problem-solving situation at one time. She showed that her understanding of odd and even numbers was not an all-or-nothing affair. Rather, through experiences such as this, Becca could deepen her understanding of this mathematical relationship as she encountered its use in other contexts. In fact, later on in this investigation, after she had tested out several other numbers, she used her knowledge of odd and even numbers to determine other possible solutions.

Generating Further Hypotheses

When Becca realized that 7 × 7 was the only multiplication factor for 49, she tried 56. "There's '7 × 8,'" she noted. Then she divided 56 by 2 and found 28 and tried to use the four factors of 7, 8, 2, and 28 to create her two problems. She set up her first problem like this:

$$\begin{array}{r} 28\ \Box \\ \times\ 2 \end{array}$$

She then realized that she needed to include an extra place in the other equation, and so she wrote this:

$$\begin{array}{r} 7\ \Box\Box \\ \times\ 8 \end{array}$$

When she then looked at the two equations together, she realized the impossibility of the two products' being the same. She drew on her sense of place value and her skill in estimating to see that the difference in the hundreds place between each equation was far too great for the products to be equivalent. Although she found that 56 was not a useful number to use, she nevertheless learned that only single-digit factors would satisfy the challenge that she had set for herself and set out again to try still other numbers. She saw that a two-digit factor placed numbers in the tens and hundreds columns and therefore made it more difficult to make both equations equal. The attitude she displayed about herself as a problem solver was healthy and demonstrates one of the important emphases of the *Curriculum Standards*, namely, that learners come to view themselves as competent problem solvers and decision makers. Instead of becoming discouraged that 56 did not work, she took what she had learned from the experience and applied it to other numbers she used. She tried to find all the factors for 20 and wrote 4 × 5 and 2 × 10. She realized from her previous work with 56 that a two-digit factor would not work, and so she abandoned 20 at this point. Being able to discard a possibility was not perceived by Becca to be a failing effort. Knowing that something would not work was certainly useful information; that insight saved her time because she did not have to bother setting up the two possible equations. She was also demonstrating perseverance and a willingness to tolerate ambiguity; it is an attitude that says, "I'm not sure if all of this is getting me anywhere, but I'm just going to keep going and see." This tolerance for ambiguity is an important dimension of the problem-solving attitude that is advocated in the *Standards* document. It is a feeling that learners have of being comfortable with the uncomfortable (Burke 1991); it is a productive tension because it involves a problem that a learner has generated herself and has a vested interest in pursuing.

Discovering Some Patterns

Next Becca tried the number 12. She found the combinations of 6×2 and 3×4 and wrote the following equations:

$$\begin{array}{r} 6\ \square \\ \times\ 2 \\ \hline \end{array} \qquad \begin{array}{r} 3\ \square \\ \times\ 4 \\ \hline \end{array}$$

Her problem then became $2 \times \square = 4 \times \square$ She chose $2 \times 6 = 4 \times 3$ and recorded the final problem as follows:

$$\begin{array}{r} 6\ \boxed{6} \\ \times\ 2 \\ \hline 132 \end{array} \qquad \begin{array}{r} 3\ \boxed{3} \\ \times\ 4 \\ \hline 132 \end{array}$$

When we discussed this part of the problem later on, she realized that other possibilities existed:

$$2 \times \boxed{2} = 4 \times \boxed{1}$$
$$2 \times \boxed{4} = 4 \times \boxed{2}$$
$$2 \times \boxed{8} = 4 \times \boxed{4}$$

"Is there anything special about the numbers that have worked so far?" I asked. She looked at the numbers she had used, focusing on the multiplier and the number in the tens column of the multiplicand (see table 1).

Table 1
Becca's First Results

$\begin{array}{r}36\\ \times 8\end{array}$	$\begin{array}{r}48\\ \times 6\end{array}$	$\begin{array}{l}3 \times 8 = 24\\ 4 \times 6 = 24\end{array}$
$\begin{array}{r}66\\ \times 6\end{array}$	$\begin{array}{r}44\\ \times 9\end{array}$	$\begin{array}{l}6 \times 6 = 36\\ 4 \times 9 = 36\end{array}$
$\begin{array}{r}66\\ \times 2\end{array}$	$\begin{array}{r}33\\ \times 4\end{array}$	$\begin{array}{l}6 \times 2 = 12\\ 3 \times 4 = 12\end{array}$

"They're all even (12, 24, 36). It must be even numbers that work," she hypothesized (she did not notice the pattern of multiples of 12 at this point).

"Yes, but '20' and '56' didn't work," I reminded her. She looked again and decided to try to find another number that worked. She felt that perhaps another example would help her see a pattern more clearly. She began with 10, trying to find four single-digit factors. She tried 11, 13, 14, and then jumped to 18, finding two combinations: 3×6 and 2×9. She recorded the following two equations:

$$\begin{array}{r} 2\ \square \\ \times\ 9 \\ \hline \end{array} \qquad \begin{array}{r} 3\ \square \\ \times\ 6 \\ \hline \end{array}$$

Her problem then was $9 \times \square = 6 \times \square$. She decided to solve it using the factors of 2 and 3: $9 \times \boxed{2} = 6 \times \boxed{3}$. Later on we discussed other possibilities:

$$9 \times \boxed{4} = 6 \times \boxed{6}$$
$$9 \times \boxed{6} = 6 \times \boxed{9}$$

Becca looked at the numbers again to see if she could detect a pattern (table 2).

Table 2
Single-Digit Factors

12	18	24	36
2×6	2×9	3×8	6×6
3×4	3×6	6×4	4×9

"I think they're adding '6,'" she observed, "so '30' has to work! " However, she found that 30 did not work because its factors of 1×30, 2×15, and 5×6 did not yield enough single-digit factors.

"Maybe '42' will work," she suggested, trying the next multiple of 6 after 36. It is interesting to note that Becca did not abandon this hypothesis about multiples of 6 simply because 30 did not work. The hypothesis was one that she had generated herself and was too powerful for her to discard this early in the investigation. She was already poised to try other possibilities, reluctant to let go of her current hunch until she generated more information.

As Becca tested out 42, she immediately knew the combination of 6×7 and recorded those numbers on her paper. She then considered each numeral from 1 to 9 to see if she could find other single-digit factors:

Possible factors
1. "There's '1×42,' but '42' is too big."
2. "No, the other number (factor) would be too big."

3. "No, the other number (factor) would still be too big."

4. "Four times '10' is only '40,' so that's not possible."

5. "No, I know that won't work, because when you multiply by '5' you have to have a '0' or a '5' at the end."

6. "This works."

7. "This works."

8. "No, because '8 × 5' is too little and '8 × 6' is too much."

9. "No, because '9 × 4' is too little and '9 × 5' is too much."

At this point in the investigation, Becca had developed an orderly problem-solving strategy; she carefully considered all possible factors for numbers 1–9 and knew that she did not need to look any further after examining these possibilities. As she considered each number from 1 to 9, she also flexibly used her estimation skills, as well as her knowledge about the divisibility of numbers, to determine all possible single-digit factors for 42. For instance, when considering the factors of 2 and 3 she did not even bother to do the division because she estimated the other factors to be too large. This flexibility in using skills and strategies is another important feature of the problem-solving competence espoused by the *Standards* document. Becca used her knowledge of divisibility rules and her skills as an estimator because they were the most efficient avenue for getting the information she wanted. Good problem solvers are flexible thinkers. They use and adapt the skills they have acquired to meet their own needs and to solve their own problems. Students need opportunities to pursue investigations that they initiate and find most interesting because oftentimes the method for solving these problems is not readily apparent and learners must use and apply their knowledge in new situations.

Becca again returned to her findings to see if any pattern was emerging (table 3). She still believed that a pattern might be behind these numbers and described her reasoning this way: "Maybe it will skip a few times and go back to its pattern. Maybe its pattern is, It works some of the time, and then it doesn't work two or three times, and then it goes back to when it works again. Maybe that could be its pattern. You know, like with blocks, it can go red, red, white, red, red, white." Becca's comments underscore the importance of working with color patterns. The *Curriculum Standards* calls for learners to represent their understandings through various representational schemes, such as art, drama, written narrative, and oral discourse.

Table 3
More Single-Digit Factors

12	18	24	30	36	42
2 × 6	2 × 9	3 × 8	No!	6 × 6	No!
3 × 4	3 × 6	6 × 4		4 × 9	

Here Becca drew on her mental image of color patterns to help her solve this current, more abstract problem.

Still hoping to find a pattern to her discoveries, Becca tried 48, the next multiple of 6, but she could find only 6 × 8. She tried 54 but could not find enough factors. As she reached 60 she remarked, "No, we're getting too high and we're going to be needing two-digit numbers." However, Becca was still not sure if she had uncovered all possible solutions, so she returned to some other numbers she had not tried. She found that 15 was not useful, but that 16 worked:

$$4\,\boxed{4} \qquad\qquad 8\,\boxed{8}$$
$$\underline{\times\ 4} \qquad\qquad \underline{\times\ 2}$$
$$176 \qquad\qquad\quad 176$$

She then tried other numbers from 17 to 35 and found no other solutions. She then listed her final possible solutions (table 4).

Table 4
Becca's Final Solutions

12	16	18	24	36
2 × 6	4 × 4	2 × 9	3 × 8	6 × 6
3 × 4	2 × 8	3 × 6	6 × 4	4 × 9

Becca's Final Reflection

When I asked Becca to reflect on this mathematical investigation, she listed three important points:

1. *"I like finding out patterns. It's neat to find out further information beyond the problem. I like to find the pattern that goes on behind that problem; it's sort of like its background, its ancestors."* What a poetic way to describe pattern explorations as searches into the ancestral background of numbers. Becca is deepening her understanding of what it means to think like a mathematician by noting that many problems have other patterns that "lurk beneath the surface" (Davis 1967). What one sees on the surface is only the tip of the numerical iceberg. Below the surface lie patterns that connect this problem to other problems. Her ancestral analogy is quite appropriate, since one problem is often seen as a "relative" to another; any given problem has a unique history with its own family of related problems.

2. *"It takes a lot of thinking. It might help you when you're doing other problems, like, 'Oh, yeah, I remember that this one is like that one.'"* Becca's comments demonstrate her understanding that work with patterns helps her see relationships that may be helpful in solving other problems. By taking this reflective stance, Becca is using herself as an instrument for her own growth. This

self-monitoring of one's own mathematical strategies is critical to the development of efficient and flexible problem solvers.

3. *"It's fun to have a challenge. It takes a lot of time and thinking."* Her comments emphasize again the important attitudinal goal advocated by the *Curriculum Standards*. Students need opportunities to engage in problem-solving ventures that are ambiguously defined; such problems force learners to raise a lot of questions and use a range of strategies. The process can be messy and can require a great deal of patience, persistence, and perspiration. But the end result is the satisfaction of having grappled with an interesting challenge coupled with the conviction that one will not hesitate to enter other such investigations in the future.

The Value of Questions

This article began with a question about some computational results. Although Becca and I constituted only a "classroom community" of two, our collaborative enterprise helped to highlight for me the importance of building learning environments that value student-initiated questions. Sometimes the questions arise when students wonder why certain mathematical results occur, as Becca's investigation illustrated. On other occasions, students wonder why not, as third grader Tammy did about the law of compensation (Whitin 1989). She knew that the law of compensation worked in addition, $8 + 5 = (8 + 2) + (5 - 2) = 10 + 3 = 13$, and so she wanted to know why it did not work in multiplication, $8 \times 5 \neq 10 \times 3$.

Sometimes teachers set up certain classroom procedures to foster the development of this questioning environ-ment. To encourage her students to ask more questions about mathematics, eighth-grade teacher Dale Anderson held a discussion group every Friday afternoon entitled "Everything You Wanted to Know about Mathematics but Were Afraid to Ask." Many of the students posed questions about certain algorithms and procedures that they could use correctly but did not understand, such as "Where did π come from?" "Why isn't there a 'oneth' place to the right of the decimal point" "Why does the invert-and-multiply rule work?" When students are respected as learners, then they ask questions that are really on their minds.

The *Curriculum Standards* calls for classroom communities that value questioning. In these classrooms, teachers and students do not accept knowledge as "ready made." Rather, they know that all ideas are open for refinement, challenge, and debate. They know that questions lead them on journeys that are intrinsically self-fulfilling. Becca's investigation proved to be one such example.

References

Burke, Carolyn. Remarks made at an Eisenhower grant–funded workshop for teachers on building interdisciplinary curriculum, Columbia, S.C., 26 September 1991.

Davis, Robert. *Explorations in Mathematics*. Palo Alto, Calif.: Addison-Wesley Publishing Co., 1967.

National Council of Teachers of Mathematics. *Curriculum and Evaluation Standards for School Mathematics*. Reston, Va.: The Council, 1989.

Whitin, David J. "Number Sense and the Importance of Asking Why." *Arithmetic Teacher* 36 (February 1989):26–30.

A Teacher's Journal

Ryan's Primes

by

Bill Juraschek and Amy S. Evans

"Why is 1 not a prime number?" This is not a question that is on the minds of most third graders, but Ryan was not your average third grader. Throughout the school year, he had impressed his teacher, Mrs. Evans, with his understanding of the mathematics they studied.

The class had been exploring multiplication and factors. After making rectangular arrays of various numbers of square tiles and seeing the connection between the dimensions of the arrays and the factors of the numbers, the class had noted those numbers for which only one array is possible. Evans told the class that these numbers were called *prime numbers* and invited her students to describe prime numbers verbally. After some discussion, the students fashioned this statement: "A prime number has only 1 and itself as factors." Later, when Mrs. Evans informed the class that 1 was not considered a prime, Ryan was the first to object.

"But 1 is only 1 times 1," contested Ryan.

"What do you mean?" responded Evans.

"Well, 1 is just like 3 and 5," said Ryan. "Three is only 1 times 3, and 5 is only 1 times 5; 1 is only 1 times 1. So 1 should be a prime. Its only factors are itself and 1."

Bill Juraschek, wjurasch@carbon.cudenver.edu, teaches at the University of Colorado, Denver, CO 80217. He also spends one day each week working with teachers. When this article was written, Amy Evans was living in Germany at Zimmerstrasse 46, 06667 Weisenfels, Germany. She was teaching at the Colorado Academy in Denver when this experience occurred. She is interested in developing students' understanding through communication and cooperative problem solving.

"You have a good point, Ryan. I am not sure why 1 is not a prime, but I do remember my math professor saying it isn't," Evans acknowledged.

"Well, your professor is wrong!" insisted Ryan.

At this point Evans suggested that Ryan write his ideas in a letter to Bill Juraschek and she would deliver it when she went to class. Ryan wrote the letter shown in figure 1.

After discussing why 1 is excluded from the set of primes, Evans and Juraschek brainstormed how to convince Ryan. They had been exploring ways to teach mathematics by emphasizing pattern recognition; this situation would be a good chance to try out a technique using carefully designed worksheets. To begin, Juraschek would construct a worksheet to guide Ryan to discover that every composite number can be expressed as the product of primes. To add some pizzazz and stretch the exploration over a few days, Juraschek would correspond with Ryan by fax. His first letter to Ryan is shown in figure 2; the worksheet follows in figure 3.

Dear Dr. Juraschek,
I think that 1 *is* a prime number, because the only way to make it is 1×1. I don't see any reason why it wouldn't be prime. If you have a reason, please write back and tell me.
Sincerely,
Ryan P.

P.S. I know that a prime number is a number that only 1 and itself is a factor of it. Examples: 2,3,5,7,11, 13, etc.

Fig. 1. Ryan's letter

Dear Ryan,

You wonder why 1 is not considered a prime number? It does seem strange. I will send you several faxes in the next few days to try to explain.

What you have discovered so far about prime numbers is true. A prime number has only 1 and itself as factors. The other whole numbers are called composite numbers. The word "composite" comes from "compose." Composite numbers are composed of prime numbers, like a song is composed of notes. The problems on the next page should show you what it means to be composed of prime numbers.

I will send another fax Friday. Bye for now.

Fig. 2. Juraschek responds to Ryan

Composite Numbers

Let's explore the whole numbers that are not prime numbers. Continue the pattern and fill in the blank squares.

$4 = 2 \times 2$

$6 = 2 \times 3$

$8 = 2 \times 4 = 2 \times 2 \times 2$

$9 = 3 \times 3$

$10 = 2 \times 5$

$12 = 2 \times 6 = 2 \times 2 \times 3$

$12 = 3 \times 4 = 3 \times \boxed{2} \times \boxed{2}$

$14 = \boxed{2} \times \Box$

$15 = 3 \times 5$

$16 = 2 \times 8 = 2 \times 2 \times 4 = \boxed{2} \times \boxed{2} \times 2 \times 2$

$16 = 4 \times \Box = 4 \times \Box \times \Box = \Box \times \Box \times 2 \times 2$

$18 = 3 \times \Box = 3 \times \Box \times \Box$

$20 = 2 \times 10 = 2 \times \Box \times \Box$

$20 = 4 \times 5 = \Box \times \Box \times 5$

$21 = \Box \times \Box$

$22 = 2 \times 11$

$24 = 2 \times \Box = 2 \times \Box \times \Box = \Box \times \Box \times \Box \times \Box$

$24 = 3 \times \Box = 3 \times \Box \times \Box = \Box \times \Box \times \Box \times \Box$

$24 = 6 \times \Box = 6 \times \Box \times \Box = \Box \times \Box \times \Box \times \Box$

$24 = 12 \times \Box = \Box \times \Box \times 2 = \Box \times \Box \times \Box \times \Box$

Now, you complete the rest up to 36, and then discuss the patterns you notice.

Fig. 3. Exercise to suggest a pattern with composite numbers

Ryan was excited as he walked to the school library to pick up his fax. After returning to the classroom, he eagerly began the worksheet. As Ryan worked, he detected patterns and shared his observations with Evans. "It looks like all numbers can be made with prime numbers," he said. He also noticed that no matter how you start factoring, you always end with the same prime factors for a number. "That is really cool," he concluded. "But that doesn't mean 1 isn't a prime." Evans relayed Ryan's comments to Juraschek; a few days later Ryan received the following fax:

Dear Ryan,

Mrs. Evans told me that when you did the worksheet about factoring composite numbers you noticed an important pattern. You noticed that every composite number can be written as the product of prime numbers. And you also noticed that no matter how you factor a number, you always get the same prime numbers for factors. For example, $20 = 2 \times 2 \times 5$ or $2 \times 5 \times 2$ or $5 \times 2 \times 2$, but we always get two 2s and one 5 as final prime factors.

Just as you did, mathematicians noticed this pattern, but they also saw a possible problem with 1. As you know, 1 behaves a special way when we multiply with it. The product of 1 and any number is the number. So we can say $20 = 2 \times 2 \times 5$ or $2 \times 2 \times 5 \times 1$ or $2 \times 2 \times 5 \times 1 \times 1$ or $2 \times 2 \times 5 \times 1 \times 1 \times 1 \times 1 \times 1 \times 1 \times 1 \times 1 \times 1$. If we call 1 a prime number, there are many different ways to write a number as the product of prime numbers. [The number] 20 could be the product of two 2s, one 5 and one 1; or two 2s, one 5 and two 1s; or two 2s, one 5, and nine 1s.

Now, mathematicians think this situation is messy. One way to clean it up is simply to say that 1 is not a prime number. If 1 is not allowed to be a prime number, we can say "Every composite number can be expressed as the product of prime numbers in only one way." (For what we are doing here, we don't consider $2 \times 2 \times 5$ different from $5 \times 2 \times 2$.) This pattern is one of the most basic patterns in arithmetic.

Suppose a bunch of third graders are playing basketball, and a big tenth grader wants to play with them. The third graders know that the tall tenth grader will make the game unfair, and it won't be much fun for them. So, they make a rule that only third graders can play in their game. This is just like the mathematicians making a rule that 1 is not a prime number. If they let 1 be a prime number, it messes up the game.

Another nice thing about saying 1 is not a prime number has to do with the way we define prime numbers. We can define a prime number as a number with exactly two factors. This makes the definition of a prime number very easy to state. Instead of saying, "A prime number is a number whose only factors are 1 and itself," we can say more simply, "A prime number is a number with exactly two factors." Mathematicians like definitions to be as simple as possible. Well, Ryan, I hope this makes sense to you. Bye for now.

Dr. Juraschek

Ideally, the story would end here, with Ryan knowingly agreeing that it makes sense to exclude 1 from the set of primes. Not so. Ryan seemed to understand what we were trying to tell him but did not find it convincing. Evans discussed the situation with Juraschek. It was time to use their ace in the hole: a magic trick.

The next day, Evans asked Ryan to take a handful of red, yellow, blue, and green colored cubes from a nearby container. "Let red be worth 2, yellow be worth 3, blue be worth 5, and green be worth 11," she said. "Now pick any four of the cubes, but don't let me see them. Then calculate the product of their values and tell me the product. For example, if you had three reds and a blue, you would multiply 2 times 2 times 2 times 5 to get 40." When Ryan said that his product was 90, Evans paused and then informed him that he must have used one red, two yellows, and one blue cube. Ryan was impressed and wanted to try again. He took a new collection of cubes and soon said that his product was 550. Again Evans could figure out exactly which cubes he used: one red, two blues, and one green.

Ryan was totally hooked. He had to know how the trick worked. Evans told him to think about it a while. He soon

Photo by Rene Galindo; all rights reserved

Ryan and his classmates revisit his third-grade investigation of primes.

noticed that the values of the cubes were prime numbers. Evans simply expressed his product as the product of primes and that told her which cubes he used: $90 = 2 \times 3 \times 3 \times 5$, so one red, two yellows, and one blue were used. He wanted to try it himself and soon mastered the procedure.

Now for the clincher. Evans informed Ryan that she was adding black cubes, which were worth 1. After choosing her cubes, Evans announced that their value was 88. Ryan thought for a moment and then said, "You have three reds and one green." Evans slowly opened her hand. Ryan was stunned to see that he was wrong. He pondered for a while, and suddenly the light dawned. With a grin, he said, "I want to choose some cubes this time."

Ryan chose some cubes and announced that the product was 3. Evans told him that she knew he had one yellow cube but that she could not tell him anything else. Ryan opened his hand to reveal one yellow and several black cubes. Filled with excitement, he said, "Aha, it doesn't work anymore. I could have a million black cubes, and you would never know!" Ryan was thoroughly convinced that 1 should not be called a prime. He finally observed, "[The number] 1 does meet our definition of prime numbers, but it doesn't fit the mathematicians' other definition."

Ryan eagerly asked if he could present the game to his classmates. The other students were impressed and amazed, but because they had not been involved in the discovery, it was merely a "trick" to them. It held little mathematical importance. For Ryan, however, the trick had significant meaning. He understood why it worked, and, in learning the underlying mathematics, he had communicated ideas, constructed knowledge, and satisfied his mathematical curiosity. In short, Ryan experienced the pleasure of mathematical power. Why is 1 not called a prime number? Ask Ryan; he knows.

What Is the Whole?

by

Nancy M. Wentworth and Eula Ewing Monroe

Photo by Jeff Niekamp; all rights reserved

Defining the unit or "the whole" in fraction examples is often confusing to students, not only because of the particular example being considered but often because of the representations teachers use as they help students construct meanings. This article begins with a brief summary of constructivist mathematics education along with a situation in which a teacher misunderstood the meaning of an answer constructed by two students. Then three examples of representations of common fractions and ways that teachers can encourage students to construct useful meanings of the fractional unit will be considered.

Constructivist Classrooms

Constructivist mathematics educators argue that teaching subject matter is not transmitting information about "the way things really are" but rather is communicating and developing knowledge that humans find useful and functional in making sense of experience and solving problems (Noddings 1990; Cobb 1988). Children construct their individual realities by reorganizing their cognitive and social experiences. Cultural knowledge is continually recreated through the coordinated actions of the members of a community (Bruner 1986).

A constructivist classroom is an environment in which students experience intuitions of mathematical reality and discover relationships (Carpenter et al. 1988). The role of

Nancy Wentworth and Eula Ewing Monroe teach at Brigham Young University, Provo, UT 84602. Wentworth works with middle school and secondary school teacher candidates in mathematics education. Monroe is interested in the role of language in developing conceptual mathematical knowledge.

Photo by Jeff Niekamp; all rights reserved

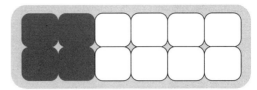

1/3 of an egg carton is shaded.

Fig. 1. Egg-carton representation of the fraction 1/3

the teacher in a constructivist classroom is to present tasks in which students think through a problem and to question students about their thinking. Cooperative-group activities are one type of constructivist activity that allows students to share their thinking with other students as they construct understandings. Students do not memorize predetermined algorithms and facts but develop and explain their own. Knowledge is both personal and socially constructed.

Maher and Davis (1990) reflected on a teacher's constructivist lesson centered on an example involving two pizzas, each cut into twelve pieces. "Seven students … are to eat one piece from each of the pizzas. What fraction of the two pizzas was eaten?" (p. 68). Maher and Davis were concerned with the teacher's representation of the unit. The teacher stated that 14/12 of the two pizzas was eaten and not 14/24 as one student decided. Reflection about the meaning of 14/12 might have convinced the teacher that 14/12 could not possibly represent how much of the two pizzas was eaten. Fourteen twelfths (14/12) is greater than 1, which implies that more than all the pizza was eaten. That result is just not possible! The unit being considered in this example was two pizzas, the amount of two pizzas eaten. The unit was twenty-four pieces, not twelve pieces. The student constructed an understanding of the unit made up of twenty-four pieces, whereas the teacher thought of the unit as having only twelve pieces.

Teachers must be very aware of the unit being represented as they present examples of fractions to their students. The following examples illustrate misunderstandings of the unit in fraction problems and contain suggestions for teachers as they aid the construction of understanding with their students.

Example 1. In an effort to use constructivist mathematics methods that include concrete, hands-on representations of mathematical concepts, many school teachers use egg cartons to represent fractional values. The fraction 1/2 can readily be shown by covering six sections of the egg carton, 1/3 by covering four sections, and 1/4 by covering three sections (fig. 1). A first-year teacher, Mary, was

asked how to represent 1/5. She immediately cut a five-section piece and a one-section piece from the carton, then covered one section of the five-section piece with the one-section piece (fig. 2).

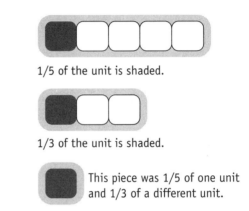

1/5 of the unit is shaded.

1/3 of the unit is shaded.

This piece was 1/5 of one unit and 1/3 of a different unit.

Fig. 2. If individual sections are cut away from the carton, the unit changes.

When the interviewer asked Mary to explain one-third again, she took the same one-section piece and covered one section of a three-section piece. The difficulty with these representations was that Mary had shown that one-third equals one-fifth. If the same one-piece section could be used to cover one-third and one-fifth, then one-third must be the same as one-fifth. This teacher recognized the error of her concrete representation by stating that the "total piece" in each problem was different. The unit or "total piece" had changed and led to the misunderstanding. Mary saw that she must keep the unit constant as she poses questions about comparison of fractions to her students.

When used carefully, concrete representations help the construction of meaning. Two mistakes in representing the unit were made in the egg-carton example. The first was in using a part of the egg carton to represent a new unit without carefully redefining that new unit. Initially the unit was the twelve-section egg carton; next a five-section piece was used as a new unit when defining one-fifth of a unit; finally a three-section piece was cut to show the meaning of one-third. The five-section piece of the egg carton made a new unit as did the three-section piece, but the teacher failed to redefine carefully the unit in the example.

The second mistake was that Mary did not keep the unit constant when comparing two fractional parts. One-third had been defined once as four sections of the twelve-section unit and again as one section of the three-section unit. A section of the whole egg carton was used to represent one-fifth of a unit in one example and then one-third of a unit in a different example. One-fifth of the whole egg carton is not one section, and one-third of the whole egg carton is not one section. The unit represented was not held constant, thus causing comparisons that confused meanings. Consequently, the inappropriate conclusion that one-third is the same as one-fifth was able to be constructed.

Students, especially young students trying to construct an understanding of fractions, have enough difficulty with the idea of the part of the whole. Keeping the whole constant will allow the focus to be on the part of the whole.

Example 2. Graph paper is often used to help students construct area-model representations of fraction multiplication (Peck and Jencks 1981). The examples 1/3 × 1/5 and 1/4 × 1/6 have different answers, but when represented on graph paper, both might have one square of the graph paper as an answer (fig. 3). When working on an assignment with these two examples, a student was overheard to

say, "Look, these two answers are the same." The teacher was not sure how to respond to the student's misunderstanding. How could the two answers be different when both were represented by one square on the graph paper?

The graph-paper representations of 1/3 × 1/5 and 1/4 × 1/6 confused the student into thinking that the fractions 1/15 and 1/24 were equal. The unit in each example was different in area; therefore, the fractional piece of the unit looked the same. The pieces were identical in area in these representations but not in their meanings as fractional parts of the whole.

Teachers should encourage students to draw their own pictures of the units and fractions. Students who did not use graph paper but instead drew their own models had less difficulty constructing meanings of answers. They usually drew rectangles of similar size for all examples then divided them into the appropriate pieces to solve the problem (fig. 4). In most cases the rectangles that represented the unit were similar in size, so the fractional pieces were smaller when the unit was divided into more pieces. The representations from example to example were more consistent with the meanings of the fractions represented. A fractional piece representing 1/15 looked larger than the fractional piece 1/24 because the unit was approximately the same in the representation of each problem.

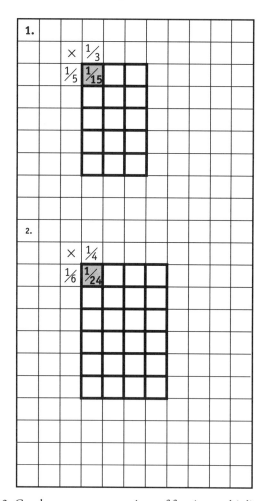

Fig. 3. Graph-paper representations of fraction multiplication

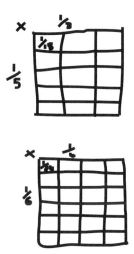

Fig. 4. Student's model of fraction multiplication

Allowing students to construct their own pictures or representations of fractions freely rather than with graph paper may eliminate misunderstandings. Student-generated models facilitate careful construction of meanings.

Example 3. Division by fractions can pose an especially difficult understanding of "one" (Clemens 1991). Consider this example: 1/3 ÷ 1/4. A useful way to restate this example is "How many 1/4s are there in 1/3?" An area model of the unit and the parts of the unit can be drawn to help students construct an understanding of this example (fig. 5). The answer is one complete 1/4 and *one-third* of another 1/4. Note that the one here refers to the unit 1/4 and the *one-third* means one-third of the 1/4 of the original unit. When students are encouraged to think through this problem with models that they construct, they can understand what the answer 1 1/3 means. The constructivist teacher should help the student think about how the one in the answer means *one* one-fourth of the original unit, not one complete original unit.

Symbols: 1/3 ÷ 1/4

Words: How many 1/4s are there in 1/3?

Diagrams:

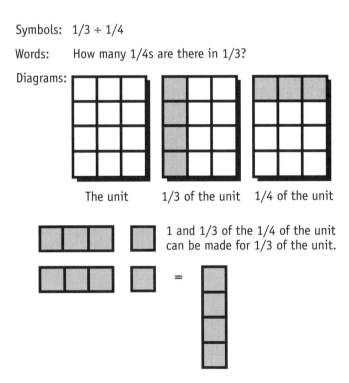

The unit   1/3 of the unit   1/4 of the unit

1 and 1/3 of the 1/4 of the unit can be made for 1/3 of the unit.

Fig. 5. How many 1/4s are there in 1/3?

Summary

In the pizza example reported by Maher and Davis (1990), the teacher did not understand what the unit was in the problem; therefore, her questioning of the students g about how the new representation of the unit might hinder the meanings of the fractions constructed by the students. In example 2, students who were given graph paper as a tool for representing multiplication of fractions incorrectly compared fractions from different units, whereas students who drew their own area models were able to construct appropriate meanings by keeping the unit size constant. In example 3, *one* had different meanings throughout the example. Initially one unit was divided into fourths and into thirds. Then *one* one-fourth and 1/3 of that one-fourth together represented the answer. A student-constructed meaning for the word *one* should be guided by the teacher, who understands how the "one" changes roles in this example.

Teachers need to define carefully the unit that makes the whole as they have students define and represent fractions in constructivist ways. Representations of the unit that remain consistent from example to example tend to help students construct appropriate meanings of fractions. As students' understanding of fractions increase and as the units vary from example to example, teachers need to probe students to define the unit, or the whole, as part of understanding the problem. Representations of fractions used in the constructivist teaching of mathematics should facilitate, not hinder, appropriate meanings of fractions for students.

References

Bruner, Jerome. *Actual Minds, Possible Worlds.* Cambridge: Harvard University Press, 1986.

Carpenter, Thomas, Elizabeth Fennema, Penelope Peterson, C. Chiang, and Megan Loef. "Using Knowledge of Children's Mathematical Thinking in Classroom Teaching: An Experimental Study." Paper presented at the annual meeting of the American Educational Research Association, New Orleans, La., 1988.

Clemens, Herbert. "What Do Math Teachers Need to Be?" In *Teaching Academic Subjects to Diverse Learners,* edited by M. M. Kennedy, 84–96. New York: Teachers College Press, 1991.

Cobb, Paul. "Multiple Perspectives." Paper presented at the annual meeting of the American Education Research Association, New Orleans, La., 1988.

Maher, Carolyn A., and Robert B. Davis. "Building Representations of Children's Meanings." In *Constructivist Views on the Teaching and Learning of Mathematics. Journal for Research in Mathematics Education* Monograph Series No. 4. Reston, Va.: National Council of Teachers of Mathematics, 1990.

Noddings, Nell "Constructivism in Mathematics Education." In Constructivist Views on the *Teaching and Learning of Mathematics. Journal for Research in Mathematics* Education Monograph Series No. 4. Reston, Va.: National Council of Teachers of Mathematics, 1990.

Peck, Don, and Stan Jencks. "Conceptual Issues in the Teaching and Learning of Fractions." *Journal for Research in Mathematics Education* 12 (November 1981): 339–48.

How Children Think about Division with Fractions

by

Mary Ann Warrington

When children are allowed to create and invent, their fertile minds enable them to solve problems in a variety of original and logical ways. When their minds have not been shackled by rules and conventions, children are free to invent procedures that reflect their natural thought processes.

Much of the research and documentation concerning children's inventions focuses on their approaches to the addition, subtraction, multiplication, and division of whole numbers. Research and practice in these areas have shown that children can develop sophisticated and meaningful procedures in computation and problem solving without explicit instruction in the use of conventional algorithms. These invented procedures have been reported not only in the United States (Kamii 1989, 1994; Madell 1985) but also in Brazil (Carraher, Carraher, and Schliemann 1985), Holland (Heege 1978; Treffers 1987), and South Africa (Olivier, Murray, and Human 1991). In the United States, some leading educators, such as Burns (1994) and Leinwand (1994), have renounced the teaching of algorithms to young children, and some researchers, including Kamii (1994), have even shown the practice to be harmful. Despite compelling evidence about children's procedures with fractions (Mack 1990; Streefland 1993), most educators still believe that to handle the more complex mathematics of the middle grades and beyond, children need to learn specific procedures, or algorithms.

As a teacher of fifth and sixth grade, I am passionately committed to reform in mathematics education and firmly

Mary Ann Warrington teaches at the Atrium School, Watertown, MA 02172. Her interests in middle school education center on children's inventions in mathematics— how they construct knowledge.

believe in the merits of children's constructing their own knowledge. Yet when I began working in the middle grades four years ago, like many I was ambivalent about whether students could continue to progress in mathematics without instruction in procedures, operations, and algorithms. Despite my convictions about constructivist teaching in the primary grades, the thought of tackling a middle school curriculum involving fractions, decimals, and percents with such an approach seemed overwhelming. However, the thought of playing it safe and teaching in a traditional manner contradicted everything I knew about how children learn mathematics. Furthermore, I was well aware of the alarming statistics regarding mathematics achievement in our schools and the apparent ineffectiveness of many currently used methods. Thus, I set forth teaching mathematics to a class of fifth and sixth graders using a constructivist approach in which the students were encouraged to think deeply about mathematics concepts and to invent their own methods of solving problems.

The purpose of this article is to let others know that contrary to popular belief, children *can* indeed construct knowledge about sophisticated and abstract concepts in mathematics without the use of algorithms. I chose to focus on the students' division with fractions because the rule of "invert and multiply" had always puzzled me, and I was concerned about students' ability to find meaning in an area that few adults understand. Most adults "invert and multiply" without any notion of why they are doing so, and students usually cannot explain the reasoning behind this frequently used and widely accepted procedure.

The following account provides insight into how children naturally think when they are encouraged to do their own thinking. The students whose ideas are expressed in this article were fifth and sixth graders in a self-contained, mixed-age, mixed-ability classroom. The children had been exposed to a variety of teaching practices in mathematics before entering my class. Some had been taught algorithms, some had worked extensively with manipulatives, and some had had two years of a constructivist approach to mathematics. The culture of the classroom and school is one that values the process of learning, and children are accustomed to sharing their ideas openly.

Children's Thoughts on Dividing Fractions

By the time this topic was introduced, the students had constructed considerable knowledge about fractions and were quite confident and proficient with respect to equivalent fractions. The work documented here began in February, so I had been working with these students for at least five months. The children had already proved capable of inventing ways to add, subtract, and multiply fractions without direct instruction on procedures or algorithms.

Because I believe that children construct knowledge on the basis of what they already know, I have always taught from this perspective; when introducing a new concept, I begin with a familiar topic and move forward. Thus, the initial discussion about dividing fractions began with a general question about division. I asked the class to think about the expression

$$4 \div 2$$

and what it meant to them. Their responses ranged from "It means if you have four things and you divide them into two groups, how many are in each group?" to the most common response, which was "It means how many times does two fit into four or how many groups of two fit into four?" This brief discussion of division informed me about how the children were thinking about this mathematical principle. It is essential to learn what your students know and how they are thinking before proceeding to new territory. Their prior knowledge about division must be used as a base or a starting point.

Next, I presented them with the problem

$$2 \div \frac{1}{2}.$$

Within seconds many children were eager to respond. When called upon, one student responded, "Four [pause] because one-half goes into two four times." Another child followed up with "I think it's four also [pause] because if you had two candy bars and you divided them into halves, you'd have four pieces." I was pleased with their thinking thus far and inspired by their willingness to attempt to solve the problems using their own devices. The students were used to relying on themselves for solutions, so the proverbial "I don't know how to do this" did not surface.

The students seemed confident about their reasoning, and I was eager to move into other problems, knowing that halves tend to be easier for children than other fractions, such as thirds and fifths.

The next problem I wrote on the chalkboard was

$$1 \div \frac{1}{3}.$$

Without hesitation the children responded, almost in unison, "Three [pause] because one-third goes into one three times." I then wrote

$$1 \div \frac{2}{3}.$$

Two responses were forthcoming. About one-third of the class said that the answer was 6, and the rest believed the answer to be 1 1/2. The reasoning of those claiming 1 1/2 was that 1 ÷ 1/3 is 3, so 1 ÷ 2/3 must be 1 1/2 because 2/3 is twice as big as 1/3 and so fits into 1 half as many times. Since they had already determined that 1 ÷ 1/3 is 3, 1 ÷ 2/3 must be half of that, or 1 1/2. This explanation seemed to convince others that 6 was not feasible. Many of those who had initially responded with 6 quickly retracted their answer, whereas others took some time to debate before noticing the flaw in their reasoning. The exchange of ideas is an important aspect of a constructivist classroom. Although constructivists believe that children learn from one another, they do not believe that children acquire mathematical knowledge *from* other people. Such knowledge has to be *constructed* by each individual from the inside. Social interaction stimulates critical thinking, but it is not the source of mathematical knowledge (Kamii 1994). In this case, the students who believed that the answer was 6 had to think about their own reasoning as well as that of their peers and determine who was correct. In deciding that 6 was incorrect, they had to *modify* their thinking. The social interaction undoubtedly stimulated these children to question their thinking; however, the actual construction of knowledge—determining the answer to be 1 1/2—was internal.

From that point the students solved 3 ÷ 1/3 with relative ease, and when asked to try

$$\frac{1}{3} \div 3,$$

they again constructed their reasoning from what they knew. One child said, "It's one-ninth because one divided by three is a third, so if you want to divide it [one-third] by three, you have to take a third of a third, which is one-ninth." Another child's explanation went like this: "I think it's one-ninth because if you had one-third of a pie left and you were sharing it with three people [two friends], each person would get one-ninth." What intrigued me about that argument was that the child took a straight computation problem and assigned meaning to it by creating a word problem.

After working through several more problems, I gave the class the following:

> I purchased 5 3/4 pounds of chocolate-covered peanuts. I want to store the candy in 1/2-pound bags so that I can freeze it and use it in smaller portions. How many 1/2-pound bags can I make?

The students were used to estimating first, so they quickly gave estimates ranging from 10 to 12. They then set out to find the exact answer. One child responded, "Eleven bags, and you would have a quarter of a pound left over, or half a bag." When I asked how she obtained that answer, she replied, 'You get ten bags from the five pounds because five divided by one-half is ten, and then you get another bag from the three-fourths, which makes eleven bags, and there is one-fourth of a pound left over, which makes half of a half-pound bag." Another student solved the problem by changing the 5 3/4 to 6 pounds and then dividing that by 1/2 to get 12 bags. He then took the 1/4 he had added and divided that by 1/2 to get the 1/2, which he subtracted from 12 to arrive finally at 11 1/2 bags.

Perhaps the invention that startled me the most on this particular problem came from a child who nonchalantly raised her hand and said, "I just doubled it [five and three-fourths] and divided by one." Her peers responded, "Can you do that?" She went on to explain that it did not change the problem. She cleverly cited how the answer remains the same when an equation is doubled, as in $10 \div 5 = 2$ and $20 \div 10 = 2$. She astutely used a mathematical relationship, without direct instruction about proportions. This sort of inventive thinking and intellectual risk taking are simply not present in classrooms where teachers impose methods on children. I also found it fascinating, although not surprising, that not one child considered converting the mixed numeral 5 3/4 to an improper fraction of 23/4, which would be the first step in a traditional algorithm. Although many advocates for teaching algorithms assert that children do not invent efficient methods to solve complex computations, the evidence cited here does not support such claims. What could be more efficient than doubling 5 3/4 to make 11 1/2 and dividing by 1?

During the next week the children continued to work with division of fractions. I was amazed by the thinking that was taking place and thrilled with how much I was learning from the children. Their work had exceeded my expectations thus far, yet I was still curious about whether they could continue this upward spiral as the problems and computation became more difficult. One day I asked them to solve the following problem:

$$4\frac{2}{5} \div \frac{1}{3}$$

By now the entire class could estimate that the answer was "a little more than twelve." After estimating, they set out to calculate the exact answer. As expected, this problem took longer than previous ones, and more head scratching, frowning, and exchanges of ideas ensued than usual. After a while we gathered as a group to discuss the outcome.

Several children remarked that they had an answer that was close but were not sure if it was exact. I assured them that I was more interested in hearing their strategies. Various children volunteered answers, which I recorded on the chalkboard. (All the answers were slightly more than 13.) One child's explanation was the following: "I got thirteen and one-fifteenth [pause]. I started with four divided by one-third and that's twelve because one-third goes into four [pause] twelve times.... Then I changed two-fifths to six-fifteenths and one-third to five-fifteenths." I interrupted her at this point and asked her to explain why she did that. She continued, "Because it is easier for me to divide them now, and they are still the same number [pause]. Then I figured five-fifteenths goes into six-fifteenths one more time, which makes thirteen, and there is one-fifteenth left over, so it's thirteen and one-fifteenth." Several children nodded with approval; some children exclaimed, "That's what I did!" Others asked to have the thinking repeated.

After a lengthy discussion about this problem, everyone seemed convinced that the answer was indeed 13 1/15 except for the child who had "doubled and divided by one" in the previous example. She raised her hand and claimed to agree with everything "except the last part." She said that "six-fifteenths divided by five-fifteenths is one, and there is one-fifteenth left over, which still has to be divided by five-fifteenths. One-fifteenth divided by five-fifteenths is one-fifth bec--- ~ve-fifteenths could fit in ~ time, so the answer is thi~ ~ was not only logical an~ ~a shining example of the~ ~hat children develop wh~ ~nselves. Here was a chil~ *for 5th grade* ~ith an entire class of peer~ ~he was not willing to acce~ ~did not make sense. Thi~ ~~~~ous products of constructivism: intellectual autonomy.

Needless to say, the debate over the answer to this problem went on for some time, and for many it carried over into recess. During the heated debate, one child looked to me and said, "Well, which answer is right?" When the class realized that I was typically not giving answers, the debate resumed. This sort of intellectual bantering among children is a desirable and typical occurrence in a constructivist classroom. This type of social interaction or debate engages children in critical thinking. It does not contribute to the sort of confusion that many people experienced in mathematics class, which resulted merely in frustration. It is a processing of ideas that results in deeper understanding. Piaget attributed great importance to social interaction. In his theory, social interaction is absolutely essential to the construction of knowledge, and it is indispensable in childhood for the elaboration of logical thought (Kamii 1989).

We continued to work on dividing with fractions, and the problems became more involved and had more complexity with respect to computation. The children continued to thrive, and eventually almost all of them had resolved their confusion about remainders (such as the 1/15 in the previous problem). Some students continued to struggle with the more difficult problems, yet they were able to give extremely close estimates, which indicates a developing understanding and excellent number sense.

Conclusion

When I first began teaching children, I was fascinated with their ability to think and reason. And their strategies for solving problems have never ceased to amaze me. In many instances and with many different topics, such as the one described in this article, students have taught me what it means to be a teacher and what it means to "think and communicate mathematically."

I want to stress to readers that children *can* and *do* invent ways to do sophisticated mathematics; however, the culture of the classroom must be one that truly values and encourages thinking. Children must feel safe if they are to take the intellectual risks necessary to construct knowledge. They must be given ample time to think and reflect about numbers and to exchange ideas with peers, and they must be developmentally ready for the material being presented. Furthermore, a child who has been fed a strict diet of algorithms and has viewed mathematics as simply calculating using a system of memorized rules cannot suddenly begin to think deeply about numbers and to invent procedures. Such children have learned to be dependent on teachers for methods and solutions, and it is extremely difficult to change such behavior.

As teachers it is our duty to provide learning environments that allow children to be successful. This obligation means that we must look carefully at the traits we value. Are we merely interested in the correct answer, and is that all we assess? Do we as educators truly value mathematics, and if so, how do we communicate that regard to students? Have we taken the time and energy to learn the mathematics we claim to teach? Do we really value and encourage intellectual autonomy?

Finally, one should not assume that the teacher's role in a constructivist classroom is one of a passive observer who sits idly waiting for children to construct knowledge. Setting up a classroom environment in which the children invent methods to solve problems is not an easy task. The teacher must strive to understand each child's thinking and must carefully determine just when and how to guide a child to a deeper and higher level of understanding. Creating such a classroom and formulating appropriate questions to probe children's thinking and lead them to new intellectual heights is perhaps the subject of a subsequent article.

References

Burns, Marilyn. About *Teaching Mathematics: A K–8 Resource.* Sausalito, Calif.: Marilyn Burns Education Associates, 1992.

————. "Arithmetic: The Last Holdout." *Phi Delta Kappan* 75 (February 1994): 471–76.

Carraher, Terezinha Nunes, David William Carraher, and Analucia Dias Schliemann. "Mathematics in the Streets and in Schools." *British Journal of Developmental Psychology* 3 (March 1985): 21–29.

Heege, Hans ter. "Testing the Maturity for Learning the Algorithm of Multiplication." *Educational Studies in Mathematics* 9 (February 1978): 75–83.

Kamii, Constance. *Young Children Reinvent Arithmetic.* New York: Teachers College Press, 1985.

————. *Young Children Continue to Reinvent Arithmetic, Second Grade.* New York: Teachers College Press, 1989.

————. *Young Children Continue to Reinvent Arithmetic, Third Grade.* New York: Teachers College Press, 1994.

Leinwand, Steven. "It's Time to Abandon Computational Algorithms." *Education Week*, 9 February 1994, p. 36.

Mack, Nancy K "Learning Fractions with Understanding: Building on Informal Knowledge." *Journal for Research in Mathematics Education* 21 (January 1990): 16–32.

Madell, Rob. "Children's Natural Processes." *Arithmetic Teacher* 32 (March 1985): 20–22.

Olivier, Alwyn, Hanlie Murray, and Piet Human. "Children's Solution Strategies for Division Problems." In *Proceedings of the Thirteenth Annual Meeting of the North American Chapter of the International Group for the Psychology of Mathematics Education*, vol. 2, edited by Robert G. Underhill, 15–21. Blacksburg, Va.: Virginia Polytechnic Institute, 1991.

Streefland, Leen. "Fractions: A Realistic Approach." In *Rational Numbers*, edited by Thomas P. Carpenter, Elizabeth Fennema, and Thomas A. Romberg, 289–325. Hillsdale, N.J.: Lawrence Erlbaum Associates, 1993.

Treffers, A. "Integrated Column Arithmetic According to Progressive Schematisation." *Educational Studies in Mathematics* 18 (May 1987): 125–45.

How Old Do You Want to Be?

by
Kenneth P. Goldberg

The *Curriculum and Evaluation Standards for School Mathematics* (NCTM 1989) recommends the integration of technology into the classroom to enhance skills and understanding. Although much of the attention on technology has focused on the computer, the inexpensive and easily available calculator, especially one like the TI Explorer with special educational features, may hold the greatest promise for positive change.

A special feature of the TI Explorer that has great potential for student exploration and understanding is the quotient-with-remainder division key INT ÷. A division operation performed with this key—for example, 13 divided by 4—results in an integer quotient Q with nonnegative integer remainder R (fig. 1). This interpretation of quotient is different from that encountered in middle grades, where the quotient of two integers a and b is a/b.

Exploring number bases using this key can lead to a better understanding of (*a*) our number system and its

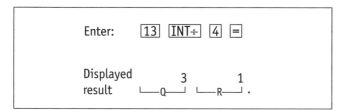

Fig. 1. Dividing 13 by 4 using the quotient-with-remainder division key

Kenneth Goldberg is the director of mathematics education at New York University, New York, NY 10003. His special interest is in using technology to enhance teaching mathematics.

place-value notational system and (*b*) the relationship between the division algorithm leading to a quotient-with-remainder result and the division algorithm leading to a mixed-decimal result. The activity, which is suitable for both fifth- and sixth-grade classes that have already done extensive introductory work with different number bases, can be completed in one day or can be used in short stages over a few days.

Growing Old Gracefully: Exploring Different Number Bases

Fifth- and sixth-grade students are usually impatient to grow up; they are eager to become teenagers like their older brothers and sisters or the junior and senior high school students in the neighborhood. To capitalize on this interest, ask students if they would like to know how they can become instant teenagers. Almost without exception the answer will be a resounding "Yes!" I have found that teachers enjoy this activity almost as much as their students. However, unlike the students who wish to make themselves older, the teachers invariably reverse the process to make themselves younger.

Begin by asking each of your students to write down their current age and to take that many unit cubes from a set of base ten blocks. Next, remind students what is represented by the digits in the numerical representation of their age in our base-ten number system, and have them divide up their individual piles of unit cubes to represent this meaning (fig. 2). Be sure to remind them that in base ten, no unique symbol exists for ten, hence we begin grouping at that point.

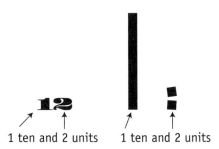

1 ten and 2 units   1 ten and 2 units

Fig. 2. Using unit cubes to represent the tens and units digits of a number

Next, suggest to the students that if they lived in a civilization that had only four fingers on each hand instead of five, they would probably use groups of eight instead of ten to keep track of the number of objects in a large pile. No unique symbol would exist for eight—that's the point where grouping would begin.

With this thought in mind, ask them to scramble their unit cubes. Have the students count the cubes out into smaller piles of eight instead of ten and see what outcome they get. One such result is shown in figure 3 from a twelve-year-old.

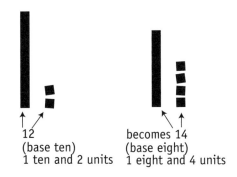

12
(base ten)
1 ten and 2 units

becomes 14
(base eight)
1 eight and 4 units

Fig. 3. Using unit cubes to model transforming a number from base-ten representation to base eight

Since more units are left over after removing groups of eight than after removing groups of ten, the students in the class should find that the numeral representing their age in base eight appears to represent a larger number than the numeral representing their age in base ten. For example, a twelve-year-old girl in the class can claim to be 14 (1 group of 8 plus 4 units) as long as she specifies "in base eight." This restriction is usually abbreviated as 14_{eight}. If a numeral does not have a subscript to show its base, it is assumed to be a base-ten numeral.

Of course, the students need to understand that both numerals, 12 and 14_{eight}, are really naming the same amount in different ways. The students are not really changing their age, just the form in which their age is written.

A number of interesting questions can then be asked, which can lead to classroom discussions about different base systems and how numbers are represented in them.

Some of these questions follow:

1. What base can you use to make yourself appear older than you are in base eight? How would this base work?

2. What base can you use to make yourself appear younger than your real base-ten age? How would this base work?

3. Find number bases that would make you appear to be at least 100 years old. At least 1000 years old.

4. If a classmate said she wrote her age as 23 in a different base, but you knew she was really 11, what base was she using to represent her age?

Using the TI Explorer

Once students understand the concept underlying the process of expressing the age in a base other than ten, they can use the integer-division key INT÷ on the TI Explorer calculator to compute quickly and efficiently. For example, to convert a student's real (base-ten) age of 12 to base eight, we enter

$$\boxed{12}\ \boxed{\text{INT}÷}\ \boxed{8}\ \boxed{=}\ ,$$

which gives the result

$$\underbrace{1}_{Q}\quad \underbrace{4}_{R}\ .$$

In other words, twelve is equivalent to one group of size eight with a remainder of four, or 14_{eight}.

The TI Explorer is especially helpful when the base is small compared with the original number and the numeral in the new base consists of more than two digits. For example, when converting 17 to base three, the result is 122_{three}, since

$$17 = (1 \times 32) + (2 \times 3) + 2.$$

Using the TI Explorer, we divide 17 two times in succession by 3 using the INT÷ key. On the first attempt, we get

$$17 ÷ 3 = \underbrace{5}_{Q}\quad \underbrace{2}_{R}\ .$$

Since no "5" occurs in base three, we must divide again by 3, using $\boxed{\text{INT}÷}$, giving

$$\underbrace{1}_{Q}\quad \underbrace{2}_{R}\ .$$

But we must remember the initial remainder of 2 and include that digit with those on the display. The procedure is illustrated in figure 4, giving the answer $17 = 122_{\text{three}}$.

If they fully understand how other number bases work, the students can next use the TI Explorer to switch numbers from a representation in one base to that in base ten

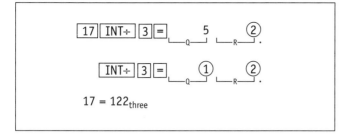

Fig. 4. Using the quotient and remainder-division key twice to obtain the base-three representation of 17

and then to that in another base. For example, the students can express the number 123_{five} in base eight by multiplying out the given number into its base-ten representation

$$123_{\text{five}} = (1 \times 5^2) + (2 \times 5) + 3 = 38 \text{ (base ten)}$$

and then use the INT÷ key to convert the number to base eight:

$$\boxed{38}\ \boxed{\text{INT÷}}\ \boxed{8}\ \boxed{=}\ \underbrace{4}_{Q}\ \underbrace{6}_{R}\ .$$

Therefore $123_{\text{five}} = 38 = 46_{\text{eight}}$.

Base Ten: Comparing Two Different Division Algorithms

Once students are familiar with the INT÷ key, it is time to ask an especially interesting question:

> How is it possible for us to get two different answers using the TI Explorer to do a division problem, one when we use the ordinary ÷ key and another when we use the INT ÷ key?

To illustrate this question with a concrete example, ask students to divide 17 by 5 using both the regular-division key, ÷, and the INT÷ key. The answers are shown in figure 5. Next, ask the students in what way the two answers are the same and in what way they are different.

Both answers have the same integral part, 3. The difference appears to be in the remaining part of the answer—

$$\boxed{17}\ \boxed{÷}\ \boxed{5}\ \boxed{=}\ 3.4$$

$$\boxed{17}\ \boxed{\text{INT÷}}\ \boxed{5}\ \boxed{=}\ \underbrace{3}_{Q}\ \underbrace{2}_{R}\ .$$

Fig. 5. Using the ordinary division key and the quotient-and-remainder division key to obtain two different forms of the answer for the same division problem

in one example, the decimal value 0.4, and in the other example, the remainder of 2. With a reminder from the teacher that the divisor in the original problem was 5, the students should be able to recognize, and then verify, that 0.4 is the result of dividing the remainder 2 by the original divisor 5 (using the ordinary division key on the calculator). In other words, just as the students' ages could be represented in different ways depending on which base was used, the decimal and the quotient-with-remainder results of a division problem are simply two different ways of representing the computed form of 17 ÷ 5.

Students can verify this equivalence by taking several division problems, evaluating them with both the regular-division key and the integer-division key, and showing that the two answers are the same by dividing the remainder by the original divisor. Interesting questions that pinpoint the students' understanding of this equivalence might include the following:

Problem 1. Suppose you used the ÷ key on your calculator to divide one number by another and obtained the answer 5.5. What would the Q-part of the answer have been if you had used the INT÷ key to perform the division?

Problem 2. Suppose, in problem 1, that I told you that the divisor I used was 4. What answer would I have obtained if I had used the INT÷ key instead of the ÷ key?

Problem 3. Suppose you used the INT÷ key on your calculator to divide a number by 4 and obtained the answer

$$\underbrace{3}_{Q}\ \underbrace{2}_{R}\ .$$

What number did you divide by 4?

Notice that questions 1 and 2 do not require any computations, whereas question 3 does require computation *if* the students really understand the relationship between the two equivalent ways of expressing the answer. The solutions follow. However, the teacher will learn a great deal more about what students do know and do not know if they are asked to think through and explain the answer orally rather than write the problem down and solve it computationally.

Solution 1. Since the Q-part of the quotient-with-remainder answer is the same as the integral part of the decimal answer, the Q-part is 5.

Solution 2. If the divisor was 4, then the remainder is 0.5 of 4, or one-half of 4, or 2. Consequently the calculator answer would be

$$\underbrace{5}_{Q}\ \underbrace{2}_{R}\ .$$

Solution 3. The original number is $4 \times 3 + 2$, or 14.

Reference

National Council of Teachers of Mathematics. *Curriculum and Evaluation Standards for School Mathematics.* Reston, Va.: The Council, 1989.

A Historical Reconstruction of Our Number System

by
Kim Krusen

Imagine your class as a "primitive society" just on the brink of civilization. Your society has been using tally sticks to represent numerical quantities. But now that your society is becoming more involved in commerce with other societies, you need an easier way to represent large numbers and some structure so that numbers can be manipulated. You need an organized number system. Creating a number system from scratch was the recent task of my sixth-grade class. My objective was to offer a more humanistic approach for my students further to understand and appreciate the structure of our number system. As the teacher, I was armed with a general knowledge of the number systems of the great ancient civilizations, and my students were armed with an enthusiasm to be cave dwellers for the day instead of mathematics students. With these resources, we began our project.

The question before the class was this: What is an efficient number system and how does its development begin? Our class began the discussion by looking at how our primitive society expresses numbers with tally sticks. I laid down eighteen pretzel sticks to express the number eighteen and asked what limitations such a simplistic method of expressing quantities would have. The students quickly agreed that I would have to go out and buy more pretzel sticks if I wanted to express a very large number! Then when asked, "But what if I did have enough pretzel sticks, as for the number eighteen on the table?" They replied that it would still be too much of a burden and that it

would be easier just to write a "number." When I reminded them that as a primitive society we had not yet invented written numbers, the discussion led to deciding how to create symbols to represent quantities.

Some students decided to create a symbol for ten.

The students assumed that we would use our counting numbers (I, 2, 3, 4, ...) as symbols, but I reminded them that they were building from scratch and must invent their own symbols. By encouraging this approach, I was hoping that they would be less likely to take our present number system for granted and would be forced to think more creatively. After all, our symbols for numbers were not even used by the early Babylonian, Egyptian, Greek, or Roman civilizations. They were not developed until between A.D. 200 and A.D. 800, by the Hindus, and the Europeans did not begin to use them until after A.D. 1200, when they were introduced by way of the Arabs. Hence, we call them Hindu-Arabic numerals.

The students filed up to the chalkboard, each responsible for making up and writing down a symbol for a number, beginning with one. (This activity could also be done in small groups.) I was delighted when the first student asked, "Can't we just use '1' for number one, since it looks like one pretzel stick?" The ancient peoples had had that same idea, and many of their symbols were designed to hint at the quantities they represented. Many of the

Kim Krusen taught mathematics at Stewart Middle School in Norristown, PA 19401. She enjoyed incorporating the history of mathematics into her lessons. She now resides at 1012 North Summit Street, Number 3, Iowa City, IA 52245.

students kept this scheme in mind as they were creating their symbols; for instance, a triangle was chosen to symbolize the quantity three.

I suppose that I should have expected the students to have such a good time drawing symbols on the chalkboard that no one would stop to question whether we needed that many distinct symbols. I asked them to think for a moment of how many letters are in our alphabet. Is it not true that all the words in the English language are formed by using only twenty-six letters? With that limitation in mind, they began to see that if they made a new symbol for each new number, we were going to have a great many symbols to memorize. That system would be as bad as having to carry around bags and bags of pretzel sticks to express large numbers. For instance, if we wanted to express the quantity of thirty-one, would we need thirty-one symbols to get there? A student said, "No, you only need the three symbol and the one symbol," and proceeded to construct the numeral for that quantity by writing the symbol for one to the right of the symbol for three. While the student was at the chalkboard, I asked him to erase all but the symbols that he thought we needed. He left standing the symbols for the numbers one through ten, as shown in figure 1. When asked if every quantity could be expressed by using these ten numbers, the general consensus was "yes." Soon, they would have to explain to me why we can make do with only ten symbols.

Fig. 1. One class chose the symbols above to represent the numbers one through ten.

Since the students had chosen to create a symbol for ten, I decided to challenge them by writing the number thirty-one using three ten symbols and a one symbol:

It took a moment for them to realize that my way required adding the value of the symbols:

$$10 + 10 + 10 + 1 = 31$$

This approach was a very common method used by the ancient Babylonians, Egyptians, Greeks, and Romans. I asked the students how the combination of the symbols for three and one implied the quantity thirty-one. It would seem to imply a total value of four. And would it matter if the one symbol was written first, followed by the three symbol? They practically screamed back what some former teacher must have screamed at them in the past, "You have to put them in the right place!" So they had hit on the concept of place value—a concept that only the Babylonians had toyed with in ancient times.

I told the class that I was impressed that they could express thirty-one using only two symbols, whereas it took me four symbols to express it, but that they would now have to explain to me what they meant by putting symbols in special places. They proceeded to explain the concept of place value in a base-ten system. Each place would stand for an increasing power of ten, and a symbol in a certain place would indicate how many of that particular power of ten you would have. As far as they were concerned, our reconstruction task was complete, but I had some more challenges to present.

The first challenge was to write the number for three hundred one. It did not take long for someone to say that we had forgotten to create a symbol for zero, as had most of the early civilizations. The students quickly created a zero symbol. Then we had a total of eleven symbols on the chalkboard. I asked them if they would write the ten symbol in the tens column to express 10 tens. Clearly 10 tens equal one hundred, so it is much more efficient to write a one symbol in the hundreds column. They agreed that the ten symbol was unnecessary in the system that we were building. (It is easy to see in our Hindu-Arabic notation that "10" is made up of the symbols "1" and "0." That observation was not so easy in our class, since the ten symbol was completely different, not a composition of symbols that had previously been used.) As the students erased the eleventh symbol from the chalkboard, it became clear that the impressive simplicity of our use of place value rests on the ability to use only ten distinct symbols that represent the first ten whole numbers in a base-ten system, using position to construct all other numbers. (See fig. 2.)

Fig. 2. After realizing that a zero symbol is needed but that a ten symbol is unnecessary in a base-ten system of place value, another class represented the numbers zero through nine as above.

The next challenge was, Why base ten? Most of the early number systems had used it. Why not something like base twenty, which was the chosen base of the ancient Mayan civilization? We discussed that a base-twenty system would require memorizing twenty distinct symbols, whereas base ten requires only ten. Then why not use base twelve? Twelve was commonly used in ancient times as a division for measurement, possibly because it has divisors of two, three, four, six, and twelve, allowing more integral fractional parts than found when working with ten. Yet the explanation historically offered in favor of a base-ten system is given by simply holding up ten fingers, no doubt the same number of fingers that the ancients had!

At this point, our newly created number system was essentially in place. *Our class had just accomplished in one class period what it had taken civilization over 3000 years to develop!* Obviously, this "primitive society" in my classroom was working with the benefit of hindsight! They had incorporated the concepts of place value and base ten with the use of nine digits and a zero symbol in a compact, easily

---

Most early civilizations neglected a symbol for zero.

---

expressed number system. Some of the early civilizations had some notion of one or more of these concepts, but not one of them had them all. One of the concepts alone cannot be used to its full potential. The beauty and efficiency of our number system comes from their combined use.

This lesson could be extended by examining more closely the number systems of the ancient civilizations which of these concepts did they use, of which were they unaware, and what limitations did their number systems have? After 3000 years of less-than-efficient number systems, the first civilization credited with embracing all three concepts was the Hindus, sometime between A.D. 500 and A.D. 800. The purpose in doing such an activity is not just to examine structure or history but to allow students to discover the sheer power and respectable efficiency of our present-day number system based on these concepts.

Bibliography

Eves, Howard. *An Introduction to the History of Mathematics.* Philadelphia: Saunders College Publishing, 1983.

Payne, Joseph N. "Ideas" (classroom exercises on the ancient Egyptian number system). *Arithmetic Teacher* 34 (September 1986):26–32.

Wilder, Raymond L. *Evolution of Mathematical Concepts.* New York: John Wiley & Sons, 1968.

Promoting Number Sense in the Middle Grades

by
Barbara J. Reys

Photographs by Nancy A. O'Connor; all rights reserved

Phrases such as "number sense," "operation sense," and "intuitive understanding of number" are used throughout the *Curriculum and Evaluation Standards for School Mathematics* (NCTM 1989) to describe an intangible quality possessed by successful mathematics learners. Number sense refers to an intuitive feeling for numbers and their various uses and interpretations, an appreciation for various levels of accuracy when computing, the ability to detect arithmetical errors, and a common-sense approach to using numbers (Howden 1989; McIntosh, Reys, and Reys 1991). Number sense is not a finite entity that a student either has or does not have but rather a process that develops and matures with experience and knowledge. It does not develop by chance, nor does being skilled at manipulating numbers necessarily reflect this acquaintance and familiarity with numbers. Above all, number sense is characterized by a desire to make sense of numerical situations, including relating numbers to context and analyzing the effect of manipulations on numbers. It is a way of thinking that should permeate all aspects of mathematics teaching and learning.

The idea of number sense is not new. As early as the 1930s William Brownell was concerned with what he called "meaningful learning." To Brownell the true test of mathematical learning was not the ability to compute but the possession of an "intelligent grasp [of] number relations and the ability to deal with arithmetical situations with proper comprehension of their mathematical as well as their practical significance" (1935, 19). He stressed the importance of instruction that is "deliberately planned to teach arithmetical meanings and to make arithmetic sensible to children through its mathematical relationships" (pp. 257–58).

Perhaps number sense, like common sense, is best described by looking at the specific behavioral characteristics of those who value and use it. A student with number sense will—

- *look at a problem holistically before confronting details.* For example, in adding 1 2/3 + 3/4 + 1/3, a student might mentally reorder the addends to 1 2/3 + 1/3 + 3/4 to take advantage of the compatible addends (1 2/3 and 1/3).

Barbara Reys teaches at the University of Missouri— Columbia, Columbia, MO 65211. Her interests include exploring and promoting a variety of computational tools including calculators, mental computation, and estimation.

- *look for relationships among numbers and operations and will consider the context in which a question is posed.* For example, in buying 4 notebooks priced at 39 cents each, the student with $2 might reason that she or he has enough money, since each notebook costs less than half a dollar.

- *choose or invent a method that takes advantage of his or her own understanding* of the relationships between numbers or between numbers and operations and will seek the most efficient representation for the given task. For example, suppose that at least 75 percent of the class of 30 students needs to agree on a plan for a school trip before it can be finalized. A student might reason that "75% is 50% plus 25%, or half plus half of that. So 15 + 8, or 23, students must agree."

- *use benchmarks to judge number magnitude.* For example, 2/5 of 49 is less than half of 49.

- *recognize unreasonable results for calculations in the normal process of reflecting on answers.* For example, 3.2 × 4.8 can't possibly be 153.6, since the answer must be about 3 × 5, or 15, so an error in decimal-point placement must have been made.

Number sense, then, is not a new topic for teachers to include in an already overcrowded mathematics program. Rather, it is an important perspective from which to view learning mathematics. *Number sense is both the ability of the learner to make logical connections between new information and previously acquired knowledge and the drive within the learner to make forming these connections a priority.* Number sense will be valued among students only if teachers believe that it is more important for students to make sense of the mathematics they learn than to master rules and algorithms, which are often poorly understood, and if they act on these beliefs. Students will begin to acquire number sense if they are engaged in purposeful activities requiring them to think about numbers and numerical relationships and to make connections with quantitative information seen in everyday life.

The Teacher's Role in Developing Number Sense

Just as number sense requires an attitude of sense making on the part of the learner, teaching for the development of number sense requires a conscious, coordinated effort to build connections and meaning on the part of the teacher. Teachers play an important role in building number sense in the type of classroom environment they create, in the teaching practices they employ, and in the activities they select.

Use process questions

Process questions—those that require more than just a factual response—can stimulate discussion of an idea, which can lead to further exploration and the use of oral language to explain and justify a thought. Consider the following classroom conversation:

Teacher: I'm thinking of two fractions. Their sum is between 0 and 1. What can you tell me about the fractions?

Greg: Both fractions are small, maybe less than 1.

Teacher: OK, what else?

Greg: Are they both less than 1/2?

Teacher: Good question, can anyone answer that?

Praveen: They don't have to both be less than 1/2. One can be 3/4 and the other real small, like 1/10.

Greg: OK, but if one is bigger than a half, the other one must be smaller than a half.

Teacher: Good point. Can anyone tell me anything else about my fractions?

Nhung: If their sum is less than 1, their product is also less than 1.

Teacher: What do the rest of you think about that idea?

The teacher's questions prompted the students to examine various examples and to prove or disprove their initial thoughts. In promoting number sense it is important for students to see that it is possible to be wrong. What is valued most is reflection on answers so that they can be proved either right or wrong. The teacher in this example assumed the critical role of posing questions, which caused students to continue reflective thought, and of encouraging other students to be involved in the process. See activity A for additional questions related to fraction computation that can be used for discussion and exploration.

Activity A: Fractions between 0 and 1

To the teacher: This activity helps clarify students' understanding of fractions between 0 and 1. It can be used as a quick warm-up for the mathematics lesson. Several questions have more than one correct answer.

Ask students questions such as these:

1. Name a fraction between 1/2 and 1.
2. Name a fraction between 1/4 and 3/4, other than 1/2.
3. Name a fraction between 1/4 and 1/2 whose denominator is 10.
4. Name a fraction between 7/8 and 1. How many can you name?
5. Name a fraction between 0 and 1/10 whose numerator is not 1.

Note: *This activity is from Reys et al. (1991, 28).*

Teaching for number sense involves a quality-over-quantity attitude toward problem completion. That is, the focus is on understanding a given problem by looking at it from multiple perspectives rather than on attempting to work as many problems as possible in a given period. Strategies offered by students must be justified, and students learn to ask, "Does this make sense?" when considering each answer (see activity B for an example from the *Curriculum and Evaluation Standards for School Mathematics* [NCTM 1989] that illustrates the need to connect information and make generalizations).

Activity B: Operations on fractions

To the teacher: This activity is suggested in the evaluation section of the *Curriculum and Evaluation Standards for School Mathematics* (NCTM 1989, 203). It is useful for clarifying students' understanding of the effects of certain operations on fractions.

Display the number line and ask students questions such as those indicated here and others that come to mind. Encourage students to justify their answers by explaining their reasoning.

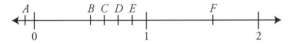

1. If the fraction represented by the points *D* and *E* are multiplied, what point on the number line best represents the product?

2. If the fractions represented by the points *C* and *D* are multiplied, what point on the number line best represents the product?

3. If the fractions represented by the points *B* and *F* are multiplied, what point on the number line best represents the product?

Note: *This activity is from Reys et al. (1991, 34).*

Use writing assignments

Having students summarize their thinking in written form is an effective method for helping students nurture their sense of number. Students can be asked to write about the results of group activities or to keep a journal in which they enter ideas generated by specific tasks. As they write, they may formulate new ideas or questions, which may serve as a reference for further question posing and discussion. Later, as they reread their journals, they can see how their conceptions have been changed and expanded by further exploration and discussion. The following excerpt from a fifth-grade student's journal illustrates how children might record their thoughts:

Today I found out that I can't count to 1 000 000 in 1 day. It would take me more than 10 days and I would even have

to count all night without stopping. A million is a lot bigger than I thought I wonder how long it would take to count to a trillion?

Encourage invented methods

Creating and exploring their own methods for calculating and solving problems prepare students to consider traditional methods at a later stage and view standard algorithms as yet another means of producing sensible answers. In a classroom where sense making is a priority, teachers become guides and moderators instead of dispensers of rules and procedures. The goal of "one right answer" derived from "one preferred algorithm" is replaced by the goal of multiple solution strategies that are generated by, and make sense to, the students. The emphasis shifts from the solution to the process. Allowing students the freedom to use strategies that are intuitively obvious to them helps them to feel more comfortable with the problem-solving process and to internalize mathematics in a way that makes sense to them. At some stage it also helps them appreciate the efficiency of standard algorithms.

Use appropriate calculation tools

Number sense can be promoted by ensuring that students learn to calculate in various ways including written, mental, approximate, and electronic methods. Alerting students to the use of approximate numbers in real-life situations underscores the value of estimates (see activity C for an example of such an exploration).

Activity C: Exact and approximate numbers

To the teacher: Ask students to investigate the use of approximate and exact numbers in newspaper articles. Use this activity to help students appreciate the everyday use of estimates.

Give students copies of the front page of various newspapers. Ask them to use a marker to circle numbers used in headlines and articles. Next, have students review the context for the use of each circled number to determine if it is an exact or an approximate value. For example, do the numbers in these headlines below refer to exact or approximate values?

U.S. population tops 220 million
Lottery winner earns over $200 000 annually
Stocks fall 5.4 percent

Note: *This activity is from Reys et al. (1991, 20).*

Both mental computation and estimation offer vehicles to encourage invention of strategies and alertness to sensible answers. For example, in calculating 5×96, one student might change the problem to $10 \times 96/2$, another might think $5 \times 8 \times 12$, whereas another might use the distributive property and compute $(5 \times 90) + (5 \times 6)$ or $(5 \times 100) - (5 \times 4)$. Probing questions and concrete analogies can be used to initiate the exploration of alternative methods of mental calculation. For example, after giving students the problem 25×49, the teacher might ask, "Can anyone create a problem from this calculation by substituting the word *quarters* for the number 25? Does it help to find the product of these two numbers if we think about the 25 as a quarter? How?"

The calculator plays an important role as an efficient tool in an environment that emphasizes exploration. By using the calculator to perform tedious computations and test conjectures, students can focus on the process of deriving a solution and on the meaning of the answer once it is computed rather than on the computational procedure. Students may be more eager to explore properties of numbers when calculators are accessible. For example, suppose the teacher poses the following question to the class: "What happens when you multiply a positive whole number by a decimal between 0.9 and 1.1? Use your calculator to explore this question, generate your conjecture, and make a list of examples that support your conjecture." Students are encouraged to generate many examples and to draw a conclusion on the basis of these examples (see activity D for elaboration of this idea).

Help students establish benchmarks

Approximate computation or estimation is another important tool for encouraging students to use what they already know about numbers to make sense of new numerical situations. Oftentimes this tactic means that students use their own benchmarks to judge the reasonableness of a situation. For example, a student using a standard protractor to measure a 30-degree angle is not likely to read the wrong scale and report 150 degrees as the measure if a 90-degree angle has been established as a referent. In the same way, a student who has been encouraged to estimate fractions near 0, 1/2, and 1 will understand that the sum of $2/5 + 4/9$ must be less than 1, since both fractions are less than a half (see activities E and F for examples focused on establishing awareness and use of benchmarks).

Encouraging students to consider these benchmarks, or referents, is a way of helping them develop better conceptual understanding of fractions, decimals, and percents. This intuitive understanding is a priority and should precede the study of operating with fractions, decimals, and percents.

Activity D: Multiplication by decimals near 0, 1/2, and 1

To the teacher: This activity helps students explore the effect of multiplying by decimals near 0, 1/2, and 1. After students have generated and verified many of their own examples with a calculator, encourage them to make generalizations from the pattern that emerges.

What Happens When ...?

What happens when you multiply by a number less than 1? Ask students to explore this question by completing the chart.

Pick a Whole Number	Multiply by 0.05	Multiply by 0.48	Multiply by 0.9

Questions to consider:

1. In general, what happens when you multiply a whole number by 0.05?
2. In general, what happens when you multiply a whole number by 0.48?
3. In general, what happens when you multiply a whole number by 0.9?

Note: *This activity is from Reys et al. (1991, 40).*

Promote internal questioning

An important role for teachers in the development of number sense is helping students learn to ask themselves key questions before, during, and after the solution process. For example, what type of number would I expect for an answer to this problem? About how large will the answer be? What is the biggest or smallest value I expect? After completing a calculation, students then determine whether the answer is consistent with what they expected. This process of self-examination may help sensitize students to order-of-magnitude errors as well as prevent them from checking their answer by repeating the same computational error a second time. For example, as students

Activity E: Establishing benchmarks for whole numbers

To the teacher: Adults often use benchmarks or common referents to process numerical information. For example, knowing the population of your town might help you judge the size of a crowd attending a concert. (For example, if the high school stadium holds 1 000 people and the report says that 150 000 people attended a rock concert, you might think of the size of the concert, crowd as being the stadium filled 150 times.) This activity is designed to see how many students are aware of the size of some commonly used referents. Encourage students to formulate additional questions and problems for studying the implications of these statistics. As an extension, you might want to review with your class the book *In One Day* by Tom Parker (1984), which contains a number of interesting numerical facts about what Americans do in one day.

Pose the following questions to students. Allow them first to estimate and then do research to determine the value that answers each question.

1. Population of the world: _____
2. Population of the United States: _____
3. Population of your town: _____
4. Population of your school: _____
5. United States government budget: _____
6. The number of 13-year-olds alive today: _____
7. The number of graduating high school seniors last year: _____
8. The number of tons of garbage generated every day: _____

Note: *This activity is from Reys et al. (1991, 16).*

Activity F: Percent benchmarks

To the teacher: Students will likely benefit from discussion with fellow classmates as they complete this activity. You may want to organize them into small groups to encourage this discussion.

Ask students to read and reflect on each statement and then to choose and answer from the answer list. The answers will vary; you may want students to continue this activity by researching each answer using appropriate sources of information or by conducting a survey.

Complete each statement using one of the following choices:

0 percent
Less than 10 percent
about 25 percent
Fewer than 50 percent
About 50 percent
More than 50 percent
About 75 percent
At least 90 percent
100 percent

Statements:

1. _____ of the students in my classroom are left-handed.
2. _____ of the students in my classroom have red hair.
3. _____ of the students in my school like hamburgers.
4. _____ of the students in my school like baseball.
5. _____ of the students in my school are wearing tennis shoes today.
6. _____ of the people in my town are over 90 years old.
7. _____ of the people in my town own a car.
8. _____ of the people in my state are female.

Note: *This activity is from Reys et al. (1991, 43).*

explore the questions illustrated in activity G, they are encouraged to predict what happens when a number is multiplied or divided by a number near 1. As conjectures are made they can be verified or refuted quickly using a calculator. Students are given the opportunity to study the effect of multiplying or dividing by a number more or less than 1 and to formulate and test conjectures.

In classrooms where number sense is a priority, students are active participants who share their hypotheses, reasoning, and conclusions. The classroom environment encourages students' exploration, questioning, verification, and sense making.

Selecting Activities

By establishing a classroom atmosphere that encourages exploration, thinking, and discussion, and by selecting appropriate problems and activities, the teacher can cultivate number sense during all mathematical experiences.

Activities that promote number sense by concentrating on process have several common characteristics. They encourage students to think about what they are doing and to share their thoughts with others. They promote creativity and investigation and allow for many answers and solution strategies. They help students know when it is appropriate to estimate or to produce an exact answer and when to compute mentally, on paper, or with a calculator. They help students see the regularity of mathematics and the connections between mathematics and the real world. Process-oriented activities also convey the idea of mathematics as an exciting, dynamic discovery of ideas and relationships.

Throughout this discussion several activities have been suggested. These activities are taken from the NCTM's

Activity G: Multiplying and dividing by numbers near 1

To the teacher: In this activity students are encouraged to fill in each blank by thinking about the effect of the indicated operation. All can be answered without calculation. Encourage students to verbalize their thinking for each problem. After completing all the problems, you might substitute ÷ for the × symbol in each problem. Ask students to reevaluate each sentence.

Ask students to study each problem. Without performing any calculation they are to decide if <, =, or > would complete each sentence. Ask them to justify their thinking.

1. 246×1.3 ❏ 246
2. 920×0.8 ❏ 920
3. 98×1.001 ❏ 98
4. $32 \times 1/2$ ❏ 32
5. $1/2 \times 7/8$ ❏ 1/2
6. $1/2 \times 7/8$ ❏ 7/8

Note: *This activity is from Reys et al. (1991, 38).*

addenda book *Developing Number Sense in the Middle Grades* (Reys et al. 1991). They are offered not as "number sense lessons" but as ideas related to number sense drawn from various topics within the middle-grades curriculum. Different ways of integrating number sense in elementary school classrooms are also demonstrated in the *Number Sense Now* videotape series available from NCTM (1993). Activities in these resources may further illustrate number sense and highlight some ways to encourage its development.

References

Brownell, William A. "Psychological Considerations in the Learning and the Teaching of Arithmetic." In *The Teaching of Arithmetic*, Tenth Yearbook of the National Council of Teachers of Mathematics, edited by D. W. Reeve, 19–51. New York: Teachers College, Columbia University, 1935.

Howden, Hilde. "Teaching Number Sense." *Arithmetic Teacher* 36 (February 1989):6–11.

McIntosh, Allistair, Barbara J. Reys, and Robert E. Reys. "A Proposed Framework for Examining Basic Number Sense." *For the Learning of Mathematics* 12 (November 1992):2–8, 44.

National Council of Teachers of Mathematics. *Curriculum and Evaluation Standards for School Mathematics.* Reston, Va.: The Council, 1989.

———. *Number Sense Now! Reaching the NCTM Standards.* 3 videotapes and guidebook. Project directed by Francis (Skip) Fennell. Reston, Va: The Council, 1993.

Parker, Tom. *In One Day.* Boston: Houghton Mifflin Co., 1984.

Reys, Barbara J., Rita Barger, Maxim Bruckheimer, Barbara Dougherty, Jack Hope, Linda Lembke, Zvia Markovits, Andy Parnas, Sue Reehm, Ruth T. Sturdevant, and Marianne Weber. *Developing Number Sense in the Middle Grades*, Addenda Series, Grades 5–8. Reston, Va.: National Council of Teachers of Mathematics, 1991.

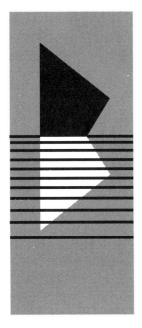

A Foundation for Algebraic Reasoning in the Early Grades

by

Erna Yackel

For many adults, *algebra* means solving systems of equations; finding the value of an unknown; using the quadratic formula; or otherwise working within a system of formulas, equations, and literal symbols. From this perspective, the suggestion that algebra should permeate the K–12 mathematics curriculum seems unreasonable and certainly indefensible if we take seriously that children should learn mathematics by making sense of things on the basis of their current mathematical understandings. Do we expect children in kindergarten and first grade to solve algebraic equations? If not, then what might it mean to suggest that algebraic thinking should be part of the mathematics curriculum for the elementary grades?

In taking the position that algebra is for all, the NCTM is calling for a complete rethinking of what we might mean by algebra (1994). In effect, the NCTM is advocating that the notion of algebra be expanded to include a range of mathematical activity. To assist in this rethinking process, in 1994 the NCTM appointed an Algebra Working Group charged with developing and elaborating a vision of K–12 algebra that would help teachers and school systems as they grapple with the process of change. Significantly, the working group deliberately chose not to begin by defining algebra or setting forth standards for algebra (NCTM 1995). Such an approach would be static, narrow, and limited and be bounded by historical views

Erna Yackel, yackeleb@calumet.purdue.edu, is a mathematics educator in the department of Mathematics, Computer Science, and Statistics at Purdue University Calumet, Hammond, IN 46323. Her professional interests include the development of mathematical explanation and justification, classroom norms, and the mathematics preparation of preservice teachers.

and perspectives of algebra. Rather, the group chose to take an emerging view of algebra. This view acknowledges the dynamic nature of mathematics in general and of algebra in particular, treats mathematics as a human activity (Davis and Hersh 1981), and puts students' thinking at the forefront. In this view, we develop our vision of algebra as we consider the mathematical activity and thinking of students. This position is consistent with the views of Smith and Thompson (in press) who argue, "We believe it is possible to prepare children for different views of algebra—algebra as modeling, as pattern finding, or as the study of structure—by having them *build ways of knowing and reasoning which make those mathematical practices appear as different aspects of a central and fundamental way of thinking*" (emphasis added). Thus, the emphasis is not on whether an activity should qualify as being algebraic but on the underlying thinking and reasoning of the students. This view is particularly helpful at the elementary school level because it eliminates the need to focus on what algebra "content" should be included in the elementary grades. Instead, the crucial issue is the nature of the children's reasoning and thinking.

The purpose of this article is twofold. The first is to explore children's thinking that might be foundational to algebraic reasoning. In keeping with the spirit of the Algebra Working Group, definitive claims are not made about what does and does not constitute algebraic reasoning. Instead, readers are invited to consider ways of reasoning and thinking that in their view might be a foundation on which to develop algebraic thinking and reasoning. The second is to describe some instructional activities that can potentially engender such reasoning and thinking. Here again, readers are invited to be active participants by asking themselves what possibilities these instructional activities might have in their own classrooms.

Thinking That Is Foundational to Algebraic Reasoning

To explore the nature of children's thinking, consider the following example that comes from a first-grade classroom-research study conducted by Cobb, Whitenack, and McClain (Cobb et al., in press) and cited by Smith (in press) as illustrating one kind of algebraic thinking. In the example, students were shown a picture of one large and one small tree and five monkeys (see fig. 1). The teacher explained that all the monkeys want to play in the trees, and she asked the students to think about the different ways that the five monkeys could play in the two trees. The children began to generate responses, such as that three could be in the little tree and two in the big tree or that five could be in the big tree and none in the little tree. The children's reasoning in generating these responses might be described as primarily numerical. Their activity involved thinking of, and figuring out, specific instances of how many monkeys might be in each of the two trees. From the observer's perspective, we might say that the children found various ways to partition the number 5 into two parts. The teacher recorded the children's suggestions by drawing a vertical line between the trees and writing the number of monkeys in each tree on the corresponding side of the line, creating a table in the process (see fig. 1). As the discussion progressed, the teacher asked if all the possibilities were already recorded and if a way could be found to ensure that they had them all.

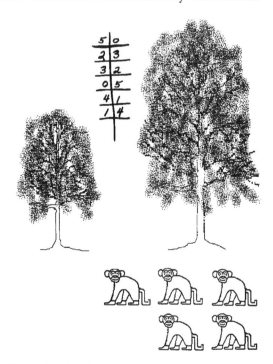

Fig. 1. Overhead-projector display showing a table with students' responses

Cobb and others note that a shift in the discourse occurred when the teacher asked this question. Jordan explained, "See, if you had four in this [big] tree and one in this [small] tree in here, and one in this [big] tree and four in the [small] tree, couldn't be that no more." He explained how every other partition of 5 into two numbers could yield two possible ways the monkeys could be in the two trees. The various possibilities that had been suggested previously by the children and recorded in the table by the teacher emerged "as explicit objects of discourse that could themselves be related to each other" (Cobb et al., in press). Cobb and his colleagues use the example to explicate shifts in discourse, but Smith uses the example to focus on the nature of Jordan's thinking. Jordan was no longer thinking about generating specific partitions of 5. Neither was he checking empirically to see if all possibilities were in the table. As Cobb and others and Smith point out, Jordan was building an understanding of the relationship between the possible partitionings of the monkeys and the possible entries in the table. Because of the focus on relationships, some would refer to Jordan's reasoning as representational or algebraic. Whether the reader concurs with calling Jordan's thinking "algebraic" is unimportant. The crucial point is that Jordan's thinking is qualitatively different from the numerical thinking in which he and the other children engaged initially when they generated the individual instances that first made up the table.

Some—but not all—students in Jordan's class made sense of his explanation. Some children might have been unable to reason about relationships as Jordan did, and this problem might not have engendered higher-level thinking that some would call algebraic. This point is significant. It once again highlights the mathematical activity of the students and indicates that qualitative differences can occur in children's thinking as they attempt to solve a problem. A task in and of itself does not elicit a particular type of thinking. Nevertheless, as the previous example demonstrates, opportunities for various possibilities can be generated by the careful selection of tasks and by the way they are developed in the classroom. The teacher's question "How can you be sure you have all the possibilities?" apparently was the impetus for Jordan's higher-level thinking. By asking the question, the teacher initiated a change in the focus from thinking about the various ways the monkeys might be in the trees to reasoning about the relationship between the various ways and the records in the table. Jordan's reasoning is evidence that the shift in focus was productive for at least one child in the class.

Promising Instructional Activities

The remainder of this article describes several problems that have been proposed by the NCTM Algebra Working

Group (1995) as potentially useful in fostering elementary school students' development of a conceptual basis for algebraic reasoning. Although activities from arithmetic or data measurement could have been chosen, these problems are set within the context of measurement. In one sense they can be thought of as focusing on dimension, perimeter, and area and the relationships among them. The purpose is to focus on how they might foster thinking that is foundational to algebraic reasoning. For this reason, possible ways that students might think about and solve the problems are included. These possible solutions and interpretations are representative of the working group members' classroom experiences with the problems.

The first problem described is intended for the early primary grades and is designed to encourage students to investigate various rectangles and their areas where one dimension of the rectangle is fixed.

Building-rectangles problem: Use some of your (square) tiles to make a rectangle with a base of 2.

The teacher might pose these questions:

- Did you all make the same rectangle?
- How many tiles did you use?
- How did you figure it out?
- What is the height of your rectangle?
- How would you build a rectangle that uses twenty-two tiles?
- Can you figure out how high it will be without building it?
- If you know how many tiles are in a rectangle with a base of 2, can you figure out high it is?
- If you know how high you want a rectangle to be, can you figure out how many tiles you will need?

To find the number of tiles used, which represents the area, some children count them one by one. Others count by twos. Still others count the number of tiles in one column and double the number. These strategies reflect the children's own understanding of, and facility with, number. To answer the follow-up questions, some children begin to reason in a more general way about the relationship between height and total number of tiles, or area. These questions shift the focus from making the rectangle to reasoning about how the dimensions are relevant.

For our purposes, the crucial feature of the instructional activity is the set of follow-up questions that encourage the children to go beyond building rectangles and even beyond producing numerical answers to questions about the dimensions and to reasoning about the dimensions and about the relationships between them. The teacher can facilitate the discussion by introducing various ways of recording children's rectangles, such as by making a table or by using grid paper.

The next problem, which is intended for the intermediate grades, involves working with relationships and constraints. Like the first problem, students are asked to construct rectangular shapes but with a fixed perimeter.

Rectangular-pen problem: Charmaine wants to build a rectangular pen for her pet using 26 feet of fence. Help her figure out some possible pens she might build. Record your results so that someone else can figure out how you thought about the problem. String, pipe cleaners, and grid paper are materials that are available for you to use if you choose.

These questions might be posed:

- What different rectangular pens did you find?
- How did you record your results?
- How does the shape of the pen change by making one side of the pen longer or shorter?
- Have you found all the possibilities?
- How can you be sure?

To find some of the possible rectangular pens, some students make a twenty-six-inch length from pipe cleaners and bend it to form various rectangles. Some record their results by tracing around each rectangle on a piece of paper. After making several rectangles, some of these students make additional rectangles by first folding the pipe cleaner length in half, then partitioning and folding the first half, and finally folding the other half to complete the rectangle (see fig. 2). Some students think about how many pens are possible by reasoning about possible ways

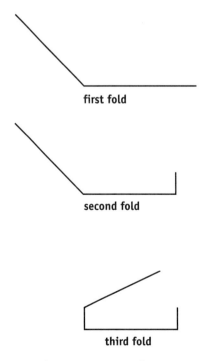

Fig. 2. Diagram depicting reasoning by partitioning and folding a length of pipe cleaner

to partition the pipe-cleaner length. Other students use grid paper to draw rectangles with perimeter of twenty-six units. The thinking of some of these students is constrained by the lines on the grid paper. As a result, they use only integral values for the length and width. Some students record their results only with their drawings on the grid paper. Others make lists of the pairs of dimensions. Very young students use square tiles, arranging them in rectangles and verifying the perimeter by counting and making adjustments as needed.

By using such materials as string and pipe cleaners, students can reason about partitioning a length without thinking numerically. By bending pipe cleaners and folding string, students can reason about how the length and width of the rectangles are related. Reasoning in this way about quantities, such as length and width, without having specific numerical values in mind, is foundational to algebraic reasoning. As students consider the question of all possible rectangles, they may abstract patterns in their own reasoning and use tables, graphs, and literal symbols to express their thinking. The teacher plays a crucial role in assisting students to develop ways to notate and record their thinking that are consistent with conventional methods. For example, students may reason that the width and the length must add to 13 or that the width can be determined by subtracting the length from 13. With the teacher's help, they can develop ways to notate this reasoning, including the use of such standard symbolic means as $W + L = 13$ or $W = 13 - L$. By introducing methods of recording and organizing as a topic of discussion, the teacher helps students focus explicitly on these means of representation. In this way, representing, notating, and symbolizing, all of which are foundational to algebra, can emerge as the instructional activity unfolds in the classroom.

The problem can be extended by asking which pen provides the most area for the pet. Discussing the maximum area encourages students to reflect on the range of possible rectangles. In some classes, questions of nonintegral values for the length and width will arise. Students can be encouraged to draw graphs and to reason from their drawings in ways appropriate to their grade levels. Some students will reason algebraically using a diagram of a rectangle as the basis of their reasoning.

This discussion illustrates that the initial choice of problem is only one of the relevant factors in the instructional activity that develops. Teacher questions, student solutions, and attempts to follow up on either or both are central to how the instructional activity is realized in action.

Conclusions

As we have illustrated, developing the foundations for algebraic reasoning in the elementary grades can be accomplished through activities that encourage children to move beyond numerical reasoning to more general reasoning about relationships, quantity, and ways of notating and symbolizing, to name but a few. In this way teachers can contribute to the emerging view of algebra for all, K–12, and to the preparation of our students for the twenty-first century.

References

Cobb, Paul, Ada Boufi, Kay McClain, and Joy Whitenack. "Reflective Discourse and Collective Reflection." *Journal for Research in Mathematics Education* 28 (May 1997):258–77.

Davis, Philip J., and Reuben Hersh. *The Mathematical Experience.* Boston: Houghton Mifflin Co., 1981.

National Council of Teachers of Mathematics. "Algebra for Everyone: More Than a Change in Enrollment Patterns." Board of Director's Statement. Reston, Va.: The Council, 1994.

National Council of Teachers of Mathematics Algebra Working Group. *Algebra in the K–12 Curriculum: Dilemmas and Possibilities.* Final report to the Board of Directors. East Lansing: Michigan State University, 1995.

Smith, Erick. "Algebraic Thinking as a Framework for Introducing Functions in the Elementary Curriculum." In *Employing Children's Natural Powers to Build Algebraic Reasoning in the Context of Elementary Mathematics*, edited by Jim Kaput, in press.

Smith, John P. III, and Patrick W. Thompson. "Additive Quantitative Reasoning and the Development of Algebraic Reasoning." In *Employing Children's Natural Powers to Build Algebraic Reasoning in the Context of Elementary Mathematics*, edited by Jim Kaput, in press.

Promising Research, Programs, and Projects

Algebraic Thinking
A Professional-Development Theme

by
Faye Nisonoff Ruopp, Al Cuoco, Sue M. Rasala, and M. Grace Kelemanik

Over a thirty-six month period beginning September 1992, teams of two elementary, two middle, and two high school teachers from each of seven school districts attended a series of biweekly seminars at the Education Development Center (EDC). The seminars, called Teachers, Time and Transformations (TTT), were held during the school day as part of a professional-development program for K–12 mathematics teachers.

This program enabled teachers to work on mathematics together, engaging in problems that focused on algebraic thinking across the grades. A general perception exists that algebraic thinking is distinct from the elementary curricu-

Faye Ruopp, fayer@edc.org, is a project director at the Education Development Center (EDC) in Newton, MA 02160. As principal investigator on a National Science Foundation grant working with K–12 mathematics teachers in Waltham, Massachusetts, and as a former mathematics teacher, she has a special interest in exploring algebraic thinking across the grades. Al Cuoco, alcuoco@edc.org, is senior scientist and director of the Mathematics Initiative at EDC. Before coming to EDC, he taught high school mathematics for twenty-four years. Sue Rasala, suer@edc.org, is a senior research associate at EDC. She is interested in early-childhood-mathematics education and professional development in mathematics for early-childhood teachers. M. Grace Kelemanik, gracek@edc.org, is a project director at EDC, where she designs professional-development programs. She is interested in providing supportive environments so that mathematics teachers can reflect on their practice.

Edited by Dan Dolan, Project to Increase Mastery of Mathematics and Science, Wesleyan University, Middletown, CT 06457, and Mari Muri, Connecticut Department of Education, Hartford, CT 06145.

This project was supported by grant no. ESI-9253322 from the National Science Foundation. The opinions expressed are solely those of the authors and should not be interpreted as official positions of the Foundation.

lum. However, as the program progressed, teachers' ideas about children's understanding of algebraic thinking, and their own ideas about algebraic thinking began to change.

The Four-Category Strategy

Throughout the project, we discussed reasons for doing mathematics together, so that teachers would better understand the purposes of each mathematical task. We separated the purposes of doing mathematics in our seminars:

1. Activities that can be taken back immediately for students to do in the classroom

2. Uncovering some reasons for possible misunderstandings that students may have

3. Learning mathematics that was new for participants, for example, investigations in algebraic structures and number theory

4. Understanding how concepts play out across the grades

Allowing elementary, middle, and high school teachers to explore algebraic themes together presented a unique opportunity to examine how algebraic thinking is developed through the K–12 curriculum. The selection of mathematical tasks, as a result, became a carefully constructed process, so that teachers from all levels could find some meaningful ways to participate.

This article gives examples of the mathematics explored and some of the other characteristics that made this project unique. We purposefully structured the seminars to highlight the important contributions that elementary teachers brought to the teams. Whenever we presented problems, we asked teachers to work in grade-level groups initially and then to work together in cross-grade teams to share approaches and solutions.

One middle school teacher commented on the value of having elementary teachers as part of the team: "The elementary teachers helped me look at math with a different viewpoint. I hope it will help me break things down and make them clearer for my kids." A high school teacher continued, "We think at the high school level that our explanations are perfectly clear, but they're obviously not for everyone. The elementary teachers helped us think about different ways to present things." From another high school teacher, "I always thought everyone else thought or should think about math exactly as I did. Watching how other teachers solve the problem, I was amazed. Sometimes the simplest way of doing it is the most elegant and sophisticated."

This impression was confirmed by an elementary teacher who commented, "I found that as these problems were presented, many of the middle and high school teachers immediately took to trying to write a formula and I reached for the manipulatives. And I usually found that I solved the problem as fast as they did, and, in fact, that my method told more the 'why' of how things worked. Somewhere along the line I got the feeling that I earned their respect."

During the seminars, teachers investigated both classic mathematics problems in algebra and innovative materials to clarify their understanding of mathematical thinking and to gain a better understanding of how algebraic thinking is addressed across the grade levels. As teachers began to immerse themselves in the mathematics, they identified the important habits of mind that students need to develop across the curriculum. At the end of the project, elementary-grade teachers articulated that they had a clearer vision of where the mathematics they taught was heading. As one stated, "I think that a lot of the problem is that between the elementary [school] and high school there is such a large gap that we are not able to see the big picture, to see how what we teach plays out later on."

Problems that emphasize algebraic thinking are illustrated in the following. Elementary-grade teachers in our project were familiar with finding, describing, and using patterns. Problems illustrating additive patterns abound in two elementary textbooks, such as "How many eyes are there on one person? Two people? Nineteen people? *X* people?"

The following problem, also involving patterns, is one that can be solved by applying algebraic thinking at a variety of levels.

A frog climbs up the side of a well that is 11 meters deep. Every hour the frog climbs 5 meters and then rests for an hour. As it rests, the frog slips back 3 meters before it climbs again. How long will it take the frog to get out of the well? Determine the answer for a well of any depth.

With such problems as the "frog in the well," teachers developed several strategies and collected numerical data. Some middle and high school teachers immediately started writing algebraic functions. As cross-grade teams solved problems together, teachers drew on their combined efforts by introducing physical models, charts, and other visual methods. Specific examples were explained in the context of a general function. Some representations included pictures and tables, such as those shown in figure 1 and tables 1 and 2.

Extending the data chart was easy, and all the teachers were able to find a solution for an eleven-meter well (7

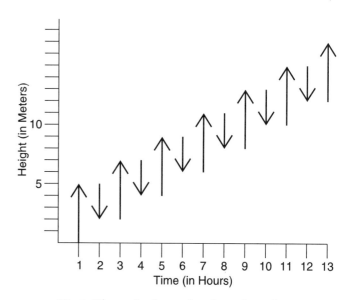

Fig. 1. The work of some fourth-grade teachers

Table 1

The Work of Some Sixth-Grade Teachers

Time (Hours)	Net Height
1	5
2	2
3	7
4	4
5	9
6	6
7	11
8	8
9	13
10	10
11	15
12	12
13	17
14	14

Table 2
The Work of Some Middle School Teachers

Depth of Well	Escape Time (Hours)
1	1
2	1
3	1
4	1
5	1
6	3
7	3
8	5
9	5
10	7
11	7
12	9
13	9
14	11

hours). As noted in figure 1, elementary teachers chose to describe the frog's height in relation to the time with a series of arrows depicting climbs and slides. This visual pattern described the frog's movement. They also found that drawing imaginary lines through the points at the heads of the upward and downward arrows was particularly interesting in describing the pattern.

Some sixth-grade teachers found it useful to concentrate on the net height after each hour (table 1). They constructed a table and found two patterns, 5, 7, 9, 11, …, resulting from odd inputs, and 2, 4, 6, 8, …, resulting from even inputs. Other middle-grades teachers took a different approach and plotted the escape time as a function of the depth of the well (table 2). However, they found that it was not easy to write a simple function to describe the table of values.

High school teachers were most interested in describing the data from their tables in formal algebraic formulas in terms of any height, any climb, and any slide length. Generalizing a method for determining the time to climb out of a well of any height is challenging. Several functional rules describing table 1 were invented. For example, if $h(n)$ is the height climbed after n hours, then

$$h(n) = \begin{cases} n + 4 & \text{if } n \text{ is odd} \\ n & \text{if } n \text{ is even.} \end{cases}$$

Teachers then explored new situations for frogs that climb and slide at different rates. They tried to write a function that covered any resting time, any forward climb, any backward slip, and wells of any depth. Teachers' questions and comments illustrated connections made among specific examples and generalizations with one variable and with more variables.

We also identified the themes that foster algebraic thinking across the grades, which included—

- finding, describing, and using patterns;
- describing and using functions;
- developing proportional reasoning;
- finding, describing, and using algebraic structure; and
- constructing appropriate pedagogy and classroom culture.

Of the five themes in the project, the notion of "algebra as structure" was perhaps the most subtle to develop for teachers at all levels. The disjunction between algebra as a mathematical discipline and as a school subject has widened to the point where university courses in "abstract algebra" that treat algebraic structures seem to have little connection to algebra as a K–12 mathematics strand. Our approach was to look at the development of modern algebra for ideas found in elementary mathematics that contributed to the evaluation of the abstract approach to algebraic structures. We searched for activities in which insights arose from thinking about the *form* of a numerical calculation rather than its *outcome*.

The "frog in the well" gave teachers a problem that they could take back to their classes; for some teachers, being able to take a problem from a workshop and adapt it for classroom use is an important aspect of a good professional-development program. Teachers at every grade level believed that they learned new mathematics by working on the problem and finding out how the same ideas could play out across the grades.

Several other problems that we investigated follow.

- A gardener builds a flower garden made up of individual square beds. She plans to put a tile border around the garden. Each tile has the same dimensions as a single square bed. She makes several models to determine the number of tiles she will need for gardens of various sizes. (See fig. 2.)

Fig. 2. A garden with dimensions of 2 × 3 beds

Use tiles or draw models to represent gardens that are 1, 2, 3, 4, 5, … beds long. For each case, determine the number of tiles needed to make the border. Assume that the equal beds are in a single row, placed end to end.

- How many trains can you make with Cuisenaire rods whose total length is 2? Or 3? Or 4? Or 10? By a train of length 3, we mean a row of rods whose length is 3, where order is important. For example, the train could be made up of rods 1-1-1, 1-2, 2-1, or 3.

Trains of any length can also be classified by the number of "cars" (rods) they contain (e.g., length = 3, 1 three-car train 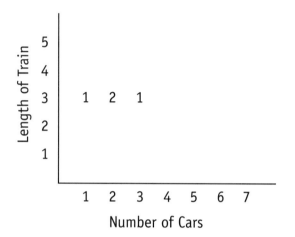, 2 two-car trains, 1 one-car train). How many trains of length 1, 2, 3, …, *n* can be made with 1 car? With 2 cars? With 3 cars? With *n* cars? Make a chart as shown in figure 3 to organize your data. For each length of train, enter the number of trains for each number of cars. Data for a train of length 3 are given as an example. Describe the pattern of numbers in the chart.

Fig. 3. The number of possible three-length trains

Conclusion

In all the mathematics introduced, we acknowledged both directly and indirectly the contributions that the elementary participants made to the cross-grade groups. Elementary teachers became aware of the complementary components of the K–12 curriculum. They also raised their level of confidence as algebraic thinkers, so that they, in turn, could teach algebraic thinking to their students. Elementary teachers agreed, "This has really made me think more about where we're heading, what I have to get my students ready for."

Bibliography

Barnett, Carne, Donna Goldenstein, and Babette Jackson. *Fractions, Decimals, Ratios, and Percents: Hard to Teach and Hard to Learn?* Portsmouth, N.H.: Heinemann, 1994.

Cuter, Ada Beth. *Teachers, Time and Transformations: First Year Evaluation Report.* Cambridge, Mass.: Education Matters, 1993.

Duggan, Theresa. *Teachers, Time and Transformations: Second Year Evaluation Report.* Cambridge, Mass.: Education Matters, 1994.

Lovitt, Charles, and Doug Williams. *The Mathematics Curriculum and Teaching Program Mathematics Task Centre Project.* Melbourne, Australia: Curriculum Corp., 1988.

Stillwell, John. *Elements of Algebra.* New York: Springer-Verlag, 1994.

United States Department of Education. *The Algebra Initiative Colloquium.* Proceedings of a conference, Washington, D.C., December 1993.

Activities

The Real-Number System

Çemen, "Adding and Subtracting Integers on the Number Line"

Refer to the rules in tables 1 and 2.

(a) Use the rules to find the answer to the following:

$$4 \_ (-8) + (-6) \_ 6$$

(b) Explain why the rules do or do not work.

(c) If the rules do not work, change the rules to make them work.

Lobato, "Making Connections with Estimation"

1. Individual problem

(a) Use your own estimation strategies to answer each of the questions in figure 8.

(b) Write an explanation of each strategy. Explain why your estimated values are either greater than or less than the values you would find if you used a calculator.

2. Group problem

(a) Write three different real-world estimation problems.

(b) Ask your friends (or children) to use estimation to answer each problem and to explain their strategies to you.

(c) Compile descriptions of the different strategies that were used for each problem.

(d) Evaluate the effectiveness of your three problems in eliciting information about estimation strategies.

Fitzgerald and Boyd, "A Number Line with Character"

1. Pairs project

(a) With a partner, play the Factor Game explained at the beginning of the article and shown in figure 1.

(b) Write a reflective account of the mathematics you used to play the game. Explain any strategies that you and your partner may have developed.

2. Group project

(a) Develop a poster displaying the "number line with character." Identify as many patterns as you can and arrange the area strips to make these patterns visible.

(b) Write a group report explaining all the patterns that you found. If these patterns have mathematical names, be sure to include them in your report.

Whitin, "Beccca's Investigation"

1. The author mentions Tammy's question about the law of compensation.

(a) Give two examples illustrating how this law works with addition and does not work with multiplication.

(b) Explain why the law works for addition and does not work for multiplication.

2. Consider the rule Invert and multiply.

(a) Explain why the rule works when one fraction is divided by another.

(b) Does this rule apply if one or both of the numbers in the division problem are whole numbers? Give examples and explain your answer.

Juraschek and Evans, "Ryan's Primes"

With a friend, play the multiplication game with red, yellow, blue, and green cubes. Encourage the friend to figure out the "trick."

Wentworth and Monroe, "What Is the Whole?"

1. Area-model representations

(a) Find a construction using area-model representations for the multiplication problems $1/3 \times 1/5$ and $1/4 \times 1/6$ that allow you to compare the relative sizes of your two answers.

(b) Explain why your constructions make the comparison mathematically possible and why the area models in figure 3 are not correct.

2. Refer to the graphical representation shown in figure 5.

(a) Use this representation to model the following problems:

• $1/3 \div 1/5$

• $3/5 \div 2/9$

(b) Check your answers by using a calculator with a fraction key.

3. Refer to the previous activities.

(a) Use pencil-and-paper algorithms to find the solutions to the problems in activities 1*a* and 2.

(b) Explain how the area-model representations embody the rules you used in each algorithm.

Goldberg, "How Old Do You Want to Be?"

1. Where appropriate, use the quotient-with-remainder division key on a calculator to answer the following:

(a) Using your age, answer the four questions relating to different base systems and how numbers are represented in them.

(b) Select two other ages, one much greater and one much less than yours, and repeat questions 1 through 3.

(c) If someone wrote her age as 2021 but you knew she was really 61, what base was she using to represent her age?

2. Suppose you had a calculator that did not have a quotient-with-remainder division key.

(a) Describe the general sequence of calculator keystrokes you would use to find the integer quotient and remainder for the following problems:

• $27 \div 4$

• $12\,965 \div 761$

• $1\,111\,111 \div 333$

(b) Explain why your method will or will not work for all three problems.

Reys, "Promoting Number Sense in the Middle Grades"

Write a reaction to this article. Include a discussion of your own number sense and how it has or has not changed after reading the articles in this section.

Yackel, "A Foundation for Algebraic Reasoning in the Early Grades"

The following problems are examples of situations that require algebraic reasoning for their solution. By not including specific numbers for the quantities described, each problem focuses attention on the relationships among the quantities.

1. In a certain town 2/3 of the men are married to 3/4 of the women.

(a) Are there more men or women in the town? Explain your answer.

(b) Find the ratio of men to women for this town.

2. Katie sorts her 52 red, blue, green, and yellow blocks so that each pile contains blocks of only one color. She then notices that she has twice as many blue blocks as green ones and four more yellow blocks than red ones. How many blocks of each color does Katie have?

Ruopp, Cuoco, Rasala, and Kelemanik, "Algebraic Thinking: A Professional Development Theme"

1. Use Cuisenaire rods to make trains.

(a) How many trains can you make whose length is 2? 3? 4? 10? (The article presents a discussion of this problem to get you started.)

(b) Describe any patterns you find.

Section 8
Data, Measurement, and Geometry

The NCTM Curriculum and Evaluation Standards for grades K–8 include specific standards for geometry, measurement, statistics, and probability. These topics, which used to be encountered only in high school courses, are now part of the elementary school curriculum. As the articles in this section illustrate, fundamental concepts in data, measurement, and geometry can be effectively developed at the elementary level.

Lindquist's article outlines changes that need to be made in the elementary school curriculum to bring it in line with the vision of the NCTM *Standards*. Five areas of concern include the view of mathematics and mathematics learning, curriculum, instruction, evaluation, and support. The author's comments are a summation of many of the themes elaborated by other authors throughout the collected readings.

Bohan, Irby, and Vogel describe the Elementary Mathematics Research Model, which can be used to structure investigative projects dealing with data collection and analysis. Specific activities are described that help students develop understandings of the concepts of mean, median, and mode. The research projects outlined in the article illustrate how real-life problems can be studied in meaningful ways by elementary school children.

The articles by Hendrix-Martin and by Shaw and Cliatt present examples of measurement activities. Hendrix-Martin illustrates how children's literature can be used as the springboard for mathematics learning. Using the book *Biggest, Strongest, Fastest,* the author creates a rich sequence of tasks that incorporates not only ideas about measurement but also estimation, the collection and organization of data, and practice with computational skills. Shaw and Cliatt discuss five principles for developing measurement sense and describe a set of versatile activities that incorporate these principles.

Imagery and spatial sense are two fundamental aspects of mathematical thinking. Wheatly discusses the important role that imagery plays in mathematics learning. He fleshes out his definition of this concept through examples of students' work and a brief discussion of related research. Andrews describes ways to build on young children's intuitive understandings about space and objects to strengthen spatial sense. These experiences establish the foundation for more-complex geometric ways of organizing the world such as that presented in the next article, by Claus. Claus describes a fifth-grade geometry activity that provides students with a review of geometric concepts as well as opportunities for problem solving and written and oral communication. The activity, which is based on forming and analyzing shapes made from triangles, presents geometric ideas in a holistic, interconnected fashion.

The articles by Berkman and by Miller highlight the importance of attending to students' use of mathematical language. Berkman describes how he introduces incorrect answers and "dumb" questions to his students to stimulate deeper levels of discussion and encourage them to develop greater precision in their use of language. Miller presents the results of a study of eighth graders' abilities to formulate definitions for common mathematical terms. She recommends that students be given opportunities to express ideas in mathematical language in order to develop conceptual understandings of such terms.

It's Time to Change

by

Mary Montgomery Lindquist

Recently, there have been many calls for reform of schooling, and in particular there has been major rethinking of school mathematics. The initial thrust for change in school mathematics was the poor achievement of students, but there are even more-compelling reasons for change. Today's technological society requires a different mathematical preparation for its citizens—and for a greater proportion of its citizens—from that of the past. Astute teachers and researchers, aware that mathematics did not make sense to many students, have found different and successful approaches to teaching and learning mathematics. Thus, exemplars on which to base change already exist. Additionally, newly articulated recommendations for school mathematics have been made by the *Curriculum and Evaluation Standards for School Mathematics* (NCTM 1989). These Standards, endorsed by many groups, provide direction from the professional organization most closely involved in mathematics education for students. Interwoven in this article is my interpretation of the Standards as I discuss five areas of needed change in the elementary school: the view of mathematics and mathematics learning, curriculum, instruction, evaluation, and support.

A View of Mathematics and Mathematics Learning

Underlying the *Standards* is a view of mathematics and the learning of mathematics that is quite different from that presently held by many people. My logical side says that the first step in implementing the recommendations is to change people's perception of mathematics and mathematics learning to make it consistent with this vision. My practical side says that the acceptance of this view will come incrementally as students, teachers, and others begin to see results of some of the changes. Common to both my logical and practical sides is the need for everyone to be aware of this view.

Mathematics is a changing body of knowledge. Some say that in five to seven years there will be twice as much mathematics as there is today. Although much of this new mathematics will not be appropriate for students in elementary school, the magnitude of change will have an impact on how we teach mathematics at this level. At present, students perceive mathematics as a set of rules to be learned and practiced. Yet children come to school with a sense of mathematics, for they have been using it to solve problems they understood. We have failed to capitalize and build on this understanding as we teach more-abstract procedures. We must help children construct meaning and sense by approaching mathematics as problem solving. They must see that mathematics is created by us and that it can make sense.

Children come to school with a sense of mathematics.

This view of mathematics as a dynamic subject must be begun as soon as children enter school. It does not take long for students to adopt the opposite view as they become receivers of procedures: "Tell me what to do, not why." The short-term payoff for students' knowing "what to do" is great because that is what we reward. The long-term payoff is a disaster, as shown by the present state of mathematical learning.

Technology has made possible many of the new creations in mathematics, and we must be responsive to technology. Students have often been seduced by the power of a paper-and-pencil algorithm; they know it will do something and they know how to do it, but they do not know what it really does or why. Thus, they perform mathematical antics with little thought about the reasonableness of answers. Technology is even more powerful, and we need to know how to use it skillfully, just as in the past we needed speed and accuracy with paper-and-pencil algorithms. Without a strong conceptual base, the ability to use technology will be severely limited.

As the amount of mathematics content increases, so does the number and type of applications. There are new applications of geometry, of measurement, of statistics, and even of sophisticated counting. We need to broaden the curriculum so that our young, beginning students do not have a narrow view of mathematics and so that they will be prepared to study a wide variety of mathematical topics.

Thus, viewing mathematics as a changing body of knowledge forces us to look again at what we are doing with mathematics for the elementary school child.

Mathematics is useful and powerful. Everyone agrees that mathematics is useful, but often our opinion appears to be that it is useful for someone else. This attitude is well ingrained by the seventh grade (Lindquist et al. forthcoming). At one time this may have been a valid opinion, but it is not one today, for every career is becoming more dependent on mathematics. Do you realize that over 60 percent of college career choices are closed if one has not taken advanced mathematics in high school? Similarly, our technical schools also require a strong background in mathematics for a diversity of career options. Even to function well outside the workplace we need more mathematics and more sophisticated reasoning related to mathematics.

Mathematics, even in elementary school, is often approached on an abstract level as students learn to manipulate symbols. Little attempt is made to have the mathematics grow out of, or be tied to, problems children have solved in other ways. For example, when being taught subtraction, children might wonder why they would *subtract* to find out how much longer a rod of nine cubes is than a rod of five cubes when they have been counting or thinking about how many more cubes would have to be *added* to the shorter rod. Even if one is imagining taking away some cubes, it is not the five cubes. With situations like this, it does not take children very long to think of mathematics as a different world from the one that once made sense.

Any mathematics is powerful if one has control over it, and one can gain control by understanding how it works. In the example described in the last paragraph, if children

trying to solve the problem understand that subtraction has many meanings including the comparative meaning, then they will have power. They will understand why subtraction can replace their more primitive method of counting and how subtraction is related to addition. The *Standards* calls for developing the language of mathematics so that students can see its power. The symbolic language of mathematics is powerful, but it is abstract; consequently, it takes time for students to develop the meanings of these symbols.

A goal of the *Standards* is for children to view mathematics as a useful subject that gives them power to solve problems. Our challenge is to create classrooms in which this will happen.

Any mathematics is powerful if one has control over it.

Mathematics is learned by doing mathematics. An underlying assumption of the *Standards* is that learning mathematics is a constructive rather than a passive activity. When students are using prior knowledge to construct new mathematical knowledge, they are learning mathematics. Otherwise, they are receiving a body of knowledge, and often in unrelated and unorganized pieces, which makes it difficult to retrieve and use.

This does not mean that the *Standards* advocates that students not be taught. It does mean a new view of teaching for many of us. The teacher must make decisions about what mathematics students are ready to learn and what experiences will help them construct meaning for this mathematics.

This approach is success oriented. Children will be learning that which they can learn and thus will develop the sense that they can *do* mathematics. Developing this self-confidence in students is critical, so that they will continue to use, study, and enjoy mathematics.

Mathematics can be learned by all. Mathematics is often viewed as a subject that can be learned only by a few. One often hears, "Either you have or you don't have what it takes to learn math." Of course abilities differ, but often all students do not have a true opportunity to learn mathematics.

We cannot afford to neglect any student or any segment of our population. Evidence from NAEP (Dossey et al. 1988) shows that since 1978 the differences in performance between some subgroups have been narrowing.

Black and Hispanic students have made progress in closing the performance gap relative to their white peers. Students in the Southeast improved significantly during this period with comparatively larger and more consistent gains than their counterparts in other parts of the country. Differences between the performance of females and males were not significant at ages nine and thirteen, but small, significant differences in favor of males were present at age seventeen. Overall, these results are encouraging, but substantial gaps in performance still exist between many subgroups and between many individuals. Moreover, much of the gain has been made in computational skills, not in higher-level arithmetic or in other areas of the curriculum.

Not only do we need to close the gap between these subpopulations, but we also need to look at our low-ability students. Any change must take into account this group. One of the most striking differences between American and Asian schooling is that the latter expects hard work. "If a child's rate of learning is slower than that of other children, it means only that the child must study even harder" (Stevenson 1988, p. 8). We need to set realistic goals for low-ability students and then expect them to reach them. One crucial goal, often not expected of these students, is that they should make sense out of mathematics. At present, we are overloading them—as well as many other students—with a preponderance of isolated nonsensical procedures.

Mathematically talented youth also need special attention, for they, with proper encouragement and background, will be the ones who discover new applications of mathematics. But the masses of students in the middle also must be given the chance to learn mathematics in a way that makes sense. They will be the users of much mathematics in their careers and in their daily lives.

Curriculum

The Underachieving Curriculum (McKnight et al. 1987) focused attention on the need to make changes in the mathematics curriculum, and the *Standards* proposes many changes. The elementary school has the greatest responsibility for their success, since it will be difficult or nearly impossible to make significant changes in the secondary school curriculum without first making changes in the elementary school curriculum.

Four aspects of the curriculum—the emphasis, placement, integration, and treatment of topics—need careful consideration in making these changes consistent with the direction set forth by the *Standards*.

Emphasis of topics. In the past ten years, interest and progress in including more than paper-and-pencil computation in elementary schools have increased. Textbooks have increased the number of story problems, included

problem-solving strategies, and made suggestions for mental math and calculator activities. Statewide tests have increased their emphasis on geometry, measurement, probability, and statistics. Teachers are attending in-service sessions on these topics. Yet elementary school students still perceive that mathematics is computation and that the goal is to get the correct answer as quickly as possible. It is evident, although we have made a beginning, that we have not overcome the preoccupation with computation.

Seven changes in the presently implemented curriculum can take us another step forward. If the two recommended decreases are made, there would be time for increased emphasis in the five areas described below. In fact, by implementing the seven proposals below, we can ensure that our students will reach the same level of achievement they now have but without spending the time they do now on computation and repetition.

1. *Increase the emphasis on building an understanding of numbers.* Central to much of mathematics is a firm understanding of numbers, yet children have a narrow understanding of numeration and little understanding of fractions or decimals. On the fourth NAEP mathematics assessment, fewer than half of the seventh- and eleventh-grade students knew that 5 1/4 was the same as 5 + 1/4 (Lindquist et al. forthcoming). The *Standards* refers to this understanding of numbers as number sense. This includes such meanings as knowing that 8 is 6 and 2, or 7 and 1 more, or 2 less than 10; that 23 is small compared to 3856; and that the sum of 57 and 71 is more than 100. This number sense permits a child to mentally add 8 and 4 by thinking 8 and 2 is 10 and 2 more is 12, or to mentally find the sum of 56 and 7 by thinking 56, 60, 63. It is the sense that permits people to make reasonable estimates, not wild guesses.

2. *Increase the emphasis on the meanings of the four operations.* Until recently, any discussion of operations usually focused only on how to develop meaning for computation. One of the greatest contributions of the *Standards* is the highlighting of operations as a separate standard, putting the proper emphasis on *concepts* of operations rather than only on computation. This missing emphasis on operations is a prime cause of students' difficulty with word problems and with a lack of understanding of computational procedures.

3. *Increase the emphasis on the variety of ways to compute and to make estimates.* In a recent national survey (Weiss 1987, p. 44), 72 percent of teachers of grades K–6 indicated that they placed a heavy emphasis on having their students perform computations with speed and accuracy. Only 2 percent of these teachers had students use calculators "in the previous day's lesson." Although the two percentages are not directly comparable, they do indicate the status of computation in schools today. It is time to educate youth in how to use the tools of today—including

their minds, paper and pencil, calculators, and computers. They also must know when it is appropriate to use each tool. For too long our students have needed pencil and paper to find the sum of 56 and 7, which indicates that this problem is not a new one surfacing only because of calculators.

4. *Increase the emphasis on geometry, measurement, probability, statistics, and algebra.* The new applications of mathematics in all aspects of society give us an impetus for reexamining the need for a broader curriculum. Just as we have laid the foundation of arithmetic in the elementary grades, so we need to lay the foundation of the other topics listed above not only for the further study of mathematics but also for use in everyday life.

5. *Increase the emphasis on appropriate, individual segments of the curriculum at each grade level.* When we try to cover everything at each grade level, we end up not covering many things in enough depth to enable children to retain the concepts and skills. A recent study (Porter et al. 1988, p. 4) found that "teachers devoted less than 30 minutes of instructional time across the full year to 70 percent or more of the topics they covered." For example, in many texts *each year* there is one lesson on *each* of these topics: pounds, quarts, liters, and kilograms. The curriculum needs restructuring so that fewer bits and pieces are included each year, thus allowing time for children to internalize the new material. Then in succeeding years we should use, not reteach, this material.

6. *Decrease the emphasis on paper-and-pencil computation.* This recommendation is not a call for doing away with all paper-and-pencil computational work. Much can be learned about numbers and the operations through such work. It does call for a reevaluation of the amount of time now spent on paper-and-pencil computation and ways to free the curriculum for other mathematics. The *Standards* gives direction to this change.

7. *Decrease the repetition from year to year.* The amount of repetition is well documented in the literature or by a look at the scope and sequence in textbooks. This repetition is partially due to the premature introduction of some topics into the curriculum. It may also be due to students' perceptions of what is important—they soon learn that it is not necessary to learn many things, since they will be retaught in time for the test the next year. It is also due to not staying with a topic long enough for students to build meanings. Certainly old topics will be revisited, but there are many ways to use previously taught material in new settings or with new twists so that students do not think it is the same old stuff. Our motto should be, Use previously learned mathematics yes, but reteach no.

Placement of topics. A careful consideration of the placement of topics may alleviate some problems with time. It is clear, for example, that if enough time is spent on

two-digit subtraction in the second grade, many children will become at least mechanically proficient. But what is sacrificed? At present, much of this skill must be relearned in third grade because students lack the foundation. Valuable time is lost that could be used for other topics, not to mention the frustration for those second-grade students who were unsuccessful and the third-grade students who had mastered two-digit subtraction earlier and must sit through it again. In general, our computational strand needs to be slowed down so that ample time can be spent developing number sense and meanings of operations as well as applying learned computational skills.

For too long our students have needed pencil and paper to find the sum of 56 and 7.

Some people question whether this slowing down of the paper-and-pencil computation strand is weakening the curriculum. I see it as just the opposite; it is opening time in the curriculum for more problem solving, more communicating about mathematics, and more reasoning. These are higher-level skills that demand much more of students.

If number sense is to be well developed, then neither the large numbers nor the small numbers (decimals) can be rushed. I am convinced that time spent on these topics will make time later; if not, at least more students will have a better understanding of the basis of much mathematics.

Appropriate segments of all other topics should be placed in each grade. As with number work, the development should be done carefully so that it is not necessary to repeat the same topic as new work the next year. This, of course, does not mean that there is no need for maintenance or review. It does mean that new topics should be clearly marked and treated differently from those needing only to be reviewed.

Integration of topics. There are many reasons why topics should be integrated. First, the integration of topics keeps concepts, vocabulary, and skills alive. It provides a natural way to review these aspects of learning. Second, integrating topics also helps children make connections between mathematical content. For example, they can see how geometry can help them visualize an arithmetic problem. Third, the compartmentalization of content encourages children to think that once they have passed a test, they can forget the material. Thus, integration would set expectations of having to know, use, and remember the different topics in mathematics.

Treatment of topics. It does not matter what we emphasize or how we place or integrate topics if the topics themselves are not treated in a way consistent with what we want children to learn. In the *Standards*, each of the usual content topics is addressed separately to indicate what children should be able to do as a result of instruction in that content area. The reader is referred to the *Standards* for further discussion and to the other articles in this book for examples of content treatment.

Instruction

It also makes little difference what we teach if we do not change how we teach. If we wish children to make sense out of mathematics and to develop confidence in their ability, then we must find a better fit between teaching children and teaching mathematics. Although the Standards focus on curriculum, they imply a great deal about instruction.

Problem solving, reasoning, and communicating. Three of the Standards are common across all the grade levels (K–4, 5–8, and 9–12) and address problem solving, reasoning, and communicating. These three Standards, crucial to the overall view of mathematics being presented in the *Standards*, are discussed in the next two articles, but let me make one point about each.

It makes little difference what we teach if we do not change how we teach.

If problem solving is to become the focus of the curriculum, then it must be central to the way we teach. We cannot expect children to solve problems unless we help them build mathematics from problems rather than teach them procedures that later can be applied to problems.

Children can reason in mathematics. That is, they can make sense of it if we give them the chance. The atmosphere of our classes should be one of both teachers and students wanting to know why and not being satisfied with knowing only how.

A classroom that encourages communicating will be one in which there is a lot of talking, listening, writing, and reading. Students can more readily communicate about something concrete. Herein lies another reason to provide physical materials that model mathematical ideas.

Building connections. We need to help students build several connections. One is the connection between conceptual and procedural knowledge. Learning rules and procedures without understanding eventually causes difficulty because there are too many isolated rules to learn and remember, too many rules from which to select, and too little chance of transfer to new situations (Hiebert and Lindquist forthcoming).

Similarly, we need to connect the concrete with the abstract. Manipulatives are of little use unless the bridge is made to the symbolic aspects of mathematics. Again, communicating is central as we help children make the connection between something that makes sense to them (the concrete) and something that makes sense to mathematicians (the abstract).

Another connection that needs to be made is between topics in mathematics. The integration of topics in the curriculum will help children make some of these connections, but we must also do it as we teach. For example, how is rounding a number like measuring to the nearest centimeter? How is finding an average like making equal groups? How is dividing by 3 like dividing by 2/3?

Still another connection to make is that of connecting mathematics with other areas of the curriculum. It is this connection that may help children see the usefulness of mathematics from the very beginning of their long school career.

Role of students. Listen to the verbs used in the *Standards: investigate, explore, describe, develop, use, apply, invent, relate, model, explain, represent, validate….* This list alone should indicate what students ought to be doing.

Role of teachers. Obviously, the teacher is the central figure in the instruction of children, but we often seem to forget this when recommendations are pronounced. The *Standards,* during its development and during the year of hearings on the draft version, had much input from teachers. Yet, without the acceptance of change by this group, no real and meaningful change will occur.

Those of you who are elementary school teachers have a great challenge. The reward will be seeing children make sense of mathematics as you become less of a dispenser of knowledge and more of a facilitator of learning. How can students be actively involved in doing mathematics if they are taught by the rule-example method? How can they communicate if mathematics classes consist mainly of individuals doing paper-and-pencil worksheets? How can they learn to solve problems and reason unless they have the opportunity?

Evaluation

Evaluation is a critical word in the title of the *Standards*, for if evaluation is not changed, then there is little reason to change curriculum or instruction. Several aspects of evaluation need to be addressed; among these are the view of evaluation, the role of evaluation in the classroom, and standardized tests.

The view of evaluation. Changing one's view of evaluation must accompany changing one's view of mathematics and mathematics learning. Evaluation is considered a driving force of curriculum and instruction; if this idea is correct, then we must use evaluation to help make changes that will improve students' learning of mathematics.

Evaluation must be a partner, not an adversary. When assessments of students are used to provide the appropriate curriculum and instruction, then the partnership is sound. Inherent in the previous statement is the need to assess students' learning of the mathematics that is deemed important. That is, if we value reasoning and communicating, then we must include these skills in our evaluation. Thus, there is a need for new approaches and techniques to assessing. When we use evaluation to help determine the overall worth of our mathematics program, then the partnership becomes profitable. We can no longer afford to have mathematics programs that do not enhance the future of all our citizens.

Evaluation in the classroom. Assessment must be an integral part of instruction if it is to be useful in providing appropriate curriculum and instruction for students. It is an ongoing process of finding out what students are doing, thinking, and feeling. This is not an easy process, but one that must accompany the changes suggested by the *Standards*. Here are a few questions that you might ask yourself to begin this process of assessment:

1. *Written tests.* Do they include a balance of concepts and procedures? Do they include problems that make the students think rather than problems that are exact replicas of the text's problems? Do they include questions calling for a written response? Do they include questions that ask why? Do you permit calculators to be used?

2. *Use of questions.* Do you use questions as you explain something to see what the students are thinking? How often do you encourage students' questions? How often do your questions probe or require higher-level thinking skills? How often do you ask students why they think this topic is useful?

3. *Observations.* How often do you make a judgment by watching children working alone or in a group? Do you use this as part of the assignment of a grade?

4. *Interviews.* Do you ask individual children to explain just to you how they are doing something or what they are thinking?

5. *Listening.* Do you listen to children as they explain to others what they are doing or thinking? Do you really listen to what they are saying as they explain to you or as they ask you questions?

6. *Understanding.* Do you *really* understand the concepts and the procedures and how children learn them?

Standardized tests. Standardized tests have become the villain in the minds of many. They can be a positive force in moving toward implementing the recommendations of the *Standards* if they change and if our use of, and attitude toward, them change. These tests must become more responsive to the need to assess in a variety of ways, must include calculator use, must assess how children do mathematics rather than only the end product, and must respond more quickly to the changing curriculum. In its turn, the education community must clearly understand the purpose of each test and use the results appropriately, realize that good instruction will produce better long-term results than teaching to the test, demand tests that are consistent with our goals, and realize that there are no easy, quick solutions to low test scores.

Support

Both the quality and the quantity of support for teachers and students need to change if we are to reach toward the goals set by the *Standards*. Although support is needed on all fronts, I have chosen four areas—time, textbooks and other teaching materials, teacher preparation, and the public—to discuss here.

Time. One of the most striking characteristics of Asian teaching is the amount of time teachers have to prepare for teaching. Few elementary school teachers here have a planning period or even any time to themselves during the day. If changes are to occur, then elementary school teachers must have time to prepare to teach each day as well as time to reflect on their teaching. They also need time to observe and work with other teachers. They need time for further study of mathematics and mathematical instruction.

Students also need time to learn mathematics. Many questions about students' time need answering. First, is enough time each day or week devoted to mathematics? Second, is that time used constructively? Third, what time of day does mathematics instruction occur? Fourth, how much time do we expect students to spend outside of school working with mathematics?

Textbooks and other teaching materials. Over 90 percent of the teachers in grades K–6 use a published textbook in their classes (Weiss 1987). The textbook undoubtedly has great influence on what is taught. It is easy to be critical of textbooks, and publishing companies must accept some of this criticism, but it is a two-way street. Textbooks cannot do everything—as they are sometimes expected to do—and textbooks will change if teachers ask and are ready for change. Both sides, teachers and publishers, must be willing to take some risks and accept change.

The *Standards* makes clear that a textbook alone is not sufficient for teaching and learning mathematics. Classrooms must be equipped with calculators, computers, physical materials, and the associated "software" to support these. Teachers must learn how to use these materials to help children learn mathematics.

Teacher preparation. Teachers are the key to effective change, and they deserve everyone's support, particularly in their preparation, whether it be initial, preservice preparation, help as a beginning teacher, or in-service programs. As initial preparation, we must provide the mathematics background they will need to teach in a changing world of mathematics. Along with this preparation they need to learn mathematics as they will be expected to teach it. They need to leave this preservice experience knowing that mathematics makes sense so that they can impart this sense to their students. Preservice teachers also need to maintain or develop their self-confidence about mathematics so they can help children develop theirs. We must provide them with ways to help children learn mathematics and let them experience children learning mathematics.

During their first years of teaching, teachers need to continue this learning process in a more systematic way. Of course they learn by doing, but there are other ways that could help them during these first years. In addition, after the first years we need to provide for ongoing, meaningful in-service programs.

It is time to take seriously the need for mathematics specialists in elementary schools, at least after grade 3. It is unrealistic to expect a teacher at these grades to have the in-depth background needed to teach eight subjects. It is even more unrealistic to expect teachers to find the time to prepare daily to teach each of these areas.

The public. The support of the public is needed in many ways. The public needs to be aware of the changing view of mathematics and the implications for schooling. As parents, we must be open to reasonable changes in the curriculum. Just because we or Sue's older sister learned the multiplication tables in the third grade does not mean that it is better for Sue if she learns them in the second grade—or perhaps even in the third grade. Just because we did not use a calculator in elementary school does not mean that our children should not use one.

We must encourage our students to study mathematics; it can be fun and rewarding, but it takes hard work. We often do not like to see our children struggling, and there is, of course, a limit. But when children give up on a problem after a minute, then they have not developed the perseverance necessary to become mathematically powerful. As I have discussed, changes must be made in the class-

room, but few gains will be made without the support from home.

In Closing

At the beginning of this century, Dewey (1901) implied that a change in curriculum is more than it appears. This is probably even more true today as we end the century. The task ahead is great, but so are our resources. Teachers, textbook publishers, testing companies, administrators, the public, and students—together we can do it. It is time.

References

Dewey, John. "The Situation as Regards the Course of Study." *Journal of Proceedings and Addresses of the National Education Association* 40 (1901): 332–38.

Dossey, John A., Ina V. S. Mullis, Mary M. Lindquist, and Donald L. Chambers. *The Mathematics Report Card: Are We Measuring Up?* Princeton, N.J.: Educational Testing Service, 1988.

Hiebert, James, and Mary M. Lindquist. "Developmental Learning and Teaching." In *Teaching and Learning Mathematics for the Young Child*, edited by Joseph Payne. Reston, Va.: National Council of Teachers of Mathematics, forthcoming.

Lindquist, Mary M., Catherine A. Brown, Thomas P. Carpenter, Vicky L. Kouba, Edward A. Silver, and Jane O. Swafford. *Results of the Fourth Mathematics Assessment of the NAEP.* Reston, Va.: National Council of Teachers of Mathematics, forthcoming.

McKnight, Curtis C., F. Joe Crosswhite, John A. Dossey, Edward Kifer, Jane O. Swafford, Kenneth J. Travers, and Thomas J. Cooney. *The Underachieving Curriculum: Assessing U.S. School Mathematics from an International Perspective.* Champaign, Ill.: Stipes, 1987.

National Council of Teachers of Mathematics. *Curriculum and Evaluation Standards for School Mathematics.* Reston, Va.: NCTM, 1989.

Porter, Andrew, Robert Floden, Donald Freeman, William Schmidt, Jack Schwille, Linda Alford, Susan Irwin, Janet Vredevoogd, and Frank Jenkins. "Elementary Math Curriculum Out of Balance." *IRT Communication Quarterly* (Winter 1988): 3–4.

Stevenson, Harold W. "America's Math Problems." *Educational Leadership* (October 1987): 4–10.

Weiss, Iris R. *Report of the 1985–86 National Survey of Science and Mathematics Education.* Research Triangle Park, N.C.: Research Triangle Institute, 1987.

Problem Solving
Dealing with Data in the Elementary School

by

Harry Bohan, Beverly Irby, and Dolly Vogel

Standard 11 of the K–4 recommendations of the National Council of Teachers of Mathematics's *Curriculum and Evaluation Standards for School Mathematics* and Standard 10 of the grades 5–8 portion of this document suggest that students be given opportunities to—

- collect, organize, and describe data; ...

- formulate and solve problems that involve collecting and organizing data; ...

- develop an appreciation for statistical methods as a powerful means for decision making (1989, 54, 105).

A basic assumption of the *Standards* document is that students will learn better through problem-solving situations that involve their doing mathematics rather than having it done to them—so that they become producers of knowledge rather than merely consumers. The Elementary Mathematics Research Model furnishes a vehicle for problem solving through real data collection and analysis.

Photograph by Shana McKay, Conroe (Texas) Independent School District; all rights reserved

Harry Bohan is a professor of mathematics education at Sam Houston State University in Huntsville, TX 77341. Beverly Irby is also on the faculty and teaches elementary science methods courses. Dolly Vogel is a graduate student at Sam Houston State University and a teacher of sixth-grade mathematics at Houser Intermediate School, Conroe Independent School District, Conroe, TX 77385.

The Elementary Mathematics Research Model

To incorporate a research component into the curriculum, two aspects must be considered. First, students need a research model that is easy to understand and apply. Second, students must have an understanding of some basic statistical tools, such as mean, median, mode, and range. At higher grade levels, measures of dispersion other than the range might also be included. Rather than being taught as isolated topics, the statistical tools are used in applying the research model to real situations. This concept is supported by Moore (1990), who emphasizes the need for statistics to be couched in realistic settings.

Getting started

The Elementary Mathematics Research Model (Irby and Bohan 1991) has students move through seven steps to produce knowledge through mathematics. See figure 1. In step 1 students must attempt to identify a problem. For the students to become involved and have ownership in the project, the first item of business is to let them think—of things that they would like to know, of some questions that they would like to answer, or of some problems that they have observed in the school or community. During this brainstorming session, establish a rule that no one is to judge the thoughts of another. Let the ideas come freely. If someone repeats an idea already on the

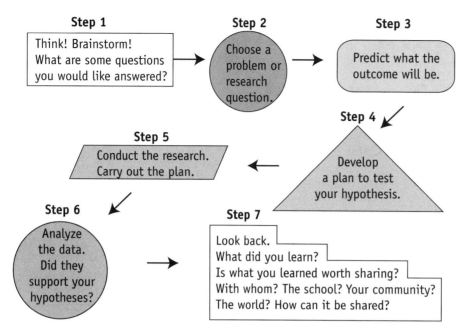

Fig. 1. The Elementary Mathematics Research Model

a grant proposal to request the money through the principal or the PTA? and (*e*) safety—what measures must we take to ensure safety, for instance, gloves and masks?

The students will need to develop an exact plan to address these concerns. In the process they may discover subquestions related to the original research question, such as, Which group is more environmentally aware—fifth or sixth graders? On which day do most students bring lunches? What buying trends should be observed by the cafeteria management on the basis of analysis of food in the garbage? Each question may call for different statistical treatments.

The teacher may have different groups in the class work on each related question, so that at the end of the research all questions will have been answered. Each subquestion will prompt the development of a specific plan.

Regarding the original question, the students decided on the following plan:

> We will have our study last for three weeks, giving us fifteen opportunities to collect data. We will check the garbage every day and request that it not be thrown out until we do so. We will request the help of our fellow students when throwing out their garbage in the cafeteria by requesting that they separate it into six different cans that are clearly marked—uneaten food, partially eaten food, Styrofoam, paper, plastic, and aluminum. We will weigh the amount of each can and keep the records each day. The number of aluminum cans will be counted.

As the students determine how they will gather the data, they need to determine what variables are involved in the research study. In this example, they might determine that the weight of each individual can would be one variable, the length of the study might be another, and so on.

Step 5 is "carry out the actual plan." During the time the data are being collected, discuss ways in which the students might report the findings. Graphs should certainly be discussed as a possibility, as should types of graphs best used for various purposes (see, e.g., Curcio [1981]). At this point, the need for statistical measures to describe the data becomes apparent. For example, since this study is to last fifteen days, it is not probable that the same number of aluminum cans would be collected each day. How can the number of cans collected daily be described without having to list fifteen numbers?

chalkboard, go ahead and write it. Never say, "We already said that," since this type of response stifles creative thinking. The job of the teacher is to see that a risk-free environment is maintained. After brainstorming, let the students take one of the generated ideas and work through the remaining steps in the design.

Step 2 is a natural outcome of step 1. One of the issues from the brainstorming session is chosen, a problem to be solved is developed, and a research question is stated. The following is a problem formulated from a brainstorming session in a sixth-grade class:

> The students were concerned with the amount of garbage produced in the school cafeteria and its impact on the environment (the problem). The research question was, What part of the garbage in our school cafeteria is recyclable?

In step 3 students hypothesize the expected outcome of the research. The teacher might ask, "What do you think will be the outcome of your research or investigation?" Students should be accustomed to hypothesizing from science classes. With regard to the first question, the students might answer, "We believe that half of the waste is recyclable."

Step 4 will find students developing a plan for how to test the hypothesis and answer the question. The following items will need to be considered in developing the plan: (*a*) permission—who will give us permission, the principal, the cafeteria supervisor, the maintenance director, or others? (*b*) courtesy—when can we conveniently discuss this project with the cafeteria management? (*c*) time—how much time can we spend on this investigation, when should we do this project each day, how long do we think it will take to gather all the data? (*d*) money—will it cost anything, how can we get the money, do we need to write

Developing Measures of Central Tendency

The mean

To teach the concept of mean, pose a situation for students in which eighty cans are collected one day and sixty the next. Have students use a meterstick and adding-machine tape to represent these numbers by cutting off pieces eighty and sixty centimeters in length. This tactic gives students a physical representation of their two-day collections. Have students attach the tapes end-to-end. Hold up the combined tapes and ask, "What does this paper represent?" (The total number of cans collected for two days) "Use this paper and the meterstick to decide the total number of cans you have collected."

"Suppose that on two other days you collected the total number of cans represented by the combined tapes. However, an *equal number* of cans was collected each day. Use the combined tape to decide what that number was." Since this paper represents two days of collecting, the combined tape can be folded into two equal parts and compared with the meterstick to find the number. Once the number, 70, has been determined, define this number as the *mean*. Repeat the activity with different numbers of cans and days; this extension is necessary because otherwise some students form the misconception that we *always* divide by 2 when finding the mean.

Present various situations in which students try to predict what would happen to the mean if, on the next day, a greater or smaller number of cans was collected. Predictions can be investigated by using adding-machine tapes. The conceptual work done with the tape can readily be connected to the symbolic procedure for finding the mean. Connecting the tapes represents finding the sum of

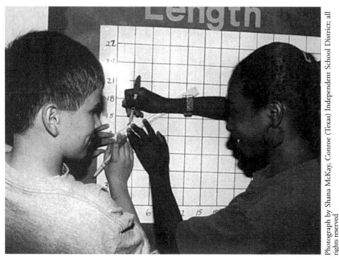

A formal presentation emphasizes the need to communicate mathematically.

Photograph by Shana McKay, Conroe (Texas) Independent School District; all rights reserved

the numbers, and folding the combined tapes represents dividing the total into equal parts. The number of parts into which the combined tape is folded is determined by the original number of pieces of tape.

Demonstrate the need for other measures of central tendency by pointing out the main weakness of the mean—the extent to which its value can be affected by extreme scores. This weakness can be demonstrated within the framework of activities discussed earlier by showing the effects that a day when no cans were collected would have on the mean of three days of collection averaging eighty cans per day. The median and mode can then be presented as different measures of central tendency that minimize the effect of extreme scores.

The mode

To teach the meaning of the mode, have students write fifteen numbers on index cards and place them in a box, for example, 76, 80, 84, 72, 85, 80, 74, 61, 72, 84, 76, 80, 91, 87, and 85. Have students pull a card at random from the box and place it on a chart. A second card is then extracted, and the question asked, "Is this number greater than, less than, or equal to the first number?" This second card is placed on the chart to the right, to the left, or above the first card depending on whether the number on it is, respectively, greater than, less than, or equal to the number on the first card. (See fig. 2)

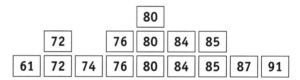

Fig. 2. A table of fifteen number cards

The students continue to pull cards, asking the same question over and over until all cards are arranged on the chart in order, left to right, from smallest to largest. Looking at all the cards on the chart, ask, "What number appeared the greatest number of times?" After identifying the tallest column, define the number of cards in that column as the *mode*.

The median

To teach the concept of median, have students use the fifteen numbers they have placed on the chart. Ask, "Where have you heard the word *median* used before?" (The median of the highway is the part that divides the highway into two equal parts.) "In mathematics the word *median* is used to tell us something about a set of numbers. What do you think it tells us?" (It is the point that separates a set of numbers into two equivalent subsets.) Have students work with a partner to find the median of the set of numbers represented by the cards on the chart.

One way is to begin removing cards from either end of the set simultaneously, one with each hand. This process is continued until only a single card remains. Have groups share their method with the class. Identify the number on the middle card as the *median*.

"If we find the median by eliminating cards from each end, will we always get to a point where a single card remains?" After getting a consensus that we would not, discuss the conditions under which this outcome would or would not occur, capitalizing on the opportunity to review the concept of even and odd numbers. Next place an even number of cards in the box, place them on the chart in order as indicated previously, and eliminate cards simultaneously from either end until only two cards remain. Give students an opportunity to discuss how the median might be identified. Try to get the class to agree that the best solution would be to call the point halfway between the two remaining cards the median. Introduce situations in which—

- the median is not a whole number, as when the two remaining cards contain such consecutive numbers as 87 and 88 (median 87.5);
- the median is a whole number but not a number on one of the cards; for example, the two remaining cards have such whole numbers as 84 and 88 (median 86).

In either case, the median is the mean of the two remaining numbers.

Dealing with the data

In step 6, at the end of the three weeks, analyze the data. The question to be answered is, Did the test support our hypothesis? The data will be analyzed on the basis of the statistical tools previously developed.

As they "look back" in step 7, students should ask such questions as the following:

- What did we learn?
- Will our findings contribute to our school, our community, or our world?
- How can we share our findings with others?
- If we repeated this experiment during a different three weeks, would we expect the same results? Why or why not?
- If we repeated this study in another school, would we expect these results? Why or why not?
- Who might be interested in our results?

The teacher should assist the students in presenting the findings to a particular audience. In the example presented here, the students presented the information to the fifth-grade students, the cafeteria workers, and the teachers. A formal presentation with charts and graphs is important in showing students that research is valuable when it can be related to the real world and put into prac-

tice. Additionally, it emphasizes the need to communicate mathematically.

A Real-Life Winner

Using the Elementary Mathematics Research Model, Dolly Vogel, a teacher of sixth-grade mathematics at Houser Intermediate School, Conroe, Texas, presented her students with the opportunity to conduct research. She encouraged her students to focus their studies on science and mathematics. All studies had to be submitted with a written report in research format and had to include statistical data that were graphically displayed. The three studies submitted for review were as follows:

Group 1—Research question: Which pollutants are most harmful? (Survey research)

Group 2—Research question: Does life exist on other planets? (Survey research)

Group 3—Research question: How much trash can the students at Houser Intermediate School eliminate by recycling aluminum and Styrofoam? (Observational research)

Significant findings were reported by each group, with the findings from group 3's research of particular interest. The students found that by recycling only the aluminum and Styrofoam, the school's garbage could be cut in half. As it turned out, the research was award winning, with the school receiving a set of statistical software from the American Statistical Association, which sponsored the competition. (For information on this national contest, write to the American Statistical Association, 1429 Duke Street, Alexandria, VA 22314-3402.) Mrs. Vogel and her students are to be commended for their award-winning efforts.

Conclusion

The Elementary Mathematics Research Model allows the students to begin early to collect, organize, and describe data. The model is founded on problem-finding and problem-solving behaviors and is designed to support the development of higher-level thinking as students' thoughts diverge and converge throughout the research process. Additionally, the appreciation for statistical methods used in problem solving can be emphasized. Zawojewski (1988) reported that when students applied memorized algorithms for finding measures of central tendency in a rote manner, they tended to make predictable errors that they did not tend to make when these measures were presented in the context of real-world situations.

The research studies may be completed as group or individual projects. As studies are developed, they may be concentrated in the community or in the school. Although in some instances the teacher's assistance may be required, research topics should preferably be chosen by students.

The teacher's responsibility should be to assist with the design of the study so that the students will be able to use statistical treatments, tools, and terms in the analysis of the data collected in the study. The format for a report and record keeping throughout the project is open.

The final thought to leave with students is that they can be researchers and producers of new information and that new knowledge can be produced and communicated through mathematics. Their findings may contribute to the knowledge base of the class, the school, the community, or society as a whole. Their findings may affect their school or their world in a very positive way.

Bibliography

Bohan, Harry, and Edith J. Moreland. "Developing Some Statistical Concepts in the Elementary School." In *Teaching Statistics and Probability*, 1981 Yearbook of the National Council of Teachers of Mathematics, 60–63. Reston, Va.: The Council, 1981.

Curcio, Frances. *Developing Graph Comprehension: Elementary and Middle School Activities.* Reston, Va.: National Council of Teachers of Mathematics, 1989.

Irby, Beverly, and Harry Bohan. "Making Math Work through Statistics in the Elementary School." Workshop for Math Cadre, Conroe Independent School District, March 1991.

Moore, David S. "Uncertainty." In *On the Shoulders of Giants: New Approaches to Numeracy*, edited by Lynn Arthur Steen. Washington, D.C.: National Academy Press, 1990.

National Council of Teachers of Mathematics. *Curriculum and Evaluation Standards for School Mathematics.* Reston, Va.: The Council, 1989.

Zawojewski, Judith S. "Research into Practice: Teaching Statistics: Mean, Median, and Mode." *Arithmetic Teacher* 35 (March 1988):25–27.

———. *Dealing with Data and Chance.* Addenda Series, Grades 5–8. Reston, Va.: National Council of Teachers of Mathematics, 1991.

Links to Literature

Students Use Their Bodies to Measure Animals

by

Eunice Hendrix-Martin

The biggest snake, the anaconda, can grow to be more than 25 feet long and to weigh 400 pounds. The smallest mammal, the Etruscan shrew, is little enough to sleep in a teaspoon. And the tiny flea can jump 130 times its own height. These are just a few of the interesting facts in Steve Jenkins's (1995) book *Biggest, Strongest, Fastest* (see fig. 1). This book is an appealing introduction to the "world records" held by fourteen members of the animal kingdom.

I shared this book with my third- and fourth-grade students, hoping it would spark an interest in using these facts to investigate comparative lengths and heights. After we read the book, a lively discussion took place about which animals the students found most interesting. For many it was the sun jellyfish, which has tentacles that are 200 feet long. Others thought that the ant was amazing; the strongest animal for its size, the ant can lift five times its own weight. The students generated a list of almost every animal in the book, along with each animal's best-known characteristic. The discussion then focused on the biggest animal that has ever lived, the blue whale. Most students were shocked to learn that it is even longer and heavier than the largest known dinosaur.

I asked the students to close their eyes and picture in their minds what a 110-foot blue whale would look like.

From *Biggest, Strongest, Fastest,* © 1995 by Steve Jenkins, published by Ticknor & Fields Books for Young Readers; all rights reserved

Fig. 1. Title-page illustration of book about animal-kingdom world records

Cynthia said, "It doesn't fit in my head." "Bigger than a football field," Russell stated with confidence. Other descriptions included bigger than a three-story building, bigger than our playing field and blacktop put together, and bigger than the canal we had been learning about in social studies. All estimations described the whale as being bigger than something, rather than smaller, a fact that I found interesting.

Finding the Mean Height of the Class Using Unifix Cubes

To help students begin developing a better point of reference, we started with their own heights. I posed the question "Could you use your own height as a way to measure some of the animals in the book to understand how big they really are?" They were excited about this

Eunice Hendrix-Martin, windsurf@intergate.sdcoe, teaches fourth grade at Paloma School, San Marcos, CA 92069. Her professional interest is searching for ideas and approaches for teaching developmentally appropriate mathematics.

Edited by Maryann Wickett, 1584 Caudor Street, Encinitas, CA 92024.

REFLECTING ON PRACTICE IN ELEMENTARY SCHOOL MATHEMATICS

idea, and many began sharing how tall they were. Tammy said, "But we are all different heights, and I'm not sure how tall I am!" Nigel suggested that we find the average height of students in the class and use that value as our unit of measure. Students had had previous experience with range, the difference between the smallest and largest value in a set of data, and with mode, the value or values that appear most frequently in a set of data. Since most students had had no experience with the mean, we defined the mean to be the value that represents the amount each would have if all the data in a set, such as the set of all students' heights in the class, were evened out. This new understanding of average height helped students decide that it would be a good unit of measure to use. I now had a great opportunity to give my students a hands-on activity using manipulatives to investigate their mean height.

Together we developed a procedure for using Unifix cubes to find the average height of students in the class. Each student lay on the floor; a partner used tape to mark the spots that corresponded to the student's feet and head (fig. 2). Using these measures, each student made a train of Unifix cubes to represent his or her height (see fig. 3). Once all the students had made their trains, we put the trains side by side to represent the heights of all the students in the class (see fig. 4). "To find the mean height

Photograph by Eunice Hendrix-Martin; all rights reserved

Fig. 2. A student marks her partner's height on the floor.

Photograph by Eunice Hendrix-Martin; all rights reserved

Fig. 3. Students build trains of cubes to represent their heights.

we need to make all the trains the same length," I explained to the class. Nikki said, "That will be easy because all we need to do is move cubes from the tallest trains to the smallest trains until they are all even."

After everyone took a turn moving a few of the Unifix cubes to make the trains the same length, students discovered twenty-one cubes remaining that could not be divided equally among the twenty-eight trains. We set these cubes to the side. The remainder helped the students recognize that we had found an approximation of the mean.

Photograph by Eunice Hendrix-Martin; all rights reserved

Fig. 4. Placing the trains side by side shows the variations in height.

After the class agreed that the trains were all of the same length, we measured the length of one of the trains to determine the approximate mean height of the students in the class. "Why don't we just count the number of cubes in a train and that will tell us the number of inches?" suggested Sean. I asked the rest of the class if they agreed with Sean. Some agreed because they thought that each Unifix cube looked like it was about an inch long; therefore, counting the cubes would tell us the number of inches. Others disagreed, saying that until we measured a Unifix cube to see if it was an inch long, we could not be sure.

Brittany volunteered to measure a Unifix cube and discovered that it was three-fourths inch long. She then used a tape measure to measure the length of one of the trains, which was fifty-four inches. Irwin responded by saying, "Four feet six inches." I wrote on the chalkboard, "4' 6" or 54", " and explained how the notation " ' " indicates feet and " " " indicates inches. Sean was still convinced that counting the cubes would give us the same information, so he proceeded to count them. He announced to the class that there were seventy-five cubes. He pulled out the tape measure again, and it showed fifty-four inches. He realized that the length in cubes and the length in inches were indeed different. Taking this time to help Sean construct his own understanding also helped others in the class to see why the relationship of cubes to inches was not numerically equal. Allowing this type of exploration of ideas also encourages students to take a risk and try their ideas.

Once we knew the mean height of a student, we were ready to begin our investigation. We recorded on chart paper animals from the book for which either the height or length was given. They listed the African elephant, 13 feet high; the giraffe, 19 feet high; the anaconda snake, 25 feet long; the blue whale, 110 feet long; and the tentacles of a sun jellyfish, 200 feet long. We developed the following problem: Given the mean student height of four feet six inches, how many students would it take to equal the height of the elephant? Of the giraffe? How many students would it take to equal the length of the snake? Of the blue whale? Of the tentacles of the jellyfish?

Problem-Solving Strategies

Everyone was excited. Most students chose to work with a partner so that they could discuss their thinking. I reminded them that they were responsible for recording their work individually using pictures, words, and numbers to help them communicate their thinking and understanding. We had done some measurement activities earlier in the year as part of a science unit on matter, and I was eager to see how they would apply that experience and their growing knowledge of multiplication and division to this activity.

Irwin began by multiplying 13 by 12. He was using the traditional algorithm to show his work. He explained, "The '13' is the height of the elephant in feet and the '12' is the inches in one foot. I need to multiply them together to find out how many inches tall the elephant is."

At another table Brian was also multiplying 13 by 12; however, he was not using the traditional algorithm to find the number of inches (see fig. 5). Brian applied his understanding of place value to the multiplication problem by viewing the number 12 as 10 and two 1's and then multiplying. He explained confidently, "The number '156' is the number of inches tall of an African elephant. This is important to know because if I know how many inches tall the elephant is, then I can just subtract fifty-four inches, which is the mean height of our class, until I can't subtract anymore." To clarify his thinking further, he wrote down "156 – 54 = 102," under the "102," he wrote "54" and subtracted again. This time his answer was "48." Thus, not ready to divide by 54, Brian intuitively used repeated subtraction. "It will take two of us and forty-eight inches left over to measure the elephant," he explained. Not certain that Brian understood what the forty-eight inches represented, I asked him to explain. He said, "You can't use another person because that would be too much, so the forty-eight inches is what you would need to finish measuring the elephant."

While Brian calculated his answer using only inches, Gladys decided to use a combination of feet and inches (see fig. 6). I wanted to know how she came up with forty-eight inches. She explained that thirteen feet minus nine feet is four feet and that forty-eight inches is four feet. Although her written explanation was initially confusing, her oral explanation showed clear understanding. Gladys used addition and subtraction to solve the problem on paper; however, her ability to convert inches to feet quickly in her head demonstrated skill in division.

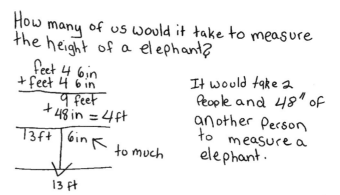

Fig. 6. Gladys uses addition and subtraction to determine the height of the elephant in "student" units.

Mia attacked the problem with a guess-and-check approach (see fig. 7) using multiplication and addition. Unlike Brian and Gladys, who saw the answer as two people plus forty-eight inches, Mia saw it as needing three people, with six inches left over. Mia's work clearly describes her mathematical thinking and understanding of

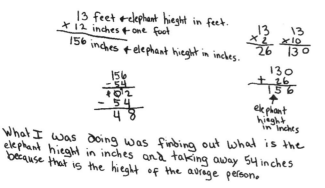

Fig. 5. Brian uses his knowledge of place value to complete the multiplication.

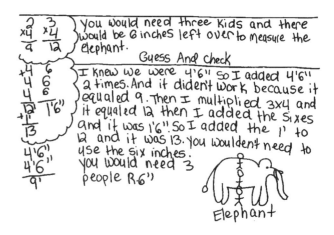

Fig. 7. Mia uses a guess-and-check approach.

230   REFLECTING ON PRACTICE IN ELEMENTARY SCHOOL MATHEMATICS

the problem. These two different interpretations of the same quantity evoked a lively class discussion.

Class Discussion

Students were eager to share their answers and justify their thinking. Their responses were recorded on chart paper so that all students could visualize the strategies. Two answers quickly became apparent. Students were given a few minutes to discuss the answers with their groups. Ashley explained her group's thinking: "We think you would have to have at least three people or you wouldn't be measuring all of the elephant that you could using people, so two people plus the forty-eight inches is wrong." Another group defended two people plus forty-eight inches as correct because not all of the third person could be used; thus, in their view, the third person should not be included. Other groups justified their thinking in a similar way. Sean's group decided that the two answers were really very similar measurements that were just written differently, because forty-eight inches was all but six inches of another person. It became clear during the discussion that many students were not yet ready to see the two answers as equivalent measurements.

Irwin, however, had an important discovery that he thought might help the others and that he wanted to share before we continued working. "Every time you add two people (4' 6'' + 4' 6'') together you get nine feet. The other animals will be simple because it's easier to add nine feet than four feet six inches. Isn't math lovely?"

As students began to work on the snake problem, an interesting connection to patterns was made. Mia shared that she had made a table (see fig. 8), which I then recorded on large paper. As students quietly studied the table, they began to see patterns. "I see a pattern counting by twos under the people," said Gladys. "In the feet column, the ones are going down by one; and in the tens place, they're going up by one ten," announced Tammy. "If you add the digits together under the feet, they all equal nine, so the next number will be thirty-six. Hey, that's a pattern counting by nines!" exclaimed Shawn.

Fig. 8. Mia's table shows the relationship of students to feet.

Almost everyone used a table to help measure the last two animals, the whale and the jellyfish. Most were able to quickly generate the list of people counting by twos and the number of feet counting by nines. For the whale, some students stopped at twenty-four people, or 108 feet, knowing they would need only 2 feet of another person. Other students said twenty-five people were required, with 2 feet 6 inches left over. Still others continued the table to twenty-six people, or 117 feet, not realizing that the twenty-sixth person was not needed. Students who finished the whale then used the table to compute the length of the jellyfish's tentacles.

Reflections

Biggest, Strongest, Fastest provided animal facts that were of interest to students and that could be used in a variety of ways. Although finding the mean turned out to be a pivotal point, other skills were involved, such as estimating; adding; subtracting; multiplying; dividing; measuring; and collecting, organizing, and using data. Measurement activities like the one my students did give students practical applications for the computational skills that they are learning.

Most students had access to the problem because they felt comfortable using a problem-solving strategy that made sense to them. This level of confidence comes when students are encouraged to solve problems in their own ways and justify their own thinking. Students' work is discussed and recorded for others to see. This process tells children that their thinking is valued and their work is important. When students are given opportunities to share their ideas, opinions, and questions, a classroom climate is created in which mathematical thinking is encouraged and valued.

One of the most valuable discussions in this lesson happened when Mia shared the table. Recognizing a pattern and applying a rule to the pattern proved to be a powerful problem-solving strategy for many students. Students who had difficulty working with feet and inches were able to use the table to see the relationship of people to feet. When students can look for patterns and express them mathematically in this way, they connect mathematics to their world.

By using themselves as a unit of measure, students had a real-world connection to the problem. Making comparisons between the length and height of the animals and themselves helped them see that measurement is never exact, that even careful measurements are approximations.

Reference

Jenkins, Steve. *Biggest, Strongest, Fastest.* New York: Ticknor & Fields Books for Young Readers, 1995.

Developing Measurement Sense

by

Jean M. Shaw and Mary Jo Puckett Cliatt

Measurement is an important, useful topic that deserves a prominent role in the mathematics curriculum. Facility with measurement is valuable because people use it almost daily throughout their lives as they cook, give and receive directions, and participate in sports and hobbies. Many people also use measurement on the job.

The focus of elementary school measurement should be on the development of concepts and understanding rather than on separate and narrow skills. Students must gain insights and intuitions about measurements and the process of measuring. This emphasis promotes the development of "measurement sense," a highly useful outcome of measurement instruction.

Measurement sense has several interrelated components. Children and adults who have measurement sense have a *knowledge of the units appropriate for a task.* They have formed useful mental pictures representing measurement units. For example, mental images of units help people decide whether centimeters, meters, or kilometers are the most appropriate unit for measuring the distance from a student's home to the school. A student with good measurement sense knows that although it is possible to measure such a distance in centimeters (or even millimeters), a larger unit such as meters or kilometers is easier to work with and communicate to others.

Measurement sense also involves a *knowledge of the measurement process.* Quantities are compared to standard or nonstandard units. Numbers are attached to units in the measurement process. Tools are often used: rulers, tapes, scales, clocks, thermometers, spoons, and cups are measurement tools with which elementary school children should be proficient.

Students with measurement sense have the *ability to decide when to measure and when to estimate.* When deciding how to dress for the day, most people want only a general idea of what the temperature will be. They are not ordinarily concerned with whether the temperature will be 20°C or 22°C, but rather that the temperature will be in the "low 20s." However, when someone is seriously ill, a single degree of temperature may be carefully monitored and measured.

Finally, measurement sense involves a *knowledge of strategies for estimating* lengths, temperature, volumes, masses, and time. Good estimators know several strategies and choose the one most applicable to a situation. According to Lindquist (1987), good estimators use at least three strategies: referents, chunking, and unitizing. With *referents*, a child might use a known quantity—her own weight of about forty kilograms, for example—to estimate whether another person's mass is about the same as, greater than, or less than her own and by how much. With *chunking*, a quantity is broken into workable parts. In estimating the area of the floor of a classroom, a student might mentally break (or chunk) the area into three parts—the area of the chalkboard and the teacher's desk, the area of the students' desks, and the area of the small vestibule. The student would combine estimates of these three areas for an estimate of the total area of the room. With *unitizing*, a student divides a quantity into smaller, equal parts. To estimate the volume of a pitcher, a student might mentally divide the pitcher into "glassfuls" of 250 milliliters each, then work with the number of glassfuls to arrive at an estimate for the total volume.

Educators must teach measurement in appropriate ways. Children need repeated opportunities to work with measurement to develop the concepts and skills necessary for building measurement sense. The following introductory and follow-up activities give children chances to develop and refine their skills and deepen their understanding of measurement.

Principles for Developing Measurement Sense

Several principles can guide educators when they work with children to develop measurement sense. These principles can help educators select a balance of measurement experiences to enhance and refine children's knowledge of measurement.

1. *Provide hands-on, "involving" experiences.* Children learn by doing. As they participate, children learn to measure rather than learn about measuring. Hands-on experiences enhance children's mental images of measurements. As children handle and read measurement tools, they directly compare quantities to units. They see that measurements can be expressed many different ways. For example, the weight of a pencil can be described as "about 10 grams," "about 0.01 kilograms," or "much less than a kilogram."

2. *Make verbal and written language integral parts of measurement experiences.* Children must talk about what they are doing. Language complements and clarifies thought. Written records of data can be referred to and can help children keep from forgetting data. Often pairs or small groups of children can compile data and then bring this information to the entire class for discussion, comparison, and analysis. As children discuss and compare measurement results, they see that measurements can be expressed in many different but correct ways. As they discuss their recorded data, students often pick out their own errors without an adult's prompting. For example, a group of students can weigh books of a set of encyclopedias and record their masses: 2 kg, 1.5 kg, 0.8 kg, 2 g, and 1800 g. The 2-g measurement "sticks out" as "way too little" to a group of children with a sense of what 2-g and 2-kg masses feel like.

3. *Compare and estimate, then measure.* When students routinely perform comparing and estimating steps before they measure, they are more careful with the measuring step than if they thoughtlessly pick up and use a measuring tool. Comparing and estimating take just a few moments, but they encourage thought about each problem and create interest in outcomes. These processes also develop sensitivity to the units being used and the number of units in the object being measured. For instance, if students are using pieces of string as units for measuring the length of a work counter, they can first think about whether the string is longer or shorter than the counter. If the string is shorter, they can next try to visualize how many strings it would take to make the length of the counter. Finally, students will lay the string along the counter, each string-unit length beginning where the last one ended, and count the number of string-units in the counter.

4. *Have children make some of their own measurement tools.* Children can make inexpensive but useful measuring tools to supplement commercially made and teacher-made tools. Child-made measuring tools can also be taken home without a cumbersome check-out system for equipment. Children usually take pride in creating and "owning" their own measuring equipment and are motivated to use it. Making tools contributes to children's measurement sense. They must decide what units are appropriate for the tool and its purpose and mark and label the tool with these units. As children make their own measuring tools, they typically handle units several times, thus increasing their familiarity with the units (Shaw 1983).

5. *Enhance home-school communication with measuring assignments.* Concerned, informed parents support school programs and contribute to their children's achievement. Creative homework activities are opportunities for building home-school communication and for strengthening measurement sense. For instance, third graders might use measuring tapes they have made to estimate, then measure, the lengths of family members' feet. The next day at school the children can report the different lengths, compare and order them, and find total lengths for their families. The ranges of foot lengths will probably be wide and generate much discussion!

Activities to Develop Measurement Sense

The following activities offer different types of measurement experiences and incorporate some or all of the suggested principles for teaching measurement. Because they are versatile and flexible, these activities can be adapted for different settings and levels.

• *"Show me" lengths.* Children with strong mental images of lengths can demonstrate different lengths with their hands. Practice with several "show me" activities will help to strengthen mental images in children who have trouble visualizing lengths. A kindergarten or first-grade teacher might show the children a new pencil, then "hide" the pencil and have the children illustrate how long it was. She can bring the pencil back out and let the children "check" the lengths they showed. Next she might ask that children show the length of a new crayon, their own shoe, or other familiar objects. Many sixth graders will be able to deal with "show me" tasks involving fractional parts and conversions: "Show me 0.3 meter," "Show me 0.5 of a meter," "Show me 80 millimeters," for example. The sixth graders can verify lengths by looking at the ruler. As students work with "show me," it is OK for those who are less secure to look at their classmates' hands for guidance. Observing classmates' answers is a legitimate way of verifying or modifying one's own answers during a practice session.

• *How many smaller ones make a larger one?* This versatile question prompts many different investigations. Kindergartners and first graders might explore the question at a "waterplay table" using small containers to fill a larger one.

They might also make investigations using a balance scale and classroom objects. For example, young children can try to see how many crayons balance a pair of scissors. Second or third graders might use a fishing pole with a magnet for bait to catch paper fish with pins or paper clips attached to them. They could see how many fish make a meter length. Elementary school students of any age might work with several sizes of plastic containers and see how many smaller ones will fill a larger one. Pouring water or "solid fluids," such as sand, cornmeal, or birdseed, from one container to the other to verify estimates makes this a sensory, motivating activity. Teachers can challenge children to make their own problems and solve them by manipulating physical objects and tools.

• *Body measurements.* Making body measurements is appealing because the process is so personalized. Children can use body parts as nonstandard measures or can relate body parts to standard measures. Young children can "step off" the lengths of such classroom objects as rugs or chalkboards by using their feet as handy nonstandard units of measurement.

Children may have read about how ancient peoples used the length of a forearm as a measurement unit called a cubit. They might investigate to see whether a distance like twenty cubits is longer than their chalkboard, shorter, or about the same length. Children can compare twenty-cubit distances laid out by several classmates and see the slight variations due to differences in the lengths of arms. To enhance mental images of standard measures of length, children can find body parts that are close to one centimeter, one decimeter, or one meter. These images will vary; one meter may be about the distance from the floor to the waist of one fifth grader but "hit" a shorter classmate in the middle of the chest.

An intriguing project for children of almost any age is recording different body measurements in a "Metric Me" booklet (Shaw 1984). The booklet can be just two to four pages. Each child can record estimates and actual measures of such vital statistics as height, mass, head circumference, the length of a smile and the length of a "serious" mouth, axillary body temperature, and the length of a foot. After individual measurements are made, the children might also examine a single measurement such as foot length. They can pool their measurements, order them, see the range, and pick the median of the set of data. Older children can figure the mean length on their calculators. Each child can compare his or her foot length to the mean: Is it close to the mean? Longer? Shorter? By how much?

Interesting comparisons can emerge from body measurements. Children might work in groups to investigate questions such as these:

> How does the length of an upper arm compare to that of a lower arm?
>
> How does the length of a lower arm compare to that of

a person's foot?

How does a person's arm span compare to height?

• *Scavenger hunts.* In this activity children find objects that fit given categories. A teacher might start by asking young children to find something on the playground that is longer than their hands or heavier than a rock. The children can compare and perhaps order all the objects they bring back. Second graders might cut out ten-centimeter-long strips of paper and "scavenge" at home for five objects, each about a decimeter long. The objects can be displayed on a "sharing table" in the classroom. Fifth graders might work in groups to find, estimate, and then measure temperatures in ten different locations in the school on a temperature scavenger hunt. Scavenger hunts either with verbal instructions or with a list of items to collect are versatile, involving, and fun!

• *Seasonal measurements.* To keep measurement skills alive throughout the year and to quantify the observations that children routinely make, teachers can make use of seasonal measurements, which can be interesting and valuable. For instance, children might record and compare indoor and outdoor temperatures for a week at the beginning of school, in midwinter, and in early spring. They can measure and weigh fall fruits and vegetables that are available. Cooking seasonal dishes is always a popular activity and enhances children's understanding of measures of volume: as they prepare foods like whipped topping or popcorn, they can see dramatic changes in volumes. Children might also compare the masses (weights) of food before and after cooking.

For other seasonal activities, children might make measurements as they construct geometric and free-form shapes for decorations for a holiday tree or a bare branch. (Of course they would estimate and measure the height of the tree or the length of the branch, too.) Children might estimate and measure the lengths and widths of several Valentine cards, then pursue different strategies to get "good" answers for their areas. As spring growth emerges or after children plant seeds, they can keep track of the heights of new plants. Alert teachers will find many seasonal opportunities to develop and reinforce measurement sense and to encourage parents to engage in measurement activities at home.

Bibliography

Lindquist, Mary Montgomery. "Estimation and Mental Computation: Measurement." *Arithmetic Teacher* 34 (January 1987): 16–17.

Shaw, Jean M. "IDEAS." *Arithmetic Teacher* 32 (December 1984): 20–24.

———. "Let's Do It: Student-made Measuring Tools." Arithmetic Teacher 31 (November 1983): 12–15.

Trimble, Harold C. "Teaching about 'About.'" In *A Metric Handbook for Teachers*, edited by Jon L. Higgins, pp. 100–104. Reston, Va.: National Council of Teachers of Mathematics, 1974.

Research into
Practice

Enhancing Mathematics Learning through Imagery

by

Grayson H. Wheatley

Mathematics is often seen as a subject in which rules are followed and symbols manipulated to achieve "correct" answers. Fortunately, this characterization of mathematics is changing, in large part because of NCTM's initiatives. As we move into the decade of reform in school mathematics, we should explore all options for enhancing mathematics learning. This article considers the role of visual imagery in doing mathematics.

Although a few teachers may supplement mathematics instruction with spatial activities, most students rarely have opportunities to use imagery in school mathematics classes. In fact, school curricula militate against such use. As Sommer (1978, 54) states, "School more than any other institution is responsible for downgrading visual thinking. Most educators are not only disinterested in visualization, they are positively hostile to it." The absence of spatial activities in textbooks is clear evidence that imagery is thought to be nonessential in school mathematics. But is it?

As described in Wheatley (1990), imagery involves (1) constructing an image from pictures, words, or thoughts; (2) re-presenting the image as needed; and (3) transforming that image. A student might decide that the two shapes shown in figure 1 are "the same" by mentally rotating her or his image of the one on the left until it is in the same orientation

Fig. 1. Comparison of two figures using imagery

Edited by Grayson H. Wheatley
Florida State University
Tallahassee, FL 32306-3032

as the one on the right. The need to make such comparisons occurs frequently in mathematics and is facilitated by the use of visual imagery.

Imagery is not just a process of taking a mental picture and retrieving the picture from memory (Wheatley and Cobb 1990). As Lakoff (1987, 129) states, "Different people, looking upon a situation, will notice different things. Our experience of seeing may depend very much on what we know about what we are looking at. And what we see is not necessarily what is there." A nine-year-old girl was asked to draw the right triangle shown in figure 2a. Each time she tried to draw it, the segment on the right slanted out as shown in figure 2b. She knew her drawing did not look right, but she was so influenced by her concept and the images she had constructed of a triangle that she could not bring herself to draw one side vertical; for her, the sides of triangles "slant." Understanding geometric concepts and relationships is, in large part, a matter of constructing images.

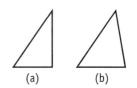

Fig. 2. A right triangle (a) and Tammy's drawing of it (b)

In a recent study (Brown and Wheatley 1989), fifth-grade students of high and low spatial ability were interviewed about various mathematics tasks. The goal was to assess students' meaningful mathematical knowledge rather than their facility for manipulating symbols. Six students were interviewed, three with high spatial ability and three with low spatial ability. The results could not have been more dramatic. The performance of the students with low spatial ability was average or above on standardized mathematics tests and in fifth-grade mathematics class. The results of the clinical interviews, however, showed that these students attached little meaning to mathematical ideas and could not solve nonroutine problems. For example, when asked to arrange thirty-six Unifix cubes in the shape of a rectangular region, one girl struggled for some time and finally made a five-by-seven region with one cube left over. She was unable to make a rectangular region using all thirty-six cubes even though she was attempting to do so. Contrastingly, the students with high spatial ability whose performance was average or below on standardized mathematics tests and in school mathematics class had an excellent grasp of mathematical ideas and were able to solve nonroutine problems, often creatively. These students with high spatial ability were not being recognized for the gifts they possessed. We interpret these findings to indicate that spatial ability lies at the heart of meaningfulness. Students can memorize facts and become proficient in demonstrated procedures, but they may not be giving meaning to their mathematical activity.

The use of imagery on a mathematics task is a function of the instructional setting. If mathematics tasks are presented in a familiar setting, students have a greater opportunity to use their prior experience in giving meaning to the tasks. For example, rather than just pose the problem 36 – 29 in abstract form, the teacher could present the task in a potentially meaningful setting, for example,

36 chairs are needed for a school party. 29 chairs are already in the room. How many more are needed?

In this way students can construct images for the numbers and use this imagery in developing a procedure for subtracting. Some might imagine moving one chair in with the twenty-nine to make five rows of six (30 chairs), then six more chairs to make seven chairs moved in. Posing tasks in a setting meaningful to students facilitates the use of imagery and the construction of mathematical relationships.

The use of imagery is also influenced by the student's intentions. Wheatley and Lo (1989) reported on a third grader who could determine the number of dots in a four-by-five rectangular pattern shown briefly by using subpatterns but who had great difficulty solving 20 – 5 because she tried to count back from twenty rather than use the imagery of 2 tens and breakup 1 ten into five and five. She was intent on using a particular procedure—counting back from twenty to fifteen—instead of imaging a set of dots to be transformed. School experiences can contribute in significant ways to the powerful use of imagery in mathematical settings.

Learning new ideas and solving nonroutine problems are situations in which imagery is particularly useful. Since dealing successfully with novelty is one of the most important competences in a rapidly changing and complex technological society, we need to cultivate the development of essential tools that allow us to deal effectively with new situations. Imagery is one of those essentials.

Just as images of landscapes, houses, and people are formed when we listen to a conversation or read a novel, images are formed when we give meaning to our mathematical activity. Consider the following problem:

Paul has a swimming pool in the shape of a rectangle. It is 31 feet long and 23 feet wide. A 3-foot-wide walkway surrounds the pool. What is the length of a fence around the walkway?

An experienced problem solver might form an image of the swimming pool with the walkway and fence around it and make a sketch based on the image. But note that a sketch can be created only if a mental image has been constructed first. In fact, a sketch can prove useful in thinking through the problem. Perhaps the imaging occurs in steps. On first reading the problem, a student might image and then sketch the swimming pool; he or she might elaborate the constructions after rereading the problem, with first the walkway and then the fence added to the image and the sketch. Finally, the numerical information might be added to the sketch to help solve the problem.

Wheatley and Wheatley (1982) found that few sixth-grade pupils drew diagrams in solving the foregoing problem. It should also be noted that few students successfully solved the problem. Yet most of these students were doubtless capable of forming the necessary images. When students are encouraged and given opportunities to form mental images, most readily do so, and when they are encouraged to use imagery, their mathematical power is greatly increased.

Some students are particularly good at forming images and are able to use them effectively in solving problems. The following transcript of an interview with Mike, a beginning first grader, illustrates the use of imagery in mathematical reasoning. In flashcard fashion, he was shown a series of cards with various arrangements of dots; after each card was briefly displayed, Mike was asked how many dots he saw. Here is how he responded to three of the dot patterns. Each card was shown for about one second.

I: (After showing figure 3) How many dots did you see?

Mike: Six

I: How did you know that one?

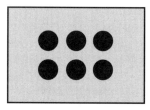

Fig. 3. Mike was shown this six-dot pattern and then asked, "How many dots did you see?"

REFLECTING ON PRACTICE IN ELEMENTARY SCHOOL MATHEMATICS

Mike: (Putting his hands up vertically, in front of his chest, as if to box in the two rows of three) They were all put together.

I: (After showing figure 4) How many dots did you see?

Mike: S-seven

I: (After showing figure 5) How many dots did you see?

Mike: Six

I: How did you do that one?

Mike: (Holding his hands up in the same gesture as before) They weren't put together right, but I figured it out.

I: You tell me what you mean by "They weren't put together."

Mike: I mean by ... those were right (pointing to the three dots at the upper left). Those ... and it came down like that (indicating that he had made a linear pattern of the remaining three dots).

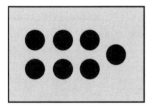

Fig. 4. Mike was shown this seven-dot pattern and then asked, "How many dots did you see?"

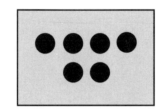

Fig. 5. A six-dot pattern that Mike mentally transformed into the pattern in figure 3

It was clear that Mike had transformed his image of the four-over-two pattern to a three-over-three pattern so as to create an image for which he knew the number. Under normal school conditions, Mike would likely be considered slow (he had to figure out the problem 3 + 1 by counting from one) when in fact he had exceptional visual reasoning and great potential as a mathematics student.

As the foregoing examples illustrate, imagery plays a prominent role in many if not all aspects of mathematics. Imagery is useful not only in coming to know a parallelogram and its properties but also in doing numerical tasks and especially in problem solving. Listed here are suggestions for incorporating imagery in mathematics instruction.

Instructional implications

Since dynamic imagery can be particularly useful as students give meaning to geometric and numerical relationships, it is important to give them opportunities to develop and use their imagery.

1. Encourage students to build mental pictures—to "imagine what it would look like." Design tasks that go beyond manipulating objects to transforming constructed images as Mike's task did.

2. Encourage students to communicate their images by building models, drawing pictures and graphs, and using verbal descriptions.

3. Design activities that promote the use of visual imagery. The *Arithmetic Teacher* offers many suggestions for building imagery into the mathematics curriculum (see especially Yackel and Wheatley [1990]). Additional suggestions will appear in "Research into Practice" in future issues.

4. Show students that you value imagery by allocating time for spatial activities, accepting imagery-based explanations, and describing your own imagery.

References

Brown, Dawn, and Grayson Wheatley. "Spatial Visualization and Arithmetic Knowledge." In *Proceedings of the Eleventh Annual Meeting of the North American Chapter, International Group for the Psychology of Mathematics Education*, edited by Carolyn A. Maher, Gerald A. Goldin, and Robert B. Davis. New Brunswick, N.J., September 1989.

Lakoff, George. *Women, Fire and Dangerous Things: What Categories Reveal about the Mind.* Chicago, Ill.: University of Chicago Press, 1987.

Sommer, Robert. *The Mind's Eye: Imagery in Everyday Life.* Palo Alto, Calif.: Dale Seymour Publications, 1978.

Wheatley, Grayson. "Constructivist Perspectives on Mathematics and Science Learning." *Science Education* 75 January 1991): 9–21.

———. "One Point of View: Spacial Sense and Mathematics Learning." *Arithmetic Teacher* 37 (February 1990):10–11.

Wheatley, Grayson, and Paul Cobb. "Analysis of Young Children's Spatial Constructions." In *International Perspectives on Transforming Early Childhood Mathematics Education*, edited by Leslie Steffe. Hillsdale, N.J.: Lawrence Erlbaum Associates, 1990.

Wheatley, Grayson, and Jane-Jane Lo. "The Role of Spatial Patterns in the Construction of Number Units." In *Proceedings of the Eleventh Annual Meeting of the North American Chapter, International Group for the Psychology of Mathematics Education*, edited by Carolyn A. Maher, Gerald A. Goldin, and Robert B. Davis. New Brunswick, N.J., September 1989.

Wheatley, Grayson, and Charlotte Wheatley. *Calculator Use and Problem Solving Strategies of Grade Six Pupils: Final Report.* Washington, D.C.: National Science Foundation, 1982. ERIC document no. ED 175720.

Yackel, Erna, and Grayson Wheatley. "Promoting Visual Imagery in Young Pupils." *Arithmetic Teacher* 37 (February 1990):52–58.

Early Childhood Corner

Developing Spatial Sense—a Moving Experience!

by

Angela Giglio Andrews

A new mother's diary includes these entries about her daughter, Emily:

(Three months) Today Emily reached up to grab my glasses. She's been flailing her arms around for awhile now, but today I am certain she took aim and was determined to touch those glasses!

(Twelve months) Emily loves to play "peekaboo" with her daddy. She moves around and behind her chair, laughing when Bill pretends he can't see her.

(Eighteen months) Emily loves to climb through my legs. Today she spread her legs apart and laughed when I could not fit through her legs. We both ended up on the floor and had a good laugh together about that!

Although she may not be aware of it, Emily's mother is not only recording her daughter's explorations in a special book but also recording Emily's beginning experiences with geometry.

Photograph by Angela Giglio Andrews; all rights reserved

Prepared by Angela Giglio Andrews, Scott Elementary School, Naperville, IL 60565; agandrews@aol.com

Angela Giglio Andrews teaches kindergarten in Naperville, Illinois, and undergraduate and graduate mathematics education courses at National-Louis University in Wheaton, Illinois. She is strongly committed to making mathematics meaningful to young learners. She is a coeditor of this department with Sydney Schwartz, Queens College of the City University of New York, Flushing, NY 11367; slsqc@qcvaxa.acc.qc.edu.

When we stop to think about young children and geometry, we realize that their first geometric experiences involve moving. They expend much effort moving about as infants and toddlers. As they develop motor skills, babies roll over and sit up in space, constantly changing their location and orientation to objects in a multispeed environment. Toddlers grasp edges and crawl through and run around shapes.

As preschoolers, children build their learning on such activities as stacking blocks, which we know to be cubes, rectangular solids, and pyramids. They throw and roll spheres. They place puzzle pieces next to each other, fitting edges together. Playing with balls that roll, blocks that stack, and puzzle shapes that fit together are integral parts of children's lives as they explore. These actions serve as the foundation for developing understanding about spatial relationships and shapes long before children are formally introduced to geometric concepts.

We can strengthen these intuitive understandings about space and objects by building on children's natural interests. Geometry instruction can begin while helping children develop an intuitive feel for their surroundings and the objects in them (NCTM 1989). For young children, geometry is a skill of the eyes and hands as well as of the mind. Motion is a major component of extending children's spatial awareness. Consequently, an important step in geometry instruction involves getting the children moving. Teachers can present activities that include opportunities for indoor and outdoor movement, movement games and stories, and moving through space with music.

Indoor and Outdoor Moving Activities

Children's ongoing and spontaneous activities on the playground offer many opportunities to investigate and describe spatial relationships. The teacher supervising the children's play may say, "Walk carefully *around* the slide," "Kelly is getting *near* the top," or "Jules went *behind* the tunnel a minute ago. Maybe he is crawling *through* it now."

Naturally occurring events in the classroom often provide the context for extending children's geometric and spatial understandings and connecting language to actions and ideas. In the following example, the teacher capitalized on a "teachable moment" by using her knowledge of outdoor games to nurture personal spatial awareness in children. At the beginning of the kindergarten year, the children were discussing their vacations. When the teacher asked what one child remembered most about her vacation to Disney World, the child quickly replied, "The crowds!" The teacher remembered a similar comment in a lecture about children's perceptions of crowds, decided that it might be interesting to focus on the concept of crowds with her kindergarten classroom. She encouraged children to recall and share their perceptions of what constitutes a crowd, where they have seen crowds, when they have been in a crowd, and how it felt to be in a crowd. The game of "crowds" resulted from this investigation.

Photograph by Angela Giglio Andrews; all rights reserved

For this activity, students divided themselves into four crowd situations: a beach crowd, a Disney World crowd, a great-American crowd, and the Fourth of July–fireworks crowd. Each crowd went to a different wall. If they were playing outside, they could have gone to a different side of the playground. The purpose of the game was to move from one side to the opposite side without touching other people. The game leader, who had a whistle, assigned each crowd a number from 1 to 4. One whistle was the signal for children at walls 1 and 3 to move toward the opposite wall or side, being careful not to touch someone else in the crowd. Two whistles signaled children at walls 2 and 4 to do the same. A real challenge came when the whistle was blown three times, which was the signal for all children to move to the opposite wall or side without touching one another. By weaving in, out, left, right, and around others, the children themselves became spatial relationships, strengthening their ability to coordinate vision with movement while gaining increased body control and a sense of other people in close proximity. Sharing experiences in response to games such as these brings children's intuitive understanding to conscious levels for examination and discussion.

Moving through Space with Music

Moving through space is one of the things that young children do best. Their interest in exploring different views of the world is boundless. They are endlessly changing their position from standing to bending to kneeling. They move forward, backward, up, down, around, toward, away, sideways, and diagonally. When children are encouraged to move to music of varying tempo, dynamics, and duration during an inviting activity, they become increasingly aware of the space within and surrounding their actions. The teacher can make and then solicit children's suggestions for different ways to move, such as "Let's move toward the center now" or "Can we think of some different ways to move forward? Between these two chairs? Over this pillow?" Since many geometric and spatial experiences depend on a child's ability to follow directions that include such spatial-language terms as *above, below, behind,* and *next to* (NCTM 1989, 49), teachers can help children understand and use the spatial terms that describe the directions, orientation, and perspectives of their surroundings and objects.

Music and movement records, tapes, and compact discs offer additional opportunities in the prekindergarten and kindergarten classrooms to emphasize spatial awareness and geometric movement while encouraging the children to move their bodies. For example, Hap Palmer's song called "The Circle Game" (Educational Activities) encourages children to walk around and stand on, under, and near a paper-plate circle. As the children repeat this circle game over time, they begin to internalize the meanings of these important spatial terms. Older children may enjoy the challenge of Buzz Glass's "Walking the Square" (Activity Records). In this musical activity, children walk forward, backward, and right and left to form a square, regularly changing orientation.

Moving into Literature

A natural extension to these investigations of space can be found by presenting *Rosie's Walk* by Pat Hutchins (1968). In this story, Rosie the hen goes for a walk around

the farmyard, closely followed by a fox who fails in every attempt to catch her. The book has an easy-to-predict language pattern and uses many spatial terms, such as *around, under,* and *between.* After repeated readings, the teacher can invite the class to set up a "Rosie" obstacle course in the room or on the playground by asking, "If we were to set up an obstacle course, what are some things we could use to walk around? Over? Past?" The children then plan, build, revise, and maneuver through the course, pretending to be Rosie and the fox and any other characters the children may invent to extend the play. Offering regular opportunities for children to repeat, discuss, and vary the activity is important to young children who need multiple opportunities to explore a concept before internalizing it. The teacher might then suggest that the children move through the obstacle course in different ways, such as hopping or skipping, and offer additional challenges to children focused on controlling their body in space.

Another resource is Tana Hoban's book *All about Where* (1991), in which colorful photographs of children in interesting tableaux graphically illustrate various spatial terms. Such terms as *between, under, behind,* and *among* are listed on the side of each page, and readers are challenged to find the spatial connections in the photograph. In so doing, the author has created a spatial problem-solving book that provokes mathematical thinking and discussion about the language. After enjoying this book, a group of four kindergarten children decided to illustrate the words *between, under, over,* and *on.* They performed their "tableau" then dictated to the teacher that "Sara is crawling *between* Jack's legs. Ian is holding the book *over* his head. Marisa is standing *under* the flag, but she's trying to reach the book. The kids are playing *on* the carpet." These tableaux can be photographed by the teacher and made into an interesting exhibit or book that can be examined repeatedly throughout the year. By definition, tableaux are motionless depictions of a scene. However, do not expect young children to remain motionless for too long!

Moving On to Graphic Representations

The foregoing example gave children ample opportunities to explore a concept through direct experience over an extended period of time. They then had an opportunity to express these understandings to others. Young children can talk about their experiences and perhaps dictate their ideas to others. Although most four- and five-year-olds are unable to record their thoughts and ideas about geometric and spatial relationships in written form, they can use "graphic language" (Katz 1995, 20) or visual representations to record their ideas about their investigations and experiences with space. According to Katz (1995, 21), "Teachers often seriously underestimate preprimary children's graphic representational capabilities and the quality of the intellectual effort and growth it can stimulate."

For example, after repeated readings of, and active dramatizations of the movement pattern in, *A Week of Raccoons* by Gloria Whelan (1990), kindergarten children were invited to recall and recreate on paper the rather detailed journey Mr. Twerkle took as he resettled a family of raccoons from his farm, *past* the tumble-down log cabin, *around* the old apple tree, and *over* the bridge to the "piney woods." The children worked individually then used their drawings as field notes while working in groups to make a large story map of Mr. Twerkle's journey. They translated their own and each other's drawings then decided how to divide the task, where to place such points of interest as the old apple tree and the tumble-down log cabin, and how to carry out their plan. The children took several days to complete their graphic representations of the movement pattern in this story. Later the groups explained their work to the class, discussing problems they encountered and how they would revise their work. These revisions were hung on the walls of a long hallway where the children could study them and even retrace with their fingers the truck's journey along the path (see fig. 1). Often children reenacted the movement sequence with their hands or entire bodies while referring to the drawings. Lots of conversation was generated as the children paused to study these maps and make comments, observations, and suggestions, which were written on speech bubbles by the teacher and placed near the work. Some comments included, "I think the part where Mr. Twerkle goes over the bridge should be more near the schoolhouse than the apple tree"; "Next time, we should start our map closer to the top. See, we ran off the page here"; and "I like the way you made the fish jumping out of the water running under the bridge. It is jumping really high." The teacher and the students did not view these visual representations as simply decorative products to be taken home at the end of the day, never to be seen or discussed again. Rather, the children used their drawings to explore, reconstruct, revisit, and deepen their understandings (Katz 1995).

Spatial understandings are necessary for interpreting, understanding, and appreciating our inherently geometric world (NCTM 1989, 48). Preprimary programs that involve children in spatial explorations, such as the ones described in this article, present many opportunities for children to explore the geometric world in which they live, to make observations and construct relationships about shape and space, and to solve problems in a spatial con-

Fig. 1. One groups's story map of Mr. Twerkle's journey

text. In this manner, young children can begin to construct the conceptual foundation for new and complex ideas that will be introduced in higher mathematics.

Bibliography

Glass, Buzz. "Walking the Square." On *Aerobic Dances for Children.* Activity Records, Inc.

Hoban, Tana. *All about Where.* New York: Greenwillow Books, 1991.

Hutchins, Pat. *Rosie's Walk.* New York: Macmillan Publishing Co., 1968.

Katz, Lilian. "What Can We Learn from Reggio Emilia?" In *The One Hundred Languages of Children: The Reggio Emilia Approach to Early Childhood Education,* edited by Carolyn Edwards, Lella Gandini, and George Forman. Norwood, N.J.: Ablex Publishing Corp., 1995.

National Council of Teachers of Mathematics. Curriculum and Evaluation Standards for School Mathematics. Reston, Va.: The Council, 1989.

———. *Geometry and Spatial Sense.* Addenda Series, Grades K–6. Reston, Va.: The Council, 1993.

Palmer, Hap. "The Circle Game." On *Getting to Know Myself.* Educational Activities AR543.

Payne, Joseph. *Mathematics for the Young Child.* Reston, Va.: National Council of Teachers of Mathematics, 1990.

Whelan, Gloria. *A Week of Raccoons.* New York: Greenwillow Books, 1990.

Exploring Geometry

by

Alison Claus

This unit began as a favor for a friend who needed some examples of children writing about mathematics, but it ended as a marvelous activity for the first week of school. The unit consisted of a series of lessons that furnished my fifth-grade students with a review of geometry and problem solving using geometric concepts and allowed them to communicate with each other about these concepts both in writing and orally.

I passed out to the students three-centimeter-by-four-centimeter rectangles cut from colored construction paper. The class discussed the properties of these rectangles—four sides; opposite sides equal and parallel; four equal angles, each a right angle. We also noted that each rectangle had two equal diagonals. Each student took a ruler, drew one of the diagonals, and then cut some of the rectangles along the diagonal, forming two congruent triangles. We also talked about these triangles—the class superimposed them and saw that they were exactly the same if one was flipped. Someone remembered the term *congruent*. We looked at the identity of corresponding sides and angles. At this point our first problem-solving experience arose. We could put the two congruent shapes

Creating various shapes with congruent triangles cut from a rectangle

back together to make a rectangle. Could we make any other shapes using the two congruent triangles placed so that one pair of congruent sides was completely shared?

I divided the class into working pairs. Students sitting in adjacent seats were grouped to work together on this problem for our second day's activity. Gradually the groups found six different shapes but no more. Several groups recognized that three sides could be put together and that each pair of sides could touch in two ways. This configuration would have been easier to see if our pieces had been of different colors on each side. Thus we reasoned that six figures could be made. At this point we had some new figures to discuss and more vocabulary to review. Our six figures included two triangles, three parallelograms (including the original rectangle), and a quadrilateral with two pairs of equal adjacent sides that was shaped like a kite (fig. 1).

In the discussion of these figures, we talked about adjacent sides; opposite sides; parallel lines; acute, obtuse, and right angles; and isosceles and right triangles. Students glued onto a record sheet the pairs of triangles that constituted the six shapes. They were then asked to list on paper as many properties of each figure as they could observe (fig. 2). The initial responses to this task were superficial. The students seemed to report whatever came into their heads in a shotgun fashion. We should have discussed more, the students should have produced the list while still grouped in pairs, and perhaps I should have modeled the kind of writing I wanted from the students.

Alison Claus teaches students from kindergarten through eighth grade in her role as an enrichment coordinator for mathematics and science in the Lincolnshire–Prairie View School District, Lake Forest, IL 60045. She also teaches courses for in-service teachers at the National-Louis University in Evanston, Illinois.

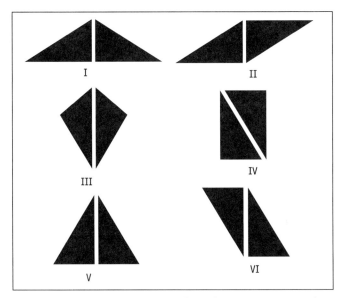

Fig. 1. Figures that can be made from the congruent triangles

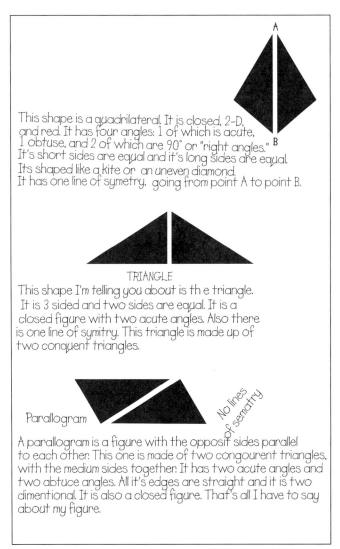

This shape is a long triangle.
It can be divided equally
1 way. It has 3 sides and
3 points. It can be made
from 2 triangles.

This object is just
like the object above
except 1 triangle is flipped
over. So instead of 3 sides,
it has 4.

This object is kind of
like a pyramid except
it is flat. It has 4 points and
4 sides. It can be
divided equally.

This is a rectangle.
It can be divided
equally 3 different
ways. It has 4
sides and 4 points.

This shape is a triangle.
It has 3 sides and 3
points. You can divide
it into 2 equal parts.
Its sides are all equal.
It can be made
from 2 triangles.

This object looks like
a slanted rectangle. it
has 4 sides and 4 points.
It can be made from 2
triangles. It can be divided
into 2 equal parts.

Fig. 2. Students' lists of properties of figures

On the third day, after reviewing the relevant concepts, students were more reflective and organized about identifying the properties for each figure. After the students had

The year doesn't have to start with place value.

finished the list of properties of the six figures, each was asked to choose one figure and, using the observed properties, write a descriptive paragraph about that figure with as much detail as she or he could produce (fig. 3).

Our final problem-solving situation occurred as the class was asked to consider these questions about the six figures:

This shape is a quadrilateral. It is closed, 2-D,
and red. It has four angles: 1 of which is acute,
1 obtuse, and 2 of which are 90° or "right angles."
It's short sides are equal and it's long sides are equal.
Its shaped like a kite or an uneven diamond.
It has one line of symetry, going from point A to point B.

TRIANGLE
This shape I'm telling you about is th e triangle.
It is 3 sided and two sides are equal. It is a
closed figure with two acute angles. Also there
is one line of symitry. This triangle is made up of
two conquent triangles.

Parallogram

No lines of sematry

A parallogram is a figure with the opposit sides parallel
to each other. This one is made of two congourent triangles,
with the medium sides together. It has two acute angles and
two abtuce angles. All it's edges are straight and it is two
dimentional. It is also a closed figure. That's all I have to say
about my figure.

Fig. 3. Students' paragraphs describing shapes in figure 1

1. Which figure has the largest perimeter?
2. Which figure has the largest area?
3. Can these questions be answered without actually measuring the perimeter and area of each figure?

The students were then asked to write the answers to the questions and to justify their answers (fig. 4).

After several days the class returned to a discussion of the figures and shared answers and reasoning about the three questions. Several members of the class had recognized that when congruent triangles are placed together with the shortest sides "inside," the perimeter equals the sum of the lengths of the two pairs of longer sides. Thus two figures (shapes I and II in fig. 1) have the largest perimeter. The students also saw that since every one of our figures is formed from the same pair of congruent triangles, they all have the same area. Thus we answered the last three questions.

(1.) Which figure has the largest area? All figures have the same area because they are all made up from two congruent triangles and from the same shape, we just cut it like this 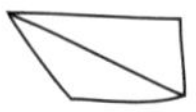

(2.) Which figure has the longest perimeter? I and II have the same perimeter because the smallest sides are together, that means that the largest sides and the second largest sides are showing.

(3.) Find a way to answer the first 2 questions without measuring. I did.

---

1 All the shapes have equal area, because each shape is make up of the same two triangles.

2 Shape number One and Two have the largest perimeter, because the smallest side on both triangles are Facing each other, and that leaves out the largest sides. (perimeter)

3A For question number one, I figured out that each shape is made up of the same two triangles and that makes the shapes equal in area.

3B For question number two, I numbered the sides and figured out that problem one and two have the largest perimeters.

Fig. 4. Students' answers to questions and their justifications

One possible extension of this activity is to use other figures as the starting shape. Students can explore what would happen if they divided a square into two triangles or can perhaps use another figure, such as a quadrilateral, that is not rectangular as the source of the two triangles. Students can also investigate what happens if figures other than quadrilaterals are decomposed.

Another possible extension to help students build their communication skills is to play a game involving a "mystery" figure. A student selects one of the given figures and describes it orally or in writing while classmates try to guess which figure is being described.

I learned several lessons from this unit:

- The year doesn't have to start with place value or a review of number concepts. The geometry experience was valuable both as a review and as a source of new experiences. It was an exciting way to begin to work together as a mathematics class.
- Geometry offers a rich medium for working on oral and written communication in mathematics. The students were eagerly involved in the discussions. They struggled to write their descriptive paragraphs carefully.
- Fifth grade is not too early to have students begin to reason informally to support a conjecture. These students were able to apply logical procedures to the problem of finding the six different figures. They were convinced that they had recognized and listed all the possible combinations of congruent sides to get the six figures they identified. Similarly, they were convinced by the argument that the largest perimeter was formed by the triangles with the two longest sides on the outside of the figure. They were also satisfied that all the areas were equal because each figure is composed of the same two triangles.
- A unit like this one enables students to integrate many concepts that they have previously studied, such as properties of angles, triangles, and quadrilaterals and perimeter, area, and vocabulary. The overall approach is holistic rather than the usual disjointed one-lesson-one-topic format often found in geometry chapters in textbooks. The framework arises naturally out of the context of the problems we set out to solve. Students respond well to this approach.
- It is possible to teach fourth-, fifth-, and sixth-grade mathematics students geometry, including definitions, properties, and informal reasoning about those properties, by having a number of two- or three-day units on a variety of such geometric topics as symmetry, tessellation, estimation of angle measure, or explorations of volume, area, or perimeter inserted into the curriculum throughout the year.

Bibliography

Dana, Marcia, and Mary M. Lindquist. "Let's Do It: Strip Tease." *Arithmetic Teacher* 25 (March 1978):4–8.

Dana, Marcia E., and Mary Montgomery Lindquist. "Let's Do It: Let's Try Triangles." *Arithmetic Teacher* 26 (September 1978):2–9.

Edwards, Ronald R. "Discoveries in Geometry by Folding and Cutting." *Arithmetic Teacher* 24 (March 1977):196–98.

Lappan, Glenda, and Pamela W. Schram. "Communication and Reasoning: Critical Dimensions of Sense Making in Mathematics." In *New Directions for Elementary Mathematics*, 1989 Yearbook of the National Council of Teachers of Mathematics, edited by Paul R. Trafton and Albert P. Shulte, 14–30. Reston, Va.: The Council, 1989.

Lindquist, Mary Montgomery. "Let's Do It: Problem Solving with Five Easy Pieces." *Arithmetic Teacher* 25 (November 1977):6–10.

Mumme, Judith, and Nancy Shepherd. "Implementing the *Standards:* Communication in Mathematics." *Arithmetic Teacher* 38 (September 1990):18–22.

Van de Walle, John, and Charles S. Thompson. "Let's Do It: A Triangle Treasury." *Arithmetic Teacher* 28 (February 1981):6–11.

Teacher as "Kimp"

by

Robert M. Berkman

Homework question #4: Draw a trapezoid.

The first student stands up and draws what can be described as a "textbook trapezoid":

I look at the figure, reach back, and put on a phosphorescent yellow baseball hat with the word "Forks" emblazoned in white. The students begin to groan. "Oh, no, he's turned into a 'kimp'!" they whisper. As defined by one of my students, a "kimp" is "being so stupid that you are not aware of your stupidity."

"So what you're telling me," I say in my best Ernest-Goes-to-Mathematics-Class drawl, "is that a trapezoid is a four-sided figure with two line segments that go horizontally and two line segments that go diagonally."

An uprising appears to be brewing among my charges. A flurry of hands is waving wildly in the air. A student goes up to the chalkboard and draws this figure:

Robert Berkman teaches mathematics and science at Bank Street College of Education, New York, NY 10025. His interests include technology in education, cooperative learning, and detracking mathematics classes.

For a discussion of a similar technique used with older students, readers are referred to the article "What Is a Quadrilateral?" by Lionel Pereiera Mendoza in the December 1993 *Mathematics Teacher.—Ed.*

"Oh, I see! So a trapezoid is a four-sided figure with two line segments going horizontally, that can have a right angle and a diagonal or two diagonals."

More moaning, more hands in the air. Another student goes to the chalkboard. A lot of chatter ensues; some students are scribbling in their notebooks, others are looking on and commenting. Others are shaking their heads at how stupid a teacher can be. Next figure:

"Oh, I get it now, a trapezoid has four sides, and two of them have to go either vertically or horizontally, and the other two can be right angles or diagonals." A student shouts, "No, no, we're just drawing it like that to show you an example!" I give him my dullest look, "But that's what your drawings are telling me." More groaning, more energy. Another student charges to the chalkboard:

A flash of inspiration flashes across my face. "Oh, I have it now: it doesn't have two line segments that are horizontal or vertical, but it does have to have four sides, and two of the sides go in the same direction, and the other two don't."

A flash of relief runs across my students' faces. "Yes, that's it!" one cries, thinking that we can now go to the next homework problem. But not so fast....

"But if it does have two line segments that are horizontal, the longer side has to go on the bottom, and if the two line segments go vertically, the longer side goes on the right!" Two more students run to the chalkboard. Two more drawings appear:

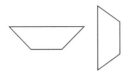

The students are sure it's all over. They've shown me every type of trapezoid that is possible to produce. They're emotionally and intellectually exhausted. But little do they know the depth of my ignorance.

"OK, that's it: four sides, two of which are going in the same direction, the other two sides are not, it doesn't matter which way you turn it around." Twelve sixth graders are happy, twelve sixth graders are relieved, twelve sixth graders believe nothing more is to be shown. But not so fast....

"And it always has to have two pointy angles on one side and two nonpointy angles on the other...."

They're obviously frustrated. While one student threatens to tell the school administrator that I don't know what a trapezoid is, most just hold their heads in their hands. "Mr. Berkman, I'll explain it one last time," one student mutters and goes to the chalkboard:

"You see, it can have an acute angle and obtuse angle on the same side, and an acute angle and obtuse angle on the other side. Or it can have a mixture of right angles and acute and obtuse angles," she explains.

"Those acute angles, they're the pointy things?" I inquire.

"Yes, Mr. Berkman, they are. You taught us that!"

"Oh yeah, I forgot. I'm a real kimp today."

She walks away from the chalkboard.

"One last question, do those trapezoids always have to be so, well, square? I mean, it looks like they can't be short and fat, or long and skinny. Are there any rules about that?"

A quiet girl from the back raises her hand. "I'm going to settle this once and for all." She heads to the chalkboard:

"See, they can be skinny or fat, long or short, in any direction—all they need are four sides, only two sides of which are parallel. It doesn't matter which way they are turned, what length their sides are, or where the angles are placed, as long as they have only one set of these parallel sides. Now, are there *any more* questions you have about trapezoids?"

"Yeah, do you always have to draw them in white?"

Is My Teacher Stupid, Smart, or Both?

One of the main goals of the NCTM's Curriculum Standards is "Mathematics as Communication"; that is, children should "reflect on and clarify their thinking about mathematical ideas and situations" (NCTM 1989). One of the best ways to accomplish this goal is to take a problem and use seemingly stupid questions to goad students into thinking carefully about how they are describing their ideas. "Kimping" is the word I use to define this strategy. The wise teacher knows that being a "kimp" means stimulating a deeper understanding of a concept or procedure.

"Kimping," if done well, forces students to be very precise about their language. By taking on the guise of one who is completely ignorant, we challenge students to reflect on their thinking and not accept "textbook" answers. In effect, students become creators of their own knowledge, uncovering complex ideas contained in seemingly simple questions. Many teachers object to this kind of struggle because they believe that mathematics is a clean, precise collection of concepts and operations. By working through these ideas, however, students emerge with a depth of knowledge that cannot be developed through conventional means.

Kimping can be used as a tool to teach by counterexample. Too often, teachers show the correct way to solve a problem without allowing students to see why the incorrect way yields a wrong answer. One good example of this tactic involves the addition of fractions. To introduce this lesson, I start by putting the following problem on the chalkboard:

Mr. Berkman says that if you add 1/2 and 1/2, you will get the following:

$$\frac{1}{2} + \frac{1}{2} = \frac{2}{4}$$

What do you think of Mr. Berkman's thinking?

In this example, I am asking students to assess my thinking. I explain that it is my belief that fractions are added in the same way as whole numbers and decimals: since we add ones and ones, tens and tens, and hundredths and hundredths, with fractions we add numerators to numerators and denominators to denominators.

Of course, the students know that I may be playing a kimp, so the discussion is lively, yet intellectual. What emerges from the students' analysis of the problem is that although the logic for the procedure seems to be consistent with other areas of mathematics, it doesn't yield correct results. How can one start out with 1/2, add another 1/2 to it, and end up with the same amount one started with? Furthermore, the students already know by their experiences that the answer must be 1, so they must then think through an alternative procedure that will yield the correct answer. By presenting a counterexample and trying as hard as possible to defend it, the students are better prepared to generate and accept the proper method for solving the problem. Furthermore, students can discard their previous conceptions of how similar problems are solved by proving to themselves that this simple method just doesn't make sense.

An International Movement?

This type of lesson is consistent with what is found in successful mathematics classrooms in countries that boast high rates of mathematical literacy, better known as *numeracy*. According to Stigler and Stevenson (1991), Asian teachers make use of incorrect answers as the jumping-off point for discussions, particularly to help reverse children's incorrect notions about mathematics. In effect, instead of regarding incorrect answers as dead ends, we must use them as opportunities to look deeper into a problem—to get at the misconceptions in our students' minds and correct them. The interesting thing about this approach is that it works for students regardless of perceived ability level. For weak students, it will clear up their misconceptions without embarrassing them (after all, the *teacher* is the one playing the idiot!), whereas for stronger students it will reinforce their understanding by forcing them to construct a rational and cogent explanation. In effect, everybody benefits when you act like a kimp.

Choose Your Opportunities

Kimping has a few drawbacks. The teacher must cease being a transmitter of knowledge and become a creator of questions that lead to clearer conceptual understanding by the students. Sometimes this role means asking a question that will cloud the issue, as did my queries in the beginning of this article about the shape of trapezoids. A good teacher will be able to keep the discussion focused and the

students motivated. The net result will be to confirm those conceptions that are correct and to challenge those that are not.

The last point brings up a second drawback of kimping—time. The homework problem we went over could have taken a minute or two of class time but instead took ten minutes to bring to its conclusion. Was the time worth it? Our discussion led to high stages of critical thinking, levels that cannot be reached in a minute or two. At the lowest level of understanding, one can recite the properties of a concept by rote: "A trapezoid is a quadrilateral with exactly one pair of parallel sides" (Serra 1989). At a higher level, one can give examples and nonexamples. At a still higher level, one can actually manipulate the attributes of a concept and determine whether it still fits into the original concept. By "kimping," I was able to move my students through these different levels of thought, resulting in their increased grasp of the concept.

Kimping changes the atmosphere of a class—it throws everyone into open discussion. It relies on the construction of convincing arguments rather than retrieval of isolated facts. Factual information works hand in hand with the explanations. For example, in my presentation of the equation 1/2 + 1/2 = 2/4, the students pointed out that this equation makes no sense because everyone knows that 2/4 is exactly the same as 1/2. Of course, being a kimp, I have to explain that I didn't know this fact, could you please explain it to me? This question leads us into a discussion of equivalent fractions, which I can continue if I perceive any weakness in this area. Kimping, although unpredictable, allows the teacher to introduce new topics, assess the class's understanding of a topic, and determine if a given concept needs reinforcement.

Kimping is not a technique one can use every day. Like any good thing, it can be overused, dulling its effectiveness. Used carefully, it can motivate a class to high levels of understanding while acting as a tool for the teacher to assess a class's level of understanding. It is also a unique way to introduce new material while reinforcing what has previously been studied. A Spanish adage says that only fools and children speak the truth. By playing the fool, we can help our students see the truth.

References

National Council of Teachers of Mathematics. *Curriculum and Evaluation Standards for School Mathematics.* Reston, Va: The Council, 1989.

Serra, Michael. *Discovering Geometry: An Inductive Approach.* Berkeley, Calif.: Key Curriculum Press, 1989.

Stigler, James W., and Harold W. Stevenson. "How Asian Teachers Polish Each Lesson to Perfection." *American Educator* 15 (Spring 1991):12–47.

Making the Connection with Language

by

L. Diane Miller

Mathematics is a language consisting of carefully defined symbols that represent fundamental concepts, for example, $A = \pi r^2$ would be read by most middle school students as "area equals pi, r, squared" and would mean, "The area of a circle equals pi (approximately 3.14, or 22/7) times the square of the circle's radius." Examine closely the specialized language used to describe this mathematical expression: *area, circle, equals, pi, times, square,* and *radius.* Also consider the multiple meanings of some of these words: square: (1) a four-sided polygon with equal sides and four 90-degree angles, (2) multiply a number by itself. Other words have meaning in mathematics and outside mathematics; for example, area: (1) the amount of surface in a two-dimensional figure, (2) the broad range of a subject, for example, the whole area of science.

In summary, students' understanding of mathematics is dependent on their knowledge of both mathematics as a language and the language used to teach mathematics. Empowering students in mathematics depends on teachers' helping students to make the connection between the lan-

SUMQUOTIENTDIAMETER
FRACTIONFACTOREQUAL
DIGITPRODUCTMEASURE
PERIMETERDENOMINATOR
CIRCLEREMAINDERWHOLE
DIFFERENCEMETERDIVIDE
AVERAGESUBTRACTANGLE

guage used to teach mathematics and their construction of mathematical knowledge. The focus of this article is on the language, particularly the vocabulary, used in mathematics instruction and the ways in which teachers can assist students in constructing, in both receptive and expressive modes, the formal language of mathematics.

Evidence Supports Increased Use of Mathematical Language

In a recent study in Western Australia, 646 thirteen-year-old eighth-year students from nine schools were asked to define twenty mathematical terms that a sample of teachers said were used routinely in the classroom under the assumption that the students understood their meanings. Although the study was conducted in Australia, the terms, given in figure 1, are probably included in the middle-grades curricula of every developed country, including the United States and the United Kingdom.

In marking the students' papers, acceptable responses were placed in one of three categories: (1) acceptable words; (2) acceptable diagram, symbol, or example; or (3) acceptable combination of words, diagram, symbol, or example. The average (mean) number of terms students

Diane Miller teaches at Texas Tech University, Lubbock, TX 79409. Her interests include the connection between oral and written language and mathematical understanding.

were able to define in their own language using only words was four. When symbols, diagrams, or examples were accepted as representing a definition of the word, the average number of words acceptably defined increased to eleven. Thus, the acceptance of such examples as 3 + 2 = 5 and the symbol "+" as representing the meaning of *sum* improved the students' correct definitions to roughly half of the twenty terms.

The results of this study are discouraging because they suggest that students are unable to define mathematics vocabulary using their own language. In light of *Mathematics Counts* (Committee of Inquiry into the Teaching of Mathematics in Schools 1982), the *Curriculum and Evaluation Standards* (NCTM 1989), and *A National Statement on Mathematics for Australian Schools* (Australian Education Council 1990), the results of this study are quite disturbing. The students in this sample have not developed a common understanding of selected mathematics vocabulary as reflected in their ability to communicate in writing.

Without an understanding of the vocabulary that is used routinely in mathematics instruction, textbooks, and word problems, students are handicapped in their efforts to learn mathematics. To illustrate this point, consider the following problem in which answering correctly does not depend on numerical computation. Instead, the right answer depends on a student's understanding of two words.

> The local community center wants to fence a park that measures 10.8 by 12 kilometers. The area of the park is 129.6 square kilometers. The perimeter is 45.6 kilometers. How much fencing will the community center need to buy?

If students understand the meaning of *perimeter*, this problem is trivial. If they do not know the meaning of *perimeter* or *area*, or if they perhaps know a meaning for both but get them confused, the situation becomes problematical. Although this particular problem was not posed to the eighth-year students in this survey, their responses when asked to define *perimeter* suggest that 64 percent of them would have had difficulty deciding how much fencing to buy.

The data collected in the study indicate that 36 percent (roughly one-third) of the eighth-year students defined

The following words have been suggested by teachers of mathematics as being words that students encounter in their studies. Please define the following twenty words. You may use pictures or give examples in your definitions. Provide whatever is necessary to demonstrate that you know what each word means. If you do not know the meaning of a word, please write "DO NOT KNOW" beside the word.

Year 8	
sum	digit
quotient	equal
angle	diameter
fraction	meter
factor	denominator
perimeter	average
measure	circle
product	whole
difference	divide
remainder	subtract

Fig. 1. Vocabulary words

perimeter using their own language. *Area* was not on their list of words to define. In the same study, 600 ninth-year students from the same nine schools were asked to define twenty mathematical terms selected by teachers as being routinely used in mathematics instruction at the ninth-year level. Both *area* and *perimeter* were on the ninth-year list. Only 214 of the 600 ninth-year students produced an acceptable definition of *perimeter* in their own language; 205 of the same group successfully defined *area*. Do these statistics suggest that only one-third of these students would have answered the preceding problem correctly? The percent of ninth-year students responding correctly for *perimeter* increased to 75 when diagrams, symbols, or examples were accepted. The percent of ninth-year students responding correctly for *area* increased to 77 when diagrams, symbols, or examples were accepted. Three responses that represent the types of definitions accepted are given in figure 2.

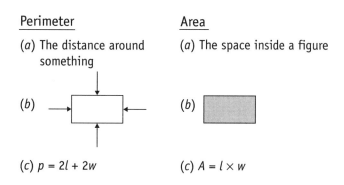

Fig. 2. Students' acceptable responses to *perimeter* and *area*

The Role of Language in Concept Development

Many mathematical words represent concepts and not objects. Such words as *quotient, fraction,* and *factor* have no unique, unambiguous representations in the real world but describe concepts. Some concepts can be embodied in real-world objects, but no guarantee can be made that students will see any connection between a real-world embodiment of a concept and the concept itself. Teachers need to create learning environments that encourage students to make the cognitive links among familiar language, real-world concepts, formal mathematics language, and symbolic manipulation.

For example, many middle-grades students are able to recite the formula for finding the area of a circle ($A = \pi r^2$) but may not have a conceptual understanding of pi and its relationship to the circumference and diameter of a circle. Various individual and small-cooperative-group activities can be used to help students develop a conceptual understanding of pi using the vocabulary and language associated with circles and pi. One example is to ask students to bring to school various circular objects or objects that have circles on them (Frisbees, plates, jar tops, coins, etc.). Perhaps architectural designs on the school grounds also represent circles. In small cooperative groups, students can measure and record in a table the circumferences and diameters of various circles. Using calculators, students can examine the ratio C/d and compute decimal values for pi.

Teachers who have used this activity say that some students are surprised and also concerned when their calculated values for pi do not equal 3.14. Thus, the activity initiates a natural discussion that uses several mathematical terms, including many from the list of words given to the eighth-year students in Western Australia. As the students use mathematics vocabulary, they should be encouraged to explain the meaning of words, both orally and in writing. Research by Garbe (1985) end by Nicholson (1977, 1980, 1989) indicates that direct teaching of the specialized vocabulary of mathematics contributes to students' conceptual understanding of mathematics. Creating opportunities for the introduction and use of mathematics vocabulary occurring naturally in classroom discourse is one way to focus on the specialized vocabulary of mathematics without distributing a list of words to be memorized.

The Language Connection When English Is the Second Language

The results of studies conducted by Dawe (1983), Garbe (1985), and Harris (1989) confirm that students for whom English is a second language have an alarmingly poor command of mathematics vocabulary. In Australia, a prominent group of culturally different students are the nonnomadic aboriginals, who generally speak English as a second language and are taught in mixed aboriginal-European classrooms in which the teaching methods, curricula, and learning styles reflect a tradition of European pedagogy, values, and sociocultural orientation that is unnatural to them. The language of instruction is English, school textbooks and mathematics syllabi are in English, and the curriculum is very much tied to a Western perspective of the world.

Students growing up using English appear to have a view of their world far more compatible with this mathematics than those students who use an aboriginal language (Kepert 1991). In the sample of eighth-year students surveyed in Western Australia, the mean number of mathematical terms acceptably defined by the aboriginal students using words, diagrams, symbols, or examples was six, compared with a mean of eleven by their nonaboriginal peers. Various reports indicate that the achievement of aboriginal students falls significantly below that of their nonaboriginal peers (Guider 1991). Perhaps part of the problem lies with aboriginal students' lack of understanding of the language of discourse in mathematics classes.

Like Australia, the United States is a multicultural society. Educational systems in general and teachers more specifically must demonstrate respect for cultural diversity. An increasing number of students in United States schools are learning English as a second language. Mathematics education cannot ignore the needs of a multicultural classroom. Mathematical literacy is essential for full participation in society. One facet of mathematical literacy is the use of language for communicating mathematical ideas. Teachers need to be aware of cultural and socioeconomic factors that may influence certain students' learning in mathematics, including any barriers posed when English is a second language. Students having English as a second language may need more attention than English-speaking students, but as the Australian study indicates, all students need to improve their knowledge of mathematics vocabulary.

Strategies to Help Students Make the Connection

Ellerton and Clements (1991) believe that when someone actively links aspects of his or her physical and social environments with certain numerical, spatial, and logical concepts, a feeling of "ownership" is often generated. Traditionally, school mathematics has been regarded by students as a fixed body of knowledge, owned by teachers, textbook and worksheet writers, and historical figures like Pythagoras and Einstein. During the 1980s, mathematics educators around the world called for teachers to establish teaching-learning environments in which students would perceive that they owned the mathematics they learned. This feeling of ownership is a key to empowerment, and evidence of ownership in mathematics is the ability to communicate one's knowledge about a concept, skill, or generalization.

When learning new mathematics vocabulary, students generally want to memorize a definition that can be reiterated on request or to represent the word by a symbol or example. For example, 26 percent of the eighth-year students in the Australian sample acceptably defined *divide* using words, whereas 51 percent of the sample used the symbol ÷ or an example like 25 ÷ 5 = 5. Several of the 23 percent who submitted unacceptable responses used a tautology like "to divide something" as the definition for *divide*. Experienced teachers know that symbols and examples do not necessarily reflect a conceptual understanding of a concept or process, much less the type of ownership and empowerment discussed by Ellerton and Clements (1991).

To assist students in making the connection between language and mathematical empowerment, teachers should implement strategies that give all students an opportunity to construct, in both receptive and expressive modes, the formal language of mathematics. The following suggestions are easily implemented.

Teachers Modeling Appropriate Language

In the Western Australian study, the word having the lowest percent of acceptable responses was *quotient*. Only 7 percent of the eighth-year students acceptably defined *quotient* using words, diagrams, examples, or symbols. When researchers reported the results of the survey to a group of teachers whose students had participated in the study, they asked the teachers why they thought the students had performed so poorly on the term *quotient*. The teachers unanimously said that they did not use the word *quotient* in their teaching because they knew that the students would not know the meaning of the word. When asked what they called the answer to a division problem, the teachers spoke in one voice and replied, "The answer." This incident raises a pertinent question. If mathematics teachers do not model appropriate vocabulary within a meaningful context, how can students be expected to use the language of mathematics?

In this episode, teachers willfully chose not to use *quotient*, a mathematical term, to represent the answer to a division problem. In one respect, the teachers were attempting to use everyday language with which they thought the students would be more familiar. In another respect, however, they were failing to assist the students in making the transition from their everyday language to mathematical language.

An example of a teacher's unknowingly using inappropriate language during oral instruction occurred in a different study in which a middle-grades mathematics teacher was implementing the writing-to-learn approach in a class of eighth-year students. During the study, he expressed frustration over the students' failure to use

mathematical terms in their writings about mathematics. For example, one day he was particularly frustrated because the students had not used the words *numerator* and *denominator* in their writings about fractions. Instead, they were saying "the number on the top" and "the number on the bottom." A few days later, a researcher observed his class. The teacher was reviewing fractions, and throughout the entire lesson, which was dominated by teacher talk, he never once used the words *denominator* and *numerator*. After class, he was asked why he had not used these two terms. He paused a few seconds and said, "But I thought I did." In all sincerity, he was oblivious to the vocabulary he had or had not used and assumed that he had included *numerator* and *denominator* in his oral instruction. He wanted to hold the students accountable for using mathematics vocabulary in both oral and written discourse but was not modeling the vocabulary for them.

Using mathematics vocabulary within a meaningful context should be second nature to mathematics teachers. Encouraging students to use their own language to define mathematical terms and initially allowing them to use everyday language instead of a mathematical word are acceptable only when assisting students in making the link between familiar language and mathematical language. At some point, teachers should expect students to use mathematical language in classroom discourse within a meaningful context.

Ask Students to Define Words in Their Own Language

During classroom discourse, teachers should encourage students to define mathematical terms using their own language. When a teacher uses a mathematical term during oral instruction, individual students can be asked to define that term to the rest of the class. For example, a teacher may ask a student what happens to a fraction when the denominator is doubled. After a student responds to the question posed, the teacher can say something like, "By the way, what is a fraction?" or "What does *denominator* mean to you?" For some words, like *denominator,* everyone in the class may be content with using the same language to define the word; for example, the bottom number in a fraction, the number telling how many parts into which the unit is being divided, or the divisor. But for words like *average* different meanings may surface, and students can proceed to negotiate on one meaning or agree that the term can have multiple meanings. In summary, students should be given many opportunities to define terms using their own language.

Using Writing to Make the Connection

In addition to verbalizing their definitions for mathematical terms, students should be asked to write the meanings and to use mathematical language in writing about mathematics. Some students are not good writers and have difficulty expressing themselves in writing. However, they should not be excused from writing assignments in mathematics class. Just like the teacher modeling mathematics vocabulary, if students do not practice communicating their knowledge of mathematics in writing, they will probably not improve their ability to do so.

Miller (1991) outlines how impromptu writing prompts can be implemented in the mathematics classroom. Using a written prompt, teachers can ask students to explain an algorithm, define a term, or express their attitudes or anxieties about mathematics. In a study examining the benefits of using impromptu writing prompts in first-year-algebra classes, Miller and England (1989) report students' use of the word *factory* instead of *factor* in their writing. When asked to explain to a friend how to factor a polynomial, one student begins her response with, "Factory. For example ..." (p. 307). Another student in the same class addressed her response to her best friend and said, "Since I don't know how to factory and you do, could you please show me how you learned?" (Miller 1990). These two examples illustrate an error that was made by approximately 12 percent of the students in two first-year algebra classes. The students were using an everyday word, *factory,* instead of a mathematical word with which they were less familiar. Even though the correct word, *factor,* was used in the teacher's written prompt, the students used *factory* in their writing.

A very natural discussion after reading students' writings is to bring their attention to the misuse or nonuse of mathematics vocabulary. For example, after reading the students' responses to this prompt, the teacher could have said to the whole class, "I noticed in your writings yesterday that some of you used *factory* instead of *factor.* Will someone tell me what a factory is?" "Will someone now tell me what *factor* means?" Without embarrassing individual students, the error can be discussed and, it is hoped, a correct definition of *factor* will be reinforced for everyone in the class.

In a large class, the teacher often finds it difficult to listen to every student talk about mathematics for a significant length of time. However, a teacher can read every student's response to an in-class writing prompt on a regular basis. Teachers having used impromptu writing prompts in their mathematics classes say that they require about ten minutes to read thirty to thirty-five responses from a five-minute writing period. They are convinced that the writing-to-learn activity benefits students by getting them to use appropriate language, as well as benefits teachers by facilitating an informal assessment of students' understanding of mathematical terms (Miller 1992).

Cooperative Groups Help Students Make the Language Connection

Talking to the teacher is not the only way to practice conversing about mathematics. Peer-group discussions are another way in which students can exercise their mathematics vocabulary and construct a meaningful understanding of the formal language of mathematics. In a statement directed to primary school teachers, Cockcroft (Committee of Inquiry into the Teaching of Mathematics in Schools 1982, 3) suggests that from their earliest days at school, students should be encouraged to discuss and explain the mathematics they are doing with their teacher and with their peers "so that by means of this discussion, they can share their ideas and develop and refine their understanding." The findings of research by Wood and Yackel (1990) are also strongly supportive of the potential of cooperative groups for using the language of school mathematics. They summarize the benefits in the following passage (pp. 244–45):

> Peer group interaction gives rise to learning opportunities by encouraging both an exchange of viewpoints and verbal elaboration. When children are committed to collaborate, they try to make sense of each other's interpretations of the situation at hand and engage in mutually supportive activity. Language plays a critical role in this process.... Additionally, language can both help children reflect on their own understanding when they give explanations (Levine 1981) and help them reconceptualize their own cognitive constructions as they attempt to make sense of their partner's explanations.

Working in small, collaborative groups gives more students the opportunity to communicate orally and helps them to make the link between language and conceptual understanding.

Encouraging Students' Use of Mathematics Vocabulary in the Classroom

As previously mentioned, students speaking English as a second language may have more difficulty making the connection with mathematical language than students speaking English as a first language. Various approaches can be taken to create a multicultural classroom environment more conducive to cross-cultural teaching. The following few suggestions can be beneficial to all students, particularly to those who speak English as a second language.

Be sensitive to other cultures. Students can sense a teacher's acceptance of cultural diversity, enthusiasm for other cultures, and genuine concern for working with students from another culture. Teachers should create opportunities to use examples from various cultures regarding the use of mathematics, the recording of mathematics, the context of mathematics, and the learning of mathematics. Asking students from non-English-speaking backgrounds to count in their own language or to identify geometric shapes using their own language contributes to the esteem of the student, as well as shows that mathematics transcends language.

Understand different cultural expectations for classroom discourse. These issues include asking and answering questions, verbal and nonverbal communications, male-female relationships, classroom groupings, and teachers' status. For example, in some cultures male children are expected to dominate over females. Appointing a female student to be the leader of a small-group discussion may offend some male students to the point that they refuse to participate in the activity. Some female students may not answer questions or participate in whole-group discussions because they would appear to be smarter than the males in the class. Other students may not ask questions in class because doing so appears to challenge the teacher's authority or way of doing things. This observation does not imply that female students should not be appointed as leaders during small-group work or that students should be ignored just because they do not ask questions. The point is that being aware that some of these problems can occur is perhaps the most important first step in handling potentially stressful situations. Students should use mathematical language in meaningful classroom discourse. Teachers who are sensitive to various cultural and social norms can establish situations that promote the participation of all students in expressive-language activities.

Encourage students to express their sociocultural understanding of mathematics. Certain teaching strategies encourage students to use mathematical language in the classroom. For example, asking students to develop their own problems to investigate allows them to cast their stories in a familiar cultural context. Students from non-English-speaking backgrounds can be allowed to write their problems in their own language first and translate them into English at a later time. Doing so frees students from the burden of having to divide their concentration between thinking of a story problem or investigation and expressing it in English. In small groups, students can verbally explain their problems to their peers and work together to express the problem in writing. This activity also furnishes an effective way for everyone in the group to

develop further language skills both orally and in writing.

Clearly write and carefully pronounce new mathematics vocabulary. The learning styles of students vary. Some learn best by hearing, whereas others learn best by seeing. When introducing new mathematics vocabulary, teachers should place each term within a meaningful context and give both an oral explanation and a written definition. Ask students to join in negotiating a definition that is more meaningful to them but maintains an accurate mathematical description of the concept. Clearly write and carefully pronounce the new word so that students do not confuse it with a more familiar, everyday term, for example, *size* for *sides* and *ankle* for *angle*. Having students pronounce a new word can also be helpful. One problem faced by students from non-English-speaking backgrounds is confusing words that either are spelled like or sound like more-familiar terms (Garbe 1985). Before introducing a new mathematical term, a teacher should determine the students' perceptions of the term. The past experiences of students in a multicultural classroom vary dramatically. Relating students' past experiences with a new word can help give the term meaning in a mathematical context.

Conclusion

Traditionally, school mathematics has emphasized receptive aspects of language, expecting students to process the verbal and written communications of teachers, textbooks, worksheets, and tests and to apply what they have been told or have read to skill-typed exercises that rarely require their own use of language. To empower students with the mathematical knowledge essential to participate fully in society in the twenty-first century, teachers must equally involve students in the expressive aspects of language by having them speak and write about mathematics. The link between the passive reception and active expression of mathematics is language.

References

Australian Education Council (AEC). *A National Statement on Mathematics for Australian Schools.* Carlton, Victoria: AEC, 1990.

Committee of Inquiry into the Teaching of Mathematics in Schools. *Mathematics Counts,* chaired by William H. Cockcroft. London: Her Majesty's Stationery Office, 1982.

Dawe, Lloyd. "Bilingualism and Mathematical Reasoning in English as a Second Language." *Educational Studies in Mathematics* 14 (August 1983):325–53.

Ellerton, Nerida F., and M. A. (Ken) Clements. *Mathematics in Language: A Review of Language Factors in Mathematics Learning.* Geelong, Victoria: Deakin University, 1991.

Garbe, Douglas G. "Mathematics Vocabulary and the Culturally Different Student."*Arithmetic Teacher* 33 (October 1985):39–42.

Guider, Jeff. "Why Are So Many Aboriginal Children Not Achieving at School?" *The Aboriginal Child at School* 19 (April-May 1991):42–53.

Harris, Pam. "Contexts for Change in Cross-cultural Classrooms." In *School Mathematics: The Challenge to Change,* edited by Nerida F. Ellerton and M. A. (Ken) Clements. Geelong, Victoria: Deakin University, 1989.

Kepert, Barry. "Mathematics for Aboriginal Students Who Have a Different World View." *The Aboriginal Child at School* 19 (April-May 1991):32–41.

Miller, L. Diane. "Writing to Learn Mathematics: Suggestions for Classroom Implementation." Paper presented at a Conference of the Australian Association of Mathematics Teachers, Hobart, Tasmania, 1990.

———. "Writing to Learn Mathematics." *Mathematics Teacher* 84 (October 1991):516–21.

———. "Teacher Benefits from Using Impromptu Writing Prompts in Algebra Classes." *Journal for Research in Mathematics Education* 23 (July 1992):329–40.

Miller, L. Diane, and David A. England. "Writing to Learn Algebra." *School Science and Mathematics* 89 (April 1989):299–312.

Nicholson, A. R. "Mathematics and Language." *Mathematics in School* 6 (November 1977):32–34.

———. "Mathematics Language (Revisited)." *Mathematics in School* 18 (March 1989):44–45.

———. "Mathematics Literacy." *Mathematics in School* 9 (March 1980):33–34.

National Council of Teachers of Mathematics. *Curriculum and Evaluation Standards for School Mathematics.* Reston, Va.: The Council, 1989.

Wood, Terry, and Erna Yackel. "The Development of Collaborative Dialogue within Small Group Interaction." In *Transforming Children's Mathematics Education: International Perspectives,* edited by Leslie P. Steffe and Terry Woods. Hillsdale, N.J.: Lawrence Erlbaum Associates, 1990.

Activities

Data, Measurement, and Geometry

Lindquist, "It's Time to Change"

Explain why you do or do not agree with this article. Include specific examples from the article in your discussion.

Shaw and Cliatt, "Developing Measurement Sense"

Select three activities you have done in your class and clearly describe how they illustrate one or more of the five principles for developing measurement sense.

Wheatley, "Enhancing Mathematics Learning through Imagery"

Andrews, "Developing Spatial Sense—a Moving Experience"

The following articles as well as those in the February 1990 focus issue of the *Arithmetic Teacher* discuss imagery and spatial sense:

- Liedtke, Werner W. "Developing Spatial Abilities in the Early Grades." *Teaching Children Mathematics* 2 (September 1995): 12–18.

- Nitabach, Elizabeth, and Richard Lehrer. "Research into Practice: Developing Spatial Sense through Area Measurement." *Teaching Children Mathematics* 2 (April 1996): 473–76.

- Thompson, Patrick W., and Diana Lambdin. "Research into Practice: Concrete Materials and Teaching for Mathematical Understanding." *Arithmetic Teacher* 41 (May 1994): 556–58.

- Wheatley, Grayson H. "Research into Practice: Spatial Sense and the Construction of Abstract Units in Tiling." *Arithmetic Teacher* 39 (April 1992): 43–45.

Write a review of two articles selected from the focus issue or from the list above. Explain, using specific examples, how the articles relate to the discussions of imagery and spatial sense presented by Wheatley and Andrews.

Miller, "Making the Connection with Language"

Refer to the twenty terms listed in figure 1 in Miller's article.

(*a*) Define the twenty terms. Use symbols or diagrams if needed.

(*b*) Reflect on this task. Which terms were easier for you to define by using symbols or diagrams than by using just words? Could you have created definitions for all twenty terms using only words?

(*c*) Compare your definitions with those given in a mathematics textbook and comment on this comparison.